THE RETURN OF SPLENDOR
IN THE WORLD

The Return of Splendor in the World

The Christian Doctrine of Sin and Forgiveness

Christof Gestrich

WILLIAM B. EERDMANS PUBLISHING COMPANY
GRAND RAPIDS, MICHIGAN / CAMBRIDGE, U.K.

Translated by Daniel W. Bloesch
from *Die Wiederkehr des Glanzes in der Welt,*
© 1989 by J. C. B. Mohr (Paul Siebeck), Tübingen, Germany

This edition © 1997 Wm. B. Eerdmans Publishing Co.
255 Jefferson Ave. S.E., Grand Rapids, Michigan 49503 /
P.O. Box 163, Cambridge CB3 9PU U.K.
Printed in the United States of America

02 01 00 99 98 97   7 6 5 4 3 2 1

Library of Congress Cataloging-in-Publication Data

Gestrich, Christof.
[Wiederkehr des Glanzes in der Welt. English]
The return to splendor in the world: the Christian doctrine of
sin and forgiveness / Christof Gestrich.
p.   cm.
Includes bibliographical references and indexes.
ISBN 0-8028-4164-3 (pbk.: alk. paper)
1. Sin. 2. Good and evil. 3. Forgiveness of sin. I. Title.
BT715.G513 1997
231′.8 — dc21   97-10580
                                        CIP

Die Herausgabe dieses Werkes
wurde aus Mittel von Inter Nationes
Bonn gefördert

This book is dedicated to my children:

Anna Maria
Daniel
Johannes
Martin

Contents

Preface

A more adequate understanding of the meaning of the words "sin" and "the forgiveness of sin" is urgent today and is also possible. In these pages I have attempted to unfold the phenomenon of sin in terms of self-justification. This relates both to the key insight of the Reformation ("the doctrine of justification") as well as to key endeavors and ways of thinking in the modern era ("self-assertion," "self-preservation"). When we examine sin, we always come to see what can deliver us as well. The goal of this study is to regain the meaning and hope for our future that have been closed off to us because of this generation's deficient knowledge of the reality of sin.

I am glad to see the considerable exegetical and even dogmatic agreements that are once again being reached in contemporary works of theology. In keeping with this newly found harmony, I felt it was no longer necessary to attempt a confessional definition of the Christian doctrine of sin and forgiveness. But it is no secret that Luther's theology has continued to point the way ahead for me on many issues.

I have tried to explain and ground my own theological statements in the philosophy of religion. In this attempt the inexplicable existence of the "good Word" in the world that cannot be explained by any cause was understood as the horizon which brings to light both the reality of God and the reality of man. It was especially important for me to analyze the main fault lines that have emerged between modern theology and philosophy in their understanding of evil and guilt.

Years ago I completed a course of university lectures in which I had gained valuable insights from depth psychology. However, I have reduced more extensive references to depth psychology for this publication. I have done this in part because I have adopted a more cautious attitude toward its significance in shedding light on the topic of sin since the publications pertaining to depth psychology have been released. I have also done this in part because philosophical and historical texts and materials should be given equal significance and space because of their ability to elucidate this topic.

The beginnings of this study are found in sections V and VII. The questions, objections, and suggestions of "church" people and "nonchurch" people, and not least of students, but also the understanding that a theologian should teach nothing new, helped me finish the fourth chapter of this book. The truth for us today does not have to be invented for the first time; it only has to be understood in light of those aspects of the truth that are of special concern for us now. Of course, this is difficult enough.

I was not able to achieve "completeness" in covering the available literature pertinent to this topic. After the book went to press I saw the following three texts which could have contributed to the discussion in the fourth chapter: Hans-Georg Fritzsche, . . . *und erlöse uns von dem Übel. Philosophie und Theologie zur Rechtfertigung Gottes* (Stuttgart, 1987) (this book was written by my colleague in Berlin, who unfortunately died prematurely in 1986. It ends with reflections on the "mission of the Christian church" to strengthen and comfort those individuals who, like Job, have to suffer from the problem of theodicy as "fate's hardship cases"); T. Rendtorff, *Ethik Grundelemente, Methodologie und Konkretionen einer ethischen Theologie,* vol. 1 (Stuttgart, 1980) (in this book evil is defined *ethically* as the "refusal to accept one another." When theological dogmatics develops its teaching on evil, it is forced to keep its focus on a point of view that is relevant for taking action); and M. Welker, "Der Heilige Geist," *EvTh* 49 (1989): 126-41 (in this inaugural lecture at Münster the forgiveness of sins brought by the "bearer of the Spirit," Jesus Christ, is the starting point for reflection on sin; even if forgiveness, for example, becomes actual as the healing of a devastated environment, it still begins *"prior to* the level of our own moral or any other kind of improvability"*)*.

I would like to send special regards to the former participants of my seminar mentioned earlier that was devoted to the topic of "sin." May they joyfully remain students of theology in their present profession! I would like to extend my heartfelt thanks to Kathrin Finke, Nanette Gosling, Michaela Köger, and Regina Köpsell for their practical help in completing the manuscript for this book.

CHRISTOF GESTRICH
Berlin, July 14, 1989

Preface to the Second Edition

Since this book was first released, quite a few additional works on sin and evil have been published. This confirms the necessity of dealing intensively with this topic. However, in the meantime the gap between a Christian understanding of sin and evil on the one hand and a secular-philosophical understanding of it not tied to the faith of the church on the other hand seems to be widening *even more*. However, from the perspective of theology both concepts cannot be secularized, at least not without missing their meaning and beating them to death. It is also a serious mistake to ignore the gulf between the two linguistic worlds or to allow the task of bridging them to cost no far-reaching effort but only a few linguistic tricks. For we cannot get rid of the following fact: Detached from their significance within the faith of the church — and here this means precisely (irrespective of the spectrum within which this faith is found): Detached from the misguided relationship to God that human beings have established, but which is not existent and virulent without God's concurrent relationship to us — "sin" and "evil" are simply dubious, at best collective, literary terms used to describe negative phenomena and experiences. They are often used by secularists as intensely ethical concepts to express a heightened degree of reprehensibility for particular behaviors deemed to be immoral. Yet ironically this "secular interpretation" has also penetrated both theology and the church. It remains an unanswered question whether this does any "good" in deterring negative behaviors or whether it should be seen as a deluded reinforcement of what only drives human beings further into hopelessness, despair, and self-destruction. At any rate, this increases the sense of urgency we presently feel in developing our own church paradigms that enable us to deal with sin and guilt and talk about evil (for example, the key phrase "a new education in repentance is needed for those who have come of age").

On the whole I still hope to point us in the direction of what is necessary today with the present book, which is being republished without change, except for a few formal corrections. The book has received a good response, especially from many pastors serving various churches in Germany, Denmark, the Netherlands, and Switzerland. Yet it is clear to me that my discussion of the prospects for the future practice of the "forgiveness of sins" and for the future of "ecclesiology" which are tied here to the concept of *substitutionary action,* elucidated in the fourth chapter (the final part of the book), needs more detailed, further development in many places. I am hoping to see further work by others, and hope to be able to present a subsequent publication on this topic in the future.

I would also like to point out an essential contribution to the discussion of several questions dealt with in this book: the monograph by Hanns-Stephan Haas, *"Bekannte Sünde." Eine systematische Untersuchung zum Theologischen Reden von der Sünde in der Gegenwart* (Neukirchen, 1992). In two large sections of his treatise Haas refers on the one hand to Wolfhart Pannenberg's hamartiology and on the other hand to mine, speaking of them as two models of a doctrine of sin in light of our responsibility to the present historical and intellectual situation that should be compared to each other. Given the diversity of approaches and positions described by Haas, he carefully recognizes the complexity of the various *problem levels* on which any proper hamartiology must now move, and in the final section of his book he submits "rules" or, better, his own proposals as to how the mixing of these levels can be avoided and at the same time how a verifiability and cogent understanding of theological language about sin can be achieved or safeguarded — a language that must precisely clarify its own "objective." In any case, one of his results, that is, that a theological doctrine of sin must start with *forgiveness,* fits in well with the stated intention of my book. Wolfhart Pannenberg, too, dealt with my doctrine of sin in volume 2 of his *Systematic Theology* (Göttingen, 1991), pp. 279ff., and addressed the question I had put to his theology. This dialogue first concerns the theological significance of Immanuel Kant's understanding of sin and evil. But then and more substantially it concerns the question how we can talk clearly and at the same time in a theologically responsible manner about God, man, and sin in the general language situation of the modern era, which is not directly and predominantly guided by Christian doctrine at all. I addressed both Pannenberg's and Haas's further inquiries in the framework of a lecture at the Barth Conference of 1993 in Schoorl, Holland, with the brevity required there ("Typologie der Sünde. Über einige aktuelle Zugangsweisen zur Hamartiologie," *Zeitschrift für dialektische Theologie* 9, no. 1 [1993]: 35-47). I am very grateful that I do not stand alone today in my quest for helpful insights in this field. I especially include in this gratitude pertinent publications by and conversations with my friend and colleague, the Zurich systematic theologian Walter Mostert, who unfortunately died in March 1995 at the age of fifty-eight. Haas as well was right to point out in his book the theological significance of several essays from Walter Mostert's pen for the contemporary discussion of sin and evil. Finally, in this context I would like to mention gratefully the significant works of our common teacher Gerhard Ebeling pertaining to this topic.

CHRISTOF GESTRICH
Berlin, Sunday Exaudi,
May 28, 1995

Preface to the
English Edition

After being largely silent for decades, theology has returned to the subject of sin with renewed intensity. There is an urgent need to make up for this lack of attention, and that is why several books on sin and evil have recently been published in rapid succession. It is no different in Europe than in America. However, it is surprising to note that the particular questions being asked are almost the same on both continents: How does the human sin and forgiveness described in the Bible relate to the emotional disturbances and misguided behaviors psychology and the social sciences research and then treat therapeutically? Based on our present level of knowledge, how should we view the biblical language about the atonement for our sins given to us by God? What can we do with an atonement that has been given as a gift? How can Christian faith help us prevent humanity from completely destroying its ecological habitat and itself and expose its blind faith in technology? How must traditional dogmatic teaching on sin be reformulated to include the questions and insights of feminist theology, liberation theology, and economic ethics? Where are the limits and the problems of such inclusiveness to be located when it comes to developing the Christian doctrine of sin and forgiveness for our day? How can we make it clear today that much more than merely questions of sexuality and morality are at issue when we talk about sin? What is the connection between sins against God and sins against human beings? What is the connection between sin and man's predicament of seeing no meaning in life? How can we talk about God, human sin, and evil *after* Auschwitz and given the technical possibility of anonymous "mass destruction"?

These many questions require a coherent, new presentation of the complete doctrine of sin on the basis of a broad, ecumenical consensus. At the beginning of the nineties I took several trips to North America to visit congregations of the United Church of Christ. I also visited various theological seminaries in Great Britain and the United States. I was able to observe how western Europe and North America have joined forces in Christian doctrine to share a common destiny of theological inquiry. At the Duke University Divinity School in Durham, North Carolina, I was able to lecture on the "Atonement" and carry on discussions, particularly with the liberation theologian Frederick Herzog (†1995), who also introduced me to additional American literature relevant to this subject. This began with Karl Menninger, *Whatever Became of Sin?* (1973), and in the intervening years has extended to Cornelius Plantinga Jr., *Not the Way It's Supposed to Be: A Breviary of Sin* (1995). In this work Plantinga examines the "masks" sin wears today and seeks to renew the language of theology used to articulate the doctrine of sin in the same way I have attempted to do. Whoever compares the book by Ted Peters, *Radical Evil in Soul and Society,* published in 1994, with my book will recognize even more common themes, although we did not yet know anything about each other when we were writing our books. In this case, what we have in common comes not only from the global problems of our time but from a common grounding in Luther's theology, which we firmly believe should be rediscovered and reinterpreted. For it is not true that Luther — as is so often claimed — portrayed man in somber colors as "twisted by nature" and "forced under the yoke of sin from generation to generation." In fact, Luther is encouraging; he stresses that it is man's destiny to be free. Luther's teaching on the creative Word of God is extremely relevant, and his doctrine of sin is the opposite of a lament on the "moral imperfections" of man.

The scales fell from my eyes when I realized that until now an important biblical concept has been completely neglected in the Christian understanding of sin. It is the term which is called "doxa" in New Testament Greek but which also appears frequently in the Old Testament. This concept can describe the glory, beauty, and splendor of both God and human beings in the Bible. Whoever wants to elucidate today what sin means can in my opinion no longer ignore the concept of "doxa." Sin leads us human beings not only into immorality but also into the loss of splendor, the loss of "doxa." This is why the meaning of the forgiveness of sins must even be stated and understood in aesthetic categories: Forgiveness must restore our splendor, our beauty! Seeing this clearly can come to the aid of Luther's teaching on the justification of the sinner. We should never disdainfully say, "After all, those are *only* aesthetic categories," because the gift of splendor is just as far-reaching as its loss, resulting in violence and destruction, and even attracting evil in a demonic way. Therefore we must reflect theologically on the beauty of man, his surroundings, and his actions! Remarkably, I found significantly fewer reflections on this subject by contemporary Protestant theologians than in many a Catholic or Eastern Orthodox work. Even if I have never quoted from it, the multivolume opus by Hans Urs von Balthasar, *Glory* (1961ff.), as well as the ideas developed by several of his students, has encouraged me.

My book was written in Berlin in the eighties — at that time an especially unattractive city in several respects. Many were of the opinion that it was interesting but ugly and without a future. As a theologian coming from the Bultmannian school, I believed that an extensive "hermeneutical translation" in the area of the theological doctrine of sin had to be made to account for the changing lifestyles in modern urban society. The last really thorough work on the doctrine of sin came from the nineteenth century. But the way in which human beings have experienced guilt and shame — and liberation from both — has drastically changed since then. Today it is no longer obvious that the word "sin" will be immediately used when a human being is proud of his own strength or beauty, when he learns to say "I," and when he aspires to obtain an affirmation of his own dignity and integrity. But then, where does the "firm boundary" run, the wall between man's necessary self-affirmation and his sinful self-justification?

When I attempted to clarify this question and distinguish between legitimate and sinful pride, two things became clear to me. First, I recognized the necessity of once again seeking serious dialogue with the respective views of classical philosophical thinkers of the modern era in the area of the Christian doctrine of sin and once again dealing undauntedly with the problems of secularization. (The Catholic theologian Eugen Drewermann did this in Germany a few years before me in his work *Structures of Evil,* parts 1-3 [1976-78], 4th ed. [1982/83], but he came to different conclusions than I. The path he took in his work led him ever more closely to psychology, but the path I took led me away from this academic discipline that is so dominant in our time.) Second, I recognized the necessity of acknowledging Karl Barth's great contributions in renewing the teaching of theological doctrine and making it fruitful for the doctrine of sin. These contributions seem to me to be even more "timely" than anything that has originated with Friedrich Schleiermacher and Ernst Troeltsch. Barth is not simply "neoorthodox," if this term is used to describe those theologians who follow Tillich. Rather, Barth is the first person in Protestant theology to make a credible case for the view that human beings realize themselves by *taking action* and in this way must bring about their freedom, self-determination, and responsibility. This is consistent with the idea Barth stressed in the same breath that all creatures are dependent on the grace of the free and autonomous God. Barth saw no contradiction in this, unlike Dorothee Sölle, for example. In my opinion he is right. In keeping with this view he tried to fashion the doctrine of the law and gospel differently than Luther. According to Barth the law even belongs in the gospel. But for me all of this represented the difficult, hermeneutical challenge of theologically harmonizing Barth and Luther, but also Barth and Bultmann (in spite of the many conflicts Barth had with the Lutheran tradition). I hope that at least to some extent I have succeeded in doing this in the present study. I would also have liked to develop the doctrine of sin completely from the perspective of the *forgiveness of sins* along the lines of Barth's theology, but this has been only partially successful. Likewise, at the end of my book I could only allude to why the reality of forgiveness is closely connected to the reality of *substitutionary action.* I think we should go beyond Barth in ontologically developing this concept of substitutionary action, which is also an important concept in Barth's dogmatics.

As a student I once had the privilege of attending the seminars of the theologians Karl Barth, Emil Brunner, and Paul Tillich, who were already in their eighties at that time. I was also able to talk to them personally and ask questions. These impressions, as well as the experience of studying Luther and hermeneutics under my teacher Gerhard Ebeling (Zurich), are still important to me. Although in the intervening years we have entered a completely new era, I think it is advisable for those of us who are modern theologians not to allow ourselves to be challenged only by our own experiences and by crime stories in the media and not to become "post-modern" too quickly in our methodology. Instead we should give an account of the new course we want to chart and explain what reasons we have for it.

A minor academic dispute with my colleague Wolfhart Pannenberg has already occurred over issues in the doctrine of sin that are of common interest to both of us. We are both anxious to do theology with intellectual depth and not only in a tight ecclesiastical corner. However, Immanuel Kant's philosophy of religion has been the focus of our discussion because our views differ considerably on this issue. Kant adopted the idea from Augustine that it is not the "physical desire" of man that is evil, but, strictly speaking, only the confusion that results when we deal with physical desire as if it were a matter of morality that had to be justified before the bar of reason; conversely, we deal with the moral imperatives of reason as if they were a matter of physical desire. This misguided thinking, Kant says, following Augustine, is evil, it is "without reason," and only a revolution in man's way of thinking can redeem human beings from this evil. This almost sounds Christian, but it is not. For according to the Christian Augustine, this confusion in our orientation is identical with man's confusion of the Creator with the creature (see Rom. 1:23). However, in Kant the question of man's wrong relationship to God is completely left out. Kant is content to note the inexplicable confusion of the material and spiritual principle in man. Pannenberg nevertheless sees the kinship Kant has with Augustine and believes Kant's understanding of evil is a stroke of fortune for theology, or at least a possible point of contact within the secular thought of modernity. However, I do not think so because I do not expect any success from such a point of contact and would prefer to think — along the lines of Barth — that a *theologically* enlightened Kant improved by Augustine would be a stroke of fortune for more recent philosophy and its post-Kantian developments up to the present. Does the Bible or does the modern secular "enlightenment" offer the more comprehensive thought?

In spite of the interpretations of Scripture offered in this book that are sometimes traced back to their various philosophical and historical contexts, I hope that it can help theology students, pastors, and others in North America and the English-speaking world to understand the phenomenon of "sin" in their thinking, in their pastoral care, and in their preaching and to radiate hope and light when confronting it.

CHRISTOF GESTRICH
Berlin, Easter 1996

Acknowledgments

I am much indebted to Daniel W. Bloesch for his excellent translation of this book. In many cases he had to reinterpret concepts and ideas peculiar to the German academic world, and he has accomplished this task with great sensibility and accuracy.

I am very grateful to William B. Eerdmans, Jr., for his willingness to publish this book in his house and his personal support during the process of publication. I owe many thanks to several others as well: Jennifer Hoffman was responsible for the friendly cooperation between Grand Rapids, MI, and Berlin, Germany. On the other side of the Atlantic Peter Bartmann and Holger Rohde, my chair and student assistants, read the proofs and made some valuable suggestions for the English edition. My friend Bruce McCallum in New Berlin, WI, was the helpful guardian angel in the time of preparations. The Deutsche Forschungsgemeinschaft (DFG) gave considerable financial support for the translation through its program "Inter Nationes." The Evangelische Kirche der Union (EKU) has also supported the English publication of this book; in so doing its president, Dr. Wilhelm Hueffmeier, wishes to contribute to the promising theological conversation with its North American sister church, the United Church of Christ (UCC). I feel gratitude to both institutions for this loyal and generous backing.

Seven Introductory Meditations

1. WHEN THINGS NO LONGER HAVE ANY SPLENDOR

> The Golden Age has passed.
>
> Georg Trakl, "Rondel"

When things no longer have any splendor their destruction is imminent. People who are headed for destruction are first deprived of their honor, stripped of their rights, and their outward appearance takes on a pathetic, ugly form.

An experience that is just the opposite of this is the shining face of a child or the promising radiance that spreads over a new day in the early morning, and especially over Sundays and holidays, renewing both space and time.

With great apprehension we register the decline of splendor in our world today. With alarming speed *everything* seems to be wearing out, and man seems to squander *everything* irrevocably. In many places even spring has become muter and duller. That is why we fear for our survival and are afraid that nothing more will be left even for our children. This fear is most pronounced in Europe. Here the signs of the destruction that has already occurred are especially obtrusive. But in principle all of humanity is threatened by the developments that have emerged from Western civilization.

Thus a universal sense of urgency is felt in this question. Can there be a return of splendor for us? *Although this sounds improbable and would seem*

1

to be paradoxical, can the inner vitality of things, relationships, plants, animals, and human beings return once again to the very place where they have already begun to recede? Although Christianity has itself become deeply entangled in this process of modern decline, can it still be a source of hope?

To the people of antiquity *world history* appeared to be a cyclical up-and-down of people and cultures that have competed against each other. The first became the last. Those cultures that had previously been small and humble in origin rose to new ascendancy. When the fateful decline of a people began, which always happened sooner or later, when at first the inner splendor of morals and religious life and later the splendor of external power faded, often visionaries appeared who warned them about their impending doom. Nevertheless it inevitably occurred. The walls of the beautiful, great city were finally torn down. The fire on the main altar was also extinguished. Never again would it burn in that place. In the end everything returned to its original condition and became an uncultivated wasteland from which something quite different emerged much later.

The vision of the "decline of the West" (Oswald Spengler) that appeared at the beginning of the twentieth century tied in with these self-evident truths of antiquity. But this vision was shocking. It touched on a Western taboo because it asserted that even the culture of Europe shaped by *Christianity,* having attained an unparalleled level of intellectual, scientific, and economic development and having ascended to the status of world power, would decline again and that it, too, is already lapsing back into an uncultivated state. This assertion shook the common conviction that was still existent in secularized Europe: Even if the previous cultures had gone around in circles, of course *WE* are on a very different path, on which sometime and somehow the highest level of development destined for humanity will be reached. Our civilization is irreversible. There is only progress and continuous self-perfection for it. The New Testament certainty that the crucifixion and resurrection of Jesus Christ were the proleptic end of world history continued to reverberate through this "faith." Concluding from this "faith" that since their history had only been moving forward under the leadership of the "Christian peoples" for the purpose of bringing in the harvest, many Westerners were and are of the wishful belief that a *Christian* people is influenced by the promise of continuing to the end of time. For Christ said in Matthew 28:20: "Surely I am with you always, to the very end of the age." Spengler's prediction of decline struck this structure of conviction like lightning. His major two-volume work, which was published between 1917 and 1922, was considered to be frivolous even by Europeans who had long been alienated from the church.

Spengler's prediction deeply affected contemporaries, who then became fascists and National Socialists. What "moved" the intellectuals among them was a revolt against the view that from now on they had to suffer the fate of a declining, late culture. In an academic lecture in Göttingen at the beginning of the "Third Reich," "the present intellectual situation in the mirror of philosophical and theological reflection" could be interpreted as follows: "This is the final secret of the bold German undertaking of 1933, that we desire to restore the power of natural ties that are characteristic of a young culture and thus overcome the life-destroying violence of late culture on the foundation of an efficient and technological late culture, utilizing all of its resources even if we are abandoned by all historical examples for the possibility of such an endeavor" (Emanuel Hirsch, 1934).

This attempt at restoration has failed. It shared this negative result with numerous modern attempts to bring about a "second naturalness." However, for a long time now inconsistencies in Spengler's own existing explanation of the "law of world history" have been documented. And yet Spengler asked contemporary Christianity an essential question with which the Western churches have not yet adequately come to terms to this day. The question is: It may well be true that there will be a Christian church, and thus Christianity, to the very end of the age. But are the Westerners, the Europeans, really Christian nations, a part of "Christendom," a society inextricably linked to the future course of the church? Should we not rather make a precise distinction between the fact that the Christianization of the Roman Empire was an *influential factor* in the continuing cultural developments of the nations of Europe, extending into all the various stages of secularization, on the one hand, and on the other hand the fact that these nations by no means simply represented *Christendom* and never differed qualitatively from other nations? Once we have arrived at this subtle view, we will perhaps conclude: Our historical linkage with a Christianity that today in many respects has assumed the status of a secularized cultural inheritance offers no real reason to assume an exceptional mission and duration of the West in terms of salvation history.

But on the other hand, can Christianity lived as a dynamic faith be clearly separated from the form of Christianity that only lives on as a cultural inheritance? In the past decades, Protestant theology has been deeply affected by this question in a subconscious way. Although the outcome is complex, as a whole the question must be answered in the negative. A separation of genuine faith from the superficially adopted Christian cultural inheritance is thus not generally possible.

However, then, there is still some theological plausibility to the old assumption that there is something special about the history of Christianity in which we have a part, even for the secularized West that has become a "late culture" long since entangled in guilt and failure. Something is left that cannot perish. An immortal aspect is left that can be regained. Christians believe that world history will never go beyond Jesus Christ, that, on the contrary, all creatures have *him* in front of them as their hope and goal. This theologically essential statement must sound aggressive in the ears of many people in this dogmatic form. It is justified only if it is not remembered as an expression of Christian imperialism. Western Christians must learn: There is still a "living hope" for the world not because and as long as there are still Christians and the church "in these parts," but because even in the future Jesus Christ radiates life and hope for the whole world, because there continue to be opportunities for life together between Christians and non-Christians, between Westerners, Asians, and African peoples.

2. CHRISTIANITY AND SIN

The very concept in which Christianity differs most crucially in kind from paganism is, . . . sin, the doctrine of sin. And so, quite consistently, Christianity also assumes that neither paganism nor the natural man knows what sin is; yes, it assumes there must be a revelation from God to reveal what sin is.

Søren Kierkegaard, *The Sickness unto Death*

Let us attempt to observe the trail Christianity has left through its history up to the present in one panoramic view. It has brought the world some experiences and images of a level of human achievement and beauty that have perhaps never been reached before, full of power to enlighten and liberate humankind. Unfortunately, when this is said, we must immediately add: The previous history of Christianity has also produced horrifying experiences and images of hell of an intensity and composition never known before. Christianity "makes the good better and the bad worse" (Romano Guardini). Thus Christianity considered as a historical force seems to demonstrate the truth of the proverb "Where there is much light, there are also many shadows."

In its doctrine Christianity is able to speak in an emphatic and comprehensive way not only of good news for the whole world but also of a *shadow* that is cast over the world. In the modern era Christianity has often been criticized for its ostensibly pessimistic assessment of the world and humankind compared to other religions. This criticism was often made with the intention of "improving" it — reinterpreted in the spirit of the Old Testament or the Enlightenment. It was asserted that the message and theology of Christianity bear a share of the blame for humanity's frequent failures, which have resulted in catastrophic explosions and "merciless consequences" (Carl Amery) in our Christianized age. Characteristically, J. G. Fichte (1762-1814) demanded: "We must take for granted that all human beings are good." With this statement he intended to *contradict* decisively ecclesiastical, but especially pietistic, traditions, though wanting to do justice to what he considered to be the actual intention of Christianity.

Today the dark world that was the very real opposite of paradise for the European of the Middle Ages is referred to reproachfully or at least with a lack of understanding — the world of "weeping and gnashing of teeth," the abyss of hell into which all would invariably descend and enter eternal torment, as the church once taught and believed, all who could not be saved in time by the remedies of the church, or, even worse, all who were not already elected before the foundation of the world and consequently were damned and rejected.

The word that linked all people to this dark world in the Middle Ages was called *sin*. Great fear of it bestowed unparalleled power on the church. Its sacraments, tied to ecclesiastical office (the office of bishop or priest), were the only means of salvation. However, sin lurked everywhere. It lurked in sexual lust and sensuality in general. It lurked in the "magic" or "witchcraft" of certain outsiders of society who were used as scapegoats. But at the same time the members of the honorable classes felt themselves to be morally and religiously impure, reprehensible on account of their everyday life. The fear they felt was excessive, and sin was felt to be real in a way we can no longer imagine today. Today we have other fears. However, in those days it was taken for granted that after our death we need the benefit of a temporary cleansing fire, purgatory, in order to pass God's last judgment and enter eternity. Even when secular judges condemned people to die at the stake in certain cases, it was often viewed as a basically charitable *ultima ratio* to save their souls.

Who would not want to criticize this today! Who could overlook the fact that "sin" in this situation was brought into play to a large extent not on the basis of divine revelation, but, to use Kierkegaard's phrase, only on the basis of human aberration and confusion! How could the great burden of guilt be overlooked that the church loaded on itself by torturing and killing human beings in inquisitions and crusades supposedly for *the glory of God!* On the other hand, who can overlook the fact that in those days the personality of each individual was discerned with a seriousness and a radical logic which we largely lack today. And who can deny that "in our enlightened modern age" we have not yet simply lost the darkest visions and most perverse mechanisms of dealing with life, of which there was certainly no shortage in the Middle Ages? On the contrary!

The *division of reality* into *this life on earth* and the *hereafter* (or into a transitory world of the material and physical and an eternal, immortal world of the spiritual and the immortal soul) became uncommon among us. If in the first half of the nineteenth century faint, final traces of this former idea about the existence of two spheres of reality had still survived (for example, belief in ghosts or fear of ghosts, the fear of returning "poor souls"), the second half of the past century and then the twentieth century for the first time brought a massive, complete rejection of *all* ideas about the hereafter, the bright ones as well as the dark ones. Both the garden of paradise and the quagmire of hell are no longer considered to be real localities in the hereafter. Instead the idea of *heaven and hell being located in existing human beings themselves,* an idea already prefigured in medieval mysticism, gained persuasiveness. Of course with this change in perspective the stamp of ultimacy was imprinted on transitory and changeable human entities.

In view of these changes it was logical that in the nineteenth and twentieth centuries the awareness of the masses that *God exists* and directs world history "from the outside" and obliges us to obey him was also permanently shaken. But the *devil* was virtually *abolished.* Because in so doing contemporary human beings place responsibility for the outcome of world history on themselves, we can say: In recent times, humanity has replaced God as well as the devil *in terms of its own consciousness.*

Have we even begun to cope with this historically very recent process of burdening ourselves with immense responsibility and investing ourselves with the brightest qualities and the darkest heinousness? Are we at all suited to bear such responsibility? Or is it even an extreme expression of sinful aberration?

At any rate, it is an especially important concomitant of these processes that when *we talk about sin and sinners* we have become vague and uncertain and sin has lost its former horrors. This kind of talk is only meaningful provided that God exists and faces us. (This kind of talk is also *possible* without this assumption, but would it still be meaningful?)

Since the beginning of the modern age the leading intellectuals have frequently endeavored to eliminate the idea of humanity's original sin against a divine authority or transcendent origin of the world. Nietzsche's philosophy represented the high point of this endeavor. Moreover, modern science furnishes so many explanations for human misbehavior that today we hardly dare to attribute personal guilt to anyone. Furthermore, science helped us defeat certain ills that used to be accepted as inevitable by our own efforts. Therefore, is Christian talk of human sin finished? My preliminary thesis is that this is by no means the case.

3. "RIDER AND HORSE" IN FREUD AND LUTHER

We could compare the relationship of the ego to the id with that of the rider to his horse. The horse provides energy for the locomotion, the rider has the privilege of determining the destination and guiding the movement of the strong horse. However, all too frequently the ideal situation between the ego and the id does not occur. Instead, the rider has to guide the horse where it wants to go itself.

Sigmund Freud, *The New Series of Lectures on the Introduction to Psychoanalysis* (1932/33)

So man's will is like a beast standing between two riders. If God rides, it wills and goes where God wills. . . . If Satan rides, it wills and goes where Satan wills. Nor may it choose to which rider it will run, or which it will seek; but the riders themselves fight to decide who shall have and hold it.

Martin Luther, *The Bondage of the Will* (1525)

Two images of the "rider and horse." Freud compared the human ego to a *relatively* helpless *rider* sitting on a wild horse (referring to the drives, the powerful unconscious id, the blind forces of nature). However, Luther characterized human will and thus man himself (!) as the beast that must always have one of the following two masters in the saddle: either God or the devil.

When compared to each other, both images seem to express characteristic differences between the modern enlightenment and the Middle Ages, or, put differently, between autonomy and a mentality placed under predetermined "eternal orders." In the modern age man is *the rider.* In the Middle Ages he seems to have understood himself to be the *animal* being ridden. Still, modern man can define his own destiny without using the "ciphers" God and Satan. However, in an earlier age he was always compelled to speak of God and the devil when he wanted to talk about his own nature and destiny. Yet, this is a more than superficial comparison! It must be immediately modified and improved when we consider the respective contexts of the quotations.

Surprisingly, both in Freud, who corrects certain idealistic concepts from the eighteenth and nineteenth centuries, and in Luther, who corrects traditional theological concepts about free will, it boils down to the fact that in a specific way man is a powerless being! Man is portrayed by Luther and Freud as a being at the mercy of a superior power.

Luther's statement about the bondage of our will was not "medieval" at all. And while Luther allowed man freedom of choice in matters of economics and civilization, if not in his relationship to God in accordance with reason, Freud of all people could not stress enough how restricted the human ego and its reason really are and how imperiled they are in the little leeway they have, how precariously the ego is situated in its complicated position between the superego and id (which is far superior to the ego in its expansiveness and force). Man is much less the master of his own house than modern man had assumed up to that time. Surely, to a certain degree Freud, too, believed in the power of human reason to enlighten and heal and in the possibility of strengthening the ego over against the superego and the id. Yet he was remarkably reserved and skeptical about the question of whether it is possible with the help of human reason to create a culture which would be able to grant individuals more freedom and happiness.

In Freud's image, the human ego is riding in the saddle of the beast on which, according to Luther, either God or an idol sits. But in Freud's image, where did God and the devil go? Both are no longer tangible at all! Here are only the concepts of a good or bright and a dark or evil demonic power. The human ego is destined to be the rider, so whatever makes it strong is good — for example, enlightening reason. What is dark or evil is mainly found in the "horse," in the powerful, sexually motivated id. Its physical superiority is a hostile factor that should be limited and controlled in the name of the good, that is, human reason.

A sufficiently profound discussion between Christian theology and Freudian psychoanalysis must begin with Freud's theory that faith in God is based on an infantile, regressive need for security. It inhibits eo ipso the vitally important human effort of strengthening the ego by using human reason and thus making it freer.

Against Freud it can be said from the perspective of Luther: Christian faith and Freud's goal of strengthening the ego in fact are not in conflict; rather, they converge. What the New Testament and the Reformers call "faith" hinders neither the process of human maturing nor the testing that occurs when we endure and shape reality. Nor does this faith spare us fear and suffering, which are essential for our maturing from one particular viewpoint. In view of pain and suffering, faith is not a defensive, repressive attitude, but a courageous one. Freud himself could not understand that a person can totally surrender himself to God without remaining dependent. Freud interpreted such a willingness to believe as a projection of the internalized image of the earthly father into heavenly dimensions (inhibiting the process of maturing). In his therapeutic practice it was important to reverse this projection and trace it back to its anthropological origin, to the early childhood desire for security.

At this point any theologically sound Christian teaching follows a different course that Freud did not take into consideration. Christian theologies assume that God encounters us as the other from outside ourselves, whereas we run the risk of "corrupting" him, obsessed with the desire to subordinate or conform him to our thoughts and desires, thus confusing the Creator himself with his creatures. However, because this is the basic pattern of sin, the comprehensive healing of man must begin with that event of faith in which human beings become willing to recognize God as the one who is in fact outside ourselves, different from us and free in relation to us. If we do not arrive at such faith, then we will by no means become or remain "our own master"; rather, according to Luther, the devil is already riding us! Then it is also inevitable that we will labor under a delusion and inflate our ego. That is not at all what Freud intends; he cannot want that at all. But we must ask whether he can prevent it or rule it out on the basis of his assumptions.

Therefore, what occupies the attention of theologians when they are dealing with "faith" and "sin" neither stands *alongside* the psychotherapeutic endeavor nor is an object *for* psychotherapeutic action; rather, it emerges *out of* psychotherapeutic action itself (and its task should be carried out by theologians in solidarity with it!). In the modern age it has become an increasingly dreadful situation that God and the devil have not simply "disappeared" but have been "lost" in the human ego (superego) and id, *which is even more problematic!*

In this situation a socially and also *politically* important new task has arisen for theology, a task that has yet to be properly fulfilled by it, the task of demythologizing human nature, resisting any ideologically or religiously conditioned human self-enlargement or self-reduction! It is essential to draw the logical conclusion from an insight with which every theologian should at least be familiar. We are on a slippery, self-destructive slope when we identify ourselves and nature with divine or demonic characteristics (partially or completely, unconsciously or consciously, in secularized or religious form). We are then expecting too much of ourselves and nature. We want to get more out of both than they can give. To reach this goal, we develop among other things a moralistic legalism without a sense of humor, without joy, without grace. The freedom we have strived for shatters beneath our hands.

However, we ourselves slip back into a kind of intellectual, moral "Stone Age," partially into gnostic, dualistic thinking, dividing reality symbolically into a realm of darkness and a realm of light, into a devilish and a divinely favored sphere (without believing in the devil or in God!), partially into a "Canaanite paganism" that excessively elevates the forces of blood and soil, nation and race. Both of these in the twentieth century! The violent conflict between both of these wrong paths ("ideologies") describes the present situation.

4. THE LANGUAGE OF THE DOCTRINE OF SIN

> We do not even talk about "sin" in the science I study. We wouldn't be able to associate anything with this topic.
>
> A Berlin medical student, 1987

In spite of and because of the existence of modern science, it is now high time that Christian theology once again speaks about sin in an informative and revealing manner. The embarrassment many modern theologians feel about their task of making accurate, thought-provoking statements about sin stands in sharp contrast to the bulk of the population. The average layman has a hunch about or an experience of unrestrained, active, evil "powers and structures" that are not understood, yet present among us. But theology is still tilting at windmills as it struggles with the rearguard of the seventeenth- and eighteenth-century Enlightenment. It allows itself to be paralyzed by focusing on the challenges posed by the Enlightenment's critique of religion. In the process, it neglects present-day challenges. Its weakness in the area of the doctrine of sin is a symptom of its tendency to live in the past. Not only its perception of reality but also its authority and presence of mind in other theological contexts, mainly in its doctrine of God, suffer from this shortcoming. Of course, the reverse is also true. If we could once again speak about sin in an understandable and definite way, theology could also win back all the other subjects of Christian doctrine for our time.

We can expect that a theologically adequate doctrine of sin will not further intensify a widespread pessimism nor paint an unsurpassably dark picture, but help its target audience to gain more hope and lead a life that can also encourage other people.

At the outset, we still face a task that has already been tackled by many in the twentieth century, the task of freeing the doctrine of sin from a *moralizing narrowness* that has become deeply ingrained in us. Sin is not to be equated with moral misbehavior that could be modified by education and the appropriate learning processes. What good educator would consider the offer of grace and forgiveness helpful when looking at sin? And is it urgent for theology of all disciplines to take an interest in this matter? However, in order to do justice to the perspectives on sin we encounter in the Bible as well as our own situation, we need a conceptuality that embraces ethical problems but is not completely absorbed in them.

Modern theology can learn various things from modern philosophical and human scientific formulations of the concept of *guilt*. But one would be mistaken to think that these formulations of the concept of guilt were as a rule clear and evident, whereas theology no longer has the chance to speak intelligibly to all by clinging to the concept of *sin*. First it must be stated that modern secular talk of guilt has by no means brought clarity to this phenomenon. Everything has remained controversial. Is there really guilt or are there only guilt feelings? How can the presence of guilt be measured? For example, when I read Heidegger I think my guilt lies in the fact that I let many possibilities life offers me slip by unused because I have to decide and then choose, for instance, the *one* possibility of writing a thick book. But *is* this guilt? A confusing and long line of various modern, secular interpretations of the guilt phenomenon faces us. One moment they stress that guilt is an essential part of being human, the next they stress that guilt means at least a temporary failure in the task of being human. One moment they teach, as especially Karl Jaspers did in the twentieth century, that man is the one being capable of changing his ways and thus overcoming guilt; however, the next moment, similar to classic Greek tragedy, they place more emphasis on the fateful character of guilt. This pluralism of interpretations indicates two things: for one it points back to its own cause, which can be seen in how the phenomenon of guilt degenerates into the private and inward realm in the modern age. A life lived in obedience to the laws of the state is the only thing that is still officially demanded of the individual in the modern era. The laws must be obeyed. How the individual incurs guilt in other ways is hardly of public interest. At best, it is of scientific interest because modern man hopes for further liberation from more extensive scientific investigations. What remain are private guilt feelings. In some ways there can no longer be any norm to understand them because of their highly individual character. However, on the other hand, contemporary pluralism indicates that the identity of meaning found in the concepts "sin" *(peccatum)* and "guilt" *(culpa, reatus)* has long since been shattered even though it erupted well beyond the time of the Reformation. Furthermore, it has frequently become uncertain whether those who speak of guilt would also like to mention sin — or whether they do not want to at all.

With all of this, we were almost thrown back to the beginning in trying to understand and speak of theological hamartiology. From many sides the inadequacy of the present state of the doctrine is partly observed, partly asserted, recently from the field of feminist theology as well where they complain about the predominance of masculine descriptions or ways of seeing sin (for example, understanding sin as arrogance and self-assertion, but not as self-neglect or self-sacrifice, which they are more likely to see as feminine manifestations of sin). Although such views are not plausible, it has in fact become necessary to rethink and reformulate the theological doctrine of sin and guilt with its many ramifications.

The nontraditional conceptuality I will try out in parts of this treatise reveals a biblically based contact with the terminology most likely encountered in the field of aesthetics. But it will not be a matter of repeating what Kierkegaard called the aesthetic existence of man, which he distinguished from ethical and believing existence. Even less do I want to put forward Kierkegaard's description of aesthetic existence as the main key to understanding (sinful) man. I also do not intend to make the case for an aesthetic justification or recovery of human beings which is supposed to be the only remaining option following the line of philosophical thinking advocated, for instance, by Schiller and, in another form, by Nietzsche. Examples from more recent history deter us from doing that! For reasons having to do exclusively with the present theological situation, I will occasionally couch the doctrine of sin in terms that are also encountered in philosophical investigations of *the relationship between the part and the whole.* Then we can draw the following analogy: Just as it is part of the experience of beauty that the greater whole of reality appears in one of its parts or partial aspects, so, too, when genuine humanity appears in a certain person, the unity between this individual and humanity as a whole and even the whole world shines forth. The problem of sin is seen in the absence, hampering, or destruction of this unity (which from a theological perspective can be traced back to a lack of unity with God).

At this point in the discussion, we can already make this general statement about sin: It somehow takes away the "satisfaction" people gain from their relationships. Their splendor disappears in the wake of sin and separation from God. Everything becomes worthless, mean, and base — even when taking place in an intelligent and orderly fashion. Fear and hopelessness enter because the future is closed.

From the perspective of the biblical data, this unusual approach to the phenomenon of "sin," though only partially new in terms of historical theology, is more obvious than perhaps first assumed. After all, Augustine wrote in the *Confessiones* (3.8): "turpis est omnis pars universo suo non congruens." This approach takes its bearings from the basic biblical concept of "glory" (Hebrew *kabod,* Greek *doxa,* Latin *gloria*).

5. *KABOD* AND THE LOSS OF *KABOD* IN THE OLD TESTAMENT

Abraham had become very wealthy in livestock and in silver and gold.

Genesis 13:2

The Hebrew word *kabod* is derived from a verb that originally meant "to be heavy" (in weight, in dignity). That is why *kabod* can mean honor and majesty as well as glory and splendor or whatever makes something imposing and attractive. Whoever has it looks impressive, whoever lacks it can be forgotten.

In the Old Testament, *kabod* is not only attributed to God but, at the same time, to certain human beings and other creatures. Abraham, for example, had *kabod*. Because God's blessing rested on him, he was very rich or (translated literally) "heavy" with cattle, silver, and gold. Israel's nobility was once characterized by Isaiah as the *kabod* of the nation (Isa. 5:13). The same prophet could also speak of the *kabod* of a forest. He prophesied that God would wipe out the glory of Assyria's forest. The splendor of his forests and fertile fields it will completely destroy, as when a sick man wastes away (Isa. 10:18). Of course, then Assyria will not only lose an external adornment but its inner vitality. This Bible verse also makes clear that when the *kabod* fades, body and soul are affected. Its loss results primarily from their disobedience to God's commandments and condemns them to infertility and extinction.

Thus in the Old Testament, the *kabod* of the creatures is their honor, splendor, dignity, and glory — in short, God's good pleasure resting on them without which they become barren and perish. Israel is taught again and again that it will come to an end if it turns away from God and his commandments because the *kabod* of his creatures stands or falls depending on whether their will is in harmony with the will of God. When such harmony is present, his creatures are bathed in splendor. Without it, they lose their splendor and cease to have a promising future.

The meaning of our human longing for God is found not primarily in an infantile need for protection and a desire for security that continues to exist even in the soul of adults, as modern critics of religion thought. Rather, it is found primarily in our desire to share in that splendor which offers us human beauty and future, strength and life. Human beings whose face and ears are

turned away from the One in whose image we are made, lack nothing at all
— except this splendor. Man without God is not a cripple. Man does not
"need" a relationship with God to share fully in human possibilities (in the
sense of capabilities) and to find happiness in his life. Statements to the
contrary make for poor evangelistic preaching! It is merely the splendor of
divine pleasure that man cannot create for himself without God. For the
Bible this is serious enough. "The ax is set at the roots" of whoever lacks
kabod or whose glory has dwindled away; he does not have the "righteousness
which counts in the sight of God." For that reason, his right to exist is called
into question or has already been terminated.

The *kabod* comes from God. With the *kabod,* God honors his creatures.
Most of all God's own honor consists in lending his creatures *kabod,* thus
sharing his own divine splendor with them. In so doing, he does not look
at their merit or worthiness. In this event he stoops down to his creatures.
That is why there are human beings among them who have a need to
praise God and thank him. This doxology is the highest expression of
worship that is possible for us on earth. When we perform this act of
worship, we ourselves are bathed in splendor.

However, when man wants to be his own Creator and when he actually
succeeds in creating his own new world for himself, he can never lend his
creatures the splendor that issues from the divine Creator of the world. The
"perfect robot" is and remains a profound symbol of human "creativity."
Adam, the representative of all human beings, does not become the one to
whom his "creatures" offer praise and honor as if man had honored them
with their splendor! No, this remains an insurmountable limit to our power.

From Greek mythology we know all too well the motive of the gods'
envy of human beings. Yet it is hard for us to be transparent ourselves in
our hidden envy of God, who brings his creatures to life and then takes
them out of it, who can lend them his splendor and then take it away
again. However, this secret human envy of God (God as man imagines
him) is the *root of human sin* that we can hardly understand, the "root of
our God complex" (H. E. Richter).

Therefore we must ask: *Is not Adam's sin precisely his attempt to continually reestablish and re-create reality on his own authority just as God did, yet
without being able to make a real creation, without even being able to fathom
fully the plan and nature of the existing creation, let alone being able to bear
it with an attitude of humility and submission and bestowing his own splendor
on it?*

Man's reluctance to work together with God, his desire to manage without the Creator and be his own creator, can indeed be called *sin*. It is an attack on God's honor that at the same time robs the sinner and the creatures affected by his behavior of their honor by taking away their *kabod* or inner vitality.

Does God simply accept such human sin by which he is robbed of the praise that is his due? It seems so. God apparently does not obstruct man's determination to live without him. In this respect he seems to allow us complete freedom. But doesn't he cruelly mislead us in this way; in fact, doesn't he destroy us with such "generosity"? Feelings of this nature were found in many of the most serious laments often intoned by devout Israelites, of all people. Christians must ultimately come to grips with such laments in dialogue with the New Testament, even though they can gain such momentum that they culminate in the exclamation "God is dead!" *The central theme of the New Testament is* its paradoxical "message of the cross": *that God came to the rescue of his humanity and his earth so critically threatened by human sin in an extreme act of divine humiliation before humankind that is hard to comprehend!*

Those who have not found the message of the New Testament in this direction but have discovered it in rationally comprehensible formulas or self-evident "ethical maxims" have not even remotely caught a glimpse of its truth.

6. *DOXA* AND THE LOSS OF *DOXA* IN THE NEW TESTAMENT

All have sinned and fall short of the *glory* of God.

Romans 3:23

I consider that our present sufferings are not worth comparing with the *glory* that will be revealed in us.

Romans 8:18

In the New Testament as well, the Greek word for "luminous splendor," "final, ultimate beauty," "glory," "honor," "weight," "fame," etc., is a concept of central importance. This Greek word is *doxa,* and it seeks to render nothing other than the meaning of the Hebrew *kabod*. To be sure, *doxa* can also mean "opinion," "view," "philosophical axiom" in classical Greek outside the New Testament. But in the New Testament itself, the frequently used word *doxa* is never found with this meaning. Rather, it always serves as the equivalent of the Hebrew *kabod*.

In the New Testament the *doxa of God*, the *gloria Dei*, is often mentioned. This underlines the fact that "glory" belongs to God first and foremost. It can be transferred to his creatures only by him — through self-renunciation. Thus, verses that speak of the *doxa* of Jesus Christ are given much attention in the New Testament. During *Jesus' transfiguration* on Mount Tabor, three disciples already see him in that luminous form which will be his own "resurrection body" *after* Golgotha. The glorification of the Son of Man who dies like a grain of wheat that is planted in the soil and then produces new life and an abundant harvest is a major theme in the Gospel of John. That is why the execution of Jesus on the cross can be ambiguously characterized as his "lifting up," as the beginning of his glorious reign over the whole world. Jesus' glory "is established in his death" (Gerhard Kittel). Yet his obedience on the cross is at the same time an event through which *God* the Father is also glorified in the man Jesus (John 13:31). For this obedience is at the same time his declaration of loyalty to God and a testimony to God's honor that cannot be imagined in stronger terms. Finally, according to the Gospel of John, the one lifted up, Jesus Christ, is also glorified in his *human* disciples, in other words, in all who believe and follow him (John 17:10).

However, at first all of humanity, says the book of Romans, is under a cloud. It has lost its creaturely splendor because of its own guilt! Jews and Gentiles have both turned away from God and thus lost their *doxa*. Because this is true, they, and consequently we too, are enmeshed in a process of self-destruction. And even nonhuman creatures are being pulled into this human disaster.

In the view of the whole New Testament — culminating in the mission of Jesus Christ — God has declared war on this human self-destruction and the destruction of creation; it is a struggle of life against death. God intervenes! With his "salvific intervention," he helps us and our fellow creatures, those of us who are not able to extricate ourselves from the consequences of sin in our own strength.

In the Bible, both in the Old and New Testament, man is perceived as the creature who, on his own, can only live in a way that is destructive to himself and his environment, yet whom God comes to rescue from this desperate situation.

In the view of the whole Bible, God has countered this destructive potential that is found in human nature with several covenants. Through the *covenant* he made with *Noah,* he guarantees — also explicitly on behalf of the plants and animals — a basic, long-term terrestrial order that is resistant to the sins of humanity: "Never again will I curse the ground because of man. Even though every inclination of his heart is and remains evil from childhood, as long as the earth endures, seedtime and harvest, cold and heat, summer and winter, day and night will never cease" (cf. Gen. 8:21f.). In the Sinaitic Covenant, God approaches the Israelite nation, to which he gives the Torah, the "law of life" (Exod. 19:8). In this covenant, God speaks to Israel on behalf of all humanity. Finally, God's *new covenant in Jesus Christ* continues these actions so that on the earth humanity as a whole is not doomed to destruction but led back to prosperity and abundance, to "life and blessedness." The New Testament's letter to the Hebrews comments on this new covenant in these terms: "In the past God spoke to our forefathers through the prophets at many times and in various ways, but in these last days he has spoken to us by his Son. The Son is the radiance of God's glory and the exact representation of his being, sustaining all things by his powerful word. After he had provided purification for sins, he sat down at the right hand of the Majesty in heaven" (cf. Heb. 1:1ff.).

The biblical certainty that God comes to our help through the covenants even though we threaten ourselves with self-destruction is not exactly close to modern self-understanding. As a rule we believe that we have to fend for ourselves totally. However, the ancient conviction of the church that Jesus Christ made the new, final covenant *in his blood,* that he overcame and atoned for our sins through his suffering on the cross, has become an extremely strange conviction to most people today.

So we must ask: How can the cross of Jesus, this sad place of weakness and dying, mean "salvation" and "life" for all of humanity? The answer to this question is what we are looking for now.

Paul Gerhardt asks us to meditate on the cross with the following words of a Passion hymn: "O world, see here your life / hanging on the trunk of the tree." Let us follow his invitation to meditate:

In meditation, you are now looking up at the one hanging on the cross. You think perhaps: Here is someone who is being executed because he trusted in vain that God would come to the aid of his suffering creatures. It was his trust in the covenant God's willingness to help that brought him to the cross. It was understandable that a few Jews asked him there: "Where is your God now?"

Had he believed too much, loved too much, hoped for too much? Was *that* his mistake?

You are willing to admit: Somehow he is also hanging there for us all. Not just because we all must base our life on trust, love, and hope. No, he was killed because his fellow human beings — we, too — are so weak when it comes to trusting, loving, and hoping. He himself is innocent. At any rate, he does not belong with the criminals but with the victims, as far as this universal human weakness is concerned. The Creator, if there is one, allowed the weakness and the failure that is in all of us to have its full impact on the one who actually loved, hoped, and trusted. He is a striking example of that.

You are still looking up at this crucified one with a quizzical look on your face. You had just thought, "He is also suffering because of me." Now your thoughts are leading you a step further. You are now thinking, "Am I doing such things only to him and others, or am I perhaps doing it even to *myself*, to my 'better self,' my true human self that I am striving to be?" The longer you think, the less you can evade this conclusion: There is something dreadful about me and all people that leads us to crucify not only others, but, in the final analysis, even ourselves. That is why we recognize in Jesus' suffering face what we also do to ourselves, how we also disfigure and ruin ourselves. To this extent we now understand the sentence, "O world, see here *your* life / hanging on the trunk of the tree."

Perhaps we could say: The life and death of us all is hanging on the cross of Golgotha: here we encounter in a vivid and tangible way the human disaster we are about to bring upon ourselves. Such a fate must befall us and our fellow companions if we persist in our lack of love, our inability to trust, and our poverty of hope (our godlessness?)!

The horizon has darkened. Now we are also thinking of the godforsaken loneliness and darkness of Jesus' hour of death in which we are implicated. He is in fact our *substitute*. But in what sense?

We can forget pseudotheological ideas about the "scapegoat" whose blood vicariously flows for those who have actually forfeited their life and now remain undisturbed because a sacrifice has been offered. Traditional claims that God's wrath had to be "appeased" in the sense of an atonement by the valuable sacrifice of the innocent Jesus are outrageous and must be banished from Christian theology.

Jesus Christ is our substitute, not so that we could go our way undisturbed but so that we would be won for God and our own human self. In the meantime, Christ takes responsibility for our true self that is no longer opposed to God but has not yet appeared. We are not excluded and "replaced" by an external victim as he suffers on the cross. Rather, as Paul clearly demonstrated, we are involved in the event if we look at him on the cross and can bear to see the conciliatory look in his eyes; then it happens to us — "our whole old self of sin" is crucified with him (Rom. 6:1-6). *We see ourselves in the suffering and with a disfigured face and recognize ourselves even as our own executioners.* But in Christ, this is not a hope-destroying but a liberating idea in which there is reconciling power.

The personal magnetism of the crucified one is such that we are not accused with a silent, bitter look but can rejoice when we see what grave danger we are in and how precious, how sacred our undestroyed humanity and our personal selves are! Our meditation on the crucified Christ enables us. And this is true although we must recognize that the "cause of God" which Jesus Christ supported as our substitute endured terrible mockery and extreme human rejection on Golgotha!

In the most vivid manner imaginable, God allowed "his cause" to come to naught on Golgotha. At first glance, he appears to be the *loser* there. However, at first glance man seems to be affirmed by living with his intention of not letting God hinder him or help him. However, this first impression can not last when we even partially focus on the cross. It is clear to those who look at the cross: God is able to impart himself and his gift sovereignly even when on the face of it "God's cause" takes second place to human interests and the human creature seems to stand alone in his sinful greatness!

Golgotha is anything but a human propitiatory sacrifice for the benefit of God, quelling or sparing him his wrath. What radiates from Golgotha and works to the present day is the divine sacrifice he himself offers: The creator of this world sends a clear signal of his intention to make a new covenant and gives up his beloved Son with whom he is intimately associated and who is intimately associated with him (contrary to the sinful separation that characterizes the rest of humanity). Jesus on the cross is the original sacrament with the purpose of winning back the rest of humanity for coexistence with God. Through this original sacrament and this effective sign of the covenant, a force is released that reconciles inwardly torn sinners with themselves and thus also with nature and with God. What radiates out into the world from Golgotha is *God himself.* God as Spirit, as a reconciling, renewing force.

However, Jesus did not attempt to change and improve the existing beliefs of the people whom he encountered so that they would receive more of God's renewing strength. Rather, the goal of his mission was enabling people to find *God* again instead of separating themselves from him. He did not begin with "a little bit of existing religion," but with the general godlessness in the midst of a situation marked by the formative influence of religion (that is why in the relationship of Christianity to other religions such as Judaism and Islam this truth must be affirmed: converting people of other faiths to one's own form of faith is not important in a single one of these religions. Rather, whoever is devout in these religions should live in such a way that perhaps others may find *access to* God in their own religion: real access resulting not from religious convention but from conquered sin).

Only God himself makes it possible for people to find him! He is also the source of all reconciliation. Making this assertion could, of course, raise the objection that almost all people lack reconciliation and, therefore, God has remained inactive as the source of reconciliation. The undeniable rarity of what the New Testament describes as reconciled human life should not be played down by stating that one day humanity will experience this reconciliation in a comprehensive fashion.

A quite different point should be made. All people can recognize in the example of Jesus Christ that even *a single* event of true, undestroyed humanity has the power to have a cleansing and reconciling impact on the broken relationships of many individuals. *A single* lifestyle in which faith comes to expression, in which God is drawn into life, is of much greater weight and has a greater historical impact than many sins. *One* friend of God can help many enemies of God. There is nothing that can allow us to affirm human existence to a greater degree than this well-founded certainty, even though intellectually it could appear to be a hopeless enterprise of nature. This is the well from which to draw courage to face life.

7. THE LOSS AND RETURN OF SPLENDOR IN THE WORLD

God saw all that he had made, and it was very good.

Genesis 1:31

The glory of this present house will be greater than the glory of the former house, says the LORD Almighty.

Haggai 2:9

I dry up the green tree and make the dry tree flourish. I the LORD have spoken and I will do it.

Ezekiel 17:24b

Instructed by natural science, we modern men and women can only picture the radiant beauty of the cosmos as it shone forth on the morning of the seventh day in praise of its Creator as a utopia, an anticipatory vision of a world that will one day be liberated from all evil. But how could the original condition of the world be called "very good"?

Nevertheless, there is something to the familiar old idea that the creatures of the earth, and especially we humans, *come from what was originally good.* There is also much truth in the traditional dogmatic proposition that we humans have fallen and still fall from this original good. There was really a creation splendor in the world which was ruined by the way human beings lived. Yet it was not so completely ruined that nothing at all remains of it. Amazingly, there is still splendor in the world which can be ruined. *However, this splendor would long since have vanished if it were not renewed in some way.*

It would surely be wrong to include in Christian doctrine the utopia of a world transformed back into paradise or evolving into a paradise. But it is possible and also important to familiarize ourselves with the secret of where and how the lost splendor can *return* to this world.

The most interesting aspect of sin is the possibility of depriving it of its power.

However, the topic of sin also raises the immensely puzzling question of the future path of humanity in the cosmos. How long will human beings be able to last in nature with their imbalanced, strife-torn existence? Where are they going? Are they under special protection?

When Christian systematic theologians develop their doctrine of man, they all come to speak of sin. In this way, they express the conviction that *anthropology* and *the doctrine of sin* must form a *unity*. They traditionally begin their explanation of humanity's path in the cosmos with Adam's fall and end it with interpretations of Jesus Christ's act of redemption. He is often described as the "second Adam" (see Rom. 5:12ff.; 1 Cor. 1:15-21). It is the conviction of the church that Jesus Christ brings this lost splendor back into the creation (Paul Gerhardt says in his Christmas song "My Heart Shall Leap with Joy": ". . . whatever is tormenting you, whatever you lack, I am restoring everything").

Especially somewhat older and very old systematic theologies make a distinction in their chapter on anthropology between the Adam who fell into sin and the *Adam before he fell into sin:* Adam in the state of highest perfection. Of course, in more recent times theological statements on this topic have often dwindled to nothing. In view of the triumphant march of the scientific theory of evolution, this is certainly understandable. Nevertheless, the old systematic theologies kept open direct access to an anthropology that should not have been buried. It was proper to first portray Adam in his glory as the being in whom God allowed his creation to reach its apex.

In contrast to this is the view that remains despicable no matter how you look at it. It believes the *first thing* we can say about man is that he is a sinner or, what is not nicer, that he has developed a little further up the evolutionary scale from his apelike nature so that he now represents a kind of "journey nature has made into the unknown." Many correct statements about man can be made along these lines. However, an anthropology that does justice to man at least to some degree should start with a sense of amazement that in the midst of the natural kingdom this being called "man" even exists at all. Especially the natural scientist has every reason to be amazed at the evolutionary origin of the human species in the universe. All of a sudden, nature recognizes itself in it. Laughing and crying commence with the emergence of this species. Love and lying, justice and its horrible counterpart, confidence and solidarity make their appearance in evolution as well as the hellish agony of a new fatal loneliness or forlornness. Yet, in spite of all this, there has also been unceasing human praise for the Creator for millennia.

Where this special being, man, appears, the phenomenon of *language* immediately appears as well, not just the language used to exchange information but also the language used to comfort and provide mutual encouragement. Finally, there is the language of falsehood that again calls into question all that is human.

In order to live, man must not only somehow be spoken to or merely be reliably informed; he must also be able to hear friendliness and a loving affirmation of his unique personal style, his individuality. This being "man" must be talked to nicely — this is his most unique feature in the realm of nature, which enables him to survive at all.

But where do these words of encouragement come from in the realm of nature? Where does this friendly form of address come from, keeping man in existence, actually creating him primordially, lifting him out of the world of animals and plants? *The miracle that this good word of encouragement even exists and, therefore, that man also exists in the cosmos is no less miraculous than if a rose garden blossomed in the middle of a glacier as a result of a sudden, enormous warming effect.* How surprising it is that so much additional warmth must have been present when sometime in the evolutionary process those words of encouragement appeared from which a real man could emerge, a biologically deficient being with a spirit. Did the biological deficiency produce the human spirit by itself? Or was the spirit added to the deficiency?

He who is not deeply moved by the miracle and the beauty of the existence of this neediest creature in the cosmos, should he be trusted to instruct us about human sin? He who does not share the feeling that we humans constitute, and should constitute, a sworn community because we are like a tiny warm island in an otherwise *ice-cold universe* (in spite of the warmth of all the animals, in spite of all the stories of gods, and in spite of the luminosity of billions of suns) — should he explain to us in a convincing fashion how we can find a way to reach a new brotherly and sisterly relationship to plants and animals or a new sense of security as children of God?

If the theologians of the modern era had felt more of this emotion with regard to humanity, the divide between Christianity and the humanistic Enlightenment that has become profoundly deep since then would not have occurred. Then modern thought would hardly have gone astray in the direction of continually suppressing evil and sin and encountering both of them more and more massively in the course of history precisely for that reason. Modern thought has failed time and again to come to terms with it and has fallen into ever greater despair.

The fundamental question with regard to man is not — even Augustine recognized this! — where does evil come from? but, where does good come from? *The origin of this good word that creates humanity is and will remain the common subject of theology and philosophy.* Both can speak productively to me and others if they debate this question and share the diverse opportunities they see to uncover this word. Even though human beings may no longer be at home in any belief about God, they never forget that they need this word to live. All of the pernicious and creative fear in human beings is related to their concern to preserve, maintain, and/or regain this word that calls us into being as men and women, promising us a human life. Man does indeed not live by bread alone (see Deut. 8:3).

Man has every reason to concentrate fearfully on preserving this essential good word because it is not as limitlessly available as are certain chemical sources of energy. The word that announces the Creator's declaration that "it was very good!," addressed to my person, is by no means found on the street in ample measure. However, I *must* have it. If it is not granted to me in a completely secure way, I will try with all my might to get it for myself. Our urge to *justify* ourselves could only diminish if we actually encountered this good word we need from outside ourselves, if we encountered it in generous measure.

In a formal sense, justification is always good news for an individual and means: *You* are worthy to exist: *Your* life is acceptable for others: There is meaning in *your* existence. It is a good thing that there is *you.* In contrast to many other things, this can be said of *you.* I like to hear this affirming word. Each person tries in one way or another to induce others to grant it to him. However, all of a sudden, sin appears on the scene during this basic human event, although it does not actually coincide with individual psychological phenomena such as ambition or the need to be appreciated. This is real sin, real evil which we all amply experience (and this is also what the Bible means!). I try with all my might to convert my relationship with other people, with God, plants, and animals and other things into an instrument that serves the purpose of justifying myself. However, this is counterproductive when it comes to establishing loving relationships. The Bible commands us to love "with all your heart and with all your soul and with all your strength" (Deut. 6:5; Lev. 19:18; Matt. 22:37-40). My uncompromising and merciless attempt to use all others to justify myself devalues and destroys my relationship to them. It robs those involved of their soul, as it were. It deprives the world of its splendor and only results in ugly chaos, ruins being left behind. Sin is anticreation, although, of course, it never completely achieves this entire goal. However, humanity has become sick over the problem of justification. This is our "sickness to death."

If a partially adequate understanding of the events leading to Auschwitz ever becomes possible, then only will we expose step-by-step the enormous need for self-justification. Especially non-Jewish Germans and the bulk of Christians turned this need "against their Jews" in a historical situation prepared well in advance. This stood in marked contrast to the Jewish attempt at self-justification that is understandable against the backdrop of a long period of suffering, although it was less disguised and less intense. Here, too, it is essential to understand that an interpretation of the Holocaust framed in moral terms or perhaps only in terms of rational psychology — indeed, any attempt to scientifically reappraise the history of the Holocaust — must at best remain insufficient. Our impression that most of these attempts to explain the Holocaust are inadequate will always linger. For the wound inflicted in this event will no longer be able to heal as long as there are human beings and it confronts us with ultimate questions about the justification of humanity.

Answers to these questions will only be found in the course of an analysis of our relationships to nature that have degenerated as a result of our human need for self-justification and only where theology takes a position on the advanced destruction of the environment common both to man and his soul in a relevant manner that transcends empty formulas. Finally, therapeutic attempts to get at the heart of the political, economic, social, and intellectual tensions between East and West, North and South are exacerbated by the presence of nuclear, biological, and chemical weapons. Therefore, if they are to have some measure of success, they must deal with the potential for self-justification embedded in these conflicts, since financial contributions, moralizing appeals for the relaxation of tensions, and intelligent compromise proposals are not sufficient to overcome the pent-up fear and oppression.

The return of splendor is possible. Our circumstances can be transformed and renewed on a rather large scale by human changes that occasionally occur.

The return of splendor in the midst of a reality demolished by sin is called *grace* in the Bible. Grace means that God is approaching and is once again making beautiful and delightful what was distorted by sin. Grace is precious and has not stopped working — something church officials more than all others must once again understand. However, grace is also identical with the *gospel,* with the good word that appears in human life and makes it prosper. In the gospel of Jesus Christ, God himself meets us in a form that should dissuade us from competing with him and living as if there were no God.

We can neither invent the gospel or the good word nor force it to appear. However, when we find it, we should guard it and cultivate it. It is essential that primarily the church and its congregational leaders commit themselves to use reverently the good word offered to the church in Jesus Christ, to keep it holy and pass it on in gratitude. For, in the end, no appeals and no educational measures can help us fight against sin. Only one thing can help. People need to encounter the precious word in which both God and his grace approach them at the same time.

The church's treasure is that it can celebrate *worship services,* that it can hear and pass on Jesus Christ as God's good word in diverse ways through the ages. But it doesn't always know what it means to guard and cultivate this treasure. Often the church only locks it up instead of opening it up. However, it often profanes it too, by "passing on" God's grace at cut-rate prices and allowing God's law to degenerate into a catalogue of important, ethical rules dictated by reason (directions). However, the real word of God heals simply by being *heard,* by being heard as the holy voice of him who has authority to call people home to himself. The real gospel is not there for us to translate into "practical rules for living." If we had done that, we would have gained nothing in our fight against sin. Rather, that "good word" must succeed and gain influence with us *as it is in itself.* This is all that really matters.

To have almost forgotten this is one reason why many Christians become embarrassed, are unable to communicate, or get into mischief reinterpreting the gospel as soon as the topic of sin comes up. Unfortunately, this complaint is often justified. The modern-day church no longer guards anything; it has become a discussion. When friends meet, they sometimes say, "I haven't heard anything from you in a long time." *The return of splendor begins when we finally hear from God again.* Man's greatest problem is hearing nothing from God. However, as soon as people feel this, they themselves can play a part in finding their way out of this deadly silence of God. Therefore, today it must be our first concern to hear the quiet voice of God in spite of the cacophony and in the cacophony of all our activities. If intensive theological work contributes to this — beyond the inflation of words that has marked the history of Christianity — this would be very much indeed.

CHAPTER 2

Developments in the
Doctrine of Sin and Evil

SECTION I
DESCRIPTION OF AN ONGOING PROCESS

A. The Rapprochement of Theology and Philosophy

In our modern era, what theologians, especially Protestant theologians, mean by the concept of "sin" was partly understood less and less and partly accepted less and less. Theologians were often accused (and not always unfairly!) of having a profoundly negative view of man. With their doctrine of sin, they irresponsibly stood in the way of the healing of human infirmities, the development of human self-confidence, and a growing self-help movement. Such critiques of theology and Christianity were not infrequently based on pertinent remarks of pietistic authors. Of course, the Reformers' original doctrine of sin would have been much less suitable as a starting point for leaving it behind.

The development of modern theological and philosophical doctrines "of man" in different directions reached its apex in the nineteenth and twentieth centuries. *The main difference is that all the material to be presented in this book is related to God/Jesus Christ in the case of theological anthropology, whereas this relatedness to God/Jesus Christ is dispensed with in the other case.* The rejection of Schleiermacher and the theology of the nineteenth century that was made after World War I by the movement of dialectical theology has further widened the language divide, and its practical repercussions

29

are still being felt. Whereas philosophy and science are in principle there *for one another* and approach the phenomena of human existence with the same kind of rationality, theological anthropology — you could think so in the first half of the twentieth century — seems to stand not only outside of but even against philosophy and science. However, this impression is objectively in need of revision — regardless of which side was most responsible for it.

Was man originally "good"? Is it only false (social) structures that corrupt him? Theology seems to assert the opposite view, and for that reason it has isolated itself in the modern era. Does man have the possibility or at least the right to "set out"[1] in freedom, to go wherever he wants, or is he originally not free and with all his plans and deeds an involuntary corrupter of his own and others' lives? Theology seems to understand man in the latter sense and, thus, communication with it has been almost completely broken off. Generally speaking, this is how the situation is portrayed.

But what if it turns out that neither a respectable philosophy nor a responsible Christian theology that draws from its authoritative sources develops the views about man just ascribed to it? What if it becomes apparent that we are simply not going *against* biblical anthropology when we human beings boost our confidence in our own strength and enhance our natural freedom from physical and mental harm, when we accept and even encourage our zest for life, our sensuality, and our pleasure in what is physically beautiful? What if we could no longer overlook the fact that the actual differences between belief and unbelief are not found where they are usually located: in a basic attitude that is supposedly a part of faith and yet is hostile to the body, discrediting the human ego's need for happiness? Could the obsolete divide between the theological and the nontheological illumination of the human condition finally be bridged again if this could be clarified?

It is not only the task of this book to chart a new theological direction as I have just indicated. This book can begin with the observation that for centuries an anthropology has been presented in leading theological works on the doctrine of sin that no longer lends any support to the aforementioned prejudices. Moreover, since the beginnings of modern existentialist philosophy there have once again been *philosophical openings* to man which are closer to the biblical-Reformational assessment of evil

---

1. Quote from Hölderlin's poem "Lebenslauf."

than many of the philosophical interpretations of this phenomenon that the Enlightenment has made over the past two hundred years.

One gains the impression from all these texts that theology and philosophy are reapproaching one another in their view of man. This development is to be welcomed because it is reducing the number of unjustified discrepancies between them. A contemporary theology which would not take an interest in the modern problems revealed in these discrepancies would be irrelevant. Well into the twentieth century, theologians were underestimating the nontheological descriptions of evil in poetry and philosophy, and they were also underestimating the insights gained by the humanities into the phenomenon of human guilt. But a change of climate even took place in the early, "dialectical" Karl Barth (who had an open ear for Feuerbach and Marx, Nostrojewski and Nietzsche, that is, for modern philosophers who clearly disassociated themselves from ecclesiastical Christianity and its theology). Furthermore, such a change of climate also took place in Paul Tillich (for whom psychoanalysis, depth psychology, and sociology already had considerable theological significance in the twenties and thirties as disciplines in the humanities, and whose theological hamartiology absorbed the concept of alienation from the tradition of left-wing Hegelianism). Surely today there is also the problem of a theological overestimation, or a false assessment, of the usability of modern human scientific and sociological data in the area of hamartiology.

Most contemporary systematic theologians across all denominational lines believe they are obligated to make drastic, yet in the modern era, necessary changes in the doctrine of sin regarding a series of traditional dogmatic approaches to humankind's creation and fall, including theological method and language. These theologians also believe they are obligated to recognize changes that have long since been made: for example, the shift from the medieval theological view of a "fallen world" or a "fallen humanity" to a concept that pinpoints sin and evil as a *problem of human identity,* or the shift from an earlier moral fear of dying in sin and guilt to the fear of dying in *meaninglessness,* or the shift from a theological doctrine that illuminates the consequences of sin in the afterlife to a hamartiology that illuminates the consequences of sin *in this life.*

Those are theological approaches to the questions and concerns that were often first raised by philosophy in our secularized, modern world. There is more. Modern man was universally appalled by the atrocities he proved himself "capable" of committing, especially in the twentieth century. In the wake of these atrocities, there is no longer any doubt for many modern philosophers and scientists even in the Marxist camp that their forgetfulness of theology (which they virtually rejected, on principle) has become obsolete and that it can be worthwhile to return intellectually, for example, to the anthropological insights of a Thomas Aquinas, Luther, Schleiermacher, Kierkegaard, or Barth. However, this has been achieved until now in only a very few exceptional cases (in the most recent past, for example, in the writings of Ernst Bloch and a few existentialist philosophers). *Theology* is probably more concerned about philosophy and science than vice versa. The "alienation" is very far advanced, and only a new, significant improvement in the public's attention — even better, only a new, basic Christianity modeled in the life of the church — will result in any far-reaching changes in this situation.

B. The Rapprochement of Roman Catholic and Protestant Hamartiology

To a remarkable degree, the earlier differences between Protestant and Roman Catholic teaching on sin are presently becoming less important, paralleling a certain convergence that can be observed in our time between philosophical-scientific and theological-ecclesiastical approaches. It is no longer appropriate in the present situation of theological teaching to juxtapose a Roman Catholic tendency to understand sin more from the perspective of individual sinful *deeds* with a Protestant tendency to conceive of sin mainly as original sin or as a general distortion of human life. The time is also past in which the confessional conflict could be described in these terms: A Catholic sins against nature, a Protestant against the grace of Christ. There is just as little reason today for comparing a Roman Catholic habit of making distinctions between sinful deeds based on their level of seriousness with the Protestant habit of judging evil/sin to be everywhere of equal weight according to the motto "*every* sin is a mortal sin."

Both confessions are equally striving for a continual biblical renewal of their dogmatic understanding of sin. Moreover, Christians and churches are demanding today that the church prove itself in the area of social ethics. This has led to growing similarities in theological doctrine and religious consciousness.

The separation of the Catholic from the Protestant understanding of original sin and justification that was made by the Council of Trent in Sessions 5 and 6 in 1546 and 1547 has not only lost its divisive relevance *in part,* but probably even *in whole.* It no longer stands in the way of a new reconciliation between the churches.

SECTION II
THE PROBLEM OF MINIMIZING
THE IMPORTANCE OF EVIL

The average citizen's attitudes toward evil in this modern era are not adequately understood when it is claimed time and again that the "secularized" modern European only knows sin in the form of "sins against one's diet" or "sins against the rules of the road." This seems to indicate that he has become unsuspecting about the reality of evil. In fact, most Europeans don't simply live in a state of ignorance, either minimizing or repressing evil. It is also not correct to assume that evil is no longer a topic of discussion for Western philosophies, science, and art. Almost the exact opposite is the case. One can often get the impression that natural scientists clearly see and discuss the completely misguided behavior of modern man, whereas many theologians and pastors hardly dare to speak of sin or are simply not willing to do so at all. The more competent ones among them actually recognize the misunderstandings that pose a threat to the church today. (As a whole, theology and Christianity in our time are in danger of failing to deal with the horror and violence of evil because they are professional experts at sin and think they possess a proven mechanism to categorize and cope with evil. Unfortunately, a special degree of mistrust of theological statements about evil, the demonic, and sin in our time is warranted!)

It is accurate to say that evil is even *the* topic of discussion within the most important intellectual endeavors of recent and most recent times; however, theological texts are to a great extent no longer a part of these endeavors. Since "God" is no longer an explicit subject in the thought of society as a whole, since "God" is consequently no longer even accused of being responsible for earthly disasters, the discussion of *human* transgressions, atrocities, and insufficiencies (including the disgust with life many feel because of it) has been pushed to the fore as a very distressing — and thus often a rejected or repressed — subject almost wherever analytic thought, anthropological research, and artistic projects are pursued.

The question is only how promising this modern (and sometimes fashionable!) philosophical and literary focus on evil should be seen. Does it begin, radically enough, at the place where the basic aspects of evil probably first become visible: at the human sin of self-justification? It is more likely that our intensive modern preoccupation with evil bears the traits of a more and more dramatic return to what could not be dealt with and is not being dealt with! There is *no* doubt that for a long time now, more is being demanded of theology and the church than merely their rapprochement to philosophy and other religions. They are being asked if the mission and authority of the church to help human beings overcome their sins can still be taken seriously today.

SECTION III
A LOOK AT CONTEMPORARY QUESTIONS IN
SYSTEMATIC-THEOLOGICAL HAMARTIOLOGY

A. The Main Concern of Contemporary Theological "Doctrines of Sin"

1. A Concise Overview in Twelve Points

a. The object of modern as well as earlier theological hamartiologies is the individual and collective misguidedness of humanity, expressing itself in suffering caused by human beings in hideous inhumanity and destructiveness. Of course, in the particulars, a more complicated picture emerges indicating divergences between contemporary perceptions and contemporary theories about sin.

b. The meaning of "sin" that seems most likely to be understood in our time and is accessible to our immediate senses is found in the virtually irreversible human damage done to long-term living conditions on earth, especially to nature.[2] Such depredations provoke not the "wrath of God" but the revenge of the environment, in the opinion of many today. In spite of or because of what has just been explained, modern men and women tend to think they are suffering "evil" from outside themselves rather than bringing it into the world by their own "sin." Above all, the corrupt condition of the environment is lamented, infecting individuals with its defects and its poison. Therefore, the task of working for a change in the situation *seems* more important than receiving the personal forgiveness of sins. Contemporary church teachings are grappling with all these ideas. However, they are largely doing this by evaluating the changes in contemporary attitudes toward evil and guilt and then asking what they should take seriously from a theological standpoint.

c. The forgiveness of sins seems to have become an embarrassment for theology and a vague experience among Christians, who desire it in de-

---

2. Statements outside of theology — for example, H. Jonas, "Ravagers of the earth are *all* modern industrial societies" — are typical. H. Jonas, *Das Prinzip Verantwortung. Versuch einer Ethik für die technologische Zivilisation* (Frankfurt am Main [¹1979], ³1982), p. 273. Quotation from English translation: Hans Jonas, *The Imperative of Responsibility: In Search of an Ethics for the Technological Age,* trans. Hans Jonas with the collaboration of David Herr (Chicago and London: University of Chicago Press, 1984), p. 153.

clining numbers. Even where it is still taught as the center of hamartiology and of Christianity itself, as well as the starting point for all real understanding of sin, its description often lacks inner credibility.

d. Theological doctrines of sin in our time are related to discourses in the social sciences and humanities in diverse ways. Embedded in *their* interpretations of humanity are older questions from the field of philosophical anthropology which in part were framed in the thought of German idealism, but also by Kierkegaard, Marx, Schopenhauer, and Nietzsche. Coming back to these traditions and implications and dealing with them from a theological perspective has often proven to be a fruitful enterprise.

e. We should always examine what guiding interest leads contemporary theological hamartiologies to seek a dialogue with the social sciences and humanities and follow their insights. Is a particular dogmatic teaching tradition merely supposed to be improved linguistically or modernized in this way, in order to make it more comprehensible for modern man, while its "objective" core remains unchanged? Or is a chapter of theological and ecclesiastical failure in the modern era supposed to be reappraised (which would have to lead to a theological hamartiology that is modified in content)? Or are the nontheological disciplines with their disparate scientific insights into the human condition supposed to be granted linguistic help from theological hamartiology, the offer of a spiritual bond, an integral, a more in-depth interpretation? Such interests are often being articulated concurrently or even sequentially in the various theological teachings of today.

f. It is theologically disputed whether sin should and can be identified as *suffering* that has reached the level of *experience* (in P. Tillich: "alienation"); moreover, whether the course of history allows us to expect an increasing liberation from such sufferings.

g. Even when they leave the traditional, exclusive orientation toward the individual behind them, most theological doctrines of sin still have a modernistic — anthropocentric and modernistic — subjectivist orientation. The distortion of humanity and the threat to *man* posed by sin are emphasized: for example, his disturbed *psychological* condition, the *development* of *society* or (human) *history* "in the wrong direction," his failure to assume personal responsibility. The slandering of God and the agony and disorder prevalent among nonhuman creatures (the disruption of world order), as well as sinful forces having a fateful effect that transcends the personal dimension of life, are less in view. One can even see the "structural sin" emphasized by political theologies as originating in persons (for example, the members of "the ruling class" and its institutions).

h. Prominent in many modern theological teachings about the *sinner* ("hamartiologies") are questions framed in the following terms: Why am I not identical with myself? And: How do I become (more) identical with myself? Or: How do we become (more) identical with ourselves as a group, as a social class, as a nation, etc.? The search for *meaning in life,* the issue of more genuine *personal freedom,* and the strengthening of the ego are all parts of this *identity problem.*

i. Here, as in German idealism, sin is understood primarily as whatever is contrary to freedom as well as whatever weakens the human ego to the point of depersonalizing it and alienating it from its actual meaning and purpose.

j. Sin should no longer be interpreted today in a moralistic sense. This is very frequently demanded in theological texts. (On the other hand, a recent understanding of sin defined in terms of moral guilt is encountered, for example, in modern "liberation theologies.")

k. At present, sin is more likely to be considered the acceptance of reality as it now exists, the deed that has not yet been done; however, to a lesser degree sin is verified by reality as it no longer exists — because of our deed! In this view, sin is perceived more as the omission of deeds or changes than as the commission of acts or an intervention in the moral order. In this way real sin is often concealed!

l. The divine *justification of the sinner* has maintained its crucial function in hamartiology in spite of all attempts to get Christian theology off this subject. In fact, sin can still be illuminated *only in its light,* as an analysis of the available texts shows. Yet, the political ramifications of the doctrine of justification must also be developed better than before.

In the area of culture shaped by Christianity, not only theological studies have been dealing with the human misguidedness that is often called "sin" in the Bible since the beginning of the modern age; that is, there are no longer only interpretations that attribute this misguidedness to humanity's wrong relationship with God. Now philosophically and scientifically based analyses have joined them. *That is why the theologians who have written the hamartiologies relevant to our modern age are spending a lot of time reflecting on the relationship of the theocentric descriptions of anthropological facts to those that are not centered on the concept of God.* What is the point of the one approach and the other? Can both approaches be plausibly combined?

2. Sin and Neurosis

Put in terms of a concrete example: What is the relationship between the understanding of man as a sinner curved in on himself and the diagnosis that a certain person is a neurotic curved in on himself? Most opinions on this problem seek a solution in the following direction: the sinner is not affected by his inner maladjustment but the neurotic is; the former can get along well in life, the latter, generally speaking, not as well; the former is primarily responsible for the bad personal situation he finds himself in, the latter is not primarily responsible for the negative factors that overwhelm him from the outside; the former would gain nothing by therapy, but the latter probably would; the former is in a perverse condition all human beings share with him, the latter is in a sick condition "with a personal note," etc.

However, the issue is not really clarified by such information and comparisons. How could the actual weight of sin become clear when it is merely said that *all* human beings are trapped in sin, but they feel fine in it? No, there is no way around the theological understanding of sin as separation or the state of being separated from God with the result that all human relationships in the real world are actually distorted, causing sorrow and suffering. If this is so, then should not the mental condition of neurotics (and psychotics) at least be encompassed by the reality of sin? The difficult fact remains: Both the neurotic and the sinner could rightfully be characterized as human beings who have missed the opportunities God has given to them. But how can they be helped?

It is known that neither the church's forgiveness of sin heals "everything," nor can psychiatric or social therapies redeem "humanity" from perverted relationships in the real world. This raises the question: How could or should both work together in particular cases? The situation is complicated. We are living in a secularized world in which the *consequences* of the general godlessness make a number of people really sick without their being able to recognize the true cause or being open to spiritual help, and in which another section of the population claims the words of comfort the church offers in the forgiveness of sins without feeling sick and without their absolution having a noticeable (socially) therapeutic effect. Why is this? For the time being, only a formal answer can be given: at present two hermeneutics, two comprehensive interpretations of humanity, overlap in our secularized world — a broader religious one and a more narrow philosophical, scientific one which not only complement each other but also disrupt each other and often even seek to take the place of the other in a questionable way.

Among the huge number of modern texts on the topic of sin, there are, in the final analysis, only a few that critically evaluate the problem inherent *in these questions* and point the way forward. This is not only due to an understandable inability of theologians to absorb all the important methods and results of the human sciences, but even more to a widespread contemporary failure to put a significant amount of time and energy into developing the theme of man's relationship to God in modern scientific studies of human problems.

3. Developments in Recent Decades

In the *sixties*, a turning point occurred in both large denominations that still shapes the contemporary landscape. It had a drastic impact on traditional ways of teaching about sin. The issue is the attempt of certain theologians to get away from a "traditional" understanding of sin in church dogmatics which was (ostensibly!) narrowly focused on the moral sin and guilt of the individual and on the ecclesiastically organized forgiveness of this sin. This shift was based on the "results" of studies conducted in the human sciences that theologians all at once rated highly interesting. Spread like wildfire through the theological press, their rallying cry was expressed in these terms: it is high time to replace an understanding of sin, grace, and faith centered primarily on the superego functions of the human psyche with an overall understanding of the Christian religion that shows it to be a force that enhances the human ego and thus can form human identity. The issue discussed by the Lutheran World Federation in Helsinki in 1963 was whether the church in this modern era should perhaps cease to talk about the justification of the sinner because modern man is no longer preoccupied by the concern "How do I get a merciful God?" but by an (ostensibly) much more radical question, "Does God exist and does our life have meaning?"[3]

---

3. See K. Rahner, *Schriften zur Theologie* (Einsiedeln, 1966), 7:11-31, here p. 20; W. Mostert, "Ist die Frage nach der Existenz Gottes wirklich radikaler als die Frage nach dem gnädigen Gott?" *ZThK* 74 (1977): 86ff.; P. Tillich, *Systematische Theologie*, 3 vols. (Stuttgart, 1956ff.).

Questions that surfaced in the sixties and the excessive theological reflections often associated with them at first (to put it mildly) led in the *seventies* to a reworking of Christian teaching on a broad front. In particular, a rich social-ethical (see liberation theology!) and educational absorption of this changed view of sin was the result. This new view was also absorbed by religious education which aimed at changing the "learning process." Christian faith was reconceptualized as the power to self-liberate the self, to change unjust structures, to develop basic trust and personal maturity (with the goal of finding one's self-identity).

In the *eighties,* developments began that could be called a cautious attempt to take stock of the theological situation by occasionally pointing back to the earlier theology. It became apparent that it was not the understanding of sin as personal guilt that had become obsolete; however, changes or expansions in the theological understanding of the nature of this guilt became possible and even necessary. It also became apparent that it was not the doctrine of the justification of the sinner that should be given up in favor of teaching about regaining meaning in life and strengthening the self; rather, the understanding of sin and justification must be conceptualized in such a way that "the issue of meaning can no longer be played off against the theme of justification, but is embraced by it,"[4] as G. Ebeling demanded as early as 1973.

The exposition of the theological doctrine of sin framed in terms of the problem of human identity is not unproblematic considering its narrow anthropocentric focus; however, it has often been retained. And it is still deemed necessary for theology to give its time and attention to human scientific and sociological interpretations of basic human experiences. However, this now takes place less and less on the basis of theological "dependence" on these scientific disciplines, but more and more by reemphasizing its own theological access to sin and anthropology. G. Schneider-Flume attempted to delineate the boundary in his study *The Identity of the Sinner* (1985) — a careful "discussion of theological anthropology in dialogue with the concept of psycho-social identity in E. H. Erikson." On the one hand, an approach that assigns to Christian faith a function in developing trust, strengthening the self, and facilitating growth toward maturity is obviously legitimate and fruitful. On the other hand, faith

---

4. G. Ebeling, "Theologie zwischen reformatorischem Sündenverständnis und heutiger Einstellung zum Bösen," in G. Ebeling, *Wort und Glaube* (Tübingen, 1975), 3:204.

cannot be "reduced to this function." "Theological anthropology speaks of the possibility of faith even when neither a mature nor a less integrated identity is developed." Also, both "the misunderstanding that faith only becomes realistic when it comes to grips with the human sciences must be countered and the view that theology only becomes tangible when it relates to the findings of the human and social sciences. Faith and theology are tangible when they talk about God — in all relationships of life in this world."[5]

However, this latter quote is more a desire addressed to theology and the church than a reference to an already existing, widespread practice. Not even the way to get there is clearly seen. *Anthropology in Theological Perspective* by W. Pannenberg was published in 1983 as the fruit of thirty years of labor (and is also to be read as a contemporary model of a theological hamartiology). This monograph has advanced further at this point in time than any other in attempting to bring together nontheo-logical and theological interpretations of what it means to be human in the *Western modern era*. On the one hand, it is able to interpret important hypotheses developed by modern science on the origin of human identity from a comprehensive point of view and to enrich them especially by reminding us of problems in the philosophy of German idealism described in part on a higher theoretical level. On the other hand, it can *meaningfully* portray the religious view of human reality (as a God-related reality) on the basis of the findings of the human sciences themselves, even though they have either fought this view or considered it unnecessary in developing their own understanding. Questions that have remained open — alter-nately the question of freedom — have found further clarification. Thus, Pannenberg's theological anthropology is already providing a service to the human sciences while at the same time promoting fresh theological insight with his ability to dialogue with this side. However, it seems questionable whether a learning process in philosophy and science will result from this in terms of a new openness to the Christian religion or in terms of a self-expansion.

Surprisingly, the great diversity of contemporary theological approaches to an understanding of sin does not convey the image of a confused

---

5. Translated from G. Schneider-Flume, *Die Identität des Sünders. Eine Auseinander-setzung theologischer Anthropologie mit dem Konzept der psychoanalytischen Identität E. H. Eriksons* (Göttingen, 1985), pp. 120, 125.

pluralism without clear and common tendencies.[6] It is more likely that the many different models have, in the final analysis, gotten bogged down with a few basic problems. There is a list of five salient questions practically every contemporary theological doctrine of sin has to wrestle with to a special degree.

4. Five Unfinished Problems

First, the standard method of verifying sin and guilt by focusing on issues of human identity formation needs further clarification. How much weight can this conceptuality bear? Is it theologically appropriate? Must sin as a collective and individual phenomenon always signify a painful loss of identity? Cannot sin at least be associated with the semblance of human identity?[7]

Second, the question of whether it is possible to verify sin empirically is connected with the first. This verification is considered essential simply because the word *sin* has faded from modern consciousness. But the connection between the experience (of alienation) and the recognition of sin is neither immediate nor evident. How is the relationship of sin to experience explicated in a theologically correct fashion?

Thirdly, a solution to this question remains unreachable as long as darkness prevails on the question of whether sin signifies a deficit in *human existence* or in *faith*. Does the sinner shut his heart to the potential given to him by the Creator to realize the opportunities inherent in human life or to God's promise of eschatological salvation? Or are both of these options *one*? This is the unfinished theological issue of the twentieth century.

The fourth problem: Is *sin* no longer a distinct word in our era; or is the actual problem the fact that *God* is no longer a distinct word? If the latter is true, what meaningful path can be followed to renew the theological doctrine of sin?

Fifth, how we answer the following question plays a role in every hamartiology: Can we expect progress in history, an increasing maturity

6. See M. Sievernich, *Schuld und Sünde in der Theologie der Gegenwart,* FThSt 29 (Frankfurt am Main [[1]1982], [2]1983), pp. 295f.

7. M. Buber, *Schuld und Schuldgefühle* (Heidelberg, 1958), p. 17; see also K. Barth, *Die Kirchliche Dogmatik,* 13 vols. (Zurich, 1932ff.), II/1, pp. 148-51; I/2, p. 290; hereafter cited as *KD.*

and identity of humanity as a whole? How the kingdom of God is understood theologically as the goal of world history determines the value and character of every understanding of sin. The question of the goal of history and the question of the proper role of Christendom on the way to this goal have created controversy in contemporary theology.

In the following section, I will more closely examine the present state of the discussion, focusing on these five main systematic problems of modern hamartiology which have all played a part in drastically undermining the church's authority to forgive sin; why its authority has faded has become a virtual mystery. However, I will not review and compare "significant models of our time." Many of them have already been portrayed and examined. Rather, it is my intention to take a closer look at unfinished problems and questions that are now being debated.

B. From Guilt Feelings to an Identity Crisis?

It seems that in recent decades an understanding of sin as *personal guilt* before God (and also before people or other representatives of the "environment") has "lost its plausibility." For example, this is the judgment of the Catholic theologian M. Sievernich on the basis of his study on *Guilt and Sin in Modern Theology* (1982) (see n. 6 above). He didn't intend to say that modern theology no longer develops the idea of guilt (it continues to do so), but that it no longer gets anywhere when it tries to explain this subject to laymen and laywomen. The first reason for this can be found in the "narrow," "at times even wrong way" the church has dealt with guilt and sin. "The Enlightenment critique of Christianity and its morality in the 19th century [*sic*] extending into our century" functions as a second reason. And the repercussions of the modern human sciences explaining, excusing, and even healing many abnormal human attitudes can be mentioned as a third reason.[8] As a fourth reason I would add the modern experience of the individual's *powerlessness* in the face of overpowering evil conditions found in the environment. The latter two reasons infect the individual and "he can't help it"; he sees no point in starting with himself when he attempts to reduce guilt. The Protestant theologian J. Scharfenberg wrote twenty years ago that the subject of guilt has recently entered

---

8. Translated from Sievernich, pp. 16-19.

the public discussion "with explosive force." This is threatening to become the "spearhead" of a new critique of religion.

"The kind of moratorium that had been negotiated, so to speak, between critical depth psychology and pastoral care in which the sick, misplaced" (Paul Tillich) feeling of guilt was handed over to the therapeutic approach but "existential guilt" remained the unassailable domain of theology, seems to have reached its limits."[9]

> If I see things correctly, the question today centers around this issue: to what extent does a Christian theology of justification that thinks it is able to monopolize the problem of guilt seem to be shaken by the appearance of a secularized competition? Must the radical solution to the problem of guilt which the theology of justification, coming from Paul, had always theoretically intended but had never realized in practice be seen as having been better realized in the secular competition? Evidently, Christian theology has displayed a fateful inclination time and again to take the wrong side in the continuous struggle for the freedom of the human spirit and has allowed itself to change sides only after fighting shameful rearguard actions.[10]

Scharfenberg raised the question of whether Protestantism, to the present day often (not always) centering on the doctrine of the justification of the sinner, must not emphatically appeal to Christians to "go beyond the guilt principle." To be sure, Christianity must not simply throw overboard the ethically indispensable function of the guilt category and also of conscience (or the psychic superego forces). But its theologians should not interpret salvation or grace in such a way that both of these serve *exclusively* to strengthen the superego forces. Otherwise, theology could confirm A. Mitscherlich's qualification of history in the Christian West as a "culture of guilt." In contradistinction to many other modern theologians who reject the idea of considering God *necessary* adequately to assume any existential task, Scharfenberg was of the opinion that "If we (nevertheless) believe we are able to discover a part of the human personality for which God is necessary, then it is the one comprising the

---

9. Translated from J. Scharfenberg, "Jenseits des Schuldprinzips?" in J. Scharfenberg, *Religion zwischen Wahn und Wirklichkeit. Gesammelte Beiträge zur Korrelation von Theologie und Psychoanalyse,* Konkretionen Bd. 13 (Hamburg, 1972), p. 189.

10. Translated from Scharfenberg, p. 207.

human ego-functions."[11] Here Scharfenberg is looking at S. Freud's theory. He asserts that the ego becomes mature and strong against the backdrop of the Oedipus complex that the individual has come through unscathed (after passing through the oral phase associated with the id, the anal phase associated with the superego, and, finally, the phallic phase). In part he is looking at P. Tillich's teaching on the three epochs of fear in church history (in *The Courage to Be:* We are now in the third epoch characterized less by fear of guilt, as in the late Middle Ages, than by fear of our existence emptied of meaning). And, in part, he is looking at E. H. Erikson's psychological-psychiatric model (in which he points out time and again that the situation of psychoanalysis has changed: Freud's patients mainly had to deal with unresolved conflicts from the realm of superego problems; present-day patients suffer primarily from neuroses or psychoses from the realm of ego-functions: they ask who/what they should/could be or become[12]).

The history of theology from the Enlightenment to Bonhoeffer teaches us: Talk of needing *God* to fill certain "gaps" in our current knowledge or in our ability to survive has to be ruled out as a possible way for Christians to "verify God." We can only understand Scharfenberg, who certainly knew this, here as trying to define the boundary between liberating and debilitating religiosity for our time.

Although Freud's model of the psychological apparatus could suggest it, guilt, the experience of guilt, and guilt feelings must not only be linked with the psychological functions of the superego. The changes in how we perceive guilt that have been observed in our time show that this would be an impermissible reduction, neglecting the possible positive relationships between the ego and guilt.[13] First I would like to pick out a few of the ten changes described by J. Schierse.

Only those moral norms that can be plausibly interpreted today as "meaningful" are recognized as an authority by which guilt is measured. Many earlier norms (for example, those dealing with sex) no longer fulfill this condition. Therefore, they produce fewer and fewer guilt feelings.

---

11. Translated from Scharfenberg, p. 207.

12. E. H. Erikson, *Identität und Lebenszyklus* (Frankfurt am Main, 1973), pp. 12ff., 189ff.; see also M. Klessmann, *Identität und Glaube,* Gesellschaft und Theologie series, Abt. Praxis d. Kirche 33 (München/Mainz, 1980), pp. 56f.

13. F. J. Schierse, "Schulderfahrung und Schuldbewältigung gestern und heute," *Geist und Leben* 49 (1976): 36.

Furthermore, the individual today can identify "practical necessity" as the cause of not a few mistakes and thus excuse himself. Furthermore, "The problem of guilt and how to deal with it is no longer considered by psychology from a merely individual perspective but primarily from a social perspective."[14]

A. Auer has observed: "Whereas until recently the nonfulfillment of any norms or requirements coming from society was experienced as guilt, today the loss of our self-identity is perceived as guilt."[15] In this case, guilt feelings result from violating our own norms and ideals. Our inability to be faithful to ourselves is certainly one contemporary component of the concept of guilt.

W. Pannenberg has shown in the context of discussing Nietzsche's views on the origin of a *bad conscience* (in *On the Genealogy of Morality* [1887]): The guilt we feel when we have fallen away from an identity that had existed earlier or when we have betrayed ourselves is to be distinguished from the guilt we feel when we have *not yet* fulfilled our own destiny. Only in the first case, the one assumed by Nietzsche, is our consciousness of nonidentity or our awareness of guilt "originating in the aggression against the self." However, in the second case, our identity is not the state of perfection that was (ostensibly) lost in the past, but the goal that has not yet been achieved. Our bad conscience indicates the distance that still needs to be covered to reach the goal. Therefore, it is useful. It has an ethically positive origin and an ethically positive goal. It drives the person who is aware of his own guilt to accept responsibility for his own development. "If we understand the doctrine of sin as functioning in the context of a still unfinished process which has human identity as its goal, we will not misinterpret this doctrine as a product of aggression turned inward. The consciousness of the failure of the self — that is, of sin — is a necessary phase in the process whereby human beings are liberated to become themselves." To be sure, self-aggression from injured pride is always natural when we live under the impression that we have incurred guilt. This self-aggression was reinforced time and again in sermons preached against sin in church. Pannenberg sees this. But under the influence of our changing sense of sin in the modern era, he draws this conclusion: "Preaching

14. Translated from Schierse, pp. 36-39.
15. Translated from A. Auer, "Ist die Sünde eine Beleidigung Gottes?" *ThQ* 155 (1975): 55.

and teaching on sin are protected against that kind of perversion only if they limit themselves strictly to fulfilling their function in the formation of human identity, where they serve as factors in the process of human liberation."[16]

It must be kept in mind that guilt feelings can also contain constructive elements of human identity formation, self-development, and self-reconciliation. Expressed in terms of Freud's model of the psychological apparatus, they primarily refer to the functions of the ego. Seen in this light, the subject of guilt cannot be separated from the subject of identity formation. One cannot be played off against the other, just as it is not correct to treat only the question of meaning in general *instead* of the question of guilt.

C. The Anthropological Concept of Identity (considering the Contribution of Kierkegaard)

We will not give special in-depth treatment to Erikson's merits in developing psychological exegesis and rapidly spreading the concept of identity that had earlier been a philosophical concept. Looking at the complicated history of the concept of identity, we can sum it up in these terms: Ultimately, the question of human identity is tantamount to the question of how to make human existence in freedom possible.

Of course, to understand the problem of identity, it is not enough that we recognize what its precise subject matter or content is. We must also ask and recognize why the problem of identity has reached such crisis proportions precisely in our modern era. Why does it occupy our attention today more than ever? The texts in the field of humanities and the human sciences clearly show it. From whatever angle this question is approached, whether, for example, from the angle of Protestant theology or Marxist philosophy, one will always encounter *a fundamental inner connection between the declining recognition of God's existence in the modern era and the uncertainty of human individuals about their identity that has become such*

---

16. W. Pannenberg, *Anthropologie in theologischer Perspektive* (Göttingen, 1983), p. 149A; quotations from English translation, *Anthropology in Theological Perspective,* trans. Matthew J. O'Connell (Philadelphia: Westminster, 1985), pp. 151-53; see also B. Lauret, *Schulderfahrung und Gottesfrage bei Nietzsche und Freud,* MMHSTh 1 (1977), pp. 15f.

a pressing problem in the modern era. It is as if souls were asking under the conditions of atheism or agnosticism: "But who will be watching over me personally with loving eyes at all times? Who will tell me the 'good news' now? Who will *always* stand by me? Who or what will guarantee my 'uniqueness' and give me the certainty that I don't have to end up as a completely exchangeable cog in the universal gear? Can or do I have to make myself into a person with my own identity?"[17] The latter was always an *unattainable goal.* In the process of seeking one's identity, the "basic law" (not only valid in the modern era) gains more distinct contours: *Man finds his identity when another makes himself identical with him,* thus intervening on his behalf with his own existence and time. But how can this be "had"? Here the religions, theologies, philosophies, etc., in ancient as well as modern times give very different answers. However, when they sin, people give *one* answer that has always remained the same down through the ages: you can try to coerce the intervention of others on your behalf in the course of a comprehensive strategy that bears the name of "self-justification" in this book.

The problem that will be extensively treated here is the following: Various thinkers of the Enlightenment and idealism ascribed an ultimately positive significance to sin, although sin destroyed an initial but naive human identity, that felt it was necessary for human motivation, especially for the emergence of human freedom (of course, today this no longer seems generally plausible). However, contemporary theologies try time and again to attribute to *God* an indispensable significance in making human freedom possible and maintaining it (although this could not yet be demonstrated with general plausibility).

Of further interest in this context, the problem of identity touches on *the difference between the ego and the self.* Man seeks himself as long as he lives. This is so because human beings always develop under the influence of two social forces that point in opposite directions: a force that confines man to himself, a second one (really a second) that drives him beyond himself. Man exists at the intersection of a centripetal and a centrifugal life force. In his personal existence he tries to do justice to two basic requirements that are difficult to harmonize: both the imperatives of *self-preservation* and the *demands of his social surroundings* which lay claim to his whole person. He

17. See Sölle, *Stellvertretung: Ein Kapitel Theologie nach dem Tode Gottes* (1965; 2nd ed. Stuttgart, 1982) pp. 40ff.

must harmonize the ascendant tendency in his life by which he draws strength from his surroundings with the descendant, which partially reduces him as an individual and partially pushes him to be there for others. All human life is ethically and religiously burdened with the question of identity because it is overshadowed by this dual aspect and dual command (and we incur guilt by not adequately noticing this). The sciences geared to individual and social therapy mainly deal with the practical consequences of this burden — the identity crisis. At the same time, theological hamartiologies also deal with them because they see here their own original field of endeavor.

A difference is found directly in the ego prior to the difference between the ego and the self. It can be explained, for example, in conjunction with G. H. Mead's "social behaviorist" distinction between "I" and "Me." It has to do with the antagonism between an aspect of the ego felt to be "close," "my own," and "free" and a second aspect of the ego felt to be more external (as, for example, my own body and its "drives" or formative influences from my social surrounding or past history) and more objective, limiting one's own existence. The unsettled conflict between these two aspects or poles of the ego results in man's not finding his self.

A contentious issue among philosophers and scholars has always been whether the initiative to overcome this primary antagonism must lie with the conscious *ego,* thus whether the initiative for a "fusing" of both aspects of the ego should be taken by that first, freer pole where the anthropological center of consciousness, the ratio, is presumably found, or whether a successful identity formation, entailing a "fusing" of both ego poles, must proceed from a *third source,* which would be, as it were, the attorney of both poles or aspects of the ego and could be called the *self* of man. Whoever thinks in terms of this latter model must emphasize that the conscious ego and the self of man are *not* the same.[18] The difference between S. Freud's and C. G. Jung's conceptions of man, for example, has to do with the fact that Freud answered this long-standing, contentious question in the former sense, Jung in the latter sense. However, not always objective but also mere differences in terminology can be present when the emergence of human identity is described on the one hand as the development of the *self* and on the other hand as the buildup of a strong *ego.* Yet, profound, objective differences of opinion can also be registered

18. See also F. Nietzsche, *Sämtliche Werke,* Kritische Studienausgabe, ed. G. Colli and M. Montinari, 15 vols. (Berlin/New York, 1967ff.), 4:40.

at this point. Ultimately, these differences of opinion can be boiled down to two opposing views. In one case identity formation is expected from a lonely ego that is endowed with illusory power. In the other case, identity formation is expected from beings and forces located outside the individual — and this is hidden behind the code phrase the "self is the actor in identity formation." In the latter case, the absence of self-sufficiency, in other words, the essential dependence of human beings "destined to be free" on others, is especially emphasized.

Here is the basic anthropological model in which *every imaginable* philosophical, theological, or scientific variant in the exposition of the anthropological problem of identity can be shown.

Diagram 1

The human being as a person

Self (previously also called spirit)

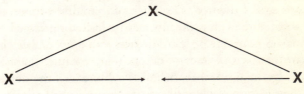

Ego (1)	Ego (2)
Subject	"ensouled body"
ratio	objective aspect of the ego
consciousness	personality components from
individual freedom	society, the human race, etc.
(emotionally/intellectually	(emotionally/intellectually
extending into the infinite	refers to the category of the
or eternal)	earthly, the finite or temporal)

But where does the *strength* come from that enables either the conscious ego depicted in diagram 1 or the so-called self placed at the top of the diagram to integrate a human being whose personality is identical with itself. In view of this question, the above-mentioned either-or is seen as insufficient, especially in theological treatments of the identity problem. Thus, recourse to the concept of God apparently becomes inevitable.

Kierkegaard's classic portrayal of the way people "become a self" — with the help of faith! — still figures as a model in many contemporary studies. His reflections on defining the relationship between the ego and the self presented in the two works *The Concept of Anxiety* (1844) and *The Sickness unto Death* (1849) form a bridge between psychology, sociology, and biblical, theological anthropology frequently traversed in our century.

In the earlier writing, Kierkegaard defines man as a unity of body and soul (see 5.4.315) as well as a unity of the temporal and the eternal (see 5.4.355) brought about by the *spirit* (of man!). However, it is a matter of a constantly endangered unity. Man is concerned about maintaining the unity of the two opposing basic forces that determine him. This concern is expressed in anxiety that as an agent of the spirit must be distinguished from the fear that reacts to tangible external threats. The role of anxiety in this regard is ambivalent. On the one hand, it serves the goal of uniting the spirit. On the other hand, it drives man into a state of giddiness in which he is afraid of his opportunities for freedom. In this way, it once again binds man to his previous disparate state. Eternity or infinity is no longer given a chance to act as liberator from the bondage of time and finitude. Kierkegaard depicts the subject of the fall described in Genesis 3 by using this figure of thought inspired by his own personal experience of life (compare *Sickness* 5.4.331f.). The later work, *The Sickness unto Death* (a sickness in the spirit of man — despair — is meant), characterizes the spirit as the *self* of man (*Sickness* 5.11.147). Moreover, the relationship of this self to the two other poles of human existence, the body and the soul (notice the objectively insignificant divergence in *terminology* in our diagram which presupposes the body as ensouled in keeping with modern thought), is apprehended by Kierkegaard more precisely than five years before: a third part, the self, is not being added to body and soul. Rather, the self signifies the *relationship* between body and soul. This relationship is now the third thing: "Man is spirit. But what is spirit? Spirit is the self. But what is the self? The self is a relationship that relates to itself. . . ."

"Man is a synthesis of infinity and finitude, of the temporal and the eternal, of freedom and necessity; in short, a synthesis. A synthesis is a relationship between two things." "In the relationship between two things the relationship is the third thing, functioning as a negative unity, and the two relate to the relationship, and in the relationship to the relationship. . . ."

"Now what is despair? It is 'an imbalance' in that relationship which relates to itself. Kierkegaard believes that this imbalance comes from the fact that man no longer consciously lives in relationship to that authority which established this whole relationship called the self: God. For those of us who want to establish ourselves the despair is inevitable. We can at best suppress it. But what follows is the formula that describes the condition of the self when despair is completely eradicated. By relating to itself and by wanting to be itself, the self is transparently rooted in the power that established it."[19]

The most interesting thing about Kierkegaard's concept of the self (which can also be read as an attempt to analyze the structure of human personality and the specific self-consciousness of man) is its coordination of *independent human activity* and human *dependence on God*. For Kierkegaard, these do not contradict each other in the least. Man relates to himself as he really is. It is *his* spirit striving for its own synthesis. But the despair that occurs when man desires to get rid of the person he really is and be another person — and finds he is not able to do either of these things — finally drives his self-reflection to the issue of the power that surrounds everything. If man succeeds in breaking through to it, despair has yielded to faith.[20]

D. Man as the Personal Image of God

The basic *anthropological model* sketched in diagram 1 can be made more precise and further clarified by linking up with Kierkegaard and especially considering the trinitarian understanding of God. See diagram 2 on page 54.

God exists and relates to himself by way of overflowing creative love. Man is created through his love and his Spirit, and man in turn is inspired to exist in a loving relationship to himself, creative in love and overflowing outward. Only in this way do we become *persons* in the full sense of the word.

In God's multifaceted personality the *Son* represents all of humanity. In our human striving for personal existence, the human *spirit* represents the side of God turned toward us.

Man is destined to exist as the creaturely, earthly image of the triune

---

19. *Sickness* 5.11.127f. Translated from translation of E. Hirsch in S. Kierkegaard, *Gesammelte Werke,* vols. 24 and 25 (Düsseldorf, 1957), pp. 8-10.

20. See also Pannenberg, *Anthropologie in theologischer Perspektive,* pp. 96-98, 113, 117.

Diagram 2

Man as the personal image of God

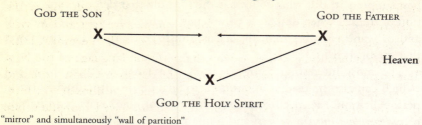

God the Son   God the Father

Heaven

God the Holy Spirit

"mirror" and simultaneously "wall of partition"

· · ·

permeable to the Holy Spirit and our prayers

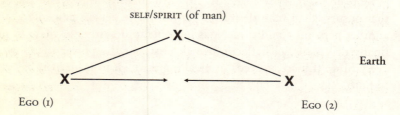

SELF/SPIRIT (of man)

Earth

Ego (1)   Ego (2)

God. However, it is not obvious that man can combine the three aspects of his being into a whole and into a personal unity as God does; indeed, we never fully achieve this.[21] The fact that we are even here at all as human *persons* with a measure of freedom, we owe to God's love and affection in the Holy Spirit (expressed in the model sketched above) — whether we use our freedom well or not, whether we are able to make something of our destiny visible or exist as persons living contrary to it. God's Spirit helps our spirit: he helps us to handle our constitutional "deficit," the fact that we, too, are not made differently than animals and plants but differ from them only in degree.

God's Spirit does not help us where we show "human weaknesses"; rather, he makes men/women into human beings. God's special loving care in the Holy Spirit lifts *all* human creatures into a personal human existence — not only believers! The latter, however, *know* about it and *let* God serve them. That is the only difference, although it is of course a decisive one!

Transition from Christology to anthropology: believers recognize the *Spirit or the self of Jesus Christ* in the Holy Spirit who makes our existence

21. See Barth, *KD*, I/1, p. 143.

as human beings possible (and saves us from our sin). They believe it is Jesus Christ who offers himself to us human beings as the one who anticipates our own *true self* that has not yet appeared. He is the substitute. He really stands where "one" would have to stand in view of our general human situation so that we, too, can "become a self." He *really* stands there, which is why the symbolic language of the New Testament repeatedly speaks of the being of the risen Christ *in us* and of our being *in him*. First, the individual comes "to himself" in him, then the whole creation "comes to itself" in the saved individual (see Rom. 8:19ff.).

Man is a flawed being. However, what he lacks through no fault of his own (constitutionally) is not a sure instinct, physical strength, and skill or the ability to adapt. *Rather, he lacks sufficient strength to be human in freedom, love, and dignity.* Put differently, he lacks the strength to maintain a reliable, constant humanity. To echo Kierkegaard, he lacks the strength to become a self on his own. *That is why he does not even want to.* Not only does he always fall behind himself but, above all, he tries to cover up his flaw.

Only at this point does his own guilt begin. At the same time, it is universal human guilt (and sin!): Man does not confess that he lacks the strength to be truly human or to become a self that really meets the *criteria of humanity* in freedom, love, and dignity. He is not truthful (*omnis homo mendax*, Ps. 116:11). As a sinner, he is also a hypocrite. And he already considers himself to be satisfactory and identical enough, although in reality he lives with surrogates who by no means remove his flaw.

It is always said that we all strive for a life of complete self-identity. But do we really do this? Perhaps Schleiermacher's famous "educated class" was never further removed from the goal of self-identity than today when they have even elevated it into a program.

E. The Concept of Salvation in the Context of Nature and Grace

Today, "salvation" has become an almost hidden word. It has also been discredited by modern German history. Before I deal with its content in greater detail, I want to point out a controversy that has especially preoccupied theology in the twentieth century and has generated repeated discussions in the present day. It concerns the old battle over "nature and grace." Across all denominational boundaries one group of theology professors assumes that even the nonbelieving sinner, in fact every person, is kept in authentic humanity by divine grace continually at work in creation. The other group wants to know nothing of such grace and calls only divine forgiveness and the defeat of human sin in Jesus Christ "grace."

But is the alternative correct? Or, are there perhaps *two* divine graces: a grace that establishes and preserves man as man and a second one that redeems man from his sins? This must be the answer: neither the alternative nor the addition of two graces is really in keeping with biblical faith. However, in order to get past this problem, even to a small degree, we must first bring it to a head.

It seems to be true of *all* people, whether they are believers or non-believers, sinful or not: man is not as firmly locked into the biological limits that are part of his nature as are the other creatures. He exceeds them all. He lives in relative freedom and assumes an "exocentric position" in nature, a point that Pannenberg makes (following H. Plessner). This special position enables man to distance himself from things, to take them as objects, *as* things. It is also the reason for his "capacity for self-reflection"; thus it is "simply another name for self-consciousness." Pannenberg (following M. Scheler, A. Portmann, and A. Gehlen) characterizes these facts as man's destiny to be "openness to the world."[22] Man's freedom is rooted in this openness. This is now the problem: Is this description of the universal human condition correct in the sense that sin — human life turned away from God — *does not change anything* about man's relative freedom and his universal ability to "take objects *as* things"? We must *not* say this! Whenever and wherever there is sin, it signifies not just the temptation but the act of seeking *more* behind the objects than mere things, attributing a soteriological significance to them. *Thus sinful man's humanity, his relative freedom, and the use of his self-consciousness are already distorted.*

This perspective sheds light on the dissension between two Protestant theologians who are currently teaching: in order to at least demonstrate the *meaning* of the idea of God, W. Pannenberg points out that we human beings must draw on an infinite reality surpassing all that exists in this

22. Pannenberg, pp. 34f.; quotations from ET, p. 37.

finite world. In order to be *human beings* we are dependent on this infinite reality which can be proven by the fact that as a being *open to the world,* man transcends the existing world in his actions. G. Schneider-Flume contradicts Pannenberg and says: "Man's dependence on salvation must be set against this dependence of man on an infinite reality asserted by Pannenberg. The former can certainly not be ascertained and recognized from the nature of man in itself, but can only be learned from God's history with man."[23]

With this recent flare-up of the old battle over nature and grace, God's revelation in creation and in salvation, we face the task of stating the problem better. This could succeed if the doctrine of sin is part of the solution in the following way: if both theological opinions as they just appeared became the foundation for a doctrine of sin, then in one instance sin would mean a violation of humanity, in the other a violation of salvation. However, this would not be a real "either-or" situation! For man's calamity is the fact that he cannot make himself *human,* but imagines that he can. From a Christian theological perspective, sin may indeed be judged to be a violation of humanity in its openness to the world or in its freedom. But the grace of Christ, salvation, may also be judged to be the salvation of human nature, that is, our basic human destiny to be open to the world or to be free. "Salvation" does not signify something beyond this. Rather, it signifies the salvation and realization of full humanity in the face of evil. It is the return of true humanity that had been lost and forfeited, the return of human freedom, love, and dignity, and all this in harmony with the environment as well!

On the one hand, we must decide — against a certain Roman Catholic teaching tradition — to see the anthropological outcome of sin *not* only in the loss of "supernatural grace" (while human nature continues to exist in an unimpaired state), but in a real disorganization and distortion of human nature. On the other hand, we must decide — against a certain Protestant teaching tradition — not to put the special history of God with human beings culminating in Jesus Christ, the grace of Christ, above, outside of, or even against a theology of creation; that is, against reality that reflects the Creator God's will and action. (Salvation in the Christian sense of the term is "a new creation" [2 Cor. 5:17] only to the extent that

---

23. Translated from Schneider-Flume, p. 105 n. 8.

it means the conquest of sin and evil *in* creation, and thus a salvation freed from sin and all evil.)

The special history of God with human beings begins temporally even *before* the appearance of the first human beings in evolution; it begins with the creation itself. The history of evolution and the history of salvation are ultimately coextensive. This is by no means to deny that God's relationship to human beings is something special. However, we believe that all of nature shares in this special relationship, is connected with it. Consequently, we decisively oppose the view — often encountered in previous theologies — that nature, developing externally to human beings, only provides the framework, the scene. The stage, so to speak, on which the *history of salvation* takes place as an ostensibly special history of God with human beings (or even with a select portion of humanity). Theology must enhance the status of the stage! It is not merely the technical facility for a dramatic game encompassing man's fall and divine redemption. Rather, nature external to human beings is included in this game — forcibly as far as man's sin is concerned; however, being set free as far as man's redemption is concerned.

Theology is and remains the attempt and task of interpreting the whole event of evolution as a history for which God accepts the responsibility. Theology really has to portray all things *sub ratione Dei* (Thomas Aquinas). An anthropocentric theology ostensibly more suitable to the modern era portraying all of reality *sub ratione hominis* would be a contradiction in terms. That is why the philosophy of German idealism is not *theology* — it carried this anthropocentric theology to its logical conclusion. However, the task of understanding reality *sub ratione Dei* means nothing but seeing theology as that science which has to discern the salvific aspect of evolution, based on divine revelation. In *this* context theology also has to speak of man's sin or his unwillingness to accept the destiny bestowed on him by God (which is at the same time his natural and evolutionary destiny).

Once again, the history of evolution and the history of salvation coincide. Whenever theology is reminded of this broad orientation that transcends traditional limitations, which has happened mainly through Teilhard de Chardin, we should affirm this theology and finally follow its lead.

F. Sin, Elemental Confidence, and Christian Faith

Human sin cannot possibly be a *necessary* part of human self-realization in freedom, dignity, and love. If human identity involves such self-realization, sin at any rate is not found along its path, but blocks its path. It disturbs, hinders, destroys the development of such an identity. Nevertheless, what leads us to our true humanity and thus to the fulfillment of our destiny or identity and what leads us into sin are separated from one another only by a hair's breadth. Indeed, they are so close together that both are mistaken for the other time and again. Then it is said: "Because I should find my own identity, I also have to sin. True, sin causes damage to me and to others, but I have to get through it." This opinion is a trap even theological hamartiology gets caught in all too easily and then dies there.

Given the incredible closeness of man's vital pursuit of his own identity to sin, Pannenberg has ventured to coin a phrase that almost exceeds the limits of what is possible: human *egocentricity (amor sui)*, which is the "essential element in sin or the failure of human beings in regard to themselves," is inextricably intertwined with the "*natural conditions* of our existence."[24] For the human being seeking his identity *must* relate the things of this world to his own ego because he shouldn't repress them or overlook their reality. He *must* place himself in the midst of the world as the center of his own awareness and see how he can manage it. This centering of the real world in the ego that is so obviously essential for the development of one's own identity does not at all contradict the *exocentric* position of man taught by Pannenberg (following H. Plessner); rather, both positions complement each other perfectly. *Because* man finds himself in an exocentric position in the cosmos, he gathers "everything" around his ego, if possible. This is really in keeping with his nature.

"This exocentric self-transcendence, this being present to what is other than the self . . . constitutes the ego or person. At the same time, however, the ego, in its identity with 'itself,' also places itself over against the other. This is the root of the break in the ego, the root of its conflict with its own exocentric destiny." If its presence to the other "now becomes" a means "for it to assert itself in its difference from the other," if it therefore signifies the desire to dominate the other or the self, then the offense

24. Pannenberg, p. 104; quotations from ET, p. 107.

begins. Now "the setting of the ego against the other becomes total," so that "everything else must be made a means to the self-assertion of the ego." Ultimately this signifies "the break of the ego from itself and its still constitutive exocentricity. . . ."[25]

Thus, the process of identity formation has found its provisional or definite end — much too prematurely. But how can this personal disaster be avoided or limited in its effects? How is human identity preserved and strengthened? How can even guilt be put to use in such a way that man can live in greater harmony with his self-identity? Today extensive literature in psychology and religious education answers that this is primarily facilitated by our ability to acquire a *fundamental* or *elemental confidence* in earliest childhood, which is the "first component of psychological health" (E. H. Erikson). The more fundamental confidence we have, the more strength we have to develop our self-identity in life.[26] Compared to this, all later therapeutic assistance or treatment is of secondary importance.

The anthropological significance of Christian faith is very often explained today in terms of this fundamental confidence. It is said, for instance, that faith establishes, justifies, and strengthens this basic confidence.[27] Often it is even identified with faith today.

The following factors seem to speak for this view: the question of the origin of this fundamental confidence extends far beyond the relationships and the people that children relate to during their earliest childhood. It seems like a miracle that this enormous confidence appeared in cosmic evolution, making it possible for our human ancestors to assume an "exocentric position." And we should *also* ask: What *justifies* this fundamental confidence that allows us to maintain the "exocentric position" so decisive for our humanity and more or less gain our identity? Neither our observations on natural processes and developments within nature nor our experiences within those parts of human history that affect us give us sufficient reason or grounds to develop such fundamental confidence. On the contrary! Of course, if this is the case, is not what the religions call "God" the origin and justification of our fundamental confidence —

---

25. Pannenberg, p. 82; quotations from ET, p. 85.

26. See H.-J. Fraas, *Glaube und Identität. Grundlegung einer Dialektik religiöser Lernprozesse* (Göttingen, 1983), p. 112; Pannenberg, *Anthropologie in theologischer Perspektive*, pp. 222f.

27. Fraas, p. 113.

which is possible to maintain even against the experience of reality? For example, the question of sufficient grounds for this basic confidence led Pannenberg to the guarded conclusion that the *question of God* is "an inalienable part of what it means to be human." Scharfenberg's reflection that man's relationship to God (which is perceived and lived in faith) is *necessary* for the development of human identity is also rooted here.[28]

Yet at this point there is a *practical* problem: a human being who has almost no basic confidence is probably also not "ripe for faith" in such a way that he could easily make the transition from a previous nonfaith or unbelief to the saving faith that provides this fundamental confidence. However, the kind of faith that is deeply moved by God is out of the question as an available therapeutic remedy for people with weak egos. On the other hand, even those who have a strong fundamental confidence are not for that reason believing human beings in a religious or Christian sense. Perhaps they of all people feel no need for faith. Perhaps they don't even like to hear that their fundamental confidence *implies* genuine, religious faith even if they don't know this themselves. Or their fundamental confidence is the fruit of the strong Christian faith of their parents, more distant ancestors, or the nursing staff that cared for them as infants.

Thus, it is difficult to define the relationship of faith to the fundamental confidence of human beings. *It can only be made transparent from the side of faith, not vice versa.* Man's confidence in the Creator and his work is certainly built up where faith in God exists. In this respect, fundamental confidence is also present. But at the same time this faith means that man ceases to place his full confidence in this world or anything/anyone in this world. The believing individual no longer bases his life on what is (supposedly) reliable in the areas of life he controls. He takes into account the sinful divisions tearing our world apart — and relies on the Creator who is at the same time the Reconciler and Redeemer of the world. Nevertheless, if in an isolated case he could be called a person having natural and spontaneous confidence in other people as well as joy and confidence in life, we are probably dealing here with a mixture of a happy disposition he received from a good childhood and a strong faith he gained later. *However, faith neither replaces such a disposition (toward basic confidence) if it wasn't present from the home, nor does faith destroy it or produce it.* Faith will support it if it is present anyway. But this is also not its actual "task"

28. See pp. 45-46.

or "function."[29] But what then is the meaning and goal of faith? Should it not, for instance, liberate us to love? And by what merely religious about-face could a person ever attain freedom and love, which are both promised to us as the fruit of faith, *without such fundamental confidence?* Therefore, must not Christian faith, if it is to mean something, be wedded to this fundamental confidence; must it not even be identified with this fundamental confidence, as even Erikson assumed?[30]

It is easy to say in terms of dogmatic correctness that faith must not be co-opted in order to support human self-development to wholeness, maturity, and happiness. But when our theology is supposed to communicate where the meaning of faith for man is to be found, it gets into trouble. Will it say that something else is more important to faith than gaining an authentic human life that makes possible or proves human identity? What is more important than deterring and healing alienation and suffering? What? Here we need careful theological thinking. Here we must not allow ourselves to be driven to "either-or" answers. But we must clearly say again in contrast to most contemporary theological literatures that real faith is first and foremost interest in *God himself* — and not in maturity, freedom, happiness, and the identity of the believing person. *Faith is not a process of finding oneself via God, but of man finding God in the process of successfully detaching from himself.* Although this first aspect is useful in acquiring our human identity, it must not be construed theologically as the actual goal! Theology together with its doctrines of faith and sin has had it if it claims to be something other than human reflection on what *God* is, wants, and does in *his* identity.

G. The Problem of the Verification of Sin and Faith — with an Initial Theological Thesis

A thesis was prepared by the preceding discussion. Here it is: *Theology should turn its back on all of its attempts to verify sin on the basis of disruptions in the development of human identity.* This doesn't mean that sin has nothing to do with the loss of identity, but that it can't be understood from that perspective. Sin is transgression against the self only in a secondary or tertiary sense. Sin

29. See Schneider-Flume, pp. 120, 123, 125.
30. See Schneider-Flume, p. 102.

is primarily a wrong orientation toward God. Of course, it then makes itself felt in destructive relationships between man and nature, in the disorder that has befallen nature itself, in interpersonal relationships and psychologically in individual human beings as well. However, if we were to portray the disunity or even disintegration of the self as the actual material problem of sin, in which various degrees of suffering, including psychosis, are experienced, we would still not have understood anything about real sin — indeed, by seeing it in these terms we sin again! For then we would be stylizing our personal nonidentity as the central, decisive aspect of sin — as if only our suffering, our self-alienation counted.

Sin will once again become a real word in our language only when we understand it primarily *as human disrespect for God's being and work,* as a reprehensible human encroachment into the realm of God's identity. A theological doctrine of sin that will have an impact on the future must not desire to make itself intelligible by moving in the direction of saying that God can ultimately "be hated and given offense only in man."[31] Rather, it must stress that *God* is offended when human beings (and other creatures as well!) are disdained and mistreated.[32] If we cannot achieve this again, the theological doctrine of sin is finished. All of our discussions about sin that are still carried on in those categories are dangerous and must even be rejected in the interest of humanity. When the honor and dignity of God do not move us, we must not assume that we are really serious about sin and forgiveness. Nor must we assume that we would really be willing to be moved to repentance by seeing the dignity and honor of man and other creatures threatened.

In the same vein, faith will once again become recognizable as a humanly significant matter only when it is not reduced to fundamental human confidence, man's conformity to himself and his world, but when faith is lived and understood as man's conformity to the other, the divine reality. Precisely because of our sin it is important that this conformity of faith is to be valued as an identity coming to us *from the outside* and not wanted or sought by us *in this form.*

---

31. D. Sölle, *Politische Theologie. Eine Auseinandersetzung mit R. Bultmann* (Stuttgart/Berlin, 1971), p. 115; quotation from English translation, Dorothee Soelle, *Political Theology*, trans. John Shelley (Philadelphia: Fortress, 1974), p. 91.

32. See G. W. Leibniz, *Die Theodicee*, nebst den Zusätzen der Bebosses'schen Übertragung mit Einleitung und Erläuterungen deutsch von R. Habs (Leipzig, n.d., 1883), p. 114.

Yet, in what way could this theological talk of a "divine reality coming from the outside" still be convincing today? Is a God who intervenes from the outside even conceivable? Could he be experienced in his coming? Does not our handling of the concept of God mean that we place God wherever man likes to or urgently needs to postulate something like God while safeguarding his "interests" (a practice recognized as harmful by modern critics of religion)? Is this perhaps *why* we assert the existence of God — because our way of portraying the *conditio humana* (especially human freedom needs a God) seems to demand him intellectually?

It is perhaps natural to suppose that because of his "exocentric position" in the cosmos, man imagines the existence of a God who has put him there and gives him support there. But such traditional "imagination" was rightly cut to the quick by the Enlightenment's demand that man should determine his own life and should not seek comfort and support from a superfather projected into the hereafter.

Meanwhile, not a few in the Christian church have learned to participate in such criticism of religion precisely for the sake of faith. This is a welcome development because God can in fact not be deduced from our needs. Everything we deduce about God from our needs in the form of hypotheses is untenable. All this only makes a statement about us, but reveals nothing about the God who exists. Our questions are also irrelevant: "Who speaks for God?" "Which of our experiences allow us to deduce the existence (of a) God?" Or: "Which observations allow God to appear intellectually conceivable?" Even if we could really *prove* God's existence from what we recognize and experience, such a proof would be inappropriate for God because asking the "God question" means not asking how God could be made plausible from the perspective of our material world and its objects. Rather, the religious "God question" is this: What meaning is shed on our material world and its objects from the perspective of divine reality? The latter question must have arisen on its own before we could ask *about it* in this way: it must have made itself noticeable and sufficiently known to us on its own! Only in this way does faith become possible and theology meaningful. All theology is a theology of revelation — or it is theological *nihil.*

The "God question" that above is relevant does not ask, "What speaks for God?" but, "What speaks for man?!" It assumes that *man* (and his existence) represents the problem, not God (and his existence). Of course, this does not mean that we humans could use something like God because of our flaws and problems. Rather, it sees certain flaws and problems in our existence *because* it is an inquiry and observation that comes from the experience of being completely taken aback by the living God.

Everything else, all our thinking and speaking about God, man, and the world that originates in our own situation of need, is fruitless. However, the God who tells us what speaks for us and why we are here, indeed, who lets us notice that we are here because *he* speaks to us because he gives us divine words which motivate us to be truly human and maintain our humanity — no theology has to go to bat for this God by demonstrating his "plausibility" to doubters, atheists, philosophers, etc. He *is* conceivable. He is a challenge for our thinking, especially for pondering finitude and the interrelationship between the world and man. The real God reveals himself — or he is silent. He speaks to us verbally or by being silent (see Isa. 42:14). One way or another he makes sure that we notice him — even if it be that we notice "nothing" of him and "hear nothing of him." This, too, has a *noticeable* effect on us.

God's silence that has often been called a special feature of our situation in the twentieth century corresponds to his self-concealment "in the moment of wrath" (at the sins of the people) mentioned in Deutero-Isaiah (Isa. 54:8). However, it remains to be seen whether God is really being silent here, really no longer talking to the people; or whether they no longer hear him on account of their sins, although he is talking. Likewise, it remains to be seen whether perhaps sinful man's deep aversion to God's goodness and even to God's existence is partially (or even primarily) expressed in the wrath of God, which, of course, cannot be an emotional, impulsive act by the Creator of heaven and earth.

H. Sin and Experience

Now we are able to pick up the theme of *religious experience* in a meaningful way. Experience is always and fundamentally experience coupled with knowledge and understanding. Mere experience, a merely dull feeling, is not yet an experience. Religious experience, too — the experience of faith, of God, and of sin — must include knowledge and understanding. The experience of sin is especially interesting in our context. Contemporary human beings often seem to "lack" it — but may we even put it and see it in these terms? The contemporary church's widespread lament over modern man's often nonexistent feeling for sin, his deficient awareness of sin, his inability to recognize his own sin is not very useful. People fully experience the lack of God. It goes to the heart of what it means to be human. The question is only how we handle and interpret it. It can also be interpreted as something quite different. However, above all, something quite different can be misinterpreted as the absence of *God* (something *that is not really sin at all)*. For example, the negative consequences of practical necessities, human weaknesses, needs and mistakes, social and psychological ills, etc., can be misinterpreted theologically and labeled as "sin." This occurs frequently in our time.

The occurrence of this misinterpretation is not to be condoned theologically, but it is understandable. The experience of God is an experience that is hidden under other experiences. For example, it *must* always be this way when God speaks to us through *silence*. However, it is also that way when God *speaks* to us because we are reached only by human words behind which God is hidden when he desires to reveal himself. This paradoxical structure of religious experience is frequently ignored both by theologians and advocates of nontheological empirical sciences. As a result they misinterpret what is happening between God and man. God's (perhaps silent) closeness to man is declared to be his absence, his unavailability; real sin is declared to be perhaps an expression of human identity or even closeness to God; ailments and disorders that can be cured by man are perhaps declared to be real sin, etc.

However, this is the situation regarding the relationship of experience to faith and sin: man feels the loss or disruption of his relationship to God, but he does not at the same time recognize and understand that this relationship is at stake. Thus, there is no direct experience of sin as sin and also no perception of unbelief in the midst of unbelief. To a great extent, Christians and theologians of all times agree with what K. Barth put in the following terms in the twentieth century: "Sin is man's self-alienation from the grace of God from which and in which he has his being. Sin consists in the fact that he neglects the grace of God and therefore his own true interests."[33]

But the same divine *grace* man rejects in sin — thus fatally imperiling himself — must be *experienced* anew in a human life; grace must take the

---

33. Karl Barth, *Church Dogmatics*, vol. 3, *The Doctrine of Creation*, pt. 2, ed. G. W. Bromiley and T. F. Torrance, trans. Harold Knight et al. (Edinburgh: T. & T. Clark, 1960), p. 35.

initiative so that this man can even recognize his sin: "Only those who taste and see how gracious the Lord is can know their sin. All others may recognise more or less clearly the preponderance of evil . . . and perhaps their inner and outer conflicts. But all these are conceived as so many evil circumstances which can be lived down or at a pinch put right. Their own sin, and therefore the real sin of real men . . . *is* known only by those who have been shown by the light of divine grace who they are and what they have done and still do." "*Known* sin is always *forgiven* sin, known in the light of forgiveness and the triumphant grace of God." Barth believes it is ultimately not so that a person who is first ready to repent and actually turns to God will *then* experience God's grace and mercy (instead of God's wrath). Rather: "We repent only as we have already found the God of grace and realised that we are His creatures."

And now Barth says pointedly: The divine forgiveness, this repeated kindness of God, His turning to man in grace, the human experience of God's grace, is necessary for man to enter into a knowledge of his sin and then to repent. His grace is not experienced here one minute and there the next, but only in one specific place: The reception and experience of that divine forgiveness are a part of the "privileges of Israel and the Church." A "message" has been entrusted to both of these by God, which they have to deliver to the whole world: The message of the *grace of God* that *triumphs* over man's sinful rejection of God's grace precisely because it forgives this sin and thus takes care of it. This message of which it is true that it does not in any way have its place everywhere could also not always be heard in world history: "It is something new which comes to believers with their recognition of the love of God in Jesus Christ."[34]

Grace understood in Christian terms is, therefore, the power of God asserting itself anew among human beings even though they have rejected it. It is a power that survives and rescinds its own negation by sinful human beings. To echo Barth, only when grace "triumphs" and rises again from its negation, does man recognize his sin; before then, as "natural man," he does *not* recognize it.

However, it remains an open question in Barth's comments whether unrecognized sin does not, nevertheless, come to be experienced as a difficulty, as a distressing situation understood in some other way. Barth seems to accept this. His tenets permit the conclusion that sin is accom-

---

34. Barth, *Church Dogmatics*, III/2, p. 36.

panied by an experience judged to be "not good." Moreover, Barth does not say that all *human attempts* to learn from such negative experiences and find relief must fail. Nevertheless, he sticks to his opinion: *in sinning we do not know what we are doing and what in fact is happening to us* (cf. Luke 23:34a). Only with the experience of forgiveness — possible in Israel and in the church — do we know who we are, what we have done, and what is happening to us. In short, sin is *initially* an ambiguous experience. However, *forgiveness* is immediately an unambiguous experience. It is an experience that interprets itself and at the same time clearly identifies the person whom it affects — by unambiguously identifying him as a sinner.

So far Barth's argumentation seems *theologically* compelling. But we would like to know more details from Barth: what is the theological importance of the human experience of being caught up in painful conflicts and negative situations marked by alienation. Barth himself mentions this experience, although it has not yet reached the point of being recognized as sin. How is the human maturing gained through such experiences to be assessed theologically? And how about the healing of much guilt, deformity, and alienation? And finally, how can the experience of the forgiveness of sins of which Barth speaks (taste and see that the Lord is good) actually be gained? Solely by devoutly hearing the "message"? Or must it be accompanied by a definite human conversion experience in the community of faith?

What impact does *the forgiveness of sins* have on human suffering and bad relationships? Does it have a therapeutic effect? Evidently it is a matter of man getting straightened out by dealing with the root cause. But must we then assume that all therapy that wants to manage without the forgiveness of sins is ultimately just rolling the sick from one side of the bed to the other? This doesn't make sense to anyone. Yet many contemporary theological doctrines of sin are not able to make themselves understood to the man on the street when the liberating power of human endeavors against suffering and alienation awaits a fair evaluation even though merely humanistic reasons are given for their efforts. Neither do they make themselves understood when they assimilate their hamartiology to certain psychiatric and social therapeutic models of sickness and healing to such a great extent that they no longer make sense as *theology*.

I. Sin in Liberation Theology

We can count all theologies that have posited a new political or social concept of sin in the last quarter century as part of liberation theology. These theologies verify sin on the basis of the suffering experienced economically, socially, and legally by groups of human beings oppressed or put at a disadvantage by racism and gender discrimination.

As a rule it can be said of these theological models what M. Sievernich has specifically written to characterize D. Sölle's political hermeneutics of sin and forgiveness: they do not accept "the inheritance of Hegel as mediated by Kierkegaard"; rather, they join the left-wing Hegelian tradition, especially the early Marx.[35] On the other hand, their tendency is not to join any "doctrinal traditions" at all, nor to participate in further dogmatic distinctions in hamartiology, but to let their own experiences speak (and, as unbiasedly as possible, to relate key biblical, mainly Old Testament statements to questions of contemporary living). In *all these models* they also seek "liberation" from a theology which is preoccupied with itself instead of with the world of today.

The relationship of liberation theology's doctrines of sin to experience *seems* simple. Obvious experiences of guilt and alienation seem to be sin; *obvious* events of liberation seem to be called grace or even salvation and redemption. But this first impression that can be gained from many models (which can quickly lead one to doubt the validity of such models) must be corrected. In liberation theology *as well*, human *blindness* in terms of not recognizing and not experiencing one's own sin plays a major role! *Consciousness-raising learning processes* must take place so that the *individual*(!) experiences and recognizes his personal involvement, his participation and collaboration in nationwide or even worldwide sin: his lethargic acceptance of injustice, his reluctance to join the organized political struggle, his insensitive suppression of immorality and oppression, his egotism.

Liberation theologies also focus on situations in which, for example, the powerful often programmatically speak of preserving freedom and experiencing freedom where a more sensitive consciousness has long since perceived an oppressive bondage and a deep involvement in coercive measures. Thus the typical starting point for liberation theology's doctrine

---

35. Translated from Sievernich, p. 185.

of sin is not an appeal to obvious experiences of alienation. Rather, in terms of this doctrine there must first be an effort to reveal that *sin* is at issue (even in seemingly harmless, everyday habits). From this kind of enlightenment about the actual character of our experiences and actions liberation theologians hope to gain new impetus for structural, political change *and* for releasing an individually better humanity!

What matters here more than anything else is the interpretation of certain experiences *as sin!* Liberation theologies want to say: You cannot possibly proceed on the path you have taken up till now, not because various things are happening that are customarily a part of life, but because what you are doing is really *sin* and because you, too, must recognize your behavior *as sin.*

Liberation theology expects *salvation* by regaining a consciousness of sin. Whatever my view of secularization may be, I should *learn* that what I am doing is *sin.* I should change my life out of respect for the old, difficult word "sin"; however, mainly to escape feelings of guilt. A guilty conscience may and should be created — whatever Nietzsche's and Freud's critique of it may be! Of course, liberation theology's critical development of the problem of hamartiological experience and understanding and the unique twist it puts on the problem are questionable! Can such exhortations that somehow seem to overlook the working of divine grace ever lead to an "understanding of sin"? Can they help us properly interpret our experiences and actions *as sin?* Do they help us understand sin correctly? In a strong anticlimax to the classical theological opinion presented by Barth ("only those who experience God's forgiving compassion, repent and recognize their sin"), the suffering of the oppressed (by us, too) seems to be laid on our souls, as an appeal for us to repent *in this way.* Does such a procedure simply signify "theological clumsiness"? Is it even dangerous and "unsuitable" in terms of its ethical purpose? Obviously we must not lump together all the models of liberation theology, and we must be especially cautious in making theological value judgments. (In fact, the theological rejection of liberation theology's exhortations could all too easily signify evasiveness in the cause that Christian ethics rightly demands that we support!)

Furthermore, remember that liberation theology's hamartiology is by its very nature immune to a mistake the traditional church doctrine of sin has made often enough. It simply cannot disregard the social relationships in which every human individual not only lives and pursues freedom but also believes, loves, hopes — and sins. Hamartiology that has *not* observed the *homines peccatores* in the surroundings of their human relationships was never theologically correct. It was not correct not only because of its isolated religious individualism. Rather, it also missed its calling because of its theoretical, academic cast, specifically its lack of and its spiritualizing and suppression of material reality. Whoever critiques contemporary liberation theology's understanding of sin — for instance, because it supposedly does not categorize *all* people as sinners, because it does not speak clearly enough of the forgiveness of sin but prefers to speak of the "responsibility" and the necessity of "dealing with" sin, or because it is not able to escape the dangers of a legalistic and moralistic understanding of sin — whoever makes this critique must first have asked whether the more theological hamartiology he has in mind, the one more in line with the New Testament, is not at least in part kept today from making grave theological errors by receiving inspiration from liberation theologies.

By their very nature liberation theologies are also virtually immune to a further danger to which theology and church have often succumbed: the neglect of history, not of church history but of world history as a whole. As a matter of course liberation theologies have grasped what many other theologies have never grasped (echoing D. Sölle): "Neither the desecrated temple nor the declining churches are our accusers, but the situation of our world."[36] Moreover, in liberation theologies the *kingdom of God* is rightly considered the goal of all history when they reflect on sin, oppression, injustice — in short, on the better and worse historical forms of our human affairs. Whoever critiques the frequently untenable theological manner in which they appeal to the kingdom of God (perhaps too synergistically in terms of the tiresome "ethical incentive") should also consider that the kingdom of God plays practically no role in many other so-called doctrines of sin and theologies advocated by church tradition and that in most cases much less damage is done by a dogmatically incorrect, heretical theology than by the nonexistence, the absence of really timely theological teaching.

It is less the occurrence of impure doctrine that usually causes disaster in the church than *the absence of pure and proper doctrine* at the right time! (How many unnecessary quarrels, how many theological slack periods would have been spared the church and humanity if the church's self-

36. Sölle, *Politische Theologie*, p. 115; quotation from ET, p. 91.

knowledge had always prevailed, the realization that pure and proper doctrine is *decisive in this sense!*)

Of course, a theological retrogression from Jesus to John the Baptist or from the New Testament's understanding of sin to the Old Testament's understanding of sin could not be a recommendation for contemporary liberation theology's attempts to strengthen our Christianity. Certainly the *justice concerns* of liberation theologians would more often be part of the doctrine of good works than of hamartiology. On the other hand, these theological models build a bridge to important and valuable endeavors of the Enlightenment (these models exist in theological forms that must be judged individually). Liberation theology's doctrine of sin that logically completes and "inwardly" resembles the hamartiology geared to the individual's pursuit of identity (a pursuit of freedom!) by pursuing social identity is an especially strong indication that the continued conversation between Christianity and the Enlightenment is a must. Both have gotten on in years and have compromised each other in various ways — but they have not yet met each other with their respective strengths. Precisely for this reason the track record of their mutual impact is not good.

J. The Significance of Eschatology for Hamartiology — with a Concluding Theological Thesis

A problem that remains open and to a large degree in need of further discussion is this: Can we assume a *plan* underlying world history in spite of all the experiences and insights that make us think the opposite is true? Is the existence and development of *humanity* the especially important part of such a plan? Do we have to assume that world conditions will radically improve sooner or later because nature is becoming increasingly hominized and spiritualized? In addition, should we (at least) believe that justice will be done for the deceased victims of history and that all tears will be wiped away by God (Rev. 7:17; 21:4)?

The less the *secularized* "plan of salvation" (that is, the restructuring of the world planned and undertaken in the spirit of the Enlightenment or a socialist utopia) is still judged to be a realistic path that could lead to "Eden," the more we ask again about *God's* providence and the meaning of the kingdom of God promised in the Bible. Does *God* have a plan?

If so, then evidently this divine plan does *not* provide hope that world conditions are continuously improving, developing "upward" step-by-step to the goal of a cosmos ultimately totally free of evil and suffering. We are not making any progress in the direction of "Eden." We have never before made any progress in this direction. What, then, could be the content of a divine "plan of salvation"? Is it only a question of *other-worldly* consolation and happiness? The latter would contradict the viewpoint of biblical eschatology. A responsible theology must not teach this because in the view of Scripture we must also ask this question: On the one hand, what does *faith* mean in terms of being gifted by the last things even now, and on the other hand, what does the biblical metaphor mean that the goal of world history is the *unification of all things with God?* (Paul writes in 1 Corinthians 15:23ff. that the risen Christ gradually defeats all the enemies of God — in a certain order — until all things are subject to him so that God is ultimately "all in all.") Is not a *this-worldly* chiliastic "hope of better times" expressed in such a metaphor? In fact, this metaphor — and theological eschatology should be guided by it! — signifies that we must not compare this world and the next or see them as alternatives. God stands and acts above this supposed alternative. (Or will we ultimately come to the conclusion, as far as the New Testament is mainly concerned, that the eschatology of all the texts placed alongside each other is so diffuse, so theologically multifaceted that it borders on being contradictory. Of course this assumption, which offers a fairly good explanation of the present state of eschatologies taught in the church, is ultimately wrong. For the *single* statement that our world of sin, evil, and death is destined for indestructible life in union or reunification with God can be clearly discerned as the main line of thought in New Testament eschatology as a whole.)

Everything that happens is thus enigmatically shaped by a continuous movement of God to the world and of the world to God. The fixed goal of these movements is the reconciliation and redemption of the world in a steadily increasing, indeed, complete participation of the creatures in God — although it can not yet be described in detail. At least this much is theologically not in doubt or in dispute.

Without certainty and clarity in eschatology the church cannot speak of sin, for the concept of sin gains its specificity and its content from the question of whether there is a clear destiny for us creatures, a purpose we can fail to achieve. Unfortunately, present-day theologies lack the power to express this purpose clearly even if there may be a minimal eschatological consensus. Theology no longer helps human beings gain certainty in this matter.

According to earlier theological teaching there are also reprobates among the human race. This is no longer true of modern-day teaching. Who can say why? Have we discerned the main contours of New Testament eschatology better than ever before — or is it just that we no longer accept what seems to us like "biblical severity"? According to an earlier theological understanding we human beings are destined by God for a life after death. Modern Christian preaching about the resurrection of the dead at the graveside has become a scene of spiritual and intellectual embarrassment. On the other hand, the chiliastic hope of "better times" and historical progress in keeping with this hope are considered today in many churches of the Reformation to be arbitrary — in contrast to an earlier strict rejection of chiliasm: It does not have to, but may claim a place in the church. (Still, a rather old verse is still sung from the German Protestant church hymnal in which, following Psalm 98, this statement is made about our earth: "God wants it to become an Eden!")[37]

The this-worldly, secular doctrines of salvation in the modern era and its imagination have been fired by religious ideas like these. They have interpreted "salvation" as an increasing moral-intellectual maturity and self-development of individuals and the entire human family. From this maturing they hoped for progress in outgrowing the alienated relationship between man and nature. Finally, they defined sin and guilt as a human behavior that inhibits this maturity and hardly saw any objective distinction between the two. Christian theology's conversation with these ideas is not yet at an end because in more recent times the Christian hope for the future was presented in such an ambiguous and disparate way.

When all is said and done, what is the reason for this ambiguity? What is the fatal flaw in modern theological eschatology and practical eschatological hope? It seems to me to be found in its faintheartedness regarding its theological statements about the world to come and a life after death, a faintheartedness that has been fashionable for some time now but is not acceptable. What is the point of the modern church's enthusiastic embrace of a naive belief in progress, chiliasm, and utopia when no hope at all can be given to the past, present, and future victims of a world situation that has *not yet* become good? The answer to this question

37. *EKG* (Protestant Hymnal), no. 186, st. 2.

should be self-evident. Individual eschatology which promises every person a specific future with God after death must regain its power in the churches — or churches will become superfluous. The most important theological tasks for the future are found in eschatology! It will become apparent that the alternative between a this-worldly and an other-worldly piety is a false one: The faith and hope of the individual beyond this life in the world (and, therefore, beyond death) are crucial sources for the kind of vitality in *this world* that can lead it to new *kabod* even though it has now lost its splendor and is threatened with complete destruction.

K. Summary and a Look Ahead

As we have demonstrated, modern theological hamartiologies have the tendency to locate the experience of faith and sin and its relationship to reality in the human pursuit of freedom and identity. It reveals a striking proximity to various philosophical models of the eighteenth century. This proximity is not without its problems. Yet the manner in which a theological model is fleshed out decides its value.

An *initial* decision which must always be made when realizing a theological project such as this reveals whether we are prepared here and now to equate faith with the feeling of a strong fundamental confidence, but to equate sin with the feeling of inner turmoil and alienation. Such an equation would not be theologically acceptable, as we have already seen. At best, we can make this theological statement: Faith and sin are related to such human experiences. *Secondly,* we must clarify whether we should ascribe an *essential role* not only to fundamental confidence but also to sin and guilt in the formation of human identity as, for example, Hegel did. The answer: from a theological point of view it is at least necessary to draw a distinction between guilt and sin (and then in spite of Hegel to state that in any case sin is *not* necessary to acquire human identity, to activate human freedom and demonstrate its success. For sin is only a disruptive, even destructive factor on the way there). We can also not come to terms with sin in the same way it is often possible to do with guilt. However, prerequisite for gaining maturity on the path to greater personal freedom is just this ability to come to terms with sin. Finally, a *third* decision is made when we ask if guilt and sin must inevitably and constantly accompany every human life — regardless of whether we expect maturity or destruction from them. In this case as well a theologically acceptable answer would assume the distinction between guilt and sin. But now in the opposite sense, it would not be proper to interpret the *act of incurring guilt* as an inevitable and constant factor or ingredient of our existence — for example, because of a conflict of loyalties in life.[38] *Man can also prove himself morally.* He can avoid guilt. He can also keep God's commandments, he can keep the law of nature and the laws of the state! To modify a famous sentence from Immanuel Kant: *Because* he can do it, he should do it.[39] As far as his moral capacity is concerned, as much pessimism as one wants may be appropriate. But fatalism is prohibited! Sin, man's turning away from God, his forgetfulness toward God, is a different matter. It is a constant companion in our existence. It is an unavoidable ingredient of our nature and striving.[40] There is no possibility that we could ever decide on our own to establish fellowship with God and prove by our actions that we have a love for God.

Those who fail to distinguish between sin and guilt, sin and alienation, as well as between faith and fundamental confidence (distinguishing does not mean separating!) will come to grief theologically. Of course, occasionally there have been significant minds and in some ways stimulating theologians who at least have come close to embracing such no longer acceptable conclusions. Our historical situation even offers us the incentive to do it because it beckons us to at last talk again about faith and sin in a way that is related to experience. Questions of this nature can be further pursued in section V in the context of our analysis of contemporary interpretations of Genesis 2 and 3 as well as further below in section VIII in the context of our interpretation of the fifth request of the Lord's Prayer.

---

38. See D. Lange, "Seinserfahrung und Gewissenserfahrung in der Sünde," *ZThK* 80 (1983): 299f.; and Julius Müller, *Die christliche Lehre von der Sünde,* 2 vols. (Breslau, [2]1844; Bremen, [6]1889), 1:43.

39. I. Kant, *Grundlegung zur Metaphysik der Sitten* A2, in *Werke,* 3:509.

40. For a different view, see D. Sölle, *Das Recht ein anderer zu werden. Theologische Texte,* RThP1 (Neuwied/Berlin, [2]1972), p. 27; and Auer, "Ist die Sünde eine Beleidigung Gottes," *ThQ* 55 (1975), pp. 53-68; see also pp. 63ff.

SECTION IV
SUPPLEMENT: THE STARTING POINTS IN THE PHILOSOPHY OF RELIGION FOR THE HAMARTIOLOGICAL MODEL PRESENTED IN THIS BOOK

God works in the world by means of calling and being silent. The divine call lifts things into the light so that they shine. It gives them shape as only love can. It is creative. God's silence drives his creatures to deathly despair and sends them into decline. It stirs in them a hunger for a renewed calling by God. But God's silence is part of his creative activity. Although it signifies the horrible fact that God distances himself and hides himself, it prepares his creatures, who learn to listen anew to reach even higher levels. Through his calling and through his silence, God is leading the world to a goal: the loving coexistence and cooperation of rivals in the struggle for sustenance. Theological tradition calls this goal of the world the kingdom of God.

God's *word* not only calls things that are not as though they were, as it says in Romans 4:17 (creation), but also calls what has come into being; it calls it to God so that he may rescue it, lead it to love, and lend it significance. It justifies what is allowed to be in evolution, and it encourages what is to develop in evolution. God gives himself in his Word that creates the world and saves it. Nevertheless, for this reason, the world is precisely not identical with God because God is also silent. Only through God's silence is there the world as a world, that is, a sphere of anxiety, a place of great distance from God.

Humanity has become what it is under conditions of evolution that can be ever more precisely defined by natural science. However, it is developing to achieve further goals that remain unknown to natural science. The findings about ourselves that can be gained by research in the field of evolution must not be played against insights about our relationship to God. The theological and scientific perspective could even be merged into a *single* perspective if we have the will to do so. Focusing on God, human beings "moved" out of the group of primates when they encountered God's calling in the form of words that encouraged them to live an ever freer life. "Words of kindness" stirred the human potential of certain primates at a certain level of evolution. Man emerged not through a rebellion, not through a defiant defection of intelligent higher beings from the life of nature regulated by instinct, but through hearing a gospel which those who were to become human beings followed. Those who object at this point that many people have just imagined the existence of such divine "words of kindness" have not understood that here a statement was made on a quite different level. It is not a question of what human beings can think or imagine if they want. Rather, a hypothesis was presented as to why human beings are even here at all (and among other things can also wonder about God!). In its total depth and breadth it deals with the issue of human origins, including the possibility of an atheistic existence!

With the emergence of humanity a *freedom* willed by God entered nature. This dignity in being able to address the world by himself as God does (the giving of names) is conferred on him, thus enabling him to interpret the world together with God, or to put it in different terms, to link evolution with the disclosure of meaning. However, in reality this freedom takes a heavy toll on human beings themselves and nonhuman creatures in multiple ways, although freedom also carries within itself the splendor of great promise. The promise of freedom is that the sufferings associated with life in nature could be overcome more and more by free, artistic human design. The fact that our freedom and our pursuit of freedom became the source of new, additional sufferings is a very sad reality human beings must never accept. Therefore, the task of reconciling freedom and love in the process of life — or not even allowing them to come apart in the first place — is the most obvious definition of the purpose and goal by which humanity can understand itself. For true humanity is rooted in their unity. By serving this task, human life is worthwhile and rewarding; the reality described by the word "spirit" emerges when love and freedom are reconciled. The spirit should increase in all the stories in which human beings have a part (it does not always do so by any means). In this sense, we human beings are all called by God. We are called from among the other creatures to realize humanity in the spirit of reconciliation — also in the terms of exercising the role of servanthood on behalf of the whole cosmos.

Reconciliation and *redemption* must be distinguished. Fortunately, oc- currences of reconciliation take place in history again and again. They constitute our highest ethical opportunity. They rescue us from great danger and lay the foundation for new human hope. It is not wrong to assume the working of the Spirit of God, or the Spirit of Christ, in occurrences of reconciliation. Nevertheless, they are at the same time a true triumph of the human spirit. One does not exclude the other, a truth that mainly idealism and chiliasm see correctly. Of course, the all-embracing permanent reconciliation of the kingdom of God remains an unachievable goal for us. Even if one day through the work of God reconciliation will have become so widespread that in fact the historic goal of an all-embracing kingdom of peace is achieved, the world would still not be redeemed. In the redeemed world justice will be given to all those who have ever lived, those who did not get their fair share at any time will receive full satisfaction, all tears will be wiped away, all things will reach their goal of blissful peace and rest in God. For us human beings the certainty of such redemption is more important than the hope of a kingdom of universal reconciliation that unfolds in history! This future realm of peace is of supreme importance to both idealism and chiliasm, but they are mistaken if they think its arrival would bring real satisfaction to the creatures. The state of universal reconciliation that will bring the development of the world to a close will mean satisfaction for God! And what will bring us satisfaction is redemption in these terms alone. All creatures must participate in reconciliation as servants of God, but only this all-embracing reconciliation will bring satisfaction to God. This redemption of all creation is God's business alone.

Sin is nothing specifically moral. Immorality is not the same as sin. Sin is a far-reaching category to which questions of morality are also related. The word "sin" describes our life from God's viewpoint. Our life does not hear "anything" from God. As sinners we stand before the silent God. Man's sin is a partial *ep-oche* in God's creative activity. It may be caused by human behavior that is not pleasing to God, but we cannot say this with certainty. Ultimately, all the events of world history are routed in God; everything serves his purpose. That *ep-oche* in his creative activity probably serves to prepare us for renewed *listening* on the road to freedom for all creation. Sin should never have been interpreted as an independent human act that went against God or that God just barely permitted and did not prevent. When theologians do this, they intellectually abolish God by way of their doctrine of sin. Sin must be interpreted by theology as a reality placed in God's loving plan of creation even though it is the reality of evil, dissolute human activity that runs counter to freedom and love. In his hiddenness, God is close to the sinner. The sinner is loved by God, and man's sin causes him great sorrow. The sin that grieves and robs God more than it does human beings produces in us that vacuum which God fills with himself. In this respect our sin is a part of the divine economy of salvation. And thus a *consciousness* of sin (not a feeling of guilt!) is the best thing we could have. It is identical with a consciousness of *God,* with the certainty of divine closeness. But even people and epochs which hear "nothing" from God do not stand outside of religion, but in the midst of it.

Faith is hearing God calling and answering him "with one's own life." In faith sin is overcome. Believers are chosen to witness to God in their surroundings. They cannot believe only "for themselves." Believers are chosen to make their common divine calling visible to all other people, their calling to model true humanity. Election certainly does not signify any personal privileges in terms of an increasing share of the riches of this world or the next. The status of being elected lays the foundation for the church to assume its servant role, enabling serving the world as to move the world toward God's goal. What human transgression against the self consists of (the self-realization of the person rejected by God) always becomes apparent in history first in the sufferings of the elect. However, by no means are "unbelieving sinners" the human beings rejected by God. God rejects the sin (whatever he greets with silence, does not encourage with his word, but rejects becomes sin in the course of evolution), but not the "unbelieving sinner." Moreover, no one has faith in such a way that he is not also a sinner, a person affected by God's silence. Faith and sin do not relate to each other as if one were a praiseworthy behavior and the other reprehensible. They are not two behavior patterns that human beings are free to choose. They both have a role in God's plan. They both contribute to the growth of God's kingdom. An egotistical individualism of salvation in which a person would especially like to find himself included in the number of saved souls is deeply repugnant to the spirit of the whole Bible.

The *world* is God's opposite. It is called into existence by God. It remains and develops as long as God continues to speak to it. He shapes it by his calling and also by his silence. His creatures answer him in many different ways. A renewed hunger for being addressed by God is created in the world (above all by sin [see Amos 8:11f.]). The evolutionary leaps by which more spirit — more love and freedom — comes into the world are being prepared in this hunger. However, we do not observe any linear evolution-ary increase of spirit in the world. On the contrary, this evolution also knows setbacks and apparent steps backward — for example, through a growing freedom without love. A theory of increasing "moral progress" and increasing "spiritualization" of the world is both unfounded and untenable. The evolutionary goal of God's kingdom in the cosmos remains unclear for our thought, knowledge, and experience. However, our certainty of salvation and our hope of redemption must be built on a completely different foundation, namely, on this statement of faith: The individual sections and branches of evolution, the individual living beings all stand in an immediate relationship to God. At all times they all find in him the one who faces them, the one who saves and redeems them — and especially, when they themselves do not experience the cosmos in its perfection!

The *church* is a divine creation. As the echo of God's call that was extended and is still being extended to Israel and the whole world in Jesus Christ, the "Word" (of God) made flesh, it is the sounding board and the repository of a treasure of divine words. But the church is also the people who gather together in response to God's call. Its mission is to comfort, heal, alleviate suffering, and help to prevent distress and misery that can be avoided in this still unredeemed world. However, above all it is empowered to absolve people of their sin, to release them from their sin on behalf of God. By carrying out its mission it gives comfort, and splendor returns to the world. It is by carrying out its mission that it is capable of moderating the silence of God and not letting it become worldwide. This is its main purpose, and the church gives up on itself more by forgetting its commission to bind and loose (Matt. 16:19; 18:18; John 20:23) than in any other way.

SECTION V
ASPECTS OF UNDERSTANDING SIN IN MODERN
INTERPRETATIONS OF THE JAHWIST'S EARLIEST
HISTORY OF GENESIS 2:4BFF.

The interdisciplinary treatment of the myth of Adam and Eve's fall from the third chapter of the biblical book of Genesis constitutes a rather large complex within the modern discussion of sin and evil. The Catholic theologian Eugen Drewermann recently examined in particular the modern exegetical, psychoanalytic, and philosophical interpretations of the archaic story of Genesis 3 in a large, three-volume study. It is part of the earliest history told by the so-called Jahwist in the context of Genesis 2:4b–11:32.

The special attention given to Genesis 3 in the entire modern era shows that this text can be a bridge between theology, philosophy, and science. This is due to a unique formal and a unique material feature. First, in Genesis 3 an open language is spoken that is not tied to particular faith assumptions and avoids a moral condemnation of Adam and Eve. Second, at the same time the text illuminates (in conjunction with the chapters of Genesis that follow it) the fall and fundamental occurrences from the beginnings of culture/civilization[41] together with their repetitions in each individual stage of human development toward maturity. Finally, the narrative of Genesis 3 portrays the human slide into sin *without reference to a redemption from sin expected in the future.* No thought, let alone promise, is given by the Jahwistic narrator to a possible return of Adam and Eve into paradise or a rebirth leading them out of sin. The Jahwist judges the conditions of Adam and Eve after the expulsion from paradise to be a hard lot. But he thinks that on the whole it is acceptable because of God's kindness, giving mankind a framework of possible survival after the fall. This soteriological limitation is the main reason for the universal comprehensibility and modern attractiveness of the Jahwist's earliest history.

Frequently exegetes of the Old Testament point out that "Genesis 3 must not be read in isolation." The Jahwist's earliest history "is characterized by a whole sequence of stories about sin: Genesis 4 recounts Cain's

---

41. See C. Westermann, *Genesis,* BK AT I, 1 (Gen. 1–11) (Neukirchen [¹1974], ²1976), pp. 374-86.

murder of his brother and Lamech's unbridled vengeance; Genesis 6:1-4 tells about the marriages with angels, leading immediately to the Deluge (6:5-9, 17)." The story of the building of the Tower of Babel (Gen. 11) comes later. "Each of these stories casts light in its own way on one particular aspect of what this enigmatic break between God and humanity means and on God's response to it."[42]

A puzzling divine restraint is part of this answer in the story of Genesis 3–11. The life of the human couple is not taken on the day they sinned even though they were threatened with death if they would eat the fruit of the forbidden tree (2:17). "Jahweh protects the murderer of his brother, Cain, by a mark (he tattooed on his forehead?). . . . "Jahweh himself takes many living creatures out of the great flood so that the whole world is given a future again. Yet at the beginning of the flood the terrible statement was made that God regretted having made human beings."[43]

Of course, *given the central significance of the Jahwistic narrative even in modern Christian theological doctrines of sin, we must ask whether perhaps essential elements of what a Christian theology of sin and forgiveness would have to say are missing in the Jahwist's view of the situation.*

Christian theology must always understand sin (and the fall) "retrospectively" from the vantage point of faith in the redemption won by Jesus Christ. Moreover, it should not let itself be blinded by the "experiential fullness" of the Jahwist's narrative so that it doesn't seek to escape an alleged "lack of experience" or an existential difficulty in conveying the New Testament's language of grace and sin. However, on the other hand, it must be conceded that nowhere else can we gain more and better insights into the modern discussion centered around the issue of sin/evil than in modern interpretations of the Jahwist's earliest history. Therefore, in the following section issues in the modern understanding (and misunderstanding) of this archaic narrative are to be discussed following an initial attempt to picture the subject matter of Genesis 3.

---

42. W. Zimmerli, *Grundriß der alttestamentlichen Theologie*, *ThW* 3 (Stuttgart and others, [4]1982), p. 148; quotations from English translation, *Old Testament Theology in Outline*, trans. David E. Green (Atlanta: John Knox, 1978), p. 168.

43. Zimmerli, p. 148.

A. What Does the Fall Narrated in Genesis 3 Consist Of?

The story of Adam and Eve's fall has two main concerns: Man's "being like God" and man's "knowledge" (which can also be translated as "recognition") of what is good and evil (Gen. 3:5).

"Recognition" or "knowledge" is called *yada'* in the original Hebrew text. Gerhard von Rad taught that *yada'* means the experience of everything and, at the same time, being in control of all things and secrets. According to somewhat more restrained interpretations, the Hebrew phrase "good and evil" mainly points to man's capability of discerning what is beneficial to life and what is detrimental to it.[44]

Man's capability of knowing good and evil is what allows him to reach a stage at which he is comparable to God. But the reverse is also true. The condition for man to acquire the capability of knowing good from evil is his attempt to place himself as a human being at a level at which he is comparable to God. The question of whether the event narrated in Genesis 3 shows man's *arrogance (hybris)* and/or *sinful desire (concupiscentia)* is brought into focus here. An additional focus is the question of whether Adam and Eve, both exemplary individuals, succeed at all in climbing to a level from which they can *really* tell the difference between good and evil. Does the so-called fall perhaps end only in the human *illusion* of being able to recognize good and evil? Aside from the loss of their natural innocence, is there any human "benefit" in eating the fruit of the tree of knowledge?

After we first point out three important models in systematic theology for opening up the whole text of Genesis 3, we will further pursue these questions on the basis of a reflection by the philosopher G. W. F. Hegel.

1. Systematic theological interpretations of the events in Genesis 3 in the modern era — first the one by the speculative Berlin systematic theologian Philipp Konrad Marheineke (1780-1846) — frequently emphasize that the anthropological result of the fall must be summarized as the *loss of the image of God in man*.[45] The basic idea here is that the created image

---

44. G. von Rad, *Theologie des Alten Testaments,* 2 vols. (München [1957], ³1961), 1:157; see a summary and interpretation of the discussion in M. Welker, "Das theologische Prinzip des Verhaltens zu Zeiterscheinungen," *EvTh* 36 (1976): 225-253; see also 247-249.

45. P. Marheineke, *Theologische Vorlesungen,* vol. 2, *System der christlichen Dogmatik,* ed. S. Matthies and W. Vatke (Berlin, 1847), pp. 182ff.

of God (Gen. 1:27) is shattered because man no longer wants to stand face-to-face with God, but himself wants to be *like God.* Classical doctrinal disagreement between Catholics and Protestants is at work here. The former teach that the creation of man both as an "image" and a "likeness" of God *(imago* and *similitudo* or *eikōn* and *homoiōsis* or *ṣelem* and *demut)* narrated in Genesis 1:26 permits the conclusion that the fall did not completely destroy the image of God in Adam and Eve. Rather, it suspended only one of the two roles humans play as bearers of the image. To be sure, it shattered the *similitudo,* that is, man's capability of having fellowship with God by virtue of being filled with supernatural grace, making him pleasing in the sight of God. However, the *imago* refers to man's natural rationality, which the fall did not destroy. In contradistinction to this view, most of the theologians coming out of the Reformation teach that man's ability to reason was also impaired by the fall; the reason of the sinner produces only what is "contrary to reason."

2. Other theological interpretations characterize the events of Genesis 3 as a confusion of the *Creator* with the *creature,* a practice that spread into humanity at this point in time: The human creature put himself in God's place. (Of course, it is disputed *why* this happened. Perhaps because of *arrogance* or *desire,* or ultimately because of *fear,* a position Kierkegaard advocated as a corrective to such views? But we do not have to decide this question at all. For only those exegetes are plausible who do not overlook the fact that all this would imply a state of corruption *before* the fall, rendering the Jahwist's narrative absurd. A moralistic explanation of the cause of the "fall" would not be appropriate for Genesis 3. We should also not derive *any* explanation for Adam and Eve's uncertainty about the difference between the Creator and the creature and the ensuing disaster from the "talking snake." Hubris and concupiscence and probably fear as well are at most *consequences* of the fall, whose occurrence remains inexplicable.)

3. Finally, many interpretations construe the loss of innocence described in Genesis 3 in terms of the *awakening of spirit in the development of human maturity.* The unity of body and soul ("dreaming innocence") that initially supported and preserved Adam and Eve's life is shattered in every person (we all repeat the fall of Adam and Eve) whereby our "spirit" intends to create a new, future personal unity marked by freedom, but first destroys the foundation on which we stand. Kierkegaard's *The Concept of Anxiety* (1844) mainly critiques Hegel's portrayal of the overall scheme of events

in Genesis without fundamentally leaving this level of interpretation. With his theological, psychological, logical queries of Hegel, Kierkegaard prepared the way for the later thought of existentialism. His own interpretation influenced (among others) Martin Heidegger's understanding of fear and Paul Tillich's understanding of sin in the twentieth century.

In the final phase of his work Hegel quoted no other word in the Bible as frequently as Genesis 3:22: "The man has now become like one of us, knowing good and evil."[46] Hegel believed he could take from this verse the idea that Adam and Eve's sinful falling away from the image of God given to them when they were created was not only a source of evil in the world but at the same time the source of a very positive opportunity for the development of humanity since now the knowledge of the good also became possible. The statement of Genesis 3:22 not only stresses the negative reason for the loss of the *imago Dei,* but also contains the positive "principle of the return to the image." In Hegel's view we must listen for this positive principle in God's affirmation: "Adam *has* now become like one of us!" Hegel complained that this Bible verse is "usually much too seldom considered in depth" by the traditional theology of the church.[47] Hegel knew that the Reformers Luther and Calvin thought that God's statement "Adam has become like one of us" was only sarcasm, God's fierce mockery. The Reformers also saw irony in this statement because in fact Adam and Eve had by no means gained a certain knowledge of what would be beneficial or detrimental to them. Against this view Hegel came up with the exegetical thesis that Genesis 3:22 is not at all meant to be taken as sarcasm or irony, but seriously describes the character and ability of man after the fall. Most modern Old Testament scholars now seem to concede that Hegel was right in this respect. But they cannot confirm Hegel's other assumption that the narrative of the fall, Genesis 3, already implies the positive component of Adam and Eve's return to the image of God. Genesis 3 does not provide any evidence for Hegel's philosophical system oriented to the autonomous dialectical movement of the spirit.

Meanwhile, M. Welker has shown that, with more recent exegetes, we can understand Genesis 3:22 as a positive, unironical statement about the postlapsarian status of man equipped with self-confident reason.[48] But this

46. See Welker, pp. 225ff.
47. G. F. W. Hegel, ThWS II, p. 239.
48. Welker, pp. 246ff.

apparent tribute to Hegel discloses a further aspect of the narrative of Genesis 3, allowing *the separation between God and man* to stand out more distinctively than ever. The narrative believes that man, with his eyes opened, can now in fact, just like God, tell the difference between good and evil, what is beneficial and what is detrimental. At the same moment, he turned a blind eye to another distinction. Since he has become "like God," he suddenly no longer has the capability of recognizing what distinguishes God and man from each other. Since he had become able to see, Adam was blinded to the nature of his relationship to God. Since then Adam can no longer tell the difference between his own realm and being, on the one hand, and God's realm and being on the other, between what is his responsibility and possible to do as man and what is God's responsibility and possible for him. With the real gain in being able to tell the difference between good and evil, man simultaneously lost the ability to recognize and keep his limits. To be sure, Adam can now strive for what is better with his reason; he can try to change his situation and avoid what is bad. He can rationally intervene in the situation. Nevertheless, this newly won power is of no benefit to him if at the same time he is no longer equal to the task of making the fundamental distinction between God and man, between Creator and creature.

Adam became more powerful through his newly won ability (Gen. 3:22a). Many interpreters presume that when God removed Adam from paradise, he wanted to protect himself from the man who had become too powerful. But this interpretation based on the motive of the envy of the gods is wrong. For God decreed the expulsion of Adam and Eve from paradise not because he was afraid that he could be completely dethroned by man through further encroachments, but because he cared for man. By taking this step, God initiated the *separation of realms* between himself and human beings that was essential for their well-being. Its purpose was to keep human beings from destroying themselves. It barred Adam from causing unending damage with his newly won freedom. It put him in a place where his freedom had to remain a "finite" freedom, a freedom within set limits.

If we want to talk at all about a positive aspect of the fall that points beyond the negative, then this is not found in the power Adam claimed for himself to know the good, but in the caring actions God implemented after the fall of Adam and Eve. As remarkable as this sounds, the expulsion from paradise was one of those actions.

The positive element associated with the event of the fall must, therefore, be defined differently than Hegel did. It is not found in a power conferred on Adam when he ate the fruit of the tree of knowledge, a power to develop back toward a perfect and unspoiled unity with God. It is also not found in the fact that Adam could really capitalize on his rational capability of knowing good and evil like God in order to live a good human life in harmony with God's will for love and justice. Rather, the positive element is found in the fact that as early as Genesis 3 it becomes apparent that God himself is willing to help human beings even though they had gotten into a situation in which they were to a large extent *blind to God.* The coverings or skirts God used to clothe Adam and Eve after the fall show this. Although man had become blind to God, and for all intents and purposes godless, God made sure that man could still survive and still have joy — even if his life as a whole was under considerable stress. Even though his unbelief and his moral failure were "givens," a wholesome restraint was imposed on man by God so that trees of corruption do not grow into the sky and the damage caused by man would be limited.

With the above-mentioned separation of realms between God in heaven and man on the earth, God responds in a positive way to that other separation which is *only* negative: the *sin* that afflicted Adam and Eve.

Sin always means separation: a turning away or being detached, isolation or division. A unity that had existed before sin came into the world is destroyed. Now Adam and Eve live separated from paradise. Understood correctly, the latter is their good fortune in the new situation! On the other hand, separation *between* the human beings will now occur as well as a deep division *between* humanity and its fellow creatures — this is their misfortune! Those idealistic philosophers who mainly noticed the happy aspect of the loss of paradise overlooked or minimized the tragedy inherent in the above-mentioned separations because they did not want to admit that overcoming this tragedy is beyond all human strength.

The separations caused by sin are most clearly experienced by man in the realm of verbal communication. The power given (*before* the fall) to human beings in Genesis 2:20 of naming all living beings gave Adam "the royal privilege of a being created only a little lower than God" (here I agree with a thesis developed by Paul Ricoeur).[49] Seen in these terms, Adam has

---

49. Translated from P. Ricoeur, *Symbolik des Bösen. Phänomenologie der Schuld II,* trans. M. Otto (Freiburg/München, 1971; originally published in French, 1960), p. 281.

not moved into a position directly under the position of God *by falling into sin.* On the contrary, Adam's authority to name all living beings and gain power over them was decisively reduced by the fall. This authority was "so profoundly disrupted that we are familiar with it and can exercise it only under the rule of the confusion of languages."[50]

A "separation of cultures"[51] came with the confusion of language. Ricoeur states it more precisely in terms of the *unity* of human language being dissolved (more precisely, the authority to name objects). This authority of language, this authority to name objects, not only splintered into several languages and cultures but, above all, a confusion of language, a conflict of namings, meanings, and interpretations of reality, etc., arose. Only this confusion, this struggle of conflicting meanings, caused trouble that even a newly introduced, standardized world language could not eliminate. This confusion signifies the fundamental breakdown of communication, the critical weakening of Adam's authority to name the other creatures. To be sure: In the state of sin this weakening is not only to be seen in *negative* terms because it also limits the damage human beings cause by exercising verbal powers.

Furthermore, in Ricoeur's opinion the fact that Adam and Eve notice their nakedness after the fall points to the breakdown in communication resulting from the fall. A "revolution" in every form of human communication is now linked with the *shame* that enters humanity as a new phenomenon: the result of this revolution is that from now on all human communication is "subject to the influence of concealment and disguise." The one who speaks now needs a protective cover, a mask. He cannot allow his innermost being to be exposed to the persons he is speaking to by way of his words. Thus, the unity of understanding between people is also lost.

But once again it can be said that the shame, the need for coverings and masks, is not only to be seen in negative terms. To some degree the other person being spoken to is protected by this shame from a far too direct influence of the speaker that could destroy *his* freedom. And the speaker himself is protected from being completely identified with his own words, from losing his own self to the "statement" that the self made.

Ricoeur does not overlook the fact that life has become *arduous* through all these consequences of the fall — and *ambiguous.* What must be said

50. Translated from Ricoeur, p. 281.
51. Ricoeur, p. 281.

through a mask is ambiguous. "This ambiguity of man who was created good and has become evil, puts a strain on every aspect of human life." From now on, "the greatness *and* guilt of man are inextricably intertwined without us being able to say: here is original human nature, this is the jinx on that nature. . . ." Or here is the actual human being willed by God and there is the twisted, unnatural, false human being.

Precisely for this reason it became an important duty of all theology and all ethics to risk making clarifying, helpful statements about the *actual boundary line between what is human and what is inhuman in this situation.* The situation of Adam and Eve after the fall is really "diabolically" confused (from Greek *diaballein* = to mix up, confuse). Man's reason is not identical with his sin. But it is also not simply his bright light. It is ambiguous. The whole person is ambivalent. What is good in one way is evil in a different way. And man is not free to choose only the good way and to leave the other. *Thus, a heavy burden lies on us — nothing we do is clearly good.* Seen from a Christian perspective, this is the basic problem of all ethics! At the same time this is the starting point of the doctrine that all people need the forgiveness of sins and that God's forgiveness of sin signifies God's gracious response to the anguish of our involvement in ethical ambiguity. But this is a position that has always been in dispute between theology and philosophy and will probably always continue to be controversial.

Let us now summarize the content of Genesis 3 (adding a few points of view that have thus far remained unmentioned). The Jahwistic narrative of the fall sees a whole series of natural and social *consequences* resulting from *the loss of God as a person who faces Adam and Eve in their practical life* — this constitutes the heart of the story of the fall. The consequences of the fall are primarily seen by human beings as difficulties in life, as "evils." Some of these consequences are also judged to be *ambivalent,* both welcomed and bemoaned. The following nine consequences must be added to what constitutes the fall. They have become the object of many philosophical and human scientific inquiries.

1. The phenomenon of the "bad conscience" arises; the original situation is in view here. Adam hides himself and gives an evasive answer to God's question about his whereabouts (Gen. 3:8ff.).
2. The loss of innocence and the phenomenon of shame develop on a sexual basis, but extend far beyond sexuality.

3. Special difficulties and inconveniences are imposed on the physical constitution of the woman; the woman is also subjected to the man.

4. The man must labor by the sweat of his brow in a cursed field. What is new in the scenario is not the phenomenon of work as such (for example, the tilling of the soil). Work as such is not a curse and not only a consequence of the fall. The "tilling and tending of the garden" was rather man's basic job even before the fall (see Gen. 2:15). But after the fall this changes. Now angels — actually God — become responsible for tending and caring for the garden (see Gen. 3:24). And now man does not even want to be his brother's keeper (Gen. 4). Under the influence of sin, work on the one hand and tending/caring for the garden on the other hand have split apart. This gap has also made work burdensome, questionable, and frustrating.

5. In the course of their endeavor to distinguish between good and evil, Adam and Eve must assume the responsibility for planning, evaluating, and organizing their life.

6. This new behavior and the underlying "practical atheism" of the man who has become like God necessitate man's expulsion from paradise. It is actually a step God took to provide for man's well-being because man could no longer live in the same realm as God with his present way of life.

7. Furthermore, death now becomes necessary in terms of a limitation on human plans for life made and organized autonomously. From now on man fearfully awaits his whole life long this "last enemy" which forces a termination of his efforts to fashion his own existence.

8. Human social behavior is subject to profound disruptions. In the Jahwistic narrative the expulsion from paradise is followed by Cain's murder of his brother Abel (Gen. 4), and finally by the withdrawal of a common language during the construction of the Tower of Babel (Gen. 11).

9. Civilization emerges with the special feature of the division of labor and with increasing technical capabilities.

As a whole, the Jahwist interprets the fall and its consequences in such a way that this occurrence, this question lies unarticulated on the horizon of this event. Will the distrust engendered between man and God make way for a new friendship between God and certain representatives of humanity in the future? Will human life once again flourish in the strength of divine blessing in spite of the fall? On the one hand, this statement is true of Genesis 3–11. "The primal history of J illustrates uncannily the rapid growth of evil, which spreads like a drop of oil on water."[52] On the other hand, an opposite inner movement can be discerned in this story: "Yahweh plans a new future of blessings for the world, which is in many ways under a curse and has no righteousness of its own that could move God to make such a decision." The Jahwist sees the divinely willed purpose of Israel's existence in these terms: "to bring a blessing into a world marked by the afflictions of God's judgment because of its alienation from him."[53]

B. A Philosophical Evaluation of the Fall as "the Happiest and Greatest Event"

In the course of the preceding discussion, it ought to have become clear that every attempt to show the authentic meaning of the narrative in Genesis 3 is subject to very difficult conditions. With a certain justification nontheological interpreters of this biblical text can make the criticism that traditional ecclesiastical exegesis of Genesis 3 has been one-sided and dogmatically predetermined. They take scant account of the vast cultural openness of the Old Testament narrative; however, in more recent philosophy, especially in modern human sciences (for example, depth psychology), several treasures of the Jahwist narrative have been lifted in which theologians have shown no interest up to now. However, such efforts to retrieve these unlifted treasures of Genesis 3 have almost always led to a struggle with theology over the entire significance of the Genesis 3 narrative. Is the Jahwist ultimately talking about freedom that has been forfeited or regained, about a loss or a gain for humanity? In most cases philosophical and humanistic interpretations have a tendency to give the upper hand to the aspect of *gain*. To be sure, the theological exegetes resist this; however, not seldom realizing at the same time that they themselves have profited from new, nontheological interpretations. The situation has been this complicated for over two hundred years! Since philosophers associated with German idealism at the beginning of the nineteenth century brilli-

52. Zimmerli, p. 149; quotation from ET, p. 169.
53. Zimmerli, p. 152; quotations from ET, p. 172.

antly paraphrased Genesis 3, the controversial viewpoints and questions have not substantially increased or changed. Time and again they are selectively picked up in modern discussions between theology and the human sciences, although the intellectual quality has not always been maintained.

At the heart of the philosophies of German idealism is the idea that human beings establish (produce) themselves by getting themselves in extreme danger, realizing themselves — apparently — and finally becoming stronger to themselves. It was assumed in idealism that in the natural history of the earth, the *first human beings* were those creatures who agreed to the dangerous experiment of no longer acting merely on the basis of habit or instinct but stepping out of the protection of an alleged (natural) sequence of events and trying out new ways of life. This idealistic paradigm of "self-generation through self-realization"[54] at the same time wants to call attention to the beginnings of humanity and the beginnings of culture/civilization as well as to the origin of each new act of freedom in history in which people courageously activate and prove their humanity while endangering their own lives and enduring pain.

Kant and the subsequent idealistic thinkers were of the common opinion that the narrative of the fall in Genesis 3 was nothing other than a successful mythological portrayal of the basic principle of human self-generation. *It is true of all these thinkers that they see the creation of man, or better, the self-production of what is specifically human, not in Genesis 1 or 2, but only in Genesis 3. Before* the event theologians call the fall, Adam and Eve were "big children," thus beings without their own responsibility and freedom, at the mercy of the eternal cycle of desire, pleasure, and rest just like the animals. The Jahwist narrator has these prelapsarian conditions in mind when he uses the word "paradise." However, when he talks about the voice of God resounding there over and over again, he means instinct making its presence felt. Thus, God is not understood as an independent being, but as a symbol of the determining power of natural laws.

In keeping with this idealistic interpretation, this is the substance of the narrative in Genesis 3: the falling away of Adam and Eve from the rule of instinct. Friedrich Schiller in "The First Human Society according to the Main Theme Running through the Mosaic Documents" (1790) made the same judgment. Theologians, Schiller believed, may see in the

---

54. I owe this phrase to my colleague R. Schröder, who teaches philosophy in Berlin.

deed of Adam and Eve a great loss. But with "no less justification," the philosopher can "congratulate human nature on this important step to perfection."[55] Philosophy even has the right to speak here of a "gigantic step forward for humanity," of immense progress. After all, through the fall man turned into "a new creation with the freedom to act" from being an "automaton in the moral realm" and "a slave of his natural instinct." After all, with this giant step, man for the first time climbed onto the ladder that "will lead him to self-rule after many millennia have passed." Schiller did not overlook the fact that Genesis 3 also deals with the entry (the possibility) of evil into history. But he thought evil *only* came into the world so that the choice of the moral good could become a real possibility. Seen in this light the fall was "without a doubt the happiest and greatest event in the history of the human race." The freedom of man, Schiller thought, is written "from this moment on"; "here the first distant foundation was laid for his morality."[56]

Schiller's evaluation of the fall (obviously running counter to the theological intention of the Jahwistic text) fits an understanding of human beings in which humanity progresses historically to ever more complete rule over nature and simultaneously to ever more complete *freedom* for the culture and civilization to fashion its life "with human reason." The cultural capability of human beings is understood and affirmed at the same time as the job or duty of man to fashion culture and as a mark of favor bestowed on the human race in order to make it happy and fulfilled.

Of course, if someone were more likely to judge our cultural endeavors to be a curse, he would have to evaluate the events described in Genesis 3 as a disaster for humanity, in partial agreement with church doctrine — based on the same logic Schiller used. For example, J. J. Rousseau was such a thinker. Of course, theologians must carefully handle the question of whether a critique of civilization that opposes Schiller's thesis can really be regarded as approval of the church's authoritative dogmatic views of the fall or as revealing an affinity to it.

In any case, Schiller wanted to put the traditional theological, dogmatic judgments of the Genesis 3 narrative in the corner of an ideology hostile

---

55. Translated from F. Schiller, "Etwas über die erste Menschengesellschaft nach dem Leitfaden der mosaischen Urkunde," in *Sämtliche Werke,* ed. G. Fricke and H. G. Göpfert, 5 vols. (München, 1958), 4:769.

56. Translated from Schiller, "Die erste Menschengesellschaft," 4:769.

to civilization and the Enlightenment. Since then such a critique of a basic Christian doctrine has on the one hand challenged many theologians to affirm freedom, the Enlightenment, and the work of building civilization, yet on the other hand to see an event of human tragedy and sin behind the narrative of Genesis 3. However, this difficult job has not yet been adequately handled to the present day. Especially in the twentieth century not a few theologians have been tempted to use historical depressions and the collapse of the modern belief in progress to demonstrate dogmatically that the traditional interpretation of Genesis 3 was the right one after all. *Such theologians overlooked the fact that neither culturally optimistic nor culturally pessimistic interpretations of Genesis 3 actually capture the intrinsic meaning of the narrative.*

However, the following four biblical-theological markers remain important for an interpretation of Genesis 3 that is in keeping with the text:

1. Every biblically based and biblically committed theology must reject the idea of identifying God with the voice or the law of an unspoiled nature, and thus with instinct, because it fails to see the clearly intended meaning of the text. As the Creator, God is different from nature. He stands opposite it.

2. Biblically based and committed theology understands the mythic story of Adam and Eve's fall not as if it were talking about the opportunity presenting itself to man in the future to *either* do what is good *or* to sin. Rather, it believes that what was narrated in Genesis 3 and brought about by Adam and Eve when they ate the fruit is a typical example of how sin is committed. It is the story of how human beings are bound by evil.

3. Biblically based and committed theology denies that the Jahwist's earliest history intends to portray the beginnings of human self-responsibility, morality, and freedom. On the contrary, it sees the beginnings of man's loss of all these things portrayed here.

4. Therefore, any biblically based and committed theology also denies that the humanization of man only begins with Adam and Eve's turning away from God. Whereas Schiller thought that by turning away from God the first rung on the ladder to true humanity had been climbed, Genesis 3 speaks in the clearest terms of man falling down, of a *fall* into sin, irrespective of how we should interpret the Bible's use of the concept of God.

The significance of the theological and philosophical controversy indicated by these positions extends far beyond the situation that prevailed at the end of the eighteenth and the beginning of the nineteenth century. Even more contemporary theories about the human condition advanced by the human sciences are affected by it in various ways. Ultimately, this conflict is about whether it is appropriate for the narrative of Genesis 3 to be used as a basic text for a dialectic understanding of existence and reality. Does the so-called fall actually signify the ontologically and existentially necessary, inevitable transition from the thesis to the antithesis (and finally to the synthesis)? The Jahwist's earliest history seems to articulate an understanding of existence and reality along the lines of idealistic philosophy, as does the story of Abraham, the narrative of Israel's exodus from Egypt, or the parable of the prodigal son. But on closer inspection the manner in which sin and its eventual conquest by God are viewed in the Bible differs markedly from the dialectic autonomous movement of the spirit which idealism seeks to grasp.

In a schematic framework the differences and disputed issues move in the following ways: diagram 3 shows that Genesis 3 puts the human situation into metaphorical language that in principle can be discussed with anyone. The "journey into a strange land," often made a subject in the Bible and emphasized in various texts, illuminates a basic human experience. Nevertheless we must be open to the idea that even this basic experience is subject not only to many possible interpretations but to genuine structural, historical changes. Thus, "earlier" and "later" forms in which this experience appeared (together with the language used to express it) could conflict with each other. For example, Genesis 3 expresses it from the perspective of Palestine around 950 B.C. (the era of Solomon). Thus their understanding of the structures of relationships between men and women and the structures of guilt and fulfillment in life is shaped by the point of view current at that time. C. Westermann ventured the thesis that "the phenomenon of sin or evil is a phenomenon belonging to the human race which has been in process for thousands of years."[57] Perhaps the three thousand years between our present day and the writing of the Jahwistic narrative can almost be neglected.

---

57. Westermann, p. 379; quotation from English translation, *Genesis 1–11: A Commentary*, trans. John J. Scullion (Minneapolis: Augsburg, 1984), p. 278.

Diagram 3: An Evaluation of the Fall			*not* thought of in the Jahwistic narra-tive of Genesis 3
	Thesis Condition before the fall: existence in paradise	*Antithesis* fall, expulsion from paradise	*Synthesis* (only in biblical texts that were writ-ten later) attaining paradise after death
Bible	*aliter:* life in the family (extended family) of one's home country, existence in the home of one's father, exis-tence by the "flesh pots"	*aliter:* Exodus, journey to an unknown land ("that I will show you"), journey to the desert, leaving the "flesh pots"	*aliter:* "return" to the Promised land, to the home of one's father *aliter:* Kingdom of God, redemption, rebirth
disputed area between biblical theology, recent philosophies, and the human sciences	raw state of nature? human life totally controlled by drives and instinct? as yet unbroken luxuriant conditions? *or (more the middle ground)* dreaming innocence (Kierke-gaard, Tillich), essential being (Tillich)	alienation, activa-tion of the faculty of reason in connec-tion with reflective self-consciousness, Oedipus conflicts, identity crises, emer-gence of the pro-letariat, impoverish-ment, destruction of nature *or (more the middle ground)* awakening of the spirit, existential being (Tillich)	"a second era of naturalness," the spirit coming into its own, perfected culture. The Oedipus complex has been success-fully passed through (Freud), "self-development" (C. J. Jung), communist society *or (more the middle ground)* reconcilia-tion, new being (Tillich)
conditions for the transition to the next stage:	sin? "autonomous movement of the spirit?" exploitation? distress? increase in fear until the "leap" (Kierkegaard)?		forgiveness of sins or grace? "revolution in our way of thinking" (Kant)? socialistic revolution (Marx)? healing or overcoming of neurosis?

Nevertheless, an understanding of the internal composition of the present era,
the condition of our own society, and the present status of civilization plays
a role in accurately grasping the phenomenon of sin and evil. Only in this
way does a recognition of sin become a real recognition of the self, does
it affect one's own self-understanding. In the modern era *theologies* were
in most cases stronger in *remembering biblical texts* (including the "journey into a strange land" testified to in the New Testament and undertaken
by God himself in the *incarnation* of Christ); in the modern era *philos-*
ophies were in most cases stronger in grasping the *reality of contemporary*
life in the flow of historical change.

Thus have we found ourselves, for quite some time now, in a situation
in which several scientific disciplines and worldviews (and Christian theologies as well) are struggling for an adequate judgment of the basic human
experiences expressed in Genesis 3.

In my teaching I have proved successful by not immediately joining
the dispute over the latest positions on the actual content of Genesis 3,
but by first somewhat more extensively presenting a text by Immanuel
Kant, who paraphrased the Jahwist's earliest history. *An anthropological*
discussion carried on as early as the eighteenth century is being repeated in
contemporary debates. Most of today's anthropological theories are probably
included in the way Kant made the beginning of the biblical book of
Genesis the basis of a philosophical anthropology and doctrine of freedom
in critical conversation with J. G. Herder and J. J. Rousseau. Conversely
we meet various *present-day theories* in the philosophical discourse of the
eighteenth century in an instructive, incipient form.

C. Immanuel Kant on the Beginnings of Humanity, with a Special Focus on Freedom (I)

We will now discuss the work of Immanuel Kant, "Speculative Beginning
of Human History" (1786),[58] which was published four years before

---

58. I. Kant, "Muthmaßlicher Anfang der Menschengeschichte," Royal-Prussian academic edition, vol. 8 (Berlin, 1923), 197-3, pp. 107-30; quotations from English translation, "Speculative Beginning of Human History," in Kant, *Perpetual Peace and Other Essays*
on Politics, History, and Morals, trans. Ted Humphrey (Indianapolis: Hackett Publishing,
1983), pp. 49-59.

F. Schiller's previously mentioned essay (and was the inspiration for it). In this work Kant provides a quasi-biblical "history of freedom's first development."[59] He attempts a philosophical answer to the question of how freedom invariably comes about in human beings. To that end he avails himself of the texts in the first chapters of Genesis, although the way he handles the texts is admittedly not tied to church dogma. At the beginning of the work Kant invites the reader to imagine that he is in a park, a garden protected from all kinds of beasts of prey "in a climate that is always mild."[60] Food is available in natural abundance in the garden. Kant's intellectual experiment now puts a human couple in this park and, for the time being, only *one* couple, so that the problem of armed conflict does not immediately appear and disturb the observation of subtle and original conditions. It concerns a physiologically fully developed human couple that can walk upright, talk, and think.[61] In the garden sketched by Kant, the *voice of God* is also present, having the effect of conveying to the inhabitants of the garden an instinctual feeling about whether the food is fit or unfit to eat.[62]

When the time was "fulfilled," *a four-staged development of humanity into ever more complete freedom began* which Kant describes in a manner similar to Sigmund Freud, who later traces the individual's development to human maturity from infant to adult (once again Freud expressly understood an individual's "ontogenetic" development to maturity as a progression from life under the rule of the "id" to life under the desirable rule of the "ego" as a repetition of humanity's "phylogenesis").

According to Kant the *first step* toward freedom takes place when human reason seriously begins to stir: *our ability to make comparisons awakens. In Kant our human capacity to think rests on our well-developed ability to compare phenomena to each other.* As far as Adam and Eve are concerned,

59. See Kant, "Muthmaßlicher Anfang der Menschengeschichte," p. 109; quotation from ET, p. 49. See also E. Drewermann, *Strukturen des Bösen. Die jahwistische Urgeschichte in exegetischer, psychoanalytischer und philosophischer Sicht*, pt. 3, "Die jahwistische Urgeschichte in philosophischer Sichte" (Paderborn, [4]1983), esp. pp. 30-53; see also E. Lämmerzahl, *Der Sündenfall in der Philosophie des deutschen Idealismus* (Berlin, 1934), on Kant's interpretation of the fall.

60. See Kant, "Muthmaßlicher Anfang der Menschengeschichte," p. 110; quotation from ET, p. 50.

61. See Kant, "Muthmaßlicher Anfang der Menschengeschichte," p. 110.

62. See Kant, "Muthmaßlicher Anfang der Menschengeschichte," p. 111.

Kant believes that their eyesight constantly showed them other potential sources of food than the ones they were used to claiming. After that the "voice of God" was regularly heard, and it advised them to refrain from eating the uncustomary food. But when the time was ripe, the following mechanism engaged: reason and imagination "feign" certain desires in man, contrary to the voice of instinct.[63] In the case of the first human couple, the cause of deserting God's voice "may only have been a petty matter" — even if it was only a "mere fruit."[64] For only in this way, Kant remarks wisely, could their falling away from the rule of instinct be handled peacefully. Reason was able to comprehend its ability to "harass" the voice of nature at will. Even if the first attempt probably did not turn out the way he expected, man nevertheless discovered "in himself an *ability to choose his own way of life and thus not to be bound like other animals to only a single one.*"[65]

The psychological reaction to this experience was ambivalent. It awakened "delight" (which would correspond to the age of defiance from the perspective of individual psychology), but also "anxiety and unease." Adam stood now "as if at the edge of an abyss." For he did not yet know anything about the hidden features and long-term effects of the things or food he approached. He knew only this one thing — from now on, there was no turning back for him from this state of freedom he had once tasted.[66]

Before I go into further detail about Kant's description of the three next steps in the development of freedom, I would like to add an interpolation that demonstrates how Kant constantly interacted with Herder and Rousseau in his treatise.

63. Kant, "Muthmaßlicher Anfang der Menschengeschichte," p. 111.
64. Kant, "Muthmaßlicher Anfang der Menschengeschichte," p. 111K; quotation from ET, p. 51.
65. Kant, "Muthmaßlicher Anfang der Menschengeschichte," p. 112; quotation from ET, p. 51.
66. See Kant, "Muthmaßlicher Anfang der Menschengeschichte," p. 112; quotations from ET, p. 51.

D. J. G. Herder's and J. J. Rousseau's Thoughts on the Biblical Narrative of the Fall

In his *Outlines of a Philosophy of the History of Man,*[67] Herder had developed a quite different anthropology one year before the publication of Kant's work mentioned above. If Kant had thought that the first step toward freedom led the first human beings out of a totally natural existence controlled by instinct and into the world of reason, and if, therefore, Kant's anthropology had a dualistic orientation based on the conflict between their natural sensuous inclination and moral reason, Herder denied that nature and reason (natural human existence and cultural human existence) were even in contradiction! Herder, the forerunner of idealism and romanticism, thought reason was a gift of nature itself! Thus he advocated the thesis that reason is not directed against nature, also not against the nature of man. In the previously mentioned work, Herder referred to the upright stance natural to human beings.[68] This is the most important requirement for man's intellectual advantages over the animals. However, man does not differ from the animals in kind or qualitatively, but only in degree and quantitatively. "Beasts are the elder brethren of man."[69] Herder regarded the emergence of highly advanced cultures not as the result of eating the fruit of the tree of knowledge in the fall. Rather, he reminded his contemporaries that in most cases religious piety and reason were originally linked together in highly advanced ancient culture.[70] Moreover, Herder interpreted the statements about the beginnings of civilization/culture included in the earliest history of the book of Genesis to the effect that piety and reason are not the result of a new capability to know good from evil originating in the so-called fall. Rather, they are the result of God's friendly *instruction* of human beings from the beginning.[71] "If the deity willed that man should exercise reason and foresight, he must have conferred on him

---

67. In Herder's *Werke,* ed. H. Düntzer, vol. 9 (Berlin, n.d.); quotations from English translation, *Outlines of a Philosophy of the History of Man,* trans. T. Churchill (1800; reprint, New York: Bergman Publishers, n.d.).

68. See Herder, pt. 1, bk. 3, chap. 6, pp. 126ff.

69. Herder, pt. 1, bk. 2, chap. 3, p. 89; quotation from ET, p. 35.

70. Herder, pt. 2, bk. 9, chap. 5, see pp. 138ff.

71. See also M. Metzger, *Die Paradieseserzählung. Die Geschichte ihrer Auslegung von J. Clericus bis W. M. L. de Wette,* APPP 16 (Bonn, 1959), p. 149; E. Lämmerzahl, *Des Sündenfall in des Philosophie des deutschen Idealismus* (Berlin, 1934), p. 36.

foresight and reason. Education, art, cultivation, were indispensable to him from the first moment of his existence." Old traditions point out "that the first created men conversed with the instructing elohim; that, under their guidance, they acquired language and sovereign reason, through the knowledge of beasts."[72] The so-called fall plays only a marginal role in this otherwise very impressive work by Herder. In passing he says that human beings were not content with the excellent faculties which make it possible for them to know fully what is good from the beginning. Beyond that they also wanted to be privy to the divine knowledge of evil, "acquired by a forbidden mode." The result was a certain amount of damage and the dawning of a new, more artificial "way of life."[73]

We find in J. J. Rousseau a completely different approach to the issue of civilization's development. For him, the *first step* into civilization was really a fall! This is clear from his response in 1754 to a prize question of the Academy of Dijon, which was phrased as follows: "What is the origin of the inequality among men and can it be established from the law of nature?"

Rousseau's thesis:[74] The fact that inequality between human beings is so prevalent must not be ascribed to the nature of man at all. The natural state of humanity which can still be observed today in several primitive peoples living far from Europe was and is not characterized by the rule of some over the others. Consequently it is not characterized by inequality. *On the contrary, the natural state must be considered a happy phase of history in which men can still live almost self-sufficiently!* They are hardly dependent on one another. Generous enough to overlook the oppressive situations of dependence in which so-called primitive peoples can live, Rousseau asserts: in the natural state, man is externally free from all technology, inwardly free from all reflection and free from worry, peacefully sitting under an oak tree and drinking from the clear water of a spring.

Unlike Kant, Rousseau assumes that humanity did not enter the realm of freedom when it took its first step into civilization, but conversely began to leave an original realm of freedom. Rousseau's work is one long critique of civilization. The reader encounters only a certain subconscious hope in

---

72. Herder, pt. 2, bk. 10, chap. 6, see p. 177; quotations from ET, pp. 285-86.

73. See Herder, p. 177; quotations from ET, p. 285.

74. Rousseau quotations are translated from J.-J. Rousseau, "Die Krisis der Kultur," in *Werke,* selected by P. Sakmann, ed. R. Schmidt, in 2 eds., KTA 85 (Stuttgart, 1956), pp. 82-96; see p. 82.

Rousseau that of all civilizations ours could one day link up with the ideals of its origin. But his main thesis is: those human beings disrespectfully called "savages" actually distinguish themselves by living an exemplary life of freedom from fear and aggression and, therefore, by the absence of any inequality as well.

1. A. Plack and K. Lorenz in Relation to Rousseau

In the spirit of Rousseau, Arno Plack developed the thesis in his book *Society and Evil: A Critique of the Prevailing Morality* (many editions of the book have been published since 1967) that the social constraints and dishonest conventions of our culture are the epitome of evil. They disfigure man and make him sick and aggressive. Plack demands that the culture and the society should be changed in such a way that the original nature of man, "which can not be evil,"[75] is able to develop in a more unimpeded way than now. The individual (or his personal sin) is ruled out as a source of evil in Plack's view. It is Plack's deep conviction that the human individual in our civilization was first made into a sinner by the false morality of the existing society.

Rousseau directed his comments on aggression and fear primarily against Thomas Hobbes (1588-1679), who had claimed that all people are by nature "defiant and think of nothing but attacking and battling." However, Rousseau also opposed Charles de Montesquieu (1684-1755), who was of the opinion that "nothing is as shy as natural man, always trembling and turning to flee at the slightest sound or movement."[76]

In the modern era Konrad Lorenz would most likely agree with the views of Hobbes and Montesquieu rather than with those of Rousseau or Plack. His book *What Is Known as Evil — The Natural History of Aggression,*[77] which was first published in 1963, clearly shows this. (This is true despite the fact that Hobbes and Montesquieu likewise contradict each other to a certain extent. This contradiction is moderated if one notices that both Hobbes and Montesquieu establish an analogy between human beings and *wild animals*. However, wild animals react to dangerous situations only partially with *aggression* and partially with *flight* as well.)

75. Translated from A. Plack, *Die Gesellschaft und das Böse. Eine Kritik der herrschenden Moral* (München [¹1967], ⁹1970), p. 339.

76. On Rousseau and Kant, see Lämmerzahl, pp. 34ff.

77. K. Lorenz, *Das sogenannte Böse. Zur Naturgeschichte der Aggression* (Wien [¹1963], ²⁹1971).

Unlike Rousseau, Lorenz would also attribute *aggressive* behavior to as yet uncivilized early man, primitive man, because in Lorenz's view man generally shares aggressiveness with most animals.

However, understood biologically, this drive is by no means identical with evil, but serves to preserve the species. Evil became associated with aggressiveness only when human beings at a certain level of development crossed the inhibition threshold that is set in the animal kingdom to keep them from destroying their own species. Yet right up to the recent past mankind learned to compensate for this handicap through the welcome development of rites, customs, ethical rules, and laws so that there has not been complete self-destruction so far. However, in the modern industrial and technological culture all of these possible compensations suddenly are in danger of failing.

Thus a new source of evil that must be recognized and combated by us has arisen in human behavior that fails to conform to our conditions (or these conditions fail to conform to us). Therefore at least a parallel to the thought of Rousseau is found even in Lorenz. He, too, is reflecting on the effects of a civilization that is hostile to man and running today in the wrong direction.

2. Rousseau against Hobbes and Montesquieu

Rousseau emphasized the following points against the anthropological views of Hobbes *and* Montesquieu: "I know, it is repeated incessantly, the idea that nothing is as miserable as man in his natural state. However, I would like to know what kind of misery a free being has to endure whose heart is not restless and whose body is healthy. I would like to know whether life in its natural state is more likely to become unbearable to the man in the natural state than life in modern society to the middle-class man. Have you ever heard of a free savage who condemned his life or sought to take his own life?" No, the so-called savages are not only free and equal but are entitled to the virtue of compassion, and only they have it in a totally pure and natural way. Only reason produces egotism, and intellectual reflection intensifies it. It causes man to curve back into himself. "Philosophy isolates."[78]

The awakening ability of man to make comparisons, so highly praised by Kant, the basis of our reason, was *not* acknowledged by Rousseau as

78. Translated from Rousseau, p. 82.

the foundation of a higher level of development for humanity! In the opinion of the Frenchman this awakening ability led humanity into a drastic worsening of their situation. The fact that Rousseau so highly praised the original, natural life in contrast to the Kantian position became a challenge for Kant, who would like to have seen in Rousseau a comrade in arms for the cause of human autonomy and freedom.

Kant felt compelled to subject the thought of Rousseau, this great prophet of *liberté, egalité,* and *fraternité,* to a somewhat maverick interpretation at the point we just mentioned: Kant developed the hypothesis that Rousseau did not conclusively locate the ideal of the natural state in the early history of man instead. He believed Rousseau was speaking of the natural state in terms of a utopia critical of the modern era. The original condition of humanity envisioned by Rousseau is actually the goal that reasonable people strive for *in* civilization. Therefore, understood correctly, the natural state described by Rousseau has nothing to do with an earlier life of humanity before the awakening of the mind or reason. Rousseau's so-called natural state describes our hope of achieving a *second naturalness* in our culture/civilization.[79]

However, let us hear what Rousseau himself said about the first sinful step of humanity, comparable to a preacher: "The first person who had the idea of fencing in a piece of property and then claiming, 'This belongs to me' and who found people simple enough to believe him, was the actual founder of the bourgeois society. But consider the man who would have torn out the posts, leveled the trench and shouted to his fellow men, 'Beware of believing this fraud! You are lost if you forget that the fruits of our labor belong to all and the earth to no one!' Imagine how much crime, wars, murderous deeds, misery and atrocities *that* man would have spared the human race!"[80] But this man who gave the warning was not there in time. Instead agriculture came, and with it the dividing up of the land. The farmers and metalworkers separated, an occurrence described in Genesis as well. (Genesis 4:22 mentions one of the descendants of Cain, Tubal-Cain, who forged all kinds of tools out of bronze and iron.) The exchange of products that now became necessary brought the division of labor, "the interdependence of the producers."[81]

---

79. See Kant, "Muthmaßlicher Anfang der Menschengeschichte," pp. 116ff.
80. Translated from Rousseau, p. 87.
81. Translated from Rousseau, p. 91.

The formerly free and independent man — in Kant the situation is reversed: man enters into the irrevocable state of freedom only through the fall; in Rousseau, however, he irrevocably loses his freedom by taking his first step into sin — this formerly free, independent man is subjugated and enslaved more and more as the demands of society steadily grow. He is enslaved both to nature and to his own fellow human beings. The *right of the stronger* — later shifted by Darwin into the *natural state,* but by Rousseau into the *cultural state* — now becomes the basis of the whole legal system. Inequality has arrived,[82] and with inequality the phenomenon of alienation as well, "self-actualization," "the rule of illusion and lies." "Man in his original state has gradually disappeared. To the eyes of the understanding individual, society can only offer the image of artificial people and artificial passions which are the work of these new conditions that do not have any roots in nature."[83]

This is Rousseau's view. Later, the French Revolution and the philosophers of German idealism were not able to catch up with him by a long shot. Thus, his mission was left unfinished, his claims unsatisfied — until Karl Marx more than any other figure gave vent to Rousseau's unfulfilled dreams and compressed them into a vision of an inevitable second revolution, an improved French Revolution. With mixed results Marxist-Leninist thinkers in the twentieth century tried to identify this vision particularly with the Russian October Revolution of 1917.

These philosophical lines of thought stretch in the form of interpretations of the biblical stories that deal with sin from Rousseau and Herder via Kant to Hegel and Marx (and far beyond these men). They all intend to disclose the truth about human nature as well as the present situation of humanity, that it may prove useful in improving our present-day conditions. One model corrects the other, in as realistic a fashion as possible, and one way of treating the problem of Genesis 3 corrects the other. *What all these philosophical interpretations of the Genesis texts have in common is that they largely keep the problem of man's relationship to God out of the discussion of what should be considered the original disaster of alienation.* A strange question follows from this fact: Must we not assume that the improvements one philosophical model feels compelled to make on the model of the preceding one have to do with the shortcomings and biases

82. See Rousseau, pp. 92f.
83. Translated from Rousseau, p. 96.

that had to occur in *all* these models precisely because they have excluded the question of God (or reduced him to deistic proportions)?

If there is something to this, we must ask a further question: By constantly correcting and outdoing those who have gone before in their efforts to dissolve the meaning of the human condition, are contemporary philosophies and modern scholarship *unconsciously* in the process of compensating for and coming to terms with the damage (the narrowing of philosophical perspectives, one-sidedness) caused by repressing the question of man's relationship to God? If this is the case, then de facto they would also be involved in theologically interpreting Genesis 3 in their own roundabout way. Theology would then face the task of developing a sufficient understanding of human alienation in conjunction with them.

Now let us go back to Kant and forward to his description of the next three phases of the event theology calls the fall.

E. Immanuel Kant on the Beginnings of Humanity, with a Special Focus on Freedom (II)

For Kant the *second step* coincides with the acquisition of the famous fig leaf in Genesis 3:7. One of the advances in knowledge gained through this act was an awareness that sexual desire can be prolonged and increased by human imagination (in contrast with the mating instinct in the animal kingdom that only occurs periodically). What, then, does the fig leaf signify? It supposedly takes our eyes off the naked body our sex drive focuses on. The more this object is removed from the senses, the more "stably," naturally the "more moderately," "the more steadily," the "business" of human sexual life is conducted. But in this way a surfeit of sex is also avoided.[84] (In contrast with Kant, Rousseau believed the *savage* is moderate in his sexuality, his love life takes place without the excessive stimulation of his senses, whereas all the swamps of vice open up to man in culture!) Nevertheless, Kant wants to trace back the emergence of human love to the discovery or use of the fig leaf. This love is a warm and heartfelt affection controlled by human consciousness.[85]

Kant further explains: "*Refusal* was the feat whereby man passed over

---

84. See Kant, "Muthmaßlicher Anfang der Menschengeschichte," pp. 112f.
85. Kant, "Muthmaßlicher Anfang der Menschengeschichte," p. 113.

from mere sensual to idealistic attractions, from mere animal desires eventually to love and, with the latter, from the feeling for the merely pleasant to the taste for beauty." "*Decency* — a propensity to influence others' respect for us by assuming good manners (by concealing whatever could arouse the low opinions of others), as the proper foundation of all true sociability — gave the first hint of man's formation into a moral creature." That's not so bad at all! Kant also adds the nice remark: "It was a small beginning that was nonetheless epochal, since it gave an entirely new direction to man's way of thinking; as such, it is more important than the entire, incalculable series of cultural expansions that follow from it."[86]

Now the *third step:* The third stage in man's break with his instinct was man's "*reflective expectation* of the future." The fact that man can plan the future is the most decisive mark of his human privilege of preparing for more distant goals "in conforming with his vocation."[87] On the other hand, this ability — Kant admits that Rousseau is right in this — is naturally also a source of constant worry that the animals are completely spared. In this context Kant also refers to Genesis 3:13-19, in which man feels the growing burden of his work and the woman suffers from the inconveniences of her gender, additionally foreseeing those troubles to which "the more powerful husband would subject her." "With fear, both foresaw in the background of the picture, at the end of a life of toil, what indeed all animals inevitably face — though without being troubled by it — namely, death." Only the hope of indirectly living on in numerous descendants who would be able to harvest the fruits of their present labor, and thus would perhaps be able to have it better, kept our progenitors standing tall.[88] However, because reason — as the ability to look ahead from this stage onward as a source of anxiety — had caused their generally unhappy situation, it appeared time and again in an unfavorable, dubious light. As Kant believes, at that time an unfortunate trend emerged. It became fashionable to label the transition from instinct to the rule of reason as a "crime," as *sin.*

Although Kant, here in conjunction with Rousseau (!), points out the

86. Kant, "Muthmaßlicher Anfang der Menschengeschichte," p. 113; quotations from ET, p. 52.

87. Kant, "Muthmaßlicher Anfang der Menschengeschichte," p. 113; quotations from ET, p. 52.

88. See Kant, "Muthmaßlicher Anfang der Menschengeschichte," p. 113; quotations from ET, p. 52.

problematic nature of this step into the "freedom" of civilization, Kant does not want to side with those who consider reason as the source of all corruption in this situation. Rather, he claims to see realistically that man has no option left but to take the risk of using his own reason (!), to find his way out of this dilemma on his own strength.

By saying all of this Kant means: As an instrument of human action used to improve social and economic conditions by carefully predicting and planning the future, science must not be incriminated but must continue to be developed!

Here Kant is clearly on the side of the (utopian) idea of a scientifically based, social planned economy (Claude-Henri de Saint-Simon, 1760-1825) that had reemerged at that time. He also affirmed the science later designated as *sociology* since the time of Auguste Comte (1798-1857). Here again there is a widening gap to Herder, who espoused a quite different understanding of civilization and culture that seems archaic today. If we could call Kant's model of culture a scientific one because it summons experimental science and technology to control nature, Herder looks back at archaic culture reflected in the Golden Age.

I now come to the fourth and final step in man's break with instinct and his entrance into freedom in my description of Kant's interpretation of Genesis 3. At this stage man recognizes himself as the actual purpose of nature: "The first time he said to the sheep, the pelt that you bear was given to you by nature not for yourself, but for me; the first time he took that pelt off the sheep and put it on himself . . . ,[89] at that time he saw within himself a privilege by virtue of which his nature surpassed that of all animals, which he now no longer regarded as his fellows in creation [as Herder demanded!], but as subject to his will as means and tools for achieving his own chosen objectives."[90]

Kant interprets the command of Genesis 1:28 in his own way: "Subdue the earth and rule over the animals . . . !" Kant's thought reaches a decisive turning point when he asserts that from now on *no one* was allowed to say to any human being something like "your fur belongs to me"![91] Here Kant is bringing to light probably the key dogma of modern thought that

---

89. Kant based this on the statement of Genesis 3:21.

90. See Kant, "Muthmaßlicher Anfang der Menschengeschichte," p. 114; quotation from ET, pp. 52-53.

91. Kant, "Muthmaßlicher Anfang der Menschengeschichte," p. 114.

no doubt had a "bracing" effect but is mainly associated with unspeakable suffering and the disastrous destruction of the environment for which it bears the greatest blame.[92] At this point Kant also expresses a particular idea about how man manages his instincts, an idea still shared by many today. The handing over of the animals to human aggression, Kant believes, makes it possible for man to create a society built "on affection and love."[93] In this way Kant agreed with the age-old *scapegoat theory.*

Sigmund Freud, a kindred spirit to Kant in many respects, would have sharply contradicted him here! In *Civilization and Its Discontents* (1930), Freud also happens to deal with this scapegoat theory. I will pick out a section dealing with the Jews. In the Christian West the Jews were often made scapegoats. Freud writes, "Once the apostle Paul had laid down universal love between all men as the foundation of his Christian community, the inevitable consequence in Christianity was the utmost intolerance toward all who remained outside of it; the Romans, who had not founded their state on love, were not given to lack of religious toleration, although religion was a concern of the state, and the state was permeated through and through with it." But when the governments became *Christian governments,* the Jewish people, Freud writes sarcastically, "rendered commendable service to the cultures of its host nations as well: unfortunately, all the massacres of Jews in the Middle Ages were not sufficient to make this age more peaceful and secure for its Christian compatriots."[94]

When we analyze these bitter lines, we are struck by Freud's opinion that all who think they can keep suffering at bay and bring good fortune to themselves by using weaker fellow human beings as scapegoats deceive themselves. In Freud's view not only the Jews have become victims of this deception, but also those Freud here calls the "Christian host nations."

Since Freud is correct here, Kant's theory in which a humane society could be erected on the basis of animal sacrifices must be sharply criticized from the perspective of our present level of knowledge! Theology should do its part as well because it must recast its understanding of *atonement* in an improved form anyway. With good reason it must take a stand

92. See K. Eschweiler, *Die zwei Wege der neueren Theologie* (Augsburg, 1926), pp. 54f.

93. Kant, "Muthmaßlicher Anfang der Menschengeschichte," p. 114.

94. S. Freud, *Studienausgabe,* 10 vols., ed. A. Mitscherlich and others, Conditio Humana series (Frankfurt am Main, 1969ff.), vol. 9 (pp. 191-270), p. 243; quotation from Sigmund Freud, *Civilization and Its Discontents,* trans. Joan Riviere, International Psychoanalytical Library, no. 17 (London: Hogarth Press, 1957; originally published, 1930), p. 91.

against Kant's interpretation of Genesis 1:28. Furthermore, it must show that Christian faith clearly calls us away from a — supposedly realistic — economic system which intends to purchase or secure our humanity (human equality, freedom, and brotherhood) by permitting aggressive and sacrificial actions against animals or plants.

Toward the end of his work "Speculative Beginning of Human History," Kant addresses the problem that Rousseau had already dealt with, the problem that equality between human beings is nonexistent. In especially tense opposition to Rousseau's thought, Kant says the fourth and final step into freedom in which Adam decided to elevate himself over all nonhuman creatures opened the door for man to "become the *equal of all rational beings,* whatever their status may be."[95] Thus, equality among human beings was made possible on the basis of the oppression of animals — and it became a duty! For now the following theory of two classes is valid. Animals have their purpose in being available to another, superior being. But man carries his purpose in himself. He exists as a self-confident, individual, and free person for his own sake. All human beings are equal in this. (That is why Kant's second version of the categorical imperative reads: "Act so that you treat humanity, whether in your own person or in that of another, always as an end and never as a means only.")[96]

For Kant this final step into full human dignity means at the same time his "release" "from nature's womb."[97] Kant reminds us that this release represents a parallel to Adam and Eve's expulsion from paradise. However, Kant evaluates the event of this release in his own way. He writes that this event "honors" man, especially since it posed serious dangers to mankind. Man agreed to expose himself to danger, realizing it is inevitable whenever human beings are pushed out of a perfectly safe environment in which they are cared for like children (or out of a garden that provides for their needs effortlessly). It signifies man's transition into a world where "he was awaited by so many cares, burdens, and unknown evils." In the future man will often long to return to the lost paradise where "he could dream

---

95. Kant, "Muthmaßlicher Anfang der Menschengeschichte," p. 114; quotation from ET, p. 53.

96. I. Kant, *Grundlegung zur Metaphysik der Sitten,* in *Werke,* ed. W. Weischedel, 10 vols. (Darmstadt, 1983), 6:61; quotation from English translation, *Foundations of the Metaphysics of Morals,* trans. Lewis White Beck (Indianapolis: Bobbs-Merrill, 1959), p. 47.

97. Kant, "Muthmaßlicher Anfang der Menschengeschichte," p. 114; quotation from ET, p. 53.

or trifle away his existence in peaceful inactivity and permanent peace."[98] (Is he thinking here of Rousseau or Herder?)

Obviously such a paradise is not to the philosopher's taste (although paradise is portrayed this way not by the Bible, but by Kant himself!). Kant ardently desires that man will free himself from such dreams! Our reason does not allow us to return to "that crude and simple state." It is good that God placed the cherub in front of the gate to this nature paradise. The cherub will put a stop to any regression. *The cherub symbolizes reason* motivating man to patiently shoulder the toil he hates . . . and to forget death itself, which he dreads.[99] Kant advises us to replace our anxiety about death with those inconsequential anxieties daily life offers us in sufficient number.

At the end of the whole essay Kant faces the decisive question of whether man has "gained or lost" as a result of that change the Bible calls the fall. His answer is that as a species humanity has undoubtedly won. For the species the release from Eden signifies continued "*progress* to perfection" or at least "*progress* from the worse to the better" conditions. But this is not true of the individual. He had it easier in the "state of ignorance" and innocence. What brings gain to the society as a whole means loss for the individual.[100]

At this point Kant expresses full agreement with Sigmund Freud's later argument in *Civilization and Its Discontents* (1930). Freud says it is true that there is no alternative to culture, but it is understandable when *individual* human beings reach the conclusion that "the whole thing is not worth the effort and that in the end it can only produce a state of things which no individual will be able to bear."[101]

But even here there is a difference between Kant's and Freud's thought. Kant goes beyond Freud when he says the individual has reason to *blame himself* for all the evils he endures and all the evils he perpetrates! At the same time he should be "admiring and praising" the wise and practical way the species are arranged.[102] Only if he does this can he cope with the

---

98. Kant, "Muthmaßlicher Anfang der Menschengeschichte," p. 114; quotations from ET, p. 53.

99. Kant, "Muthmaßlicher Anfang der Menschengeschichte," p. 115; quotation from ET, p. 53.

100. Kant, "Muthmaßlicher Anfang der Menschengeschichte," p. 115; quotations from ET, p. 53.

101. Freud, vol. 9, p. 269; quotation from *Civilization and Its Discontents,* pp. 142-43.

102. Kant, "Muthmaßlicher Anfang der Menschengeschichte," p. 116.

apparent contradiction in Rousseau, who on the one hand correctly emphasizes that culture is in conflict with the physical nature of man, and on the other hand correctly writes in his work *The Social Contract* (1762) that culture must be further developed to elevate humanity morally so that ultimately culture and man's physical makeup are no longer in conflict.[103] Kant says this harmony sought by Rousseau will be achieved when one day "art so perfects itself as to be a second nature."[104] *For Kant the moral destiny of man is fulfilled when he achieves this second naïveté.* In the era *after* Kant the thought of the philosophers of German idealism also basically moved in this direction.

F. Kant's Perception of Radical Evil in Human Nature

In Kant the humanization of man is only brought to a conclusion when the first human beings disassociate themselves from their former companions in creation, the animals. In Kant's view nothing evil has taken place so far. Rather, man has developed as a being with a special nature, as a unity of dependence and freedom,[105] belonging to nature and intellect. This human being who has emerged from the events of Genesis 3 is a citizen of two realms, though they relate to each other in an antinomian fashion and find their way together in the human beings forming a kind of unity in contradiction under the leadership of freedom and intellect (reason). The dual character which the now fully developed human being possesses first *makes* evil *possible,* man's falling into sin. As a citizen of two realms, he is capable of certain actions which suggest unjust maxims, evil principles in his inner being.

But how can this universal "inclination to evil" be better explained? Regarding this question Kant proved his extraordinary knowledge of human beings. In relation to this question as well he ironically moved into the vicinity of the church's theological teaching tradition, a fact that seemed questionable to many admirers of his other work. Kant did not simply

103. Kant, "Muthmaßlicher Anfang der Menschengeschichte," p. 116.
104. Kant, "Muthmaßlicher Anfang der Menschengeschichte," pp. 117f.; quotation from ET, p. 55.
105. For Tillich's view, see *Gesammelte Werke,* ed. R. Albrecht, zit. als GW mit nachfolgender röm. Bandzahl (Stuttgart, 1957ff.), GWIII, 199.

explain the origin of evil with the ancient, Gnostic-dualistic theorem which would have been an obvious choice for his system. In this view the realm of the flesh or the senses or matter or the determinism of natural law still brings its influence to bear so strongly in human beings claimed by mind and spirit that human beings are forced off the path of their spiritual destiny and are tempted to fall back into their prehuman state, into the realm of dependence on instinct and nature. Kant did *not* describe the mechanism of the human inclination to evil in this traditional way. However, he also did not consider the opposite theorem denying that evil could result from man's elevation of himself over his basis in nature. Thus he also does *not* see the inclination to evil being active in a way that human beings think they are freer or more intellectually powerful than they are and to the greatest possible extent force "everything" to serve what appears advantageous and reasonable to them in a hybrid love of self.

In his work *Religion within the Limits of Reason Alone* (1793/94), Kant further explained that evil is rooted neither in man's nature or instinct nor in his use of reason and rule over nature. However, evil is realized in such a way that human beings reverse the internal order inherent in *both* their driving forces — nature and reason. Man acts as if what is reasonable and moral were his lust and what his sexual desire urges him to do were his moral duty. In this way he makes life easier for himself as he views both his nature and his reason as ways to gain superficial approval of his existence, his behavior, more easily. In Kant, the root of evil, the root of all sin is this self-deluded way of making life easier.

"Human beings (even the best ones) are only evil by reversing the order of their driving forces and incorporating them in their maxims: To be sure, they incorporate the moral law alongside the law of self-love. However, since they realize that one cannot exist next to the other, but one must be subordinated to the other, they make the driving force of self-love and *its* inclinations the condition of following the moral law. . . ." "By this reversal of driving forces," their actions can even turn out to be in "such conformity to the moral law that it seems as if they had arisen from genuine moral principles" — yet suddenly evil has appeared on the scene![106]

In Kant evil is defined not by the quality and the effect of human actions but by the *attitude* underlying them. Kant is an ethicist motivated by moral convictions. Man is morally evil on the basis of an inner

---

106. Translated from Kant, *Werke*, 7:685.

dilemma in which his moral convictions are reversed and confuse his maxims: "Real evil consists of not *wanting to* resist those inclinations which invite us to violate the moral law, and this attitude is actually the real enemy."[107]

The main strands of the church's teaching tradition have always attributed sin and evil to a process that involves the culpable reversal of two basic reference points in our life: *sin begins with the event of inverting the relationship that would be appropriate to creation or fellow creatures and the relationship that would be appropriate to God, the Creator.* Even the whole Christian-Jewish teaching tradition is of one mind in seeing the key event of sin in this inversion (amounting to a violation of the first commandment). Therefore they agree with Kant to the extent that their theologies also teach that *sin or evil is not to be attributed to an autonomous evil substance or matter that is said to exist in the world.* Seen in these terms sin or evil is without substance and empty. As the by-products of distorted relationships they both are nourished not from something existent in the world but from an "as if," from false pretenses. *That is why the motive for lying is rooted in the soil of sin.*

Kant's interpretation of evil formally comes from this traditional theological view of things. Nevertheless, where the theological tradition speaks of the Creator whom human beings do not obey, Kant now speaks of (practical) *reason,* whose voice people do not dutifully heed. At the same time the Bible and church theology focus on man's involvement in his own conviviality, orders of creation, and God's command that man live in harmony with them, Kant is focusing on the unceasing effectiveness of man's natural instincts and sex drive. In Kant evil appears on the scene as soon as man "rationalizes" his sexually motivated behavior, covers it with the appearance of reasonableness, and simultaneously surrounds the behavior demanded by his reason with the illusion that it gives him pleasure. *Thus, in Kant the reversal of man's relationships to the Creator and the creation lamented by the Bible is turned into a reversal of two basic forces in the inner being of man himself, who is understood in dualistic terms.* Our broken relationships with the Creator and our fellow creatures (such as animals and plants) have been dropped from our understanding of evil in this both anthropocentric and inward-looking change of focus. This change is not only tantamount to a narrowing but to a loss of our understanding of sin,

107. Translated from Kant, *Werke,* 7:710.

and it has resulted in far-reaching consequences.[108] But Kant also calls the phenomenon perceived in this reductionist form "original sin," *peccatum originarium,* and even "radical evil" ("because it corrupts the basis of all maxims" and arises from the universal "folly of the human heart"). All this is to be understood as a "natural inclination" human forces are not able to eradicate "because this could only happen through good maxims. The eradication of this inclination can not take place if the supreme subjective ground of all maxims is assumed to be corrupt."[109]

If, then, the *inclination* to evil cannot be eradicated by any man's power, man can and must nevertheless, in Kant's view, *resist* this inclination on his own strength with the help of *good will.* This good will is articulated in dutiful behavior triumphing over one's own inclinations. Kant spoke of this good will with an extraordinary emphasis — almost as if its existence were a miracle from heaven.

G. Two Critical Inquiries Addressed to Kant

For Kant the miracle[110] that there is *clearly* good in the world at all (and not only "mixed good" or "ethically neutral good") depends on the phenomenon that human beings can have a "good will." "It is not possible to think of anything in the world, indeed, even outside the world, which could be considered good without limitation except a *good will alone.*"[111]

This *good* will is not one which could match our inclinations and desires; rather, it must — *contrary* to our inclinations or wishes — match what reason recognizes as dutiful action in conformity with the moral law. This good will corresponds to an unreserved, unlimited "respect for the law." It is by no means available to everyone at all times; rather, its existence and its effectiveness presuppose a "revolution in our way of thinking," tearing the roots of our maxims out of the ground of their sinful corruption.

---

108. Pannenberg makes a more positive judgment; see *Anthropologie in theologischer Perspektive,* pp. 91ff.

109. Kant, *Werke,* 7:675-88.

110. Kant, *Werke,* 7:695.

111. Translated from Kant, *Werke,* 6:18.

There is human *dignity* in the world because, in Kant's opinion, such good will is astonishingly encountered in the real world. A person is worthy if he, under no circumstances, allows anyone to buy from him what is above any price; not giving in to his desires, such a person has "greater inner worth of his person."[112] It is obvious that the elevation of man to a status of dignity and thus to the activation of his good will is anything but easy. Is it even humanly possible?

The *one* critical or problematic place in Kant's teaching about the good and the dignity of humanity is found in the question of the *revolutionary transition* from corruption to the human heart's freedom from sin. How is it made possible? How does it become real? The *other* problem is found in Kant's bold preview of the ideal of a *second naturalness*. We saw that Kant had held the sober view that, in the process of building a civilization becoming more and more enlightened, the individual citizen had to accept more suffering than pleasure, more ascetic restrictions than cultivation of his natural inclinations, more personal misfortune than good fortune for the sake of a general improvement in living conditions. *This would last only until one day a completely perfected civilization and his skills would once again lend man's social existence the form of a fully natural life.* This utopian hope became well known in Germany, especially through Heinrich von Kleist's later "Essay on the Puppet Theater." (Kleist thought we must "eat from the tree of knowledge a second time to fall back into the state of innocence.") But does this philosophical vision of salvation have the slightest chance of being realized? To be sure, in Kant himself it figures only as a marginal utopian idea, an ultimate goal of hope mentioned for educational reasons. However, Kant's idealist students were deeply convinced that human life in the mode of a "second naturalness" could be realized. If it was still an open question in Kant whether the establishment of a second naturalness governed by moral reason could be actually realized in the course of history, for the German idealists it was no longer a question at all. They had already assumed this second naturalness in one leap. They no longer saw reality any differently than it presents itself in the plan of moral reason.

112. Kant, *Werke,* 6:88; quotation from *Foundations of the Metaphysics of Morals,* p. 74.

H. Developments beyond Kant: Circular Thoughts Nourished by the Problem of Evil, Yet Repeatedly Thwarted by It

If Kant was the philosopher of the dutiful *struggle* of moral reason against the inclinations and desires of man, the German idealists proclaimed the inevitable victory of morality over man's physical nature reshaped by the human spirit. With Schiller and Fichte, Hölderlin and Hegel the actual Age of Enlightenment in Germany is already at an end. The train has moved on from a critique of traditional religion and a critique of man's ability of reason to a philosophical redefinition of religion to the creative invention of a new culture of reason and a new constitution for the state. This is true in spite of the fact that in Feuerbach, Marx, and others, a *critique of religion made by the nineteenth century* appeared on the scene (looking at Kant and Hegel, it was actually lagging behind) and that the idealist's extravagant dreams for the state and society never really ripened.

1. J. G. Fichte on Sin

J. G. Fichte (1762-1814), the founder and first of the idealist philosophers who related to Kant but were new in comparison to him, presented a model which was supposed to be "only an analysis of freedom from beginning to end."[113] Consciously and intentionally Fichte no longer perceived reality any differently than it is *presented* by the plan of moral reason. *Only* that which is thought and recognized within the moral order of things has reality. Everything else is insubstantial pretense. The whole world is nothing but "the materialized realm of our duty."[114] It has its reality by matching the moral will of the self. The self and all of humanity gain reality by re-creating the world in accordance with moral duty.[115] However, the idea of a created reality already given to us, a belief in the creation of the world by the divine Creator, was contrary to the system and became incomprehensible for Fichte.[116] Belief in the moral power of man became considerably more intense in Fichte than in Kant. Indeed,

---

113. Translated from I. H. Fichte, *J. G. Fichtes Leben und literarischer Briefwechsel* (Sulzbach [¹1830], ²1862), 2:279.

114. Translated from J. G. Fichte, *Collected Works,* ed. I. H. Fichte, 8 vols. (1834ff.; reprint, Berlin, 1971), 5:185.

115. J. G. Fichte, 7:64.

116. J. G. Fichte, 5:479.

by basing *all of philosophy* — even the theoretical, intellectual work to be done by "pure reason" — on the work of *practical reason,* he believed he had overcome the famous antinomies remaining in Kant's thought. For him even Kant's epistemological boundary line drawn at the thing in itself became baseless.

The train had moved on. The French Revolution *was* here, Napoleon *is* here, romanticism is beginning, and the age of the critiques is being replaced by the Age of Imperialism for the new ideas. A new era has dawned, and its key word is no longer *reason* but *history.* This appears to be the scene of a tumultuous development of expanding freedom and of an improvement in the civilization. Of course the next generation is left to ask the question of whether such optimism proved successful. Schopenhauer is already born (in 1788), for whom this optimism will turn into sheer pessimism. And in 1818, Karl Marx is born, the one who will attempt to turn the intellectual world of idealism around by 180 degrees.

Fichte's philosophy went through two stages: in the first stage it understood evil/human sin as sloth, or man's refusal to participate in the cultural work of changing nature for the purpose of realizing human freedom.

In the second stage — a mystical change in Fichte had preceded it shortly after the beginning of the nineteenth century — Fichte totally eliminates the concept of "sin" from his thinking. In the work *Instruction on a Blessed Life* (1806), he tried to solve a problem that had remained open in the first phase of his thought. He tried to show to what extent a *limit* is set to the human being who is free.[117] Fichte finds this limit in God.

God serves him as the guarantor of a limit that should not cost man his freedom. In a mystical slaying of himself man was supposed to transfer his freedom to God. In this way man experiences his rebirth, which can only be acquired through this "death." Here Fichte probably makes the last possible change in the philosophical doctrine of freedom. The end result is that man proves to be free by sacrificing himself to God. According to Fichte the act of transition to a "higher morality" and to the "blessed life" that can already be achieved in this earthly existence takes place in this act of self-sacrifice. In this new life man is fully free of all sin because, says Fichte, in apparent harmony with the Bible and church dogma, sin is life outside of God. But, correctly understood, there cannot be such a life outside of God for man. An existence outside of God would be death.

117. J. G. Fichte, 5:413.

Fichte's final conclusion is that no person is able to fall out with God. If this could succeed, we would be totally insignificant, but once again we would not be able to sin because we would be nobodies.[118]

For Fichte *Christianity* as the *religion of life* is the one faith that does not know sin and should no longer be permitted to know it. As the lamb Jesus carried sin and the illusion of it out of the world. Likewise he carried the fear of a Godhead who arbitrarily punishes and rewards.[119] By spreading this news, Jesus founded a new world and a new era.[120]

The religion of the ancient world, writes Fichte in *The Essential Features of the Present Age* (1806), knew God only as an enemy of man. The ancient peoples, even the most educated, found the most terrible fright there; they found the Godhead to be their enemy when they had happily escaped the horrors of external nature and "returned to the secret depths of their heart." They tried to bribe, to pacify, this being who was jealous of all human well-being by enduring servile humiliations, by sacrificing what was dearest to them, by voluntarily inflicting torture on themselves, by offering human sacrifices.[121] But who was it who eradicated this widespread delusion and thus first made possible the philosophy, science and the morality of freedom in the new era? "The Christian religion . . . alone."[122]

Christianity has done away with the difference between the outcast and the elect, sinners and the righteous. Sin and with it the removal of sin was totally eradicated from the world by Christianity. There has no longer been any sin since God's decision declared by Jesus that he would receive everyone who approaches him. However, God would remain the tyrannical, obstinate despot and magical God with the means of removing sin such as consecration, circumcision, baptism or whatever else there may be that is common even in the modern era.[123] God, however, is in fact the heavenly Father whom man may approach as he is, "with childlike faith and without fear."[124] Christ has died to sin — Romans 6; what he lives, he lives to God. "In the same way, count yourselves dead to sin but alive

---

118. See Barth, *KD*, III/2, pp. 113-121, esp. p. 121. Barth misses the limit set to human beings in Fichte's thought.

119. J. G. Fichte, 5:490.

120. J. G. Fichte, 5:419, 4:557ff.

121. See J. G. Fichte, 7:44.

122. J. G. Fichte, 7:53.

123. J. G. Fichte, 4:557.

124. J. G. Fichte, 4:558.

to God in Christ Jesus" (6:11). "We know that anyone born of God does not continue to sin . . ." (1 John 5:18). But not even the one who lives by his fleshly nature should think that he sins. His life is an empty sham, but it does not deserve the name of sin. For as Fichte says in his *Doctrine of the State* (1813), it is man's sinful arrogance to believe that he could sin and really disturb the divine plan for the world.[125]

The former candidate of theology, Fichte had a special predilection for a "Johannine Christianity" that understands God as Spirit and Christianity as the religion of love.[126] By taking this position he did the groundwork for an important current in the Protestantism of the nineteenth century. Fichte believed he was contributing to the historic worldwide recognition Christianity would achieve in the present day by giving certain theologumena of the New Testament their philosophical form. From the perspective of "Johannine Christianity" he also considered the confessional divide in existence since the Reformation to be outdated.[127] He also did the groundwork for Hegel in that he wanted to turn Christianity from a religion of faith into a religion of knowledge following his Johannine Gnosticism. He thought *faith* given by God as a precondition of salvation belonged to a past era.

Let us now return once again to Kant! *His* already optimistic teaching on the power of good will is in contrast to the Christian view. The miracle of good that exists in the world comes from *God's creation*. Adapting Kant, we could say of creation understood in *Christian* terms: *Everywhere there is nothing that could be considered good without reservation except being itself that is created and exists by God's Word. In the case of separation from God, man returns to God in response to God's call (see Ps. 90:3).* And everywhere there is nothing in the world, even outside the world, that could be considered *evil* except being itself that is *not* created from *God's* Word, that does not exist from him nor follows his call to turn back — in the case of separation from God.

Human beings receive the splendor that justifies their life, they receive the dignity that confers on their person its indestructible "inner worth," the "second nature" the New Testament calls *rebirth* or *new creation,* only from the "good word," the gospel that in the beginning elevated human

125. J. G. Fichte, 4:562.
126. J. G. Fichte, 7:98ff.
127. J. G. Fichte, 7:104.

beings above the other creatures and then speaks to them afresh of God's closeness and love even in their remoteness from God, their entanglement in sin, and their loneliness in the cosmos.

In Kant the human inclination or opportunity to sin is the abyss from which man can keep himself only by good will, but not at all by "grace alone" in his true humanity, in human dignity. In the Christian view, divine grace — made concrete in God's "good word" — is the sole *foundation* on which humanity can endure in dignity — in spite of the reality of sin. Christian teaching thus sees the splendor given to humanity as the result of a gift granted by God from the outside.

If Kant's teaching on the good and on dignity is of an almost illusory ethical severity, Christian teaching offensively stresses the all-embracing relatedness of human beings to God. In the generation after Kant many thinkers and poets often sought a middle road that was meant to avoid Kant's severity and the even more rigorous theocentrism of the Christian doctrine of grace. For example, Friedrich Hölderlin made an effort in this direction, seeing in Kant a *second Moses* who tried to bridle a stiff-necked people with the holy law and keep them alive.

2. F. Hölderlin's Desire to Create a New Mythology

Hölderlin was not satisfied with Kant's rigorous way of planting the high moral demands of the Enlightenment in the people. He felt that Kant's method of educating the people was too one-sided in its intellectual rigor. An all-embracing form of religion that also speaks to man's emotions, his feeling for beauty, and his religious hope must be "created," for the holy cause of the Enlightenment, which gets partial support from Christianity, however, partially goes beyond historic Christianity (carrying on where Greek classicism left off). "We must have a new mythology" that "no person has ever thought of before," "a mythology of *reason*" in order "to make the philosophers sensuous," allowing the ideas of the Enlightenment to become "aesthetic, that is, mythological," so that it could take root in the still unenlightened masses.

"Then eternal unity will prevail among us. Never more the disparaging look, never more the blind rage of the people at their wise men and priests. Only then does *equal* training of *all* forces await us, both of the individual and of all people. No force will any longer be oppressed, then universal freedom and equality of minds will prevail! — A higher spirit, sent from heaven, must create this new religion among us. It will be the final, greatest work of humanity."[128]

In spite of Hölderlin's own efforts to establish it, this new Western religion he had in mind has not yet been created, perhaps because Christianity simply does not tolerate the synthesis Hölderlin proposed, perhaps because his attempt to go beyond the rigorous form of Kant's ethics has not proven to be possible. The goal Hölderlin was striving for, his longing for a new, holistic life, is thoroughly understandable and still touching even today. But it covers up, no, with its unattainable idealism, it accurately describes a fundamental difficulty in ethics and anthropology that began with Kant.

3. Kant and Schiller in the Nineties

It is understandable that the critique of Kant began at this point. It aimed at Kant's unresolved "antinomies" between the assertion of a radical corruption in humanity and the assertion that man was able to gain the victory of his good will. Furthermore, it aimed at the antinomy between man's belonging to the realm of natural law and its determinism and his belonging to the realm of freedom. In his *Critique of Judgment* (1790, 1793, 1799) Kant showed a way that *seemed* to lead out of these antinomies: Kant called the *powers of judgment* a third way of knowing which made possible the transition from theoretical to practical knowledge, from the concept of nature to the concept of freedom. The powers of judgment (connected with the feelings of pleasure or lack of pleasure) reside between *theoretical knowledge* and *practical reason* which targets the good will. Kant remarked that the phenomenon of pleasure could go along with the feeling of the beautiful, which is why Kant laid out the first part of this book as "the critique of aesthetic judgment." He began this section with an "analysis of the beautiful," expanded it from section 40 on with studies about art, and concluded it in section 59 with a part titled "Beauty as a Symbol of Morality."

Friedrich Schiller then used this pointer given by Kant to think further independently about Kant's rigorous teaching on the law. In *Grace and Dignity* (1793) and *The Aesthetic Education of Man* (1793/94), Schiller

---

128. Translated from F. Hölderlin, *Sämtliche Werke und Briefe*, ed. G. Mieth, 2 vols. (München, [2]1978), 1:918f.

outlined an *ethic that was to come close to the ideal of life in a second naturalness.* With the help of the categories "art," "beauty," and "play" he developed a teaching about life in which the moral could be lived naturally and the natural morally. Schiller said "beauty belongs at the same time to the two worlds . . . to one by the right of birth, to the other by adoption."[129] This beauty can be naturally given as well as produced by human work, and therefore it can link together the two worlds that are poles apart in Kant.

Like Hölderlin, Schiller lamented the imperative form of Kant's moral law, which is more likely to condemn and humiliate man than to elevate him. This form creates the impression in the practice of life — *against* Kant's declared intention — that an alien norm is being forced on human beings from the outside. In contrast to Kant, Schiller thought that moral man does *not* live in a continual conflict with his nature. *Man's nature is willing to allow itself to be educated by the spirit and thus to gain grace.* Even the less well proportioned or frail individual has the opportunity to become beautiful in a moral endeavor.

As soon, then, as in man the *person,* the moral and free agent, takes upon himself to determine the play of phænomena, and by his intervention takes from nature the power to protect the beauty of *her* work, he then, as it were, substitutes himself for nature, and assumes in a certain measure, with the rights of nature, a part of the obligations incumbent on her. When the mind, taking possession of the sensuous matter subservient to it, implicates it in his destiny and makes it depend on its own modifications, it transforms itself to a certain point into a sensuous phænomenon, and, as such, is obliged to recognise the law which regulates in general all the phænomena. In its own interest it engages to permit that nature in its service, placed under its dependence, shall still preserve its character of nature, and never act in a manner contrary to its anterior obligations. I call the beautiful an obligation of phænomena, because the want which corresponds to it in the subject has its reason in the understanding itself, and thus it is consequently universal and necessary. I call it an anterior obligation because the senses,

---

129. F. Schiller, "Über Anmut und Würde," in *Ausgewählte Werke in 6 Bände* (Cotta-Ausg.), ed. K. Buchmann and H. Missenharter (Stuttgart, 1950), 4:187; quotation from English translation, "On Grace and Dignity," in Schiller, *Essays Aesthetical and Philosophical* (London: George Bell and Sons, 1879), p. 178.

in the matter of beauty, have given their judgment before the understanding commences to perform its office.

Thus it is now free arbitration which rules the beautiful. If nature
has furnished the architectonic beauty, the soul in its turn determines
the beauty of the play, and now also we know what we must understand
by charm and grace. Grace is the beauty of the form under the influence
of free will. . . .[130]

The architectonic beauty does honour to the author of nature; grace
does honour to him who possesses it. That is a *gift,* this is a *personal merit*
by virtue of which the mind moulds the body and the structure is forced
to modify itself according to the *play* that the soul imprints upon the
organs, so entirely, that grace finally is transformed — and the examples
are not rare — into architectonic beauty.

*In this paradigm of Schiller evil is located in the insufficient and uneven
biological endowment given to the individual at birth, putting him at a
disadvantage.* In this paradigm evil is the opposite of neither the concept
of faith or virtue, but it is the exact opposite of the concept of *freedom,*
the human freedom to shape oneself and select a way of life for oneself.
Schiller adopted the concept of freedom in the terms the philosopher
Fichte defined it: as the ability to change oneself according to one's own
desires by working at it. It was Schiller's heroic faith that man is "a free
being, capable of determining his modifications by his own will."[131]

In the book by Dorothee Sölle, *The Right to Become a Different Person*
(1971),[132] this idealistic confidence is identified as the actual substance of
the New Testament gospel. This is true at any rate when Schiller's talk of
the voluntary efforts by which man can change himself is understood in
terms of human freedom defined by the individual. Sölle understands
"repentance" and "the forgiveness of sins" as an introduction to the learning process that leads to self-acceptance, the autonomous structuring of
one's own life and rebellion against all that threatens to do violence to
one's own life. This also includes an introduction to a process of learning
how to love, do justice, and awaken one's social conscience. Sölle's starting
point is her attempt to "catch up" with the perspectives that split off from

130. Schiller, "Über Anmut und Würde," pp. 191f.; quotations from ET, pp. 181-82.
131. Schiller, "Über Anmut und Würde," p. 217; quotation from ET, p. 205.
132. D. Sölle, *Das Recht ein anderer zu werden,* Sammlung Luchterhand 43
(Neuwied/Berlin, 1971).

the church's theology in German Idealism and restore them to the New Testament gospel. Her intention in doing so is to improve the contemporary theology of the church. It ought to be almost self-evident that both a proper element and an element bound to fail can be detected in her work.

Schiller, unlike Kant, promises a gracious ease in ethical living. Moreover, he promises the *individual* so harried in our civilization that he, too, can achieve the personal happiness that in Kant's opinion will only come to a perfected human *species*.

Schiller's clever trick comes from his assumption that there is a human behavior toward nature that is free from the urge to subject nature immediately to certain purposes. For example, an artist could enjoy the beauty of nature without desiring to possess it; he could imagine it, reproduce it in its inner being, without wanting to use it for any specific purpose. Thus there is an artistic "similarity to nature" that can be utilized in an aesthetic education of human beings. What counts is not only granting the ethical "good will" its "own absolute authority to make the law," but also, beyond Kant, granting the same authority to the imagination.

Of course, Schiller does not avoid circular reasoning. The whole person (and not just a human will opposing human nature) must really realize himself so that the whole person, including his physical nature and natural beauty's effect on it, can be educated aesthetically and become good in this process.

Yet it remains an open question why human beings can be so one-sided and biased that they simply do not act "holistically," that on the contrary, their inclination and duty, natural drives and spiritual purposes are actually in fierce conflict. As a theologian, I am tempted to ask: Is it *faith* that makes the personality good and whole (totally), or is it faith in the *whole personality* that solves the problems?

It is apparent in Schiller's transition from the concept of gracefulness to the concept of *dignity* that the desire to go beyond Kant on the basis and with the tools of Kantian philosophy is not a very promising enterprise. If Schiller interpreted gracefulness as a match between duty and inclination marked by *ease,* he understood dignity as our personal capability to resist the disruptions and obstructions of our moral desire caused by our natural drives and instincts. For Schiller, dignity meant acting on the basis of what one was ashamed of, not in one's (own) nature, but in one's own "raw nature." *Shame* thus produces the motivation and the strength enabling us to achieve human dignity. But not only the theologian would put a big question mark here.

Is shame really sufficient to preserve or give back to human beings the splendor, the significance that true dignity possesses? To put it more concisely: Can we depend enough on shame to make itself felt? Day in and day out, shame fails to provide a possible source of resistance to instincts that detract from our moral desire, and not only in our individual life. In the twentieth century, we have to speak of an alarming absence, even failure, of shame in the dynamics of inscrutable sociopolitical processes to which whole peoples fall victim.

The unsolved problem in Schiller's method is the unanswered question of why people can be so one-sided and so inwardly torn that their inclination and duty, natural instinct and spiritual purpose in fact enter into fiercest conflict with each other. Therefore, by what objective right does Schiller see human possibilities a few degrees more idealistically than Kant? This remains an unanswered question.

But in the end it is only a question of secondary importance whether resistance to radical evil is best understood with Kant, as a most difficult undertaking that requires a revolution motivated by moral convictions and a holy imperative, or whether it is best understood with Schiller, as a humanly possible activity that is beneficial to the people. Furthermore, it is only a question of secondary importance whether evil is better understood with Kant as "radical," as undermining and corrupting the foundation of human moral convictions, or whether it is better understood with Schiller, as not quite as "radical," because it does not corrupt *all* promising human tendencies. Finally, it is only a question of secondary importance whether evil (defined here as the inhibitor of one's own free self-realization and self-change) is understood in a certain analogy either to statements in the Old Testament or New Testament. All of these possible differences do not change the fact that the biblical understanding of evil is not maintained *at any level of thought*. Ultimately, Kant, too, is not any closer to the biblical teachings about sin than Schiller is (whose efforts to put a certain amount of "good news" into his ethics should meet with understanding and good will even from Protestant theologians).

Both Kant and Schiller understood the conquest of evil as a task exclusively for man himself. They have ignored the key religious event of evil and sin — human separation from God. They also read the biblical stories in Genesis 2–3 not as explanations of the relationship between man and God but as coded statements about man becoming mature that must be judged from a purely anthropological perspective. Thus they also fail to appreciate *God's* essential part in overcoming evil and its consequences.

In the nineteenth and twentieth centuries no other question has set philosophical thought in motion and kept it in motion to the same extent as the problem of evil — a problem that Kant and his mainly idealist successors seemed to have finally solved from an intellectual standpoint. Yet it is obvious that time and again philosophers in the nineteenth and twentieth centuries gained the impression that this problem had not been sufficiently understood, let alone mastered. Thus, the systems of thought that kept appearing were always attempts to hold their ground better against the phenomenon of evil.

This dissatisfaction also extended to the relevant answers of contemporary theologians! Although it is their duty to consider the original religious circumstances and the historical roots of our discussion of evil, they have often spoken of evil and sin in a much too superficial way, following the trends of the zeitgeist. Or their contributions were not seen as being helpful or noteworthy for other reasons. One of these reasons was a widespread arrogance among theologians that made them believe they were not at all affected by the aporias of the philosophers, but with the help of the Bible and the teaching tradition of the church were in full possession of unparalleled dogmatic insights into the problem of evil. Such arrogance has forgotten two truths. First, "correct dogma" does not represent tradition that is always available like a full bank account and valuable in itself irrespective of changes in the spirit of the times. Secondly, the existence of more recent philosophy is one prolonged comment on the shortcomings of Christian dogmaticians' regarding of their knowledge of the truth.

Our present European theology is thus deeply caught up in the lack of movement in the thought of the nineteenth and twentieth centuries — revolving around insufficient philosophical theories about the nature of evil. Thus far it has not been able to exercise far-reaching influence on the thought of the industrial societies shaped by the West in a way that genuinely improves our understanding of evil. Not only rapidly spreading unbelief is to blame for this, but also the wrong way the theologians see themselves.

I. Excursus: Eugen Drewermann's Understanding of Sin and Evil

Starting with his insights into the experience of evil yesterday and today, while affirming the inadequacy of traditional theology, Drewermann allusively submits several proposals to restore a relevant theology and a piety that is helpful for everyday life. The goal of Drewermann's three-volume work *Structure of Evil* is this: The meaning of the Jahwist's earliest history in Genesis 2–11 should be developed for modern man in the light of exegetical, psychoanalytical (depth psychological), and modern, philosophical interpretations or paraphrases of this Bible text. However, never before were so many findings, questions, and methods brought together to create an ensemble and an overall view of Genesis 2–11 that are so useful for an interpretation of these texts. Words and phrases characteristic of relatively recent as well as the latest literary fiction and poetry have also been included in the presentation in rich measure. The same is also true of myths and parallels in the history of religion related to this topic, together with their discussion in various modern-day academic disciplines. Drewermann has thus brought together the *human condition* in a great language panorama. In so doing he expressed the hope that theology could regain a part of its competency "regarding the task . . . of interpreting human existence and intellectually fathoming it, based on the word of the Bible."[133]

What are the objective results of this well-written work that is so full of material and that wants to meet its goal as a work of systematic theology and at the same time as a Roman Catholic textbook? Because Drewermann thought he could show on the basis of the earliest history in J how man *must* destroy himself without God, he could in conclusion give the following admonition: "Instead of following Kant's program of reducing religion to a merely moralistic teaching 200 years after the Enlightenment in an exercise of intellectual self-mutilation and instead of increasing the amount of guilty feelings by discussing what we have to 'do' to save church and society, what initially counts more than anything else is reinforcing the insight of the Jahwist's earliest history that for the moment 'nothing can be done' because man can not be 'moral' unless the anxiety he feels about his existence has first been allayed by faith. The only crucial subject in life . . . is the issue of man's relationship to God; all the issues of morality

133. Translated from Drewermann, pt. 3, p. 565.

and action . . . come later." The direction in which Drewermann is pointing makes sense theologically. But can a fresh perspective for the postmodern churches be directly gained from an analysis of the story of the fall found in J? Making the transition from exegesis to exhortation, Drewermann speaks in the following way:

"The truth is that we can love and accept neither ourselves nor another person nor anything else in the world if we ourselves have not found love and acceptance in God. In a life without God every kind of neurosis will follow hard on its heels. Sin is the epitome of mental illness. . . ." Even the two most important human drives, "aggression and sexuality," must acquire "a function that is contrary to their biological purpose . . . if human consciousness, without finding sufficient support in the security of instinctive regulators, reflects a world that — without God — seems to be deeply infiltrated by fear, futility, threats, hostility and meaninglessness."[134]

Time and again Drewermann returns to his basic premise: Living without God means sickness, primarily "mental illness." It means being human contrary to human nature; it is missing one's purpose in life. From a theological viewpoint the teachings of psychoanalysis about neurosis constitute a single phenomenology of sin. As such they should be incorporated into theological dogmatics; psychoanalysis can function as an auxiliary science for theology. It can inform theology about "the basic attitudes which psychologically destroy or heal human beings." It can show theology "how the fundamental decisions made for or against God are converted into psychological states of mind."[135] For example, the crucial significance of the so-called doctrine of original sin should be seen in the fact "that by including psychoanalytical insights it teaches us to understand man as a being who must become *sick from the fear pervading his consciousness* if he does not learn how to conquer this fear that fundamentally characterizes it through an act of confidence." "In theory it is a matter of using the psychology of neurosis within the framework of psychoanalysis as a hermeneutical method to understand the doctrine of original sin. With its help psychoanalysis can demonstrate how fear originating in a life without God can be interpreted in terms of the individual forms that neurosis takes. . . ."[136]

134. Translated from Drewermann, pt. 2, pp. xivf.
135. Translated from Drewermann, pt. 2, p. xx.
136. Translated from Drewermann, pt. 3, pp. lxxixf.

A truly self-confident self-definition of theology and its role! It is considered to be an integrative, higher science and the irreplaceable fundamental philosophy regarding the question of what allows man to be human at all. Even more astonishing than this when first reading it is the fact that the only results of this three-volume work with its multifaceted distinctions should be found in a stereotypical phrase, "life doesn't work without God." It seems hardly possible that after Drewermann first states in volume 3 with Kant and other thinkers that Adam and Eve lost their sure instinct as creatures in the so-called fall, he now single-mindedly latches onto this thesis — unlike Kant and more recent philosophy: Now that his instinct is missing man absolutely needs God to find direction in life. The man of the fall must make his own basic decision for God. Otherwise he is lost. *And then he himself is to blame for his own downfall!* His line of reasoning is: "Every external shortage (for example of jobs, markets, etc.) may define a situation in which I am blameless and yet must accept (historical) guilt that lies outside myself in my real-life experience; but I am always to blame for a shortage of God, especially when the absence of God as a fact, as an historical reality of absolute irrefutability collides with my freedom from the outside."[137] How is all this meant? Do not this teaching on freedom and this declaration of personal guilt miss the essential point that real human beings are marked by sin?

It is strange that Drewermann draws the lesson from the earliest history of J that man must have a believing relationship to God if he does not want to destroy himself and his surroundings. On the contrary, does not the Jahwist speak of man's becoming totally incapable of living with God, deciding for God, or drawing God into his own life as a result of the fall? And does it not become clear from the perspective of the Jahwist's description that the man who has become a man of sin is now totally and exclusively dependent on *God's* willingness to reach, support, and rescue him? Is *this view* of things merely a Protestant underestimation of the strength and inner freedom even of sinful human beings? I think this is not true at all. Rather, a theology that advocates a different view of things does not have the Bible on its side in this case. What, then, could Drewermann have meant by it? The most obvious explanation for his line of reasoning is that in his own peculiar way he links questions of modern secularism, atheism, and agnosticism with questions that were once dealt

137. Translated from Drewermann, pt. 3, p. 360.

with by the Jahwist — mainly in Genesis 3. For Drewermann our modern way of life in a climate in which God does not "appear" seems to represent an analogy to Adam and Eve's break with God. Just as these two cut into their own flesh in the story of the Jahwist when they tried to lay the foundations of their own happiness and success without God, the atheist or agnostic of our modern era seems to do this as well. Drewermann seems to see the overall scheme of things in this way. But can this view be theologically maintained even if it is not uncommon among theologians?

Here is a possible objection to this view: Even though the *modern loss of God consciousness* may be caused in part by individuals, but also by "weak" theologies, it nevertheless signifies a *necessary phenomenon,* not in terms of "inevitable" (because of the futility of the developments and changes that have emanated from modern Europe), but in terms of "theologically desirable" (to the extent that it signified a break with a more philosophical than Christian concept of God which understood God not in terms of Jesus' cross but in terms of oppressive absolute power). Although modern man may be involved in the modern (alleged) collapse of the idea of God in some way, modern man is not "more godless" than people were in an earlier time. This is why the hypothesis posited by Fichte that there is a special analogy between the event of the fall in Genesis 3 and the modern Enlightenment is untenable. In all of its ambivalence, even its moral ambivalence, the event of the Enlightenment did not bring about any new and special sin that was any different from the sins or godlessness of the premodern *corpus Christianum.* Is not Drewermann's appeal "back to God" questionable in this situation?

Drewermann has his own theory about these modern events, especially about the origin of modern atheism. This theory above all else offers the key to his approach:

"Modern atheism, the struggle of the denominations and the inner turmoil of man in the modern age" are "fruits of a contradiction which was rooted in the development of Christianity from the beginning when it rejected the pagan myths and the forces in man that create myths."[138] By literally "demonizing" the mythic ideas of their pagan surroundings as products of human fantasy and passion precisely because of their obvious resemblance to the teaching of Christ, early Christian apologetics had to drive a wedge of deep skepticism into man's soul regarding his

---

138. Translated from Drewermann, pt. 3, p. 528.

own emotional makeup. Not the world of dreams, longings, feelings, and emotions was supposed to help man find and accept divine truth — rather, it was essential to suppress it as something that was hostile to Christianity; the philosophically trained *intellect* and the morally trained *will* alone seemed to have prepared the way for faith in Christ in the pagan world.[139] Subsequently even mythic church dogmas such as the incarnation of God through a virgin were interpreted *rationally* by theologians and in the form of a supposedly historical fact — a further dilemma for Christianity on account of its completely wrong beginning.[140] As long as the church lived in an environment in which the tradition of the myths actually still lived, a "polemical opposition" was neither inevitable nor humanly tolerable. However, to the extent that Christianity destroyed the cultural assumptions of the pagan world, the attitude that was hostile to myths gained a stridency that had to turn increasingly against the assumptions of Christian faith in the human soul as well.[141] Everywhere adopting opinions similar to those of C. G. Jung, Drewermann considers the modern crisis brought about by man's loss of direction in life and the shock waves sent out by atheism and nihilism (among others) to be the result of this development. He believes the Catholic church as a whole has contributed somewhat less to this outcome, but Protestantism clearly more. Drewermann calls it an act of destruction of the human psyche carried out "in the name of God."[142]

From this vantage point Drewermann's demand that we all should find our way back to a relationship with God so that we do not have to live in a sick, neurotic, and destructive way becomes somewhat understandable for the first time. This demand is not simply an appeal to return to faith in God from unbelief. It does not at all mean that we could rescue ourselves from sin and evil in our freedom and our own strength. Rather, Drewermann's stereotypical saying "only those who live with God live humanly" is obviously first and foremost a plea for a radically different theology and piety in Christianity. His concern is to ensure that Christian teachings and symbols no longer appear as a form of internalized violence imposed on and drilled into man from the outside, as fixtures of the "superego," but

139. See Drewermann, pt. 3, p. 521.
140. See Drewermann, pt. 3, pp. 522f.
141. See Drewermann, pt. 3, p. 524.
142. Drewermann, pt. 3, p. 527.

that they regain their inner truth by proving to be the reality that is planted in the depths of the human soul, thus uniting human beings of all nations and all times. Otherwise it can be foreseen "that the population explosion of the next three decades alone will devalue Christianity and turn it into a strange entity at the periphery of historical development."[143]

He is not demanding that Christianity should finally become pagan but that with the power of faith to create a new synthesis it should learn to combine the historical with the eternal, the individual with the collective, the human with the divine. The soil in which Christianity is rooted is after all just this union of the archetype of the divine Redeemer with a historical individual. And Drewermann — quite loosely — calls *faith* the power which makes this synthesis so effective in us that *fear* is banished, "the fear threatening to pull man back into a mythic neurotic-psychotic dependency on the forces of the unconscious, forcing him to assert his endangered ego in a rigoristic one-sidedness against the assault . . . of the unconscious." In contrast to the pagan religions which remain in the collective, Christianity, having produced so much fear by its antimythical frame of mind, has within itself the power "to banish fear as the power that actually deforms man, turning him into a devilish caricature of himself, and that degrades him to a mere object of demonic tyranny, which is also true in the myths. The merit and the task of Christianity [are] to have conquered this fear in principle and to conquer it again and again in every individual." This is why Christianity should not have fought the — invincible — pagan myths until now but "the *fear* which brings man to the point where he defines himself or allows himself to be defined in a mythical or neurotic way by things, persons, and forces which are not God."[144]

Now Drewermann's arguments have come full circle. We have arrived again at evil and at man's first contact with evil that is the subject of the Jahwist's earliest history. Drewermann would like to agree enthusiastically with Kierkegaard's interpretation of Genesis 3 insofar as he developed the idea that it is *fear* that makes man fall into sin and become evil. If Christianity is to be a force for the grace that can accomplish something against sin, indeed, that in faith allows the victory over evil to begin, Christianity must above all conquer fear in us. *In doing so* it places man before God. And by placing each individual as a unique historical person

143. Drewermann, pt. 3, pp. 529f.
144. Translated from Drewermann, pt. 3, p. 533.

before the eternal God of the universe, it also banishes fear. To echo Kierkegaard, fear could be missing in human beings only if they were stupid and dull — and then there would also be no sin.[145] But where sin and evil result from fear, then its unbearable consequences can be managed somewhat only by a single "human remedy": if we have not found our way (back) to God by restricting our freedom.[146] (The great pagan alternative to faith is wiping out man's fear "by destroying his freedom.") But man cannot live humanly without freedom. . . .

Ultimately man's fear is to be seen as the great *chance* that man will encounter God in it and discover "what he really lives by." This would also allow man to *continue* in freedom. "This is the step of *faith:* that I can discover myself, my contingent, not necessary, superfluous existence as created, affirmed, willed and authorized by the infinite and that this discovery makes it possible to accept myself. . . ." "The experience that I . . . do not need to create the justification of my existence because this foundation already exists . . . makes it possible for the movement of transcendence in which the finite . . . was lost to come back to myself again" — so that I no longer have to feel "disgusted" at my finitude or have to be "ashamed forever" of it. "Thus it is possible that the fear that is necessarily a part of being human does *not* lead to despair but to faith."[147]

Drewermann appeals to Kierkegaard, but of course Kierkegaard would not have said the latter in this way. He would have said that man can only break through to faith by passing through despair — and that this is grace! But the following remarks by Drewermann show that at this point he himself basically means what Kierkegaard says. Drewermann writes little about forgiveness. It does not play a significant role in his model. This may have to do with the peculiar two-track approach Drewermann uses to describe evil: One minute he wants to say that it comes from the sin that is part of all human beings (and can only be overcome or forgiven by God's grace). But the next minute he wants to say that it wells up from a fear for which traditional Christianity bears the blame by inadequately dealing with the mythical element of faith (from which we would have to draw the conclusion: we need a different theology and radically different forms of piety so that we banish this fear and do not continue to incur

145. See Drewermann, pt. 3, p. 546.
146. See Drewermann, pt. 3, p. 175.
147. Translated from Drewermann, pt. 3, pp. 546f.

guilt by supporting a theology that leads to such dire consequences). One minute he appeals to God's grace, the next minute he appeals to our understanding — but both aspects are woven together in Drewermann in a peculiar way. At this point we must try to be more selective. Otherwise we risk opening the floodgates to a triumphalist or a pietistic "You-too-need-God" theology. On the other hand, we are in danger of at least giving the impression that we expect to gain something by characterizing the entire modern world as a large hospital in which the atheists are in the intensive care unit — without noticing it and without as yet having found the right doctors. (It would obviously be best if they were theologians and psychoanalysts rolled into one.)

The crucial question we must discuss with Drewermann on this subject is what it means "not to be without God as a human being." Undoubtedly this is first a calling which God himself gave and gives to man. And in the end this will never become a calling we will give to ourselves on the basis of a decision of our own will.

This is why I take a cautious approach to Drewermann's way of reminding us of his belief in our responsibility to save the world! "The issue of humanity's survival will be a question of faith. Does man possess the strength to solve the ancient conflict between nature and culture? . . . Will the groups of those who believe (according to J, the people of Israel; in the New Testament, the church) succeed in fighting the inclusion of our biological inheritance in the blueprint for man's self-deification or will man have to solve the problem of his evolutionary origin with purely biological methods, i.e., by voluntarily eliminating freedom instead of exercising the freedom that comes from faith? The actual decision between the national destiny of Babylon and the principle of life exemplified by the holy nation of the Bible, the decision between the Apocalypse and the kingdom of God remains as ever . . . the key problem of history."[148] Israel's faith in its one God (who for Drewermann is fully identical with the God of the church and already developed in the Jahwist!) is "the mission and guiding principle of our history," because the modern world "lives deeply absorbed in a world of mythical inhibitions and collective obsessions; in comparison to Israel it lives behind the times." "The history of God with his people does in fact replace the history of the nations and places a merely natural understanding of man in its merciless cruelty and unwarranted

---

148. Translated from Drewermann, pt. 3, p. 561.

superfluousness on a new foundation; only now do we recognize what man can actually be. . . ."[149]

All of these assertions are summary repetitions of idealistic philosophical views. The history of their influence extends to the present day and has several strands. One of these strands leads to certain types of contemporary critical social science by way of left-wing Hegelianism. Another leads to today's depth psychology by way of the natural philosophy of German romanticism in the late Goethe era and by way of certain forms of the philosophy of life. Drewermann's assertions are located at the temporary end of this one strand of depth psychology. Their intellectual basis is thus very narrow, and this initially gives them impetus. But it is a real pity to see how many facets of the entire range of problems are lost in the end since this study had *begun* on such a broad basis.

I see a twofold danger: God could be reduced to a "therapeutic remedy" that can be "prescribed" or "released" from the unconscious, and a new religious individualism could be cultivated which might treasure the discovery of God in the soul as a compensation for the frustration felt in today's societies and social surroundings, yet this individualism is not likely to have a healing impact on the abuses found in politics, in social services, and in nature, etc. I have no objection to Drewermann's demand that the church's liturgy and pastoral care should pay (renewed) attention to symbols and myths in Christianity. On the contrary, the churches must reactivate their old knowledge in this area. Yet even if they should be successful in doing this, the problem of the evil that corrupts and undermines all of our structures in life will still not be solved. Contemporary humanity will still not have come to grips with the "vital issues" it faces today; and fear would not diminish. What can really be hoped for is more modest: It is the hope that in our fear we will have fewer illusions about its causes and that more people than today will gain the strength to see real evil. Then we would act the wrong way less often and act more often in the direction that is necessary to tackle our problems. But in between, Christians would have to pray, worship, and build each other up.

---

149. Translated from Drewermann, pt. 3, pp. 555f.

SECTION VI
UNDERSTANDING EVIL IN OUR TIME

A. A Review of Modern Interpretations of Evil and Where It Can Be Located

At this point we will cut short our presentation of several interpretations of the Old Testament narrative of the fall in Genesis 3 that have become paradigmatic in the modern era. We have considered only a small section in detail: the path leading from Kant into the German idealism that followed him. Of course, the hypotheses, questions, and conflicting positions that have appeared on this short path will still occupy our attention. Today we cannot see only the differences of opinion about evil that have already emerged within this narrow part of the history of contemporary thought. Rather, from a historical distance we can also see what the positions described in the previous chapter have in common: tracing their path from Kant to German idealism, all its interpreters have commonly understood the so-called fall as *culturally necessary*. Our capacity to sin was characterized as our ticket of admission into the realm of possible freedom and self-responsibility. It was said that the so-called fall was an evolutionary leap, leading humanity out of the animal kingdom or, at any rate, out of its uncivilized periods. But in the time frame just discussed (and far beyond it into the twentieth century), the following formal concept of evil was devised: When human beings do evil, they are violating the higher level of existence that has opened up to them through the so-called fall. They are not, or not consistently enough, assuming responsibility for the tasks of a humanity that has come of age. They are falling back into behavioral patterns which man can no longer afford to repeat after the "spirit" and "mind" of man have awakened. They are "regressing" or are "slothful" in their behavior by following archaic "physical" impulses rather than moral reason. In a formal sense this evil actually consists of an *inopportune backwardness* in their moral development. As the source and cause of this evil, man is not on the high level that would not only be intellectually and socially appropriate for him *after* the so-called fall, but also necessary for his survival.

This constitutes a radical, far-reaching *innovation* in comparison to the traditional, Christian ecclesiastical interpretation of the fall — breaking with God and damaging or impoverishing formerly good structures of life: evil is no longer interpreted as leaving a good original state (even if it is transhistorical or supernatural) that occurred in the so-called fall of Genesis

3. Evil is thus no longer perceived in a protologic, but in a teleologic, frame of thought! This change in the system of coordinates which to a large extent has found its way into contemporary theologies made our understanding of evil and sin subject to increased moralizing.

In their attempts to conceive of evil Kant and his idealist successors held on to the *concept of God*. The significance of this philosophical concept of God appears to be easy to see through (custodian for general conditions that have not yet been understood for axioms, etc.). In reality it is not easy to shed light on the significance of their concept or to judge it. On the one hand, the word "God" was obviously used as a symbol for certain forces in nature or also attributes in man (for instinct, the voice of conscience, reason, etc.). On the other hand, they spoke of God because they could not explain and give sufficient reasons for the ethical purpose of man by observing human nature and human destinies (of what use is it for the individual to support the cause of good?) *and* because they did agree with important intentions of biblical Christianity and thought they were renewing the intellectual foundations of Christianity. Within the framework of this view, evil was understood without exception as being opposed to human nature, contradicting the "divine" in man. The concept of God was withdrawn from the philosophical interpretation of evil only with the critique of religion made by Feuerbach and by the vast majority of the proponents of so-called left-wing Hegelianism.

In the end Nietzsche considered any understanding of man that compares God with man to be the source from which *real* evil emerges in the first place. The latter is to be distinguished from the *so-called* evil of moral-religious convention. The limitation of man by God, especially by God as understood in Christian terms — the "Christian concept of a god," says Nietzsche in *The Antichrist*, "is one of the most corrupt concepts that has ever been set up in the world: it probably touches low-water mark in the ebbing evolution of the god-type. God degenerated into the *contradiction of life*. Instead of being its transfiguration and eternal Yea! In him war is declared on life, on nature, on the will to live! God becomes the formula for every slander upon the 'here and now,' and for every lie about the 'beyond'! In him nothingness is deified, and the will to nothingness is made holy![150] — first *produced* hopeless confusion on earth. Moreover,

---

150. See Nietzsche, *Sämtliche Werke,* 6:185, see also *Sämtliche Werke,* 5:93; quotation from Nietzsche, *The Antichrist,* trans. H. L. Mencken (New York: Knopf, 1918), p. 67.

what Christianity calls "evil" is almost a human virtue; man's best strength is the source of good.[151] Nietzsche delivered the message that there *must* not be God for the sake of human development that corresponds to our own possibilities.

However, in the philosophical developments of the twentieth century influential today, Nietzsche's hope of overcoming real evil by man's courage to be godless has not grown any more intense. To be sure, there has been no philosophical return to the theism postulated by Kant and the idealists. But in recent historical, programmatic philosophy confidence has waned that man liberated from the idea of God and faith in God would develop into a rich, humane being who could be called good — most recently even in several models of Marxist philosophy. Political upheavals and enormous crimes often expressly committed in the twentieth century in the name of a militant *atheism* have largely finished Nietzsche's well-known ideal of the "superman" and his "will to power" that had been adopted by many in a misunderstood form. Today there is no longer any question that we still experience real evil, even if people no longer relate to God or are reminded of him. As Nietzsche knew, real evil comes from human beings, but this is true not because they believe in God but because they try to fulfill their egotistical but shortsighted desires by using power and violence — this can be clearly experienced in one's own life. In the course of the modern interpretation of reality *etsi Deus non daretur*[152] the understanding of evil is subject to an increasing politicization. Time and again individual foreign nations, but also members of a certain strata of society or a certain political ideological alignment in one's own country, are identified with the "evil empire." Not my own heart, nor the thoughts and strivings of *all* people since they were children, is assumed to be the source of evil, but the violent and egotistical claim to power made by certain groups of which I am not a part or over which I think I have no influence whatsoever. If I were to have become evil myself, it is only because such sinister centers of violence oppressed me when I was not yet evil (for example, this is how A. Plack argues).[153]

"Evil does, in fact, come from human beings — but not from all human

151. Nietzsche, *Sämtliche Werke,* 4:359; see also 4:40.

152. For further details on this formula that can be traced back to Hugo Grotius and was important in D. Bonhoeffer's thought, see E. Jüngel, *Gott als Geheimnis der Welt. Zur Begründung der Theologie des Gekreuzigten im Streit zwischen Theismus und Atheismus* (Tübingen, 1977), pp. 21f. with n. 7.

153. See Plack, pp. 103f.

beings and only the smaller part from me." This is the way humanity probably thinks today. The Enlightenment thought that the fall into sin affects *all maturing human beings* was thus abandoned in the twentieth century at the instant. The attitude that if you're not for us you're against us gained renewed currency. Yet another idea from the Enlightenment was retained, the idea that evil can and must be *defeated* and *abolished* in a laborious struggle (against the evil groups and ideologies).

With this imbalance our situation has dramatically worsened in comparison with the Enlightenment, whose optimism about the human capacity for self-improvement was already too great. The danger has increased that the illusionary struggle against evil located in "the others" will be fought with violence, possibly even with devastating military weapons. For here the focus is no longer on God against whom we *all* have sinned and in whom *we* (and the members of other classes and groups of human society *as well*) find forgiveness of sins.

B. What Kind of Questions Do We Need to Ask to Stimulate Fresh Thinking?

Given this modern development of views on the question of evil up to the present time, we must once again come back to the question strongly emphasized by Nietzsche: *Does the idea of God represent an obstacle in dealing with evil?* Does the process of associating evil in the world with our sinful relationship to God — generally accepted in an earlier era — represent a blockage of our moral strength, an additional moral burden? Does the danger of an even deeper involvement with evil result from faith in God? Although in view of such questions the reader would expect a theological book to reject them or answer them with a "no" in the end, we must seriously ask these questions in light of a common failure of philosophical metaphysics and the church's doctrine of God in the modern era.[154]

In fact, at first glance it seems as if there is something to be said for the idea that the postulate of God's existence makes it more difficult to explain and combat evil. God can be used by believers as an alibi, allowing them to wash their hands in innocence. The reality of evil seems to speak more against than for the existence of God. In earlier times the question

154. See Jüngel, pp. xiif.

was often asked with the wording of Boethius: "If God exists" — and that was considered fairly certain — "then where does evil come from?"[155] Today it is more natural to ask the opposite question: "If evil so obviously exists and afflicts us — how can there be a God! Where do you intend to get arguments for his existence?" Therefore it is no longer *si Deus — unde malum?* but *si malum — quo modo Deus?* It seems that on closer inspection the problem of theodicy or the task of justifying God, given the evil/evils found in the world, has not proven insoluble; rather, it appears to be *solved* in terms of a rejection of faith in God that had become inevitable. Even contemporary theology is of the opinion: ". . . what bad is in Christian understanding only comes to light when he is revealed as a superior power over evil in the world."[156] But where is this happening?

The front lines seem to be straightened out, and the task seems clear now that the majority of those belonging to Western civilization sees evil as an exclusively *human* concern, mainly as a task for education, therapy, and government. Now we know where we stand. Now human endeavor and demonstration of success are in demand — and nothing else.

But what if evil originates in a hole, an absorbing emptiness, a flaw that is *always* there and stays there in spite of all our human efforts to improve conditions? What if even in the ethical experience of secular man without God, evil proves to be a hydra on whom more heads grow back than are chopped off by the ethical fighters against evil? Therefore, what if *nothing at all* helps unless God himself would bridge this chasm of evil by reapproaching the human beings separated from him and would fill this hole that had been torn open in human existence. Then the issue of God would again need to be dealt with as the key one in confronting the reality of evil today. However, this is not said as an assertion but as an initial hypothesis in need of further elaboration.

C. The Knowledge of God and Evil

In this section we will attempt to make the further elaboration we just asked for. The basic statement of all Christian and Jewish dogmatics is

---

155. Boethius, from his *The Consolation of Philosophy*, bk. 1, prose 4.
156. Translated from T. Koch, "Das Böse als theologisches Problem," *KuD* 24 (1978): 287.

this: God is the Creator and Redeemer of the world, the Sustainer and Savior of all beings that come into being and pass away. Knowing God means trusting *the* source of love and beauty, the deliverer who governs and restores the world. Knowing God is trusting *against* the appearance that the living beings of this world are condemned to an existence in which they have been sold down the river, having to fend for themselves. Certainly, it seems to be the case that God forsakes *us*: "Why have you forsaken me, Father," the dying Son of Man laments. But his Easter is already dawning there, because the God who does not answer him identifies himself *at this moment* (not only three days later!) with this forsaken dying person! We forsake *God*: "Why do you want to die in your sin?" God laments according to the testimony of the Old Testament prophets. But then he is not as close to anyone as he is to the sinner suffering the consequences of his culpable separation from God. Only first he must have hit rock bottom. This means we could *not* know God if we did not have to experience separation from God and the inaccessibility of God. If we existed in a symbiotic union with God, the knowledge of God would be just as impossible as the self-knowledge of man if he were a being totally different from God.

Man is the creature called to know God. Man finds himself — if at all — solely in the knowledge of God. This is why his heart is restless until it finds its rest in God. This key idea in the theology of Augustine can never be dispensed with. We can dispense with the issue of God himself. In sovereign splendor it will rise from the ashes and ruins of *old questions* and *familiar answers* (and from feelings of union with God that had become routine — for example, our Christmas theology!) and assume *new forms* because God as the Living One never loses his way of surprising us in his encounters with us.

Fichte's mystical hypothesis that there could not be any separation from God at all for living creatures, including human beings, is surely false, but it gets at the heart of the problem of evil: could God himself have pushed human beings into the agony of separation from him so that this species of living beings is able to "find" him and *know* him? Then the evil actions of human beings living in separation from God would be the price willed by God or accepted by God to bring about human knowledge of God?! Imagine the terrible sufferings and trials of God's creatures stricken by evil that God would have to answer for! This distressing conclusion cannot be easily dismissed, especially since it is a generally accepted Christian conviction that God's deity is incompatible with the view of those dualistic philosophies that posit a second, sinister world principle besides God, the demiurge who is responsible for evil. Dualistic thought "explains" the puzzle of evil much more easily than Christian thought (notice Augustine's Manichaean starting point on his way to the Christian life and the knowledge of God!), but it takes leave of God's omnipotence, of God as the Creator of heaven and earth. Therefore we have no other choice than to enter into a discussion of these difficult questions Christianity has always faced when it treated the reality of God and the reality of evil with equal seriousness.

We have just rejected *a limine* the intellectually alluring possibilities for explaining the existence of evil which the dualistic cosmologies offer. However, in the previous paragraph we had already rejected the theories developed in the Enlightenment and in German idealism in which evil is only a *so-called* evil because it always has "its good side" as well and even lays the foundation of our freedom. This interpretation that looks on evil as something that must be accepted (and thus downplays it) would be an intellectually elegant and satisfying solution. We felt compelled to take a stand against it: not *because* we human beings activate our intellect and want to exercise the freedom that is a part of our humanity do we have to go through the "negative experience" (Hegel) felt to be evil. Rather, we fall into evil when we activate our spirit and exercise our God-ordained freedom while at the same time not knowing God, not standing firm in the faith. (The activation of the human intellect and human freedom are *not* consequences of the fall but have been a part of our human nature *before* it and are jeopardized *by* it.)[157]

Therefore we say of evil: Evil is not the price of freedom, but its loss. Properly understood, humanity's exodus from the realm of plants and animals which laid the foundation for freedom does not have anything at all to do with Adam's fall into evil. Indeed, man's exodus out of the complete control of instinct can be regarded as humanity's God-ordained path into self-consciousness and intellectual achievement. There is nothing

---

157. See Jüngel, referring to Herder's phrase "the first creatures released from captivity." In Jüngel the first ones released from captivity are not the parents of mankind, Adam and Eve, who fell into sin, but those who believe. See also J. G. Herder, *Ideen zur Philosophie der Geschichte der Menschheit,* pt. 1, bk. 9, in *Sämtlich Werke,* ed. B. Suphan (Berlin, 1887; reprint, 1987), p. 146.

negative or evil about it! On the contrary, *this* exodus was made possible by the special loving care God lavished on the hominids. This loving care was expressed in divine words of kindness. Motivated by these divine words, the hominids ventured forth, taking their first step into freedom. However, evil only begins when man turns away from God and his Word. Evil is unbelief. Such estrangement is always fed by the *illusion* that the danger of once again losing his freedom and humanity together with his attachment to God is not so great after all. On the contrary, in the course of turning away from God, his humanity can develop even more richly than before. Genesis 3 furnished the pseudojustification for the opinion that disobedience to "God's voice" leads to demonstrable progress in civilization. And civilization is of demonstrable usefulness in the fight against illness, violent breaches of the law, and natural disasters. It increases general prosperity. In short, civilization is an effective human invention to counter the ills God has unfortunately not (yet) removed from his creation.

What is tragic and defective about this opinion is how it confuses man's troubles with evil. But civilizatory improvements were also confused with human good, with not being evil. Human freedom of movement increased by civilization was also wrongly equated with an increase in human freedom. The increasingly civilized human race stabbed itself in the back by nurturing the illusion that it could get rid of evil at the same time it achieved its successes in combating its ills, thus believing that it could become increasingly good by forgetting God. We now want to turn our attention to the complicated question of the relationship between evil and ills.

D. Can a Distinction Be Made between Evil and Natural Evil?

Malum can be rendered in German either with "Böses" or with "Übel." In the last request of the Lord's Prayer, we face the question in German of whether we should pray "deliver" us "vom Bösen" or "vom Übel." At the same time we face the problem of discerning the difference between evil *(Bösem)* and natural evil *(Übel)*. It is frequently said that evil is the event, but also the result of human guilt/sin; the natural evils, however, are the consequence of a certain defectiveness or temporal imperfection of nature (epidemics, earthquakes, death, living creatures eating each other, etc.). On the basis of this distinction we could conclude: man has to answer for evil, but God, as the author of nature, has to be responsible for natural evil. But then, to be honest, we would immediately have to ask: Why then isn't God also responsible for all the evil (and good) that human beings initiate? Human beings, too, are part of nature.

Yet in the end it is proper to distinguish between "evil" and "natural evil."[158] This is subject to several irrefutable objections only if it takes place in the manner indicated above. For it is logical and scientifically not compelling to separate our human ability to incur guilt and produce evil from the rest of nature's flaws. Even man's ability to sin originates in the evolution of nature. It is perhaps one of the major weak points in nature — this is a natural evil par excellence. But this human foible does not represent a special category of the negative; rather, it is a natural evil.

On the other hand, those who would like to proceed in a completely different manner and paint a more optimistic picture of humanity will be eager to avoid making a distinction between evil and natural evil. They will prefer the translation of *malum* with *Übel* (natural evil), as the philosophers Leibniz and Wolf did in the Enlightenment, so that they do not have to put a negative label on man (but can characterize him as a moral champion especially qualified to fight against the present shortcomings of nature).

In his *Theodicy* (1710), Leibniz totally reduced *malum* to the concept of "Übel." But at the same time, Leibniz made a distinction between *moral evil* (human sin or guilt), *physical evil* (suffering), and *metaphysical evil* (imperfection of things in only the best of all possible worlds).[159] These three kinds of evil are dependent on each other — a point disputed within the history of Western thought — in *Leibniz:* moral evil follows from metaphysical evil, but physical evil follows from moral evil.

It was natural for Leibniz to derive moral evil, that is, sin, from metaphysical evil: the root of sin is not being able or wanting to accept one's own imperfection and the imperfection of the world which in terms of the creation was inevitable, necessary, and ultimately good. Of course, it would also be conceivable (in contrast to Leibniz and in agreement with many human scientists) to see the experience of suffering and the fear of suffering (that is, physical evil) as the primary cause of human guilt/sin.

---

158. Cf. Barth, *KD,* III/3, pp. 362f.
159. Leibniz, vol. 1, sec. 21.

But as we said, Leibniz understood physical evil as a consequence of moral evil and not as its precondition. In his estimation physical illnesses are punishments for moral transgressions, but also teaching tools. But on the other hand, it would have been conceivable to derive physical evil from metaphysical evil, from the imperfection of the world at its core. Moreover, an identification of physical with metaphysical evil is always worth considering — for example, when one wants to say: the imperfection of the world is its nature, which allows living creatures to suffer.

Looking at the question whether we should distinguish between evil and natural evil, the point is this: Do we decide to see human beings who incur guilt more as *victims?* In other words, do we want to understand human evil not as a result of individuals' *own* corruption but as the result of an evil reality damaging individuals from the outside? *If we want to do this, we don't need to distinguish between evil and natural evil.* In the modern era an anthropological trend unparalleled in its influence is going precisely in this direction.

A note on this trend. Who would deny that violence perpetrated on human beings can warp them and drive them into antisocial behavior? And who would deny that suffering and warping influences that can be evident *should* be avoided. There should be no quarrel about this — also not with theology. On the other hand, we must not accept that the problem of evil can be solved and explained the way the following hypothesis implies: "Evil comes from the violent warping of human personality by other people or by anonymous conditions and structures!" Those who consider this an adequate explanation overlook the circularity of their own approach, "Why do the tormenters torment? Why do the oppressors oppress?" This response can be made: Because they endured a similar experience when they were children. And why this? Answer: wrong ideas, inhumane religious norms and customs are ultimately to blame for it. But where do these come from? In the end, we must face the fact that individuals can be and are evil of their own accord. Pushing back the causes of evil onto others also has a logical limit!

Hans Blumenberg has called attention to another context. He correctly writes that in the course of the modern era evil has changed from a negative originating in *nature* to a negative flowing from *human nature*.[160] The less

160. H. Blumenberg, *Der Prozeß der theoretischen Neugierde* (Frankfurt am Main, 1973), p. 68.

our living conditions depend directly on nature, the more frequently we experience evils that are traced back to human beings.

This process has already advanced so far that by now it no longer seems appropriate to limit such natural evil to distressing situations caused by God or nature. In fact, in many airplane crashes or massive pileups on the expressway we endure evils that are not caused by any individual human being, but that all the same are traced back to a civilization forced on nature by human beings. *The idea that the evil resulting from the sinful human heart can be distinguished from evils not resulting from human planning and responsibility but caused by nature, breaks down at this point.* In this way we can no longer tell the difference between evil and natural evil. We can make this statement with Blumenberg: more and more frequently we experience an *evil (Übel)* that is clearly forced on us externally as an alien power, but which is also clearly anthropogenic and for which there are hardly any "guilty persons" and hardly any remedy. By now we know: It is often a matter of experiencing the inevitable flip side of originally good, humanistic endeavors and realizations — for example, the negative consequences of the "dialectics of the Enlightenment"!

Here theology and the church are at the heart of present-day language problems with evil: the old distinction "evil comes from the inner being of human beings and natural evil is encountered from the outside" no longer works. Consequently, preaching that always offers a general appeal to believe and repent no longer works when we look at the negative and destructive acts that well up from human beings. As Blumenberg has shown, it is no longer a priori clear whether *our* "sinful evil deeds" are at issue here. Consequently, theology and the church must learn a new hamartiological language which in *view of these anthropogenic negative and destructive* acts can tell the difference between sin and nonsin, between what we need forgiveness for and what we need to come to terms with. However, this amounts to a *new ability* to tell the difference between evil and natural evil.

As a philosophical borderline problem, it remains an open question whether the *increasing anthropogenic* evils Blumenberg points out should ultimately be regarded as a vital expression of great, mysterious Mother Nature which can barely "afford" to accept these destructive human beings. However, this borderline idea does not seem to get us anywhere, for in this situation, not a new philosophical naturalism and determinism is helpful, but only the attempt to find out which negative and menacing phenomena in our world might be conquered or eliminated; moreover, how and by whom the struggle against them should be waged.

Thus it is valid for theologies no longer to assert objectively false "interconnections" between the sinful heart of the individual and the general weak points in the systems of modern civilization. Church dogmatics must no longer create quasi-naturalistic dogma about *the* evil human nature. Theology must reexamine where confession, forgiveness of sin, and divine redemption really belong. It must work toward ensuring that in confession it is not the individual who seeks liberation from negative forces which are either not at all his fault, not *his* evil, or which should be approached by him in a quite different way than by asking for forgiveness; for example, by personally participating in the shaping of public opinion in the political arena.

We may stick to the idea that the concept "Übel (natural evil)" stands solely for the dimension of *malum* that is properly understood as a *task* for our morality, science, and technical skill. But we must also stick to the idea that we can still "handle" that dimension of *malum* which we can never get under our control. We only recognize this dimension by recognizing God at the same time — God as the ground of being whose honor as the Creator we human beings violate in an unfathomable way (although the latter image is only an inadequate one).[161] Only when we also grasp this dimension of the *malum* do we cease to deceive ourselves completely about the reality of evil and strive to combat it in a direction in which we only entangle ourselves in it even more deeply. The beginning of our real liberation from the entanglements of evil is found exclusively in the knowledge of God. No other way is possible. The way that leads to the goal can only be embarked on from the starting place where God and man have met each other as the "kind father met his lost son."

If our liberation from the entanglements of evil is to be *possible* and if combating various manifestations of evil or various kinds of natural evil is to become successful, then the noose of evil must be *loosened* in advance from God's side. Put in traditional theological language: deliverance from evil which we ask for in the Lord's Prayer must *precede* our struggle against evil (if this struggle is not to bring about the opposite of what was intended). Whoever struggles against evil must begin by personally coming

---

161. See G. Ebeling, "Das Problem des Bösen als Prüfstein der Anthropologie," in G. Ebeling, *Wort und Glaube* (Tübingen, 1975), 3:223.

into contact with the God who forgives if his struggle is really to bring forth good and not just heighten the reality of evil. Evil has a dimension that transcends the world, not extending to the existence of a devil but to the existence of God. The devil would be at no great loss if human beings did not grasp this transcendent dimension of evil, but *God* would be, or, more precisely, the good coming to *us* from him.

It is not unlike people in the world to inflict hurt or injury on the Creator of the world, figuratively speaking. Again, figuratively speaking, it is not unlike people to act in such a way that the Creator is moved to rip "something" out of his own divine "heart" and give it to human beings so that they can exist. (If only we could express this more appropriately than was done in the images just used!) Of course, you could consider what I have said as mere speculation or a "simple matter of faith" that cannot be proved by anything. The latter is also true. If you want, you can dismiss everything that is said about this subject in Christology as being irrelevant. But man will never, ever be genuinely successful in his struggle against the ills of the world or against "evil" without recognizing this special affection of God for us. The key is found in God, not in us.

In conclusion: It is not a matter of sorting out the negative phenomena in our world and calling some "natural evil" and others "evil." Such a distinction, and the problems associated with it that we saw at the outset, is ultimately neither necessary nor possible. But it is a matter of distinguishing a transcendent dimension concerning God from the immanent dimensions when we look at what is negative. When in our recognition of God's existence we reach this transcendental abyss of evil that "wounds" the ground of being, then *all* appearances of *malum* in our world become *mere natural evils,* no longer having anything mysterious or demonic about them, nothing that would prevent us from struggling against them even when they seem so frightening.

E. *Unde Malum?*

For millennia human beings have been seeking to fathom the mystery of where evil comes from and how it enters the world. The desired goal in this search is ultimately to eliminate and defeat the evil that has been understood and exposed. But this goal is not achieved. The conceit of thinking that evil can be brought under control is always tantamount to an unnoticed and unwanted increase in evil. For man himself is the origin of evil. His exocentric position in the cosmos (his specific intellectual faculties) causes him to be tempted time and again to turn his own merely fleeting and relative significance deceitfully into absolute significance. In this way he disrupts the cosmos and destroys himself and others. In this way, too, he sins and forfeits his relative freedom because he yields to temptation and deludes himself about his true condition. Then it is said — even Augustine said it — that his *will* brings forth evil. But even the will is no *primum movens*. Man succumbs to temptation, he overestimates himself, he finds no limits on his misguided endeavors, his striving is everything.

Certainly Plato's brilliant and consequential intuition of the existence of *two worlds* — on the one hand the transitory world of earthly, material phenomena tainted with many flaws and imperfections, on the other hand the perfect, complete world of the intellect or ideas — opened up a multitude of possibilities to explain the essence and origin of evil and the ills of this world. Even after 750 years Augustine experienced this intuition as a great and fresh source of help in his thinking and writing about evil. In a sense he rediscovered this intuition within the framework of Christianity. He more than any other person has continued to mediate it to the present-day world.

However, after Augustine had found his way out of Manichaeanism and its influence on his thought, he emphasized how inappropriate it would be to ask *where* evil comes from. The ultimate cause of evil's emergence in the world, especially in the human will, cannot be found. Inquiring into the cause of evil is also not in the best interest of Christianity. It is advisable to examine the question, *"What* is evil?"[162] instead of dealing with the question, *"Where* does evil come from?" Moreover, Augustine believed that human beings should give more thought to the question, *"unde bonum?,"* to the origin of the many good things we depend on for our existence. Our attention would then be directed to God's activity as Creator.

What the Christian bishop Augustine *also* left behind is the endeavor to come to grips with evil intellectually and epistimologically, make its status and function transparent in the world process, and thus practically defeat it, an endeavor which is the vital center of all Gnostic systems. The

---

162. Augustine, *De natura Boni, contra Manichaeos,* book I, chap. 4, Migne, *Patrologia Latina,* 42, 553, and see chap. 2, Migne, *Patrologia Latina,* 32, 1345f.

Gnostic, Manichaean question "unde malum?" is not good for us in Augustine's opinion because it allows us to overlook how we ourselves cause and represent evil at the core of our personhood without being able to attribute this to external causes. Man will only entangle himself more deeply in evil by coming under the influence of the inquiry into supposedly external ultimate causes of evil. He will only delude himself more.

This pointer confirms once again that it is appropriate in any case to distinguish between evil and ills. For no theologian has the right to claim that we should *not* inquire into the causes of the ills in the world. It would be *against* the Bible if Christians did not want to be concerned about the causes of suffering that could be avoided or overcome. It would be a gross misunderstanding of Matthew 5:39 if, for example, Christians would consciously miss opportunities to protect themselves from lightning "in order not to resist evil." The desire to investigate the origin or the causes of ills is also one of the most valuable motives of modern science. However, the exploration of possible *side effects* resulting from the elimination of hardships we experienced and combated as ills and turning out to be new evils is part of the ethos of the scientist conducting such investigations. This means that an ethos must finally be developed that can endure these ills and share their burden fairly in order to avoid even greater ills. A largely unfulfilled but urgent desideratum!

It is known that Augustine not only taught that the origin of evil is unfathomable but also that a special substance constituting evil within the creation is nonexistent.[163] The creation is not a mixture of good being and evil being, but all created things are good, and evil undermines this good. Evil is parasitic on the good. It does not have its own substance, but is *privatio boni,* a lack and absence of the good, a hole in the comprehensive good representing all that exists or has been created, a hole that can only be produced by man (by man's will). The Protestant theologian W. Mostert, for example, teaches even today along the same lines as Augustine: "The place of evil is where the good should and could be. The good is robbed of its place."[164] This displacement of the good happens because we ourselves wish to take its place with our plans and our activity and imagine that in doing so we *create* good in the first place. It is just this attitude that is the root of evil.

---

163. See Koch, pp. 294ff.
164. Translated from Mostert, p. 465.

Evil is the partial absence of the good in the cosmos — a result of robbery. "The robber of the good is man": "That there is evil where good was and should be is a reality caused by man."[165] However, if man is seen from this perspective, he is at the same time seen as a sinner. As a sinner he actively commits the *privatio boni,* the dismantling of being, the destruction of parts of creation. This predatory activity is so fateful "because man himself is a good created by God."[166] He destroys himself, he ultimately contradicts himself when he sins. He, the human being, enters into nothingness when he sins, and he draws his fellow creatures into this realm. Christian theology must never distance itself from these basic statements about evil.

But we can now ask whether this doctrine of evil is compatible with the acceptance of a devil's or Satan's personal existence. Moreover, we can ask whether the definition of evil as *privatio boni* does not misjudge the effectiveness and power of evil in its autonomous existence. Perhaps the hypothesis that a devil or an independent satanic principle must exist in the world lies much closer to modern intellectual presuppositions than is generally believed. We will deal with this question in the next section.

F. The Church's Language Problems with Evil — The Devil and the Incarnation of Evil in the Soul

Now we must discuss the difficult question how theology and the church should speak of the epitome of evil extending into the realm of transcendence, that is, deeply affecting God under the conditions of the modern era. Is the religious and dogmatic language of the church out of date? Does a theological terminology that not only sees evil in the human, secular realm but claims that in the leading figure it affects and violates God take into account the conditions of modern thought (for example, subjectivism and anthropocentrism)? Does it not also fail to address, for example, the insights of modern depth psychology? Does the church become an agent of evil by no longer facing it at its virulent focal points? The church's language seems to have been overtaken by secular speech in two ways. On the one hand, "belief in the devil" — reckoning with Satan's reality — is

---

165. Translated from W. Mostert, "Gott und das Böse. Bemerkungen zu einer vielschichtigen Frage," *ZThK* 77 (1980): 467.

166. Mostert, "Gott und das Böse," p. 469.

gaining greater attraction and new plausibility in many places as the church makes less of a case for recognizing a satanic personality. On the other hand, not a few depth psychologists are asking us to recognize the reality and numinous power of evil in our own soul. Following C. G. Jung we recognize this reality not by praying for redemption from evil or by praying to be spared this evil but at most by praying for the strength to *integrate* it. And this evil is not only a *privatio boni,* but a powerful reality sui generis.

Today theology and the church should definitely prove capable of carrying on a dialogue with both sides.

1. "The Evil One" — Our Language Problem with the Devil

Three theoretical models are relevant:

1. It is not worth taking up this topic.
2. Those who consider "God" a reality should also do this with regard to the devil in order to be consistent.
3. God exists, but not the devil. For the "Evil One" is absolute nothingness. Nothingness is about reality but not about a person because personhood presupposes relationship. Nothingness, however, is that which is totally unrelated. . . .

The modern era mainly speaks in favor of the first model. The danger of a Counter Enlightenment and a regressive demonization of realities inflamed by fear becoming associated with a "belief" in the devil is greater than the danger that the masses are being held by the throat by *him* because they hardly "feel" the devil at the moment.

The second model is the most questionable: It is not clear how it could even be corroborated by logic, let alone history and theology. The Old Testament gives us a beautiful example of how a religion knew God during many centuries but not a devil. Then it began to reckon with the existence of Satan at a certain point in time and under certain influences. The case *for* a devil who must be thought of as God's opposite is supposed to serve the *theological* purpose of "exonerating" God and human beings. In this way God is not supposed to be a possible source of evil. And in this way man is supposed to be rescued intellectually as a being in whom goodness and the freedom to do good dwells (according to the motto "we can't be so bad that all the horrible things we do are completely our fault"). Thus, with feeble logic, the devil is "pushed forward." But, correctly understood, this does not change the problem at all: God is not "exonerated" because, why does he allow the devil? Man is not exonerated because, "what religion that is taken seriously would allow him to attribute his evil deeds to another person who is then made responsible for them (and who even dwells in another world)?"

The Heidelberg speculative theologian Karl Daub (1765-1836) probably mounted the most thoughtful defense of the devil. It emerged from the critical discussion of the concept of God F. W. J. Schelling developed in his *Philosophical Inquiries into the Nature of Human Freedom and the Objects Associated with It* (1809).[167] Schelling, who on his part endeavored to overcome the aporia of earlier views, was looking for a conceptual derivation of evil in God, avoiding any dualism in explaining the world and yet *not* declaring God to be the cause of evil. In Schelling's view, a dark ground of being came together with God's radiant and orderly will in the event of the creation of the world. The dark ground of being is an exclusively wild, selfish, and yearning desire to achieve a breakthrough into existence. However, God's will is already shaped by love and understanding. The creatures thus have a double origin in God. They are free to detach both these principles from their harmonious and meaningful coexistence *in God* and to turn them against each other. Evil flows into creation from creatures who do this.

In his strange work *Judas Iscariot or Evil in Relation to Good* (1816/18),[168] Daub tried to improve this theory because it ultimately did not separate the origin of evil from God. Daub's correction consists of the introduction of Satan's existence, which proves to be intellectually compelling and necessary! But how did Satan come into being? He was created by himself without a reasonable motive as a "nasty miracle." He did not emerge *from* creation which is "good," but he was created *in it* on his own initiative (vol. 1, p. 136; vol. 2, pp. 96f.). In him Schelling's dark ground of being became a living being by "spontaneous combustion," bypassing God's will. Because he is not associated with the creation, he is the "absolutely accidental being" standing *against* creation and its divine

<hr />

167. *Philosophische Untersuchungen über das Wesen der menschlichen Freiheit.*
168. K. Daub, *Judas Ischarioth oder das Böse im Verhältnis zum Guten,* 2 pts. in 1 vol. (Heidelberg, 1816, 1818).

author from the beginning (vol. 1, pp. 171ff.): "God is not God to him, but he is God to himself; He considers not eternity to be reality, but temporality with its scandalous chronology, called history; not what is holy, but what is spatial is essential to him; not love . . ., but hate is love to him; not the truth . . ., but lies are the truth to him" (vol. 2, p. 446).

Since the so-called spirit of the times always causes theology a great deal of trouble, Daub's assertions had the welcome side effect of being able to unmask the "spirit of the time" as the "spirit of lies." But it is sufficiently clear: Even Daub was only able to put into the existence of "Satan" what others understand as the essence of sinful *man:* lies, enmity toward God, unfounded hatred of God's creation, etc. As a whole Daub's arguments *for* the devil live more on the problems observed by Daub in Schelling's system than in a solid exegesis of Scripture and dogmatic foundation. This is especially apparent in his questionable theory: as Christ has to be considered the incarnation of the good, the one who opposed him, Judas Iscariot, was the incarnation of evil. Judas — "in the end only a shell of a person" — committed suicide, a supposedly logical step for him considering his nature (vol. 1, pp. 22ff.).[169]

As a theological interpreter of contemporary history in his era, he paid attention to miscarriages and other biological and physical abnormalities — signs of Satan! However, on the basis of his system he could demonstrate to a citizenry unsettled by natural science with great dogmatic certainty that "chance" cannot be considered the Creator or Cocreator of the world (vol. 2, p. 427), for chance is supposedly the devil's origin and nature!

The third model contains two difficult questions that must not be dismissed. The first one is: Is God ultimately the author of evil? The other one is: Is the impersonal, evil power of nothingness a component of every human person which we either *suppress* to our own detriment or *consciously incorporate* into us in the process of personal maturing? We should not dismiss the first of these questions because we must seek to show those who ask it how senseless it is. It can never lead to a reasonable conclusion because we could never rule out the *feeling* that when he is working for our good, the Creator of the world is nevertheless the source of evil. The

---

169. Quotations from Daub translated from R. Schanne, *Sündenfall und Erbsünde in der spekulativen Theologie. Die Weiterbildung der protestantischen Erbsündenlehre unter dem Einfluß der idealistischen Lehre vom Bösen,* Theologie im Übergang, vol. 1 (Bern/FFM, 1976), pp. 160ff.; see also Jüngel, p. 30 n. 15, as well as p. 35.

origin of evil is not a problem that can be clarified intellectually. But it is not easy to accept this. The only person who can do this is the one who recognizes himself as a sinner. The second question leads us to the problem of whether theology and the church should finally move closer to the ancient idea that evil, too, must become flesh, be incarnated, taking into account the recent findings of depth psychology. This complex problem will be examined now.

2. Incarnation of Evil or Redemption from Evil?

On the basis of texts such as C. G. Jung's *Answer to Job* (1952),[170] we can illustrate the wide-ranging nature of the question to be discussed here: *Experience* seems to support the idea that not only a radiant, friendly, reasonable, ethically constructive, and law-abiding divine force desires to be "conceived" in man (just as Mary conceived the Son of God), but also a dark, anarchistic, destructive force. "God" has two "sons," Christ and Satan, and we human beings must pay dearly (with inner turmoil and a failed existence) if we permit only one of the two to become flesh and blood in us. The prerequisite for gaining the strength to "accept" *my* evil is becoming more and more the person I, myself, should unmistakably become and, above all, becoming a person of peace and finding peace myself. According to Jung,

> The Christian "idea" that evil is merely *privatio boni* does not agree with the psychological findings. Psychological experience shows that whatever we call "good" is balanced by an equally substantial "bad" or "evil." (Characteristically Jung does *not* make a distinction between the two.) If "evil" is nonexistent, then whatever is must necessarily be "good." Dogmatically (referring to the dogma of the church), neither "good" nor "evil" can be derived from man, since the "Evil One" existed before man as one of the "Sons of God."[171] The idea of the *privatio boni* began to play a role in the church only after Mani. Before this heresy (of the church!), Clement of Rome taught that God rules the world with a right and a left hand, the right being Christ, the left Satan. Clement's view is clearly *monotheistic* as it unites the opposites in one God. Later Christianity, however, is dualistic, inasmuch as it splits off one-half of

170. C. G. Jung, *Antwort auf Hiob* (1952), in Jung, *Gesammelte Werke,* vol. 11, *Zur Psychologie westlicher und östlicher Religion* (Olten, ²1973), pp. 385-506.

171. Jung is wrong at this place: According to the dogma evil *has* its origin in man.

the opposites, personified in Satan, and he is *eternal* in his state of damnation. This crucial question forms the point of departure for the Christian theory of redemption. If Christianity claims to be a monotheistic religion, the presupposition of the opposites united in the one good is inevitable.[172]

Jung's description of the dogmatic development does not get the historical facts adequately right. Apart from the fact that Clement of Rome did not signify a "turning point in the concept of God" that would have changed everything "later," too little consideration is given to the fact that Augustine decisively moved away from a dualistic concept of God at the same time he turned away from Manichaeanism and reconciled this with his description of evil as *privatio boni.* Because Jung probably took concepts of God from nineteenth-century liberal theology as his standard, he also did not see that influential Christian theologians — I think of Luther or the Occamists — endeavored to hold together the idea of the God revealed in Christ and the hidden God. They did this precisely because they assumed and sensed the "conflict" in God himself.

For Jung it was significant that his own father failed as a pastor and as a human being because he was not able to meet the faith requirements and ethical demands of his God, or so it seemed to Jung. His profession was his ruin. The duty of being a witness for God was too much for him. From a psychoanalytic point of view, what Jung saw happening was a person in his relationship to God being put under a lot of pressure by *God's* dark side. (See the corresponding figure of thought in *Answer to Job,* p. 489.) A person was "identified" with that evil that is actually God's evil. Only when a person learns to accept this evil as *his* evil in the process of so-called individuation can he cope with this burden. This is what Jung meant by the idea that it is necessary for God's dark side to be incarnated in us.

But how does Jung think about man as the *source* of evil? And how about man's redemption by God? Is he seriously advising Christianity, which sees God's triune nature defined by the man Jesus, to understand God not only as love but as love and Satan in one being, and to honor him in this way as well? Is confidence in God, is love for God ever possible in this way?

We will only make headway and can only take Jung seriously when,

172. Jung, *Antwort auf Hiob,* pp. 505f.

first, we share his concern that excessive demands placed on human beings by the divine should be considered unacceptable (and objectively not a given), and second, when we notice precisely the location of his discussion about the incarnation of God's dark side (which is necessary, given the conditions of Christian history).

"Sin" and "evil" play a role in the experiences of so many modern men and women only when *detached* from the knowledge of faith and a believing relationship to God. What is "sinful" or "evil" is determined in their mind by more or less irrational conventions, traditions, and external authorities. In fact, this is true of modern society: evil no longer has any official definition; in the course of the modern era it has fallen into the unconscious, subjective, and private realm. The individual is alone with his evil. Because he lacks the language to express "his dark side" or make it public and because he carries his dark side inside himself partially for historical reasons that are not his fault, he runs the danger of being torn apart emotionally. Thus, Jung considers him not only entitled but also obligated not to have to deny one-half of himself. For this would be good neither for him in general nor for his humanity in particular. Theology can also agree with this without any problem.

Must we understand Jung a little better than he understood himself in order to see *in this* the crucial point in his discussion of the incarnation of God in us (beyond Jesus Christ)? At any rate, we *must* understand him in this way and not as a teacher of religion who posited a new concept of God which makes God unworthy of our honor and worship. It is helpful, for example, when a doctor encourages individuation and helps a patient to cushion and withstand the fears associated with it where there is no faith or vital relationship to God based on the gospel that leads to an understanding of our own sin (what would make the above-mentioned problem superfluous — the problem of an earlier faith and ethos sinking into the realm of the unconscious). Providing help so that human beings are able to integrate their second side shrouded in darkness is without a doubt what Luther would have called "a good work." The fact that such an occurrence is experienced as "numinous" is anthropologically understandable. The fact that in our culture it is frequently associated with remnants of Christian symbols and language was historically bound to happen. The result is the present inflationary use of the term "incarnation." All this must be accepted by a sensible theology after it has become clear about the situation. People who are helped in Jung's way to resist their shadow and their opposite sex arche-type and grant both entry into their own *conscious* being are not con-demned right from the start to turn their back on the Christian God and make use of "self-redemption." It is conceivable that they become capable of knowing themselves as sinners before God and thus as a source of evil only at an advanced stage of individuation. Only then are they capable of enjoying divine forgiveness and grace. The test of Jung's statements on all these questions is whether in the end man knows how to be grateful for his life and for the undeserved "wings" that have been spread over and under him and others. Therefore, the question is whether man experiences grace and whether he learns to appreciate what he has received without having earned it. In addition, we must ask if man now understands that how he can find himself is *not* the only problem but that it is flanked by the equally important problem of how he can avoid diminishing the life of other creatures or depriving them of life. The test of Jung's good work of helping man develop his self is also that the person who receives such support no longer pushes responsibility for evil away from himself and onto an external authority, but that he recognizes his responsibility, becoming more humble in the sight of his neighbor and giving God the honor. The following concluding section is intended to show that only this goal is hopeful and respectable and that it is urgent to strive for it.

G. Shoah — Absolute Evil

The theological books of earlier times know little or nothing of what we are now going to focus on. Absolute evil is the destruction and desecration of human life, including his soul, *without any recognizable reason*. In all of us there is a need to assume that evil is at least anthropologically *under-standable* if it can't be avoided, defeated, and abolished. But a great illusion is hidden behind the idea that we can at least theoretically get evil under control!

There are two classical "attempts to understand." They see the root of evil in man's being seized either by hubris or by soul-destroying drives (concupiscence). Numerous, very diverse theological, philosophical, and human scientific interpretations of *why* the conditions of human existence virtually provoke him to exceed his limits follow these classical interpretations. Because we are compelled to elevate our ego to a place at the center of our world, the way we live our human existence all too easily leads to an excess of egotistical behavior and, thus, to evil. In the past century, for example, J. Müller, in his significant model of a doctrine of sin, vehemently advocated the view that the anthropological reason for the origin of sin and evil is to be understood in no other way.[173] His (somewhat less) scholarly antipode was R. Rothe, in whose ethics the classical concupiscence theory is developed just as emphatically and with equally good reasons.[174] But S. Kierkegaard went a step beyond both positions. Driven by the intellectually unsatisfying situation that the reason for the origin of evil is supposed to be something that itself represents a part of sinfully corrupt life — as hubris or as concupiscence — Kierkegaard attempted to locate the reason for evil at an even earlier stage. It originated in man's *fear* of the possible, real consequences of his freedom — thus fear of nothing (at all), of what has not yet occurred.[175] It was a brilliant move for Kierkegaard to use the terms "fear" and "nothing." But did Kierkegaard actually find the root of evil/sin that is neither good nor bad?

In the present era, E. Drewermann emphatically defends Kierkegaard's attempted solution,[176] whereas W. Pannenberg[177] does not see any real progress in Kierkegaard's attempt to go beyond the classical models of understanding evil. Kierkegaard, too, made an intellectual mistake because he portrayed fear as something supposedly neutral in relation to good and evil, whereas even in Kierkegaard's own portrayal it is in fact subject to the same objections as hubris and concupiscence (if it is to be the origin of evil). Fear, too, is negative, for man's concern for himself is articulated in it. In Kierkegaard's view it is selfishness itself.[178] Therefore, does it not also signify human corruption since it is fundamentally foreign to animals in Kierkegaard's view? This could be further debated. Of course, Pannenberg's objection does not mean that we should now go looking for the anthropological origins of evil and track them down even more thoroughly than the classical attempts were able to (of which Kierkegaard's presenta-

173. Müller, 2:199.

174. R. Rothe, *Theologische Ethik,* 5 vols. (1845; Wittenberg, [2]1869-71), 3:12ff.

175. S. Kierkegaard, *Der Begriff Angst* (1844), *Gesammelte Werke,* trans. E. Hirsch, pt. 11 and 12 (Düsseldorf, 1965), pp. 38ff. (4:312ff.).

176. Drewermann, pt. 3, pp. 436ff.

177. Pannenberg, *Anthropologie in theologischer Perspektive,* pp. 99f.

178. Kierkegaard, *Der Begriff Angst,* p. 61.

tion of the concept "fear" is now a part). Furthermore, it seems unproductive if in the future the arguments gleaned from J. Müller and R. Rothe are repeated in ever new variations in the hope that they can help one of these two explanatory models to gain general acceptance.

We should ignore the patent explanations for the origin of evil that are offered time and again. For example, psychoanalysis holds that evil arises when human beings are put under pressure from their sufferings. Enumerating *particular* factors in life as the *cause* of evil from the very beginning should be regarded as a failed venture. Whoever would want to go further would have to find a formal concept, as Kierkegaard did, in which many and various individual phenomena in life can be explained and their contradictions resolved. If I were to consider it proper to continue thinking along these lines, it would seem most obvious to me to interpret the task of existing as a human person as a basically excessive burden — and, in the end, I would then say: evil comes from this excessive burden. But, ultimately, this whole line of thought is misguided because it originates more in the hygienic need of psychology to bring intellectual order into the actual disorder of our life than in actually tracking down evil itself. This line of thought also very clearly reveals the old idealistic desire to find "something" that avoids the excessive burden (and thus evil).

If there is no other way, we must clarify the problem by using Hitler as an example. Did Hitler become evil because life was an excessive burden for him as a human being? Is it appropriate to illustrate the anthropological reason for the origin of evil on the basis of a concentrated social scientific examination of his life? Psychoanalytic and similar studies of his personality are already existent. But is there an interpreter who could find the real reason for the evil radiating from Hitler in such ways?

The reality of evil is such that even our need at least to understand its power over us remains unsatisfied, and we can hardly prevent it from happening. We are not right if we think the significantly evil figures in history were just sick people with a neurotic childhood and unsuccessful socialization in their youth. We would like to have it that way, but it is not so. Certainly evil often *appears* in forms which must be considered to be such a sickness. But this sickness is a result, not the reason for evil. Evil is absolutely without any reason. Fortunately, it does not always appear so. It is a special mercy of God to keep a certain window of our spirit half closed most of the time so that we hardly get to see the abyss of our own self. This abyss would show us: we do not enter life in such a way that the good is normal and evil is the exception. It can also be the reverse. Everything is possible because the hoped-for ultimate orderliness of things does not appear in that abyss, but instead their complete indifference. In his natural desires and in the quiet of his soul, *one* human being is a cruel agent of evil, but the *other* loves people and spreads warmth. Or both are found in one and the same person. But only in exceptional cases — thank God! — does evil appear to us in its absolute unrestrained and unchallenged form in which it *impassively* nullifies all that is human as if it were mere dirt: our humanity — not safeguarded by any Platonic idea not secured by any educational work of the millennia.

The reason for evil is so clearly beyond our human control that nothing but God — likewise beyond our human control — can possibly be conceived as being helpful regarding evil. Wherever absolute evil appears because God is not in front of it, there is no other choice but immediate death, whether it occurs by suicide or some other way. Wherever absolute evil appears, the creature perishes perhaps not with a cry for God, but as a cry for God. Whoever knows this will hardly cease praying and being grateful for every word from God.

* * *

Filip Müller, a Czech Jew, is a survivor of the five liquidations carried out by the so-called special commando unit of Auschwitz. In the camp he was one of the people who had to do the work in the gas chambers and crematoria. Müller, at that time a robust twenty-year-old, appears in Claude Lanzmann's documentary *Shoa* as a miracle of survival and as an unforgettable witness and reporter. He saw the most horrible things. His hands had to perform the most monstrous deeds — even to the point of "stirring" human bodies in the ovens. But he tells about this in a calm and warm, very melodious voice, articulating the German language in a refined and elegant fashion — what a contrast! The viewer wonders how it is possible for this man looking back to keep his composure. Evidently the memory of the victims being surprised every time (as he believes) by the deprivation of their life in the death chamber helps him. From what Müller observed, they had hope to the end.

But one time he had a different experience. A rather large Czech "family shipment" that had come from Müller's home region, of all places, was "treated well" in Auschwitz for months on account of specific instructions.

An SS officer gave the group his word of honor that Auschwitz was only an intermediate stop until they could be brought to a permanent place for resettlement. A few of the members in the shipment knew Müller personally. However, to his horror, one day they all appeared together in the "undressing room." Müller reports: "For once most of these people did not follow the order to undress. Shouting in a loud voice, they accused a group of officers who had shown up to be observers: 'We were lied to! We want to live! We want to work!' And as they protested, they looked right into the faces of the SS executioners."[179] Their boldness in looking into the faces of these thugs was unusual.

In response these "unfortunate people" were beaten with "unusual ferocity" while the officers looked on as if they were not involved. "And suddenly I heard a choir beginning to sing. A song spread through the undressing room; they began to sing the Czech national anthem and the 'Hatikwa.' It moved me so deeply, this . . . this. . . ." *Now* Müller can suddenly no longer keep on telling his story. He demands of the film crew: "Turn off the cameras!" He is crying. The unbelievable contrast between what these people had to suffer and their song was beyond all comprehension. Their song seemed so meaningless, so unrealistic, appealing once again to a caring human community, evoking basic human hope that reverberates in a vacuum. When Müller's report touches this point, the striking composure he once had is instantly a thing of the past. The mere memory of this scene seems to break his heart and soul all over again.

When filming can be resumed later, Müller explains that at that very moment, many years ago, his strong will to survive completely collapsed. "This incident with my countrymen made me understand that my life no longer had any value." All of a sudden, in a very loud and very harsh voice, he utters an additional question: "What was I supposed to live for?" When the last sparks of hope are stamped out, evil is perfected. Müller was dragged into the experience of absolute evil. No one can survive such an experience. It was not the physical destruction of thousands and thousands of human beings that brought him to this question, "Why live?" and to this end — an experience that led him to become hardened — *but experiencing the complete uselessness of all human values,* both the spirit of love

179. This quote and the following quotes translated from C. Lanzmann, *Shoa,* with a foreword by Simone de Beauvoir (originally published in French, 1985; German edition, Düsseldorf, 1986), pp. 218-20.

and the spirit of hope. Its uselessness manifested itself in an indifferent, hopeless room ("the undressing room"). The human element together with the sparks of a higher being supposedly dwelling in it proved to be dirt. That is why Müller involuntarily detached himself from his "work unit," and, at that very moment, he decided to die and went into the gas chamber with the others.

One of the women who recognized him in the gas chamber said to him (according to Müller's report): "You want to die. But that doesn't make any sense. Your dying will not bring us life. This is no way to act. You must get out of here, you must keep telling the world about our suffering here, what a great injustice has been done to us . . . what has happened here." At the last moment Müller returned to his unit. A spark of hope remained in that woman who persuaded him to return, and that hope was pinned on Müller. In contrast to him, that woman still clung to the hope that reality is a structure of meaning. A future reporter could announce the injustice occurring now to the whole world. In so doing, absolute meaninglessness would not descend on these murders like darkness. Justice and injustice, humanity and inhumanity would once again be separated in a just judgment. The woman died. But she did not recognize absolute evil — the denunciation of humanity as filth.

*   *   *

Theological doctrines and the churches must not speak of *sin* in such a way that their language unintentionally becomes a denunciation of humanity as filth. May theology beware of ever judging any people or humankind *ad maiorem Dei gloriam* to be "bad" or unimportant. The believer may really apply this biblical word only to himself: "Because of your wrath there is no health in my body; my bones have no soundness because of my sin" (Ps. 38:3). And he may say this only if hope still glimmers within him because he already knows God is an "eternal refuge."

In view of *evil,* the language of the church must endeavor to use this term exclusively for the bad contingently erupting from the individual, the malevolence which man cannot attribute to an external cause. Theology should not be allowed to consider what C. G. Jung calls evil and, at the same time, "God's dark side" as real evil! Although it is true that our self can be flooded by dark and "numinously" active forces, and although it must be conceded that much of what is not good ultimately flows from us through no fault of our own due to external conditioning; nevertheless, theology must not consider all this evil. Theology must distinguish between real evil and the fragments of an ancestral religiosity that act as a poison in which these fragments unfold their valences without being integrated into our own intellectual and emotional life. It must distinguish between what can be treated by means of psychotherapy (and this is not a question of evil) and what the foundation of all love — God — must redeem us from (and only this can be evil). When the churches learn to make this distinction, their theology will gain an unpolemical as well as independent and cooperative relationship to the human sciences whose purpose it is to support people in their efforts to be liberated from a dark and malicious captivity. It will not fight over concepts such as "incarnation" with these human sciences. Rather, it should do this in intramural theological discussions. For its part, such theology will once again concentrate more on the issue of how the church can speak of God today in such a way that this truth becomes apparent: We, together with all of our sciences and therapies, do not have to perish ultimately in absolute evil. It is the task of theology to give reasons for this hope and the freedom to be truly human associated with it. The theological doctrine of sin is part of this task and supports it, but what actually constitutes this doctrine is to be discussed in the last two chapters of the book.

CHAPTER 3

Systematic Development: What Is Sin?

The arrangement of paragraphs in this chapter needs an explanation. After the discussion of Genesis 3 in the previous chapters, laying a New Testament foundation would have been the obvious thing to do, followed by a historical *tour d'horizon* of church history and the history of this doctrine, finally speaking of sin from the perspective of systematic theology and making the application to our responsibility at the present time. I did not choose this path. It would have detached the dogmatic component from the exegetical and historical components in an inappropriate way. Therefore, right at the outset — in the middle of the book — the systematic theological approaches to the hamartiology I intend to develop here are together in a concentrated form. Of course, the following seventh section assumes the prior study of hamartiology in the New Testament and in the history of Christianity (especially the Reformation). The results of this study were incorporated into the following discussion. Nevertheless, three paragraphs will follow that are devoted to more specialized questions from New Testament texts as well as texts from the history of dogma. The last of these, section X, will make the transition to the final chapter on *the forgiveness* of sins, with which a theological book on the doctrine of sin could well have begun. Perhaps hamartiologies of the future will proceed in such a fashion.

SECTION VII
THE EVENT OF SINNING — ITS ESSENTIAL ASPECTS

A. The Comprehensibility and Recognizability of Sin

Sin can be explained and understood even outside the realm of faith. We have to distinguish the question whether a person can *understand* sin from the question whether a person *recognizes* his own sin in particular. With regard to the latter question, this principle is valid: The event of sinning can be made comprehensible not only to believers. The anthropological, cosmological, and theological implications of this event can be developed in such general terms that everyone can clearly see why it is not just of importance for people shaped by antiquated religious ideas. It will then be apparent: The fewer "human deficits" there are anywhere, the less ignorance there will be as far as sin is concerned. The more personal freedom, openness, and strength are available to handle one's own fear without suppressing one's memories to any great extent, the more familiarity may be expected with the disaster of sin that destroys everything. This insight was the first fruit of Kierkegaard's intense preoccupation with the dark greatness of sin.

However, what has been said seems to contradict an often quoted sentence of Luther which states that our sinful condition is only disclosed to us with the help of *faith,* because this is not evident to us.[1] Nevertheless, it is not a matter of being in conflict with what has just been discussed. For Luther speaks here of how man recognizes *himself* to be a sinner. Luther ties this to faith. I would, however, like us to beware of misunderstanding — even of misunderstanding Luther. I advocate the position that even the event of faith must not be understood in a narrow sense. The essence of faith is misunderstood when that faith appears as a system of guidance characteristics only of committed members of faith communities, something added on to "normal" human self-understanding. In fact, belief and unbelief are universal human attitudes. Faith is higher than all reason neither in a mysterious way nor beyond all experience. Of course, it is true: not always does a person know that he believes. He especially does not know that his attitude represents unbelief. However, the fact that someone categorizes himself as a Christian and thinks he believes in God does not yet mean that he really believes and recognizes his sins.

---

1. *Luthers Werke,* Weimarer Ausgabe, 56:231, lines 8-11; hereafter cited as WA.

Luther's sentence mentioned in the preceding paragraph certainly does not mean that only such Christians who are given the gift of loyalty to the church and who believe in God within the community of faith are capable of recognizing their sinfulness. Rather, Luther's statement is to be unfolded in the following direction. Recognition of one's own sin *cannot* be expected when human beings are in an acute situation in which they have lost confidence, are weighed down by depression or feelings of guilt, or accuse themselves. In an acute state of disintegration sadness, regret, or anger may be felt, but the strength and freedom to recognize one's own sin is lacking. However, the chance that this strength and freedom will appear is found where goodness is experienced in the midst of guilt — which is almost unimaginable — and where God allows faith to emerge in the context of *this* experience.

"Sin" (and also "evil") is more unmysterious than mysterious,[2] more banal[3] than interesting, more superficial than deep-rooted — and yet we cannot get it under control.

The word "sin" also does not mean the kind of human misbehavior that can be "explained" today in psychological terms and "treated" therapeutically, whereas in an earlier age it was still exploited and combated with irrational mythological or religious formulas against the backdrop of the church's lust for domination. In fact, sin cannot be dealt with *scientifically*[4] because, although it is superficial and banal, it has long since been playing its destructive role in us when we get down to the task of opening up reality scientifically for ourselves. In relation to sin, science comes too late. Sin casts a shadow on everything human at an early stage, before we develop our interests. Later we will get to know this early stage of our life better as "self-justification."

We all have no spontaneous interest in this shadow and thus in the subject of sin — even if we think we are highly fascinated by the phenomenon of evil. This is the main reason why sin is so unknown and the word "sin" is so little appreciated among us — only secondarily is this because we have often foolishly misnamed relatively harmless or scientifically solvable events with the word "sin."

Understanding real sin, and recognizing one's own sinful condition

2. Against R. Blomme, *Widerspruch in Freiheit. Eine Analyse des heutigen Sündenbewußtseins und der Sünde,* Werdende Welt 5 (Limburg, 1965), pp. 49, 52. Sin and evil are a "mystery" because they touch "the deepest" part of us.

3. G. Mann, *Erinnerungen und Gedanken. Eine Jugend in Deutschland* (FFM, 1986), pp. 320ff.

4. Sin cannot be dealt with but only forgiven.

besides, is of great significance for all life on earth. Not the act of sin itself seals our doom. But invariably the knowledge of sin is no longer pursued by anyone, by any group that could act as a representative of society as a whole — it is this lack of knowledge that seals our doom. This is the main reason I am writing this book. I will attempt once again to expose the most important conditions necessary to understand, recognize, and speak of sin in a situation where any capability of finding a language for the reality of sin has been largely buried for historical reasons. (If a proper study is successful, the goal of *understanding* sin can be achieved again. However, unfortunately, no book can cause a person to recognize his or her own sin even though this is infinitely more important.)

What will be discussed in the following section is the kind of theological work that ranges through the field of the general anthropological discussion and searches for truth in our time without looking for "secret loopholes." But I also want to show that this kind of approach does not have to cut back on biblical truth but, on the contrary, does more justice to it than any other approach. This kind of theological work does not prevent us from *reflecting* on God and the creation. There is no question about whether a modern awareness of truth that does not dispense with scientific inquiry could do this. Rather, the question is *how* it can engage in this reflection.

B. Man's Primordial Longing and Unrestrained Quest for Affirmation

Although sin has to do with God or represents the human desire to have *nothing* to do with God, we shall not immediately and first *speak* of God when the event of sin is described. It lies in the nature of sin itself that a premature, precipitous mention of God could only be perceived as meaningless. Initially we will have enough work developing the anthropological, ontological, and cosmological contours of that experience which can only be properly designated by the word "sin," a term that could really not be replaced by any other German word thus far.[5]

---

5. See P. Tillich, *In der Tiefe ist Wahrheit. Religiöse Reden,* 1st series (1952) (Stuttgart, [6]1975), p. 144: "There is no replacement for words such as 'sin' and 'grace.' But there is a way to rediscover their meaning. It is the same way that leads us into the depths of our human existence" (translated from German).

Sin is the inappropriate relationship of all human beings to other living beings and things established (or accepted) in the course of their fearful anxiety about themselves.

But what does "inappropriate" mean? Are we, for example, to think of aggressive relationships, or relationships controlled by our physical urges? By no means! For example, sin is something other than the consumption of other beings resulting from man's desire for food. Man's swift action to take the life of other beings is subject to the laws of nature and thus cannot be described as an "inappropriate relationship." *The actual event of sin puts too great a strain on the creatures involved in it, resulting in mutual destruction.*

We human beings kill animals in the interests of our nutrition and the preservation of our life (according to Genesis 9:3 legitimately and under certain reservations). We are not sinning at all when we human beings feel obligated to follow the natural law "all of life lives on life." The human infant who literally lives on the life of his mother obviously does not sin by doing so. In this early stage of life infants cannot sin (thus doing away with the reminiscence from the history of Christian dogma that "man is conceived in sin," a dogma misunderstood most of the time anyway). To be sure, infants are human beings who will one day sin as all others do. But the fact that infants temporarily keep caregivers busy does not label them as sinners because it is a physical or instinctual act not subject to the free will. *Sin cannot at all be characterized as the naturally conditioned use we make of one another, but only as an abuse which can often be recognized as contrary to nature and in which power over others is exercised in an exploitative, one-sided way that disrupts all relationships.* Unfortunately, the killing of animals and the destruction of plants by people can be driven by this bad attitude, which we can verify today in an industry manufacturing luxury articles that go far beyond the concession of Genesis 9:3. Our "human misery" is that we only rarely succeed in making purely natural use of things. Rather, our use of natural resources verges on being contrary to nature in diverse ways.

Of all living creatures, the act of sinning is solely reserved for human beings. It is closely tied to our exocentric intellectual and spiritual nature, which is unparalleled in the natural kingdom. A wise old aphorism says it takes intellect to sin. *Sin does not emerge in life only where our biological self-preservation is at stake. Rather, sin has more to do with our intellectual self-assertion as human beings.* To the extent that the concept of "metaphysics" expresses something of what seems to point beyond what is *only* physical, *only* natural law to specifically human intellectual needs, sin can be put in these terms: *Sin is not the physically conditioned use but the abuse of other beings and even of our own nature, that is, the physical nature we ourselves possess, driven by metaphysical human needs.* (Moreover, we are not exempted from perpetrating this abuse by rejecting the concept and the cause of metaphysical thinking or an actual metaphysical realm, as even Marxists and other philosophical materialists concede. For the generally well known, tremendous danger that accompanies the specific human need for freedom is at issue here.)

Freedom is not only tied to the condition of our human ability to make our own decisions, but also to the condition of a limited, surmountable resistance on the part of the environment. No human being can be objectively free against the determined resistance, against the rejection of a hostile environment. Not even freedom of thought would be possible then because the environment holds a seat and a vote even in the thoughts and conscience of an individual.

Therefore, it is a characteristic of human beings to court the approval of others for their own existence and desires. Man's pursuit of affirmation from outside himself is indispensable. Taken by itself, there is nothing reprehensible about it. For example, it could originate in and serve the intentions of a human being or a group wanting to protect itself and others from unjust and harmful infringements on their rights and wanting to lead a life that is beneficial to the general public. But this is an abstract approval. In fact, individuals and intentional communities always exert pressure on the environment to ensure their own recognition. As a rule they pursue it in a completely unrestrained fashion — and that is where sin begins. Even God can be "used," "harnessed" for the purpose of self-aggrandizement by, for example, pointing out to others that God did not choose *them,* but those whose human quality and right to exist are supposed to affirm them.

Sinning becomes a compulsive act for man time and again because he endeavors to ensure an all-embracing affirmation of his person by others — in spite of all that may be worth criticizing about him — by using any means, including cunning and tyranny. Of all living beings, only man acts like he still needs affirmation. And this behavior is not a "psychic need" of human beings that occurs in only isolated cases, sometimes more intensely, sometimes less so; rather, it is a general human orientation. It also exists without the equivalent psychological moods. In the kingdom of nature, human beings appear as the still-unaffirmed creatures whose most intense hunger is not for biological nourishment but for the acquisition of their own affirmation. *Man's hunger for his own justification is that primeval place in human existence where sin first casts its shadow on all that is human.*

This all-embracing affirmation man strives for means that others are supposed to affirm me and my behavior by *judging* both *to be good* in a way that is audible to me and reassures me.

From my perspective, this acclamation should ignore the fact that no one is able to give my life the quality grade "good." Moreover, the fact that, objectively speaking, not everything is good about me should be disregarded. Perhaps I ask others for constructive criticism of my person. Nevertheless, from my perspective, even the criticism requested from others must serve to establish or reestablish my unreserved affirmability. I long for and need this affirmation so much that I let my capacity to *distinguish between good and evil* become *indistinct.* Perhaps I even suspend this capacity for discernment as far as my own person and my behavior acquired through the fall in Genesis 3 are concerned.

But, strictly speaking, I first *become* a sinner by doing this. The so-called *fall* occurs for each individual only at this point, and the outcome of this fall is not the gain but the loss of the knowledge of good and evil — this must be said against Hegel's interpretation of Genesis 3:22a: "The man has now become like one of us, knowing good and evil." By basically playing a part in the world around me in the mode of my pursuit of self-justification (in spite of the self-criticism I may carry around in my consciousness), I have already disqualified myself as a subject that can tell the difference between good and evil. Thus, it is not proper to emphasize the power of discernment between good and evil as "the outcome of the fall."

According to the Old Testament this is also the reason why God later solemnly enacted and inculcated special *divine commandments,* enabling Israel to recognize and do good and avoid evil in spite of man's acquisition of his own moral discernment since the fall of Adam and Eve. This took place to help human beings deal with the problems they face in life because as sinners they block their capacity for moral discernment in practice even though it is *theoretically* at their disposal. Of course, *holiness* and not, amazingly, new subject matter, is the crucial point of the Sinaitic laws.

Whoever thinks through this general scheme of things will have a hard time being convinced of the autonomy thesis enthusiastically advocated in the Enlightenment of the seventeenth and eighteenth centuries. This thesis held that "man" basically does not need any commands or laws enacted "externally" because his awakening intellect "by itself" comes to recognize and practice the distinction between good and evil. Contrary to this view — today more than ever — the holiness, beneficence, and necessity of the ethical law given to humanity by God must be acknowledged and proclaimed. But the emphasis must not be placed on the "ethical law" (which can always be given a philosophical foundation) but really on the authoritative law "given by God"! Evangelical theology is mistaken whenever it denies or weakens this authoritative givenness and validity of the law by declaring the law to be either ethically self-evident or in harmony with man's own reasonable understanding, or outdated by the gospel because Christ is the goal and end (telos) of the law (Rom. 10:4).

Let us summarize: the pressure human beings exert on their environment, asking it to give them the response that they are good people worthy of living, is the sinful substratum of all the evil that enters the world through human beings. Real evil, not so-called evil, originates in man's desire that the world around him affirm his own goodness. He desires this affirmation so anxiously that he is filled with fear and thus will with ultimate, frightening anxiety coerce it, if necessary, by manipulating others for his own purposes. Whenever human beings act this way, they have begun to be sinners. This root of sin is universal; it is the same in all human beings. The hypertrophied traditional way of speaking about *original sin,* or *peccatum originale,* must be cut back to this root. Even then the problem is troubling enough.

C. Sin as Self-Justification

The boundary between God-ordained human liberality/reasonableness/ethical competence on the one hand and sin on the other hand seems *fluid.* That is why sin so often remains unrecognized. That is why there is often such indignation, lamenting the fact that theology drags the best strengths of man through the mud of sinfulness — his pursuit of freedom and his will to achieve moral autonomy. This is the reason for that defiant spirit which expressly congratulates man for his ostensible sin. Because the boundary between human existence that is desirable and genuine and that which has turned sinful has such subtle contours (it is fluid and yet *not* random, *not* a matter of indifference and *not* nonexistent!), it should be our urgent endeavor to use a magnifying glass to bring this boundary line into sharp focus. It should be the main concern, especially of all theologies, to serve as this magnifying glass and to bring out and then impress on our minds the boundary between nonsin and sin, between good and evil, even though it is so hard to discern. Unfortunately, the achievement of dogmatic theologies has diminished at this point, yet they could be the ones who, dogmaticians themselves, could produce the most excellent system of ethics!

The results of our search for an initial understanding of the crucial boundary between good and evil thus far have established this fact: *making use of the world around us to justify ourselves is the basic form of sin that is universally experienced — whether it is committed by the individual or by groups of human beings.* It has immediate social, political, and even ecological results. It puts a strain on man's social surroundings and demands from them what is unreasonable and unfair: man's social surroundings are especially supposed to acclaim *individuals,* lavish praise on *them,* classify *them* as "good," and thus underline the worthiness of their life.

To be sure, man *needs* recognition. Man's pursuit of it is also not eo ipso reprehensible. The verdict of his social surroundings and his neighbors with whom he should be associated in loving relationships can and must not be a matter of indifference when he examines himself. But it does not follow that human beings should also be able to coerce their own affirmation. Nor does it follow that human beings should safeguard their freedom by holding in their own hands absolute control over the justification or affirmation of their own life and its worthiness. Even less does it follow that fellow creatures are really able to justify our existence for us.

In the sense intended here, self-justification is a wrong human attitude. A more precise understanding of this basic human attitude can be promoted by cooperative studies in the human sciences, but, at any rate, it also needs theological analysis. Theology must demonstrate what happened to the foundation or origin of humanity that affects us all in terms of setting us on a pernicious, misguided course. Self-justification must be construed by theology as a false sign looming before *all* our decisions in life, but not as an (for example, psychologically interpretable) individual human behavior alongside many other human behaviors (which, for example, could be interpreted in psychological terms).

Because the whole process of our basic human pursuit of justification is about the affirmation of individual human goodness (and not merely certain human actions!), the question arises: Who among the creatures of the earth could ever pronounce the verdict "Behold, this person is very good" (see Gen. 1) without crossing the boundary? *When I press others to signal to me the justification of my existence or my current appearance, I am looking for something from them that human beings, animals, plants, and things cannot reasonably do, nor want to do.* Therefore, theology must teach that sin always and everywhere happens in such a way that human beings and their surroundings are expected to do too much and are worn out. The act of sinning always signifies that too great a strain has been placed on God's creatures.

The epistemological boundaries of studies in the human sciences are *not* violated when the explanations given thus far are also described this way: in the event of self-justification, I abuse others because I use them *as if they were God.* But probably theology will be the first discipline to *conclude* from this: I am demanding a performance from them that is inappropriate for beings who are not God! From time immemorial, our language calls an abuse of earthly beings which demands the work of God from them idolatry! *Whoever (or whatever) is harnessed into an event of self-justification is also made into an idol in the process.*

The basic human pursuit of self-justification occurring as a result of the fear that the worthiness of one's life will be denied or not affirmed, perhaps even as a result of the fear of not being a person — *this basic human behavior cannot be sufficiently understood without perceiving its close contact with the question of God!* This is true irrespective of whether one is convinced of God's existence or not. For the process of making idols has always been accessible to the philosophical and scientific critique of religion.

The act of making idols itself not only affects those who are co-opted into human processes of self-justification, but also those from whom it comes. By making idols of others for the purpose of self-justification, I cross my own boundary line. I have already elevated myself to inhuman proportions; indeed, I have made myself into an idol to the extent that I strive to procure my own justification through trickery, cunning, or power. We all take the place of God when we make the world into a world centered around us, which has to be seen in relation to us and should effectively function as the chorus to add splendor to our existence.

Theologically speaking, the self-justification of man means nothing but a violation of the first commandment. Human beings concoct "other gods" for themselves in the belief that they are strengthening their grip on life in this way. This *pagan decision* — and I do not mean by this historical polytheism from ancient Greece, but an anthropological, ethical process in which both Israel and Christianity are always capable of getting involved — was classically described by Paul in the first chapter of Romans: "Human beings (pagans) avoid honoring God and his invisible qualities." They consider themselves to be wise when they exchange the glory of the immortal God for images made to look like earthly creatures and used in the place of God. In fact, the people who do this become "fools." All their relationships in life are turned into "unnatural ones." Their life is destroyed (Rom. 1:18ff.).

D. Torah and Sin

The Torah and the law of God — the heart of the Hebraic Bible/of the Old Testament — can *only* be *properly* understood as a salvific divine gift (expressing God's loving-kindness to a humanity whose existence is threatened by its own sinful actions). This means God did not give the Torah to Israel with the hidden intention that Israel would fail because of this "law" and thus be totally cast upon God's free, compassionate grace.

The solemn divine revelation and establishment of the Torah on Mount Sinai is described in Exodus 19 as a holy event in which God's *covenant* with Israel was established in the midst of thunder and lightning and a loud trumpet blast (Exod. 19:16). In the Old Testament, "covenant" always means the divine initiative on behalf of those with whom the covenant is made. Israel always rightly felt that the divine establishment of the Torah was a mark of distinction and a help, but not God's veiled threat to all human beings who would not obey the instructions of the Torah in the future.

A clue to defining the relationship of sin to the law properly is found in this truth. *Human sin is not first "established" when individual commandments of the Torah are violated, but the Torah was "established" by God because of the prior sinfulness and poverty of human beings.*

It was always a theological mistake when sin was understood *only* in terms of the *transgressio legis,* that is, the crossing of the boundaries set by God's commandments to control our arbitrary human actions. For man is a sinner even before he has violated these instructions for living God gave him *because of* his sinfulness. Not just the discrepancy between God's ethical demands on Israel and the actual life of Israel stamps Israelites, and today Christians, as sinners. Neither does a spiritually fruitful recognition of one's own sins result from observing this discrepancy. Rather, such a recognition always and everywhere occurs only as we observe our own *ingratitude* given the divine closeness and assistance we have already experienced, given God's loving-kindness across the "gaping chasm" between us and God.

It was always a theological mistake when, in teaching Christian doctrine, the divine *justification of the sinner* was limited to those who are able to trust God's grace "alone" after failing to do the works required by God's law. That makes it seem as if faith were easier and doing the "works of the law" were harder. The whole direction of this teaching is wrong. The divine decision in favor of the justification of the sinner was already made *before* the issue of keeping or breaking God's commands ever became a pressing concern for the sinner. Luther's correct intuition regarding this issue found concise expression in his hymn "Nun freut euch, lieben Christen gemein": "God has great pity on my misery *in eternity,* he thought of his compassion, he desired to help me" (author's italics).

However, God's help does not exclusively mean help in Jesus Christ, who in Luther's view had been "sent" to *counter* an emergency supposedly caused by God himself when he gave the Torah. (If Luther ever meant *this,* his theology would have to be corrected at this point.) Rather, the Torah *as well* is one of God's many covenanted gifts which all unite to form *one* eternal divine will to help man, who is separated from him (and this is the basic meaning of the word "sinner") in his particular historical situation.

If we do not notice this, all who take delight in the good, holy gift of God's commandments and desire to be obedient to the commands bear an unfounded stigma: It seems as if they are attempting something that has become superfluous, or from the very beginning it seems as if they are under suspicion of attempting to justify themselves. However, the law of God — summarized in the love commandment (Deut. 6:5; Lev. 19:18; Matt. 22:37-40) — must be deemed unreservedly "holy, just and good" (Rom. 7:12) and thus also universally binding.

All sin is first and foremost a broken relationship that has occurred between man and God, God and man — a broken relationship in which man "wants to" get God's gifts and help elsewhere and above all safeguard them on his own. Indeed, he cannot help safeguarding them until God spares him this by bridging the gap and healing the broken relationship.

Therefore, the first (and basically the sole) help that is needed as far as sin is concerned is that God himself draws near to us beyond the broken relationship. The basic need sin represents for man is a need for God. He himself always draws near to human beings in his gifts, whether he establishes salutary commandments or raises up his Son, the human Son, as the *Savior.* With these gifts, he at the same time rescues them from disaster and makes splendor return to their lives; splendor from his splendor *(kabod).* By keeping the commandments, by believing, by being baptized and incorporated into the body of Jesus Christ, human beings are drawing God himself into their lives and gaining a share in his blessings.

Keeping the commandments is both an opportunity to draw God and his blessing into their lives and also an opportunity to answer and thank God because he *has* already shown his favor and the benefits of his kindness. Without God's having already testified to his nearness and favor, no one would be able to get anything out of his commandments. First and foremost, God reveals himself as a merciful, kind God before he takes further action to help us with the gift of his commandments, giving us an additional opportunity to find him, be close to him, and gain his blessing. No human being sets eyes on the commanding God *first,* and after that the God of grace, who has compassion on the sinner. On the contrary, God's free, compassionate grace is the foundation of the divine commandment!

Does this boil down to the doctrine of the so-called *third use of the law?* Does this mean that God's commandments can *only* be kept of our own free will in terms of gratitude for the grace, justification, and rebirth received from God, or at least kept in a way that benefits man? This is how it may look at first glance. But the teaching on the "third use of the law" by those who have been born again should rather be challenged by what has been said. It is theologically problematical. Are the people *coming from* God's nearness or beneficial self-revelation because they believe they have experienced it, always exclusively those who have been "born again"? Or only those who found their justification in faith "without the works of the law"? Is it exclusively those Christians who have been "converted"?

It is precisely this view that should be implicitly challenged by what has been presented. Why? Because even before someone has received and knows God's commandments and before someone has come "to faith," he could have already sensed God's kindness and nearness.

Thus the opposite is also true: God's commandments are not only able to light the way for and be helpful to chosen Israelites and people awakened to faith by Jesus Christ; they are universal. Of course, the Torah in the Hebrew Bible also contains cultic instructions which would be an exception to the statement on its universality. And the *Decalogue* of Exodus 20:1ff. — surely the heart of the Torah — makes a distinction between duties to God and duties to man. This distinction also makes us wonder whether all these commandments can be equally universal. It is always a question of *where* the recipients of God's words and instructions are located: Have they just gotten to know God and his favor *anew,* which is specifically assumed in the first commandment ("I *led* you out of Egypt"); or is this imminent for them? Or are they to be reminded of the fact that God has already healed the broken relationship between them and God, or are they in need of such healing anew, etc.?

At any rate, the first commandment seems to be addressed in a specific way to people who *have* just (!) sensed God's kindness and nearness. The hermeneutically rather complicated position of this commandment within the Decalogue as well as the concomitant problem of how the first commandment relates to sin, and sin to the first commandment, will be examined in the following section.

E. Sin as a Violation of the First Commandment

A special position[6] in the Decalogue is given to the first commandment, which actually encompasses all the others in itself. Whoever could really keep it could also not violate the other nine; he would not even need them. Only *because* our behavior toward God is generally deficient, the

---

6. The first person to stress the "absolute primacy" of the first commandment in a way that was not customary up to that time was Luther. It was also "unusual" that Luther said of this commandment, it is fulfilled "by faith alone." On the other side, sin, too, experienced a "centering . . . on our relationship to God" (translated from G. Ebeling, *Wort und Glaube* [Tübingen, 1975], 3:182).

well-known series of ethical instructions, beginning with the commandment to honor our parents, has become necessary. We call it the *second table* of the Decalogue.[7]

The entire human race feels that the ethical instructions of this second table of the Decalogue referring to human social behavior are laws which can be understood as meaningful even without the commandments and prohibitions of the first table, and, thus, ought to claim universal recognition. However, the commandments and prohibitions relating to *God*, especially the first commandment, stand there like a luxury article in this judgment that has been made worldwide. Its universally binding nature does not seem to be a given. Its internal linkage to the other commandments and prohibitions also does not seem to be a necessary linkage. A secularized ethics in particular sees something in the first commandment that could be considered every individual's "private matter" in the context of morality.

What is being expressed in such an attitude toward the biblical Decalogue that severs the internal linkage between the two tables? In any case, a point is being made here. The instructions of the *second table* are relevant precisely when and because it is difficult to follow the instructions of the first table. Man's attempt to "at least" follow the instructions of the second table is even legitimate! After all, the reason they are even there is that God foresaw man's universal failure to keep the first commandment. On the other hand, Christ's remarks in the Sermon on the Mount relating to the subject of keeping the commandments show that man also has considerable trouble keeping the instructions of the second table. The Sermon on the Mount has impressively demonstrated: What it would really mean not to kill, not to commit adultery, not to lie, etc., does not come into play where the first commandment is renounced in the practice of living.

Therefore, the path often followed in philosophical ethics is legitimate, taking the second table of the Decalogue by itself and judging its contents to be "morally crucial" and "universally accessible and binding," as well as the attempt made by Christian theologies to demonstrate the unity of both tables. The philosophers have this argument in their favor: the instructions in the second table are so important because what is

7. This division is in keeping with the ninety-third question of the Heidelberg Catechism: "How are these commandments divided? Into two tables. . . . The second has six commandments, teaching us what we owe our neighbor."

demanded in the first table somehow "doesn't work." The theologians could make the opposite claim. Of course, here theology is in the worst position because, although it can provide its exegetical findings, it cannot provide the power that is needed to keep the first commandment. At best it can uncover and decry — with the Sermon on the Mount — a hasty and hypocritical self-satisfaction that occurs when people superficially fulfill the moral instructions concerning their fellow man. *However, only where joy in God is encountered does the unity of both tables really make itself felt.*

This statement should be seen in conjunction with a problem which the traditional *Christian interpretation* of the first commandment (Exod. 20:2f.) cannot shake off. As a rule this interpretation suppresses the fact that God's remark to Israel is placed *before* the prohibition of having other gods: "I am the LORD, your God, who brought you out of Egypt, out of bondage." With this remark a *historical event* is being emphasized, Israel's good historical experience that *justifies* the commandment prohibiting other gods!

Because Christendom did not think for the most part that it was affected by the exodus from Egypt, its theology frequently based the first commandment — on nothing. This was a serious mistake. After all, the first commandment is a directive in the Bible that was expressly based on a good experience of life that could be reenacted in the Passover celebration: a good experience would be hard to imagine without God, just as it would be hard for Israel (and for the Christian Bible reader as well) to imagine its liberation from Egypt without *God.* Christian theology must likewise base the first commandment on a gracious act received in history that cannot be imagined without God — and *it* may and should do this with reference to Christology!

Rejoicing in God is surely not a part of the general biological makeup of humanity (something, for example, we can say about our ability to cry and laugh or walk with an upright posture). It is not even true that very many people consciously or unconsciously wish there were a God. And if many people were once grateful to him in a particular situation in their life, it is *always* quickly followed by forgetfulness and *ingratitude* (see Rom. 1:21).

It is easiest for us to cope with this by rationalizing this process and by demonstrating to ourselves and others that the assumption of God's existence cannot actually "be justified by anything." We act as if we could actually imagine our experience without God even though God once seemed to "appear" in it; we act as if he must be replaced by better contemporary insights in a larger psychological perspective. Even a philosophically and scientifically so elaborate enterprise *can* be so trite! By "proving" scientifically that God doesn't exist — as painfully as this may affect our childish mind that wishes for God's existence — we veil the fact that we really don't want God to exist at all. Luther was right to point out that the existence of God cannot really be important to us human beings at all; we could honestly not have this desire because it competes with our human need for self-realization. Luther explained our general human difficulty with the first commandment in the seventeenth thesis of his "Disputatio contra scholasticam theologiam" in the following terms: "Non potest homo naturaliter velle deum esse deúm, Immo vellet se esse deum et deum non esse deum."[8] Not God should be God, but we ourselves. This is even our "natural striving" when we are socialized in religion or perhaps in the church and in religion. Sin as a violation of the first commandment is "not merely not acknowledging that God is God, but not desiring that God is God. It is not merely turning away from God, but rebellion, against him, in aversion to God, and a hatred of him."[9] (The Hebrew word *pescha'*, the harshest of the words the Old Testament uses to name sin, best describes this state of affairs.)[10]

F. Confusing the Creator with the Creature and the Need for a Theological Critique of Religion

In the history of theology the violation of the first commandment was often succinctly described as a somehow inevitable *aversio a Deo* for the entire human race (a turning away from God because of an "aversion" to him) and a simultaneously realized *conversio ad creaturam* (a turning to the creature — however, in an only apparent love for it in spite of the opposite statement in the Prometheus myth). *Because in this event the place God could or should have in our lives is occupied by our relationship to the*

---

8. Luther, WA, 1:225, line 1f.

9. Translated from Ebeling, 3:182.

10. See the careful examination of this in R. Knierim, *Die Hauptbegriffe für Sünde im Alten Testament* (Gütersloh, 1965), pp. 113-84.

creature, the problem of idolatrous behavior and in general the problem of failed relationships arise for us.

The benefit for man in keeping the first commandment — and why should we not inquire about it? — should be sought in the direction of helping man to perceive his own significance more properly and more completely fulfill his own role in the cosmos. The first commandment works to counter ruinous exaggerations of the significance of living beings, conditions, and the individual hearing this commandment, but also the ruinous declarations of their alleged inferiority. Since all people are conspicuously bad at seeing themselves objectively when it comes to their relationships with their fellow creatures, they constantly succumb to illusions about themselves and about everything. Human beings seek and see themselves far too much in all others; thus it would be mistaken to think that these illusions would be easy for them to avoid. Not only do we for the most part see and seek only ourselves in other creatures, but also in God, the Creator, if we are religious.

Therefore, a critique of religion that can illuminate why man seems to make statements about *God* but in fact is speaking about *himself* has the greatest relevance today. This is a critique of religion not limited to Feuerbach's question whether someone speaking about God misses himself and fails to understand himself and his human needs because he projects onto a God of his own invention what belongs to man or should be given to him. Rather, this critique of religion extends even further to the question of whether someone definitely is missing God and is in the process of committing an absurd act because he is in fact only speaking about his own needs and, coming full circle, unmistakably only about himself. An "anthropology of the first commandment" would move in the direction of such a critique of religion. Indeed, all theological work should implicitly engage in such a critique of religion.

Luther once said: "Human beings sin against the first commandment because they do not seek what is God's. Instead they seek what belongs to themselves — they even seek this in God . . . they are their own final goal and idol . . . ; they use God and enjoy themselves."[11] Following this line of thought Luther went into more detail about the sinful confusion of the Creator with the creature. He argued that a sinner not just makes an idol out of creatures, but in the end he makes an idol out of himself.

---

11. Translated from Luther, WA, 1:425, line 2.

If a person were to be of the opinion that he is not guilty of this practice because he honors God, Luther would say to him: "Certainly, but you do not honor God in an appropriate way, you seek God and understand by Him something that is merely created in your own image and reflects your particular interests. You also treat God like an errand boy, even like an object that is put completely into your hands. You think you are honoring God, but in fact you are not reckoning with the real, the totally other living, God!"

In this context the "Augustinian monk" Luther picked up a term he got from Augustine's work *De doctrina Christiana:* the distinction between *uti* and *frui*.[12] Augustine distinguishes what we use from what we should enjoy. Only those things that are to be loved for their own sake are meant for our enjoyment. However, this is true only of the triune God. Only those things that are not enjoyed for their own sake are meant to be used, but we are to use them as a means to achieve the final goal of our human journey through life, the enjoyment of God. According to Augustine, all creatures, all temporal goods are ultimately destined to be used in this way.

Therefore Augustine does not distinguish between our appropriate relationship to the animals and plants, which are only means to any ends we may have, and our appropriate relationship to our fellow human beings who carry their end in themselves and therefore may not simply be used in the service of any interests we may have. In contrast Augustine distinguishes between a relationship appropriate among creatures on the one hand, and the relationship appropriate to the Creator alone on the other hand. For Augustine it is not of importance to develop the difference between rational and nonrational creatures. Rather, what counts to him is setting apart the quality of man's relationship to God from the quality of all other human relationships. However, in Kant neither man's relationship to God nor the concept of God receives consideration in this context. Kant assumed man would settle down if he could use the subhuman creatures given into his hands any way he liked. In doing so he would find peace for his soul! In Kant we thus actually find that the first commandment focuses not on God, but on the living being "man."

But must this be said so sharply? Can modern anthropology be lambasted in this way? Was the concern of Kant and many others to emphasize man as a qualitatively incomparable and especially honorable being wrong

12. Augustine, *De doctrina Christiana,* bk. 1, chaps. 3 and 4.

in every respect? In *one* respect this attitude was not wrong, even though the terrible and unrestrained destruction of nature in the modern era must be attributed to it: Whoever has the interests of man at heart, whoever fights for the well-being and honor of human beings does not on that account set himself against God. Thinking very highly of man and his worth and wanting the best for him or giving God the glory — this is not an either-or proposition. We should not play one off against the other.

The seeds of a huge ethical conflict are planted in Luther and Augustine's anthropology and doctrine of the world on the one hand and that of Kant and people of like mind on the other hand. It is this conflict that is tearing apart many people shaped by the modern age, in an intellectual sense as well! We are all sick because we constantly fail to achieve a proper balance in the focus of our thought and action, focusing more on our relationship to our fellow creatures than on our relationship to the Creator. How could this insight be given practical consideration in our modern world? What can we do in a practical sense with the conclusion that *for this reason* our earthly relationships as well are subject to unnatural changes? How could such an insight become relevant today in the realm of international politics and social ethics? No answer can be given to these questions, which only describe a common aporia. For the moment we will continue to listen to Luther and once again compare him to Kant.

G. What Does It Mean to Do Good? A Reference to Luther's Contribution to the Understanding of Sin

Luther became the Reformer by way of the better theological understanding of sin that he had acquired. But his understanding of sin is obviously at odds with the anthropocentrism of modern thought. For example, whoever compares Kant's and Luther's view of man and ethics gains this impression. Nevertheless, Luther's understanding of sin contains an important message for present-day humanity.

The three most important reasons why Luther's doctrine feels strange to modern man are:

1. It seems as if Luther labels man (in contrast to Catholicism and humanism) as a sinner in a way that leaves little chance for ethical improvement or positive change in our situation brought about by intentional human effort.

. 2. It seems as if Luther inadmissibly relativizes the moral significance of individual sins, the so-called actual sins. His theology of sin seems to place hardly any emphasis on an ethically discriminating discussion about the quality and effect of human actions; rather, it seems to place its sole emphasis on a discussion of the condition and worth of the sinful human person in general. *Original sin* seems to be Luther's master key to understanding sin. His generalizing talk of sin and *the* sinner does coincide with language that is also widely used in the New Testament. But it is foreign to at least large sections of the Old Testament because sins are viewed there as tangible, individual deeds of unrighteousness.

3. It seems as if a disqualifying verdict on modern attempts to comprehend the structures of human *alienation* and take measures to overcome them that seem politically or therapeutically suitable is a direct result of Luther's thought. A certain mood seems to pervade Luther's theology: You modernists cannot heal the contradictions you find in your social and individual lives in spite of all your efforts because you overlook the fact that they emerge from a violation of the first commandment. Thus even your alleged therapies only turn bedridden patients from their left side onto their right side for a change.

Of course, these three perspectives on Luther's understanding of sin are not likely to reveal Luther's contribution accurately. I will limit myself to a few concise remarks since Luther's understanding of man and his theological doctrine of sin have been frequently and extensively described elsewhere.

1. It is not correct that Luther tended to make a pessimistic assessment of human strengths. Even though he recognized human reason as being impaired by sin, depriving it of its complete effectiveness, he simultaneously praised it as an outstanding force for good, as the source of distinguished civilizatory achievements and skills. Only those who measure Luther's theology by the standard of their own (pre-Reformation and yet modern?) view of man, which Luther did not share, cannot see how good Luther rated man's prospects for the future and how talented he actually believed human beings to be.

According to this view of man that Luther rejected, man is formed by his deeds, which means that by force of habit he gradually acquires the mark his deeds leave on him. (Whoever frequently does what is wrong becomes a bad person.) That is why man should do as many good works as possible, so that in the end he is not left looking completely like a sinner. This view assumes that man possesses an intact capacity to reason and a certain freedom of the will to guard against the threat of sinfulness. It was just this view of human nature that Luther completely rejected. This is also why statements on how sin has led our reason astray do not mean what they would say *within* the view of man he rejected.

Luther's greatest concern did not focus on the danger that Christians would not exert themselves enough in doing good. Rather, it focused on the danger that Christians could miss what is good in spite of their great efforts! *Probably the most significant ethical contribution of Luther's doctrine of sin is found in its attempt to ask anew the question of what is really good.* Luther inquired anew about the conditions required for a good work against the impression that it is obvious what we mean by good actions and against the impression that it is evident that good, virtuous behavior is possible for human beings. He found these conditions in faith, and what this objectively means will preoccupy our attention in what follows.

2. Since Luther's doctrine of sin with its radical inquiry into what is good practically leads us right into the field of ethics, we must not misunderstand it in the following direction: Because this doctrine of sin looks less at man's specific, individual acts of sin but instead concentrates on the person of the sinner, its main concern is probably the inner condition of individual humans, that is, their life of faith and the eternal salvation of their souls; of less concern is the ethical quality of their works that is so significant for society as a whole. This is an incorrect assessment!

Whereas the medieval theologians before and during Luther's time only looked at the socially so significant good or sinful works with the greatest attentiveness because they could deduce the *quality of individual human beings from* them alone (and their *actual* concern was the salvation of their souls!), Luther's whole perspective was the exact opposite. Luther did not want to emphasize the fact that man's bad deeds or sinful works have a harmful effect on his soul (which is certainly true in a psychological sense); rather, Luther wanted to emphasize this truth: Because man is a sinner, he commits bad deeds — even if his works look good. As long as his heart is not right with God, as long as *faith* is not bridging man's sinful separation from God, a man is fruitless, indeed, harmful to all even with his philosophically and ethically convincing and illustrious deeds. We have to grapple with this special contribution of Luther to ethics!

It is correct to say that Luther's theology of sin proves to be a doctrine of the sinful human *person* (hamartology, from *ho hamartolos*) rather than a doctrine of *sins* (hamartiology, from *hai hamartiai*). But this theological approach to sin is not without consequences for social ethics. And strictly speaking, its offensiveness to modern man is not the mistaken notion that Luther did not care to draw ethical distinctions between the human deeds or lifestyles. Rather, it is the fact that Luther asserted: *Without faith, no good works!* Good works can only flow from faith, only from a situation in which the first commandment has been erected in the heart of the person who acts! Of course at this point Luther is under suspicion of having denied unbelievers or people of other faiths the capacity to do good works.

But in fact Luther is not the one who would deny that there are standards of natural law by whose norms one could discern good, very good, and not-so-good deeds right across the spectrum of the entire human race. Luther did not see any problem in observing exemplary humanity and moral good, for example, in the Turks, who were considered to be almost human monsters in western Europe in the sixteenth century. He actually felt the theological need to do this. This gives us an indication that we must look for the actual message of his thesis that *good* works are tied to faith in a different direction because it is clearly wrong to assert that Luther suspected nominal and non-Christians of moral insufficiency.

We must consider how this thesis ties in with Luther's doctrine of justification. If this center of his theology is considered, it clearly reveals what Luther actually wanted to achieve here. Luther saw that the realization and the performance of ethically good works is tied to certain conditions: *A "good work" is one that is not made to serve the (mostly hidden) goal of self-justification.* Works that seem good but are contrary to creation and actually damage it can be objectively ruled out only where this second motive for works is *not* admissible; that is, besides serving their direct effect and goal indirectly also serving the self-justification of the one who acts.

3. But how can the aforementioned doctrine be reconciled with modern ethical theories shaped by the Enlightenment? How does the intention of Luther's theology of justification relate to the modern hope of being able to change reality *more and more* for the better and to use therapy *increasingly* to treat the ills found in human beings?

If we once again inquire in this context about Kant's position on Luther — as a paradigm — this has a special attraction and a special difficulty. The philosopher Kant, standing in the Lutheran tradition, had a special appreciation for the general direction of Luther's anthropology and ethics: It was also *not* Kant's concern to deduce the goodness of the individual from good works or works that appear to be good. For example, Kant would not have recognized charitable financial donations to the poor eo ipso as good works. Whether they really were charitable depended for him on whether they were conscientiously performed and were morally consistent with the maxims to be followed by the person who acts. Only the correct way of thinking qualifies *works* that *appear to be good* as *really good* works. However, according to Kant, the person who does them remains ethically justified even if contrary to all expectations his action should bear unpleasant fruit in the midst of practical success.

In Kant the proper, conscientious *attitude* ("good will") produces good works in the core of the person; in Luther it was *faith* in the core of the person that produced good works. Both the ethicist of character and the theologian of faith assume a transcendentally based, ultimate unity between subject and object, between individual, subjective truth and goodness and objective truth and goodness. Nevertheless, Kant's philosophy is not simply a continuation of Luther's theological heritage on the basis of modern thought and with its conceptual tools. It is precisely what they have in common that also contains profound, objective differences.

Luther's ethics of faith differ from Kant's ethics of character in that Luther lays the emphasis on man's dependency on God. It is precisely this emphasis that is missing in Kant. Rather, it is a viewpoint that is once accentuated only by Schleiermacher in terms of a fresh intellectual revisioning of the Reformation. Kant on his part understood (as Fichte did later) the natural surroundings of man as the material that man had to organize in a conscientious, ethical fashion in order to prove his freedom. But for Luther what was really decisive was understanding *man* as the *materia* of God before this ethical problem of conscientiously restructuring reality even comes into view. The history of humanity and the world may reveal several dimensions, but the fundamental one for Luther is that God the Creator is working on the future shape of life in the world process. God in his freedom does this not arbitrarily, not haphazardly, not with the open possibility that the outcome of world history could be devastating for human beings, but in keeping with his promises recorded in the Bible.

In Luther's theocentric worldview the actions of human beings turn into sin whenever they, in attempting to prove their freedom and change reality on the basis of ethical maxims, ignore the fact that they themselves are the "products of God's work" in the fundamental dimension of the world process: material in the hand of the Creator who is leading the world toward its promised goal.

Luther's faith assumes that before human beings create new realities, before they build themselves up on the basis of their own blueprint for living, they *owe* all that is real and even their own selves to God. In ethical terms faith means expressing these truths in ethics, thus taking human action with an attitude of grateful praise to God and self-limitation.

Luther did not teach the bondage of man. He taught that man's freedom is surrounded by the freedom of God. This kind of transcendental foundation for world history is not found in Kant. Kant would have rejected it as a fundamental diminution of human autonomy, whereas in Luther God's freedom is seen not as a freedom *against* but for man's freedom. *Of course, Luther's faith puts human beings back into the total realm of God's creatures.* Although human beings can make their own history, humanity is first an object of God's eschatological work, leading the *whole* of creation to the goal determined *by him*.

If it is in keeping with Luther's theology to state the concept of *sin* more precisely *as man's unwillingness to admit that when he takes action he is at the same time material in the hands of the Creator,* then a critique of Kant's ethics is implied because in Kant the man who takes action ignores his creaturely solidarity with the rest of God's creatures. Luther's theology puts human beings back into the realm of God's creatures and works. This reminds us that the moral quality of our works (good or evil) is problematic right from the beginning, a priori, when the man who takes action ignores his creaturely solidarity with all of his fellow creatures. Luther makes us more sensitive to the realization that the moral quality of human actions primarily depends on how man understands his position in the cosmos.

The position of human beings in the cosmos is objectively characterized by the fact that they do not carry their justification in themselves, and thus are not an "end in themselves" as Kant thought, but need to be justified by the One who alone can grant it. God alone is authorized and capable of granting it because he "needs" all human beings each in their own way for his work of transforming creation (whether they turn against God, provoking his wrath, and therefore contribute to the destruction of the old world — also necessary for the new creation — or whether they are united in faith with God's eschatological goal and therefore directly participate in the emergence of the new creation).

Allowing oneself as a human being to be justified by God means *believing*. Justifying oneself as a human being means separating oneself from one's fellow creatures. *Unbelief* is objectified in such a separation from fellow human beings, in such social division and isolation.

Luther's message is relevant for our modern era, calling us back to an ethic which serves not to deepen the chasm between human beings and their fellow creatures, but bridges it. Luther's ethics reach their goal when the person who takes action, who intervenes in life to change it, has first seen his life and the life of all as a gift and mandate from God. Luther also teaches a special position of man within nature. Yet this does not only mean that he is vested with special powers, but even more that he is specially needy and must be dependent on God's love and affection in his Word, which is "the gospel" for us.

It is probably not wrong to laud Kant's anthropocentric ethics, since a case can be made that its approach mobilized man's best resources in the modern era, perhaps even eliciting everything humanly possible that could be thought and done to effect moral change. What Kant wanted to achieve in this matter does not at all conflict with Luther's ethics — at least to a large extent. But if we are able to look at the historical impact of Kantian ethics on the environment only with mixed feelings, we must at the same time concede that its environmental consequences are in keeping with Kant's anthropocentric *approach*. On the other hand, Luther's contrasting approach (thus giving us reason to have hope for the "environment") has thus far remained esoteric on the stage of world history. At the moment, it is still an open question whether his approach together with his Christology and theocentrism could be rather refined in the future and even acquire the form of (relatively) common intellectual knowledge in the same way it is granted to Kant's ethics.

H. The Violation of the Prohibition against Images with Reference to the Theological Structure of What Is Known as the Environmental Problem

From today's perspective, it is to be regretted that Luther decided not to include the second commandment (Exod. 20:4-5) in the catechism. As you may know, Luther subdivided the last commandment (Exod. 20:17) into two commandments to maintain the number ten. But he suppressed the text that begins with the words, "You shall not make for yourself an idol in the form of anything in heaven above or on the earth beneath or

in the waters below. You shall not bow down to them or worship them."
But to what extent is this prohibition of idols still relevant in our society?

It seems as if modern civilized humanity is no longer tempted to make
idols and worship images of creatures in nature. At most such creatures
are depicted in an artistic context or for scientific purposes — or as sen-
timental photographs. Where, then, is the looming danger to be found?
A New Testament text can put us on the right track.

When Paul in the first chapter of Romans came to speak of the form
in which godlessness is generally encountered in pagans, he characterized
their sin with the words: they "exchanged the glory of the immortal God
for images made to look like mortal man and birds and animals and
reptiles" (Rom. 1:23). Man sinfully reversed the relationship owed to the
creatures and the relationship owed to God. This basic event is cited as
the *reason* why man made the images. Pagans do not react to God's own
testimony about himself and his deeds of kindness with love for God or
with respect for God. "For safety's sake," they prefer to rely on the benefits
of an idol, an earthly replacement for God. This was happening everywhere
in Israel's Canaanite environment. However, the Jews violated the first
commandment no less than the second. They constantly violated the whole
Torah given to them by God, even though the Torah was their pride. They
even misused it. To top off the misuse, they derived the claim of having
"earned" the justification of their own existence from "the accomplishment" of having followed the commandments (or having accepted God's
kindness in showing them the right way).

If the violation of the first commandment usually leads directly to the
worshiping of images in the case of pagans, it leads to self-justification by
misusing the Torah in the case of the Jews. And in a more sublime sense,
the self-justification syndrome leads them to make mental idols "in their
hearts," as we will soon see.

The first three chapters of Romans illustrate in a monumental way how
human self-justification, the violation of the first commandment, the ex-
changing of the Creator for the creature, the misuse of God's name, and the
violation of the prohibition against images are all merely facets of a single
phenomenon — the godlessness of human hearts from childhood on.

We *always* visualize the things, conditions, and living beings we use to
justify ourselves. We see them the way we want to see them, the way we
must see them. In our relationship to them we attempt to tailor their
appearance and their reality to our interest in them. When we visualize a

person, we don't see him as he is in himself. We try to hail him down and interpret him in such a way that *we* receive justification from our relationship to him. We are anxious to get from him what only God can accomplish. We want him to pronounce the verdict "see here, a very good creature" on our existence. This can include our attempt to flatter others and initially make them into imposing figures. Whoever is elevated in this way is later brought down. However, since our perception of the other is reduced to the measure of our own desires projected onto him, we harm those we make into idols.

We make a mental impression of others. We primarily see *ourselves* in them. However, they no longer connect with us and fall silent. This behavior of our counterpart — whether it be God, our fellow human beings, or nonhuman creatures — is a sure sign that we are living as sinners. We and the other remain lonely in such so-called relationships. Sinful relationships are ones whose signature is precisely the lack of any real connection to one another. If sin has achieved its goal, the partners in the sinful relationship are dead (with the exception of God, who at most falls silent).

The Protestant Reformers recognized the prohibition of images as an instruction from God that remains important for Christians, too. It was incorporated into the Heidelberg Catechism and respected in Reformed places of worship, for they renounced all symbolic representations, especially of the crucified Jesus Christ. Of course, the latter hardly addressed the core issue of the commandment that man should not make for himself an idol and not worship any. The *opponents* of visible, graphic, and religious symbols in church do not live up to this commandment better than their advocates. The author Max Frisch, who lived in the Reformed cultural surroundings of Zurich, describes in numerous texts how the practice of making mental images of one another[13] is a basic problem and stigma in human global society.

For example, today the souls of many women are deeply hurt by not being noticed and addressed as women with their own distinctive character in a culture dominated by men. Instead they are being unceremoniously *subsumed* under male structures and notice the consequences of violating the prohibition against idols, a prohibition which is still the norm among

13. See the diary entry of 1946 in M. Frisch, *Tagebuch, 1946–1949* (FFM, 1963), p. 37.

us today. Here, too, the pain reaches down into the depths of the subject of justification. Women experience themselves as being forced into a certain image that reflects who they "are" and springs from opportunities for male domination and their need for self-justification.

The completely unchecked, widespread violation of the still valid and still relevant divine commandment "you shall not make for yourself an idol" is manifested today in the form of our immense ecological difficulties, that is, in what are known as our *environmental problems*. As soon as living beings or things enter into the zone of possible control by human beings, they immediately become "objects," of whom an image is made. In recent years, *science and technology* were accused of objectivistic thought or understanding. Their encroachment on nature negated and broke the shared identity of subject and object. A narrow understanding of reality gained acceptance in them: a one-sided interest of one-sided human beings in which the human instinct to take possession of nature ("having") was absolutely dominant. In the process nature fell silent and became terminally ill. However, even before this happened, the human beings who did this to nature were and are terminally ill.

What is wrong with this line of reasoning is that it completely overlooks the merits of natural science in combating and overcoming prejudice and ingrained worldviews as well as widening our horizons, enabling us to resist or track down even unpleasant realities that we have suppressed. We have not yet done an adequate job of singing the theological praises of this aspect of natural science (and also, for example, of the historical sciences) in our time!

What is right with it is that since the beginning of the modern era, nature has become a preferred object on which human beings have taken out their anger at their failed relationships to God. Since nature hardly confronts us any longer as a formidable threatening power, nor as a creation with its own language and dignity, but has become a material and energy provider (an *image* we have made of it!), it has become the highly welcome substitute for *human* slaves who were formerly pressed into service. The moment we lost respect for nature, we could magnanimously begin to call the conscription and possession of human slaves an injustice that lies "beneath our dignity." The invention of the steam engine and the modern recognition and establishment of basic human rights and freedoms fall in the same time frame. The *abuse* of *nature* that has grown to immense proportions since the eighteenth century does not document only the rapidly increasing material requirements of a fast-growing humanity, as many have so often claimed. Rather, it is first and foremost *the result of a misguided satisfaction of our metaphysical hunger.* The natural economy must continue its steady *growth,* natural science and technology must continue their steady *progress,* nature must continue to be exploited to an ever greater degree because we would otherwise not know intellectually or spiritually where to go and how to live. *Soteriological significance* is attached to progress and economic growth! In a most comfortable way they now relieve us of asking and answering the question about the meaning of life. They also keep the disturbing issue of God from becoming apparent. (But if that is the situation as far as the modern abuse of nature is concerned, then how much improvement in the condition of the environment can we expect from political attempts at reform and ecological programs to protect nature? The truth is that most of those who pretend they no longer want the present system secretly affirm it!)

In recent decades not only the labor issues of the nineteenth century have returned in the form of environmental issues. On top of that it only seems as if working people have gained more freedom and more quality of life by having nature more and more take their former place as slaves in the workforce. For by exploiting nature the exploiters themselves must soon enter the "loss zone." Once again, a supposedly less worthy part of creation is dominated by a supposedly more justified part. But the *curse* of alienation and destruction will be imposed on the exploiters as well. The outcome of such sin, which consists of violating the first commandment, the prohibition against idols, or the prohibition against misusing God's name, is certainly what the Bible calls a *curse,* but what might be called alienation, destruction, or fatal isolation in modern usage.

At the moment, nature is our most important idol. We honor it and we destroy it. We elevate it and humiliate it. It can offer all of humanity a pseudosubstitute for God and for the good word that human beings need to live. It provides us with the progress by which our existence seems to find peace and justification. We have built comprehensive safeguards into our existence by exploiting its forces and yet, in reality, we have allowed our existence to become less secure than ever. *It is characteristic of the basic sin of our broken relationship to God that it amounts to an increase in security that from the outset paradoxically undermines our security in a drastic way.*

A violation of the prohibition against idols is inevitable the moment we demand more from them than they can give, extorting from nondivine beings the benefit or gift God himself reserved the right to grant us: our justification.

Whoever makes for himself an idol loses himself in an illusion. He puts the real world into false categories. He spreads a cloak of deception over the world. He is a perpetrator of deceit and empty illusions (sin is a lie!). He distorts everything, and everything is distorted to him. He treats a part of creation he has made into an idol as if it were God. He classifies the finite and temporal as if it were the infinite and eternal. In his egocentricity he calls good what seems to be good to him now — his ability to discern good from evil crumbles. He does not see what is good in his vicinity; rather, he assumes that goodness is found at a spatial and temporal distance. *As a person who loses his own self* he seeks goodness wherever it is not found. He has an insatiable hunger for time and space and goes through a lot of time and space. Locked into this pattern, he consumes human beings, animals, plants, and what are known as raw materials. He uses others and loses himself. He controls others — and becomes deeply dependent on them; he loses his freedom in his attempt to find it by exploiting others.

I. Human Dignity, Self-Respect, and Shame

Semantically, dignity and self-respect can move closer together in daily usage. They can both be rendered by the Greek word *doxa*. They are also both included in the Hebrew word *kabod*. Nevertheless, their meaning is not simply identical.

The dignity of man is what sets man apart by nature as a human being — not speaking theologically. We speak of human dignity and mean by this something that sets all human beings apart. It is not the result of special achievements some people would be capable of making but others would not. Thus we can precisely indicate to whom human dignity is due: to all human beings. However, we run into considerable theological difficulties, even dead ends, when we are supposed to say what the *content* of human dignity is.[14]

---

14. G. Picht, "Erziehen — was ist das?" in *Hier und Jetzt II* (Stuttgart, 1981), p. 484, and postscript to "Zum geistesgeschichtlichen Hintergrund der Lehre von den Menschenrechten," in *Hier und Jetzt II,* p. 135.

Self-respect is less firmly rooted in general human nature than dignity. To be sure, almost all people think they need "at least" self-respect, need it even more than physical food. But we human beings are constantly struggling to preserve and keep self-respect. It is not as commonly "available" as we think. Self-respect is also more flexible and malleable than dignity. It can be enlarged and reduced by special achievements. "Give credit to whom credit is due." We can acquire "special honor" and get "credit," which enhances our self-respect, whereas human dignity cannot be increased. Moreover, it is not hard to say what the *content* of human self-respect is: it is to our credit when we do not egotistically insist on exercising the privileges we possess, but rather share them with those who have not reached our level. True self-respect breathes the spirit of self-limitation for the sake of solidarity and love. True self-respect is indeed a manifestation of the spirit.

We can surely speak of the dignity of nonhuman creatures, but it would be hard to speak of their self-respect.

A specific dignity is inherent in every creature. Every creature has his own significance *(kabod),* which has been bestowed on him by the Creator. This is also the best way to explain why we should have "respect for life" (A. Schweitzer). Consequently, an important insight must follow from this: no living being has to thank other creatures for being allowed to exist, not even his parents. Moreover, whoever exists does not have to justify himself for this or have others justify him. By being here, each creature is already entitled to exist ("worthy to live"). Therefore, no being should "do penance" (Anaximander) to others for the alleged guilt of his mere existence. Of course, this is strictly ruled out only when it is clear that the dignity of living creatures, especially of human beings,[15] is the "significance" *(kabod)* they each have in themselves because God created them.

The *issue* of man's dignity usually is missed when human beings must live in conditions/structures of power which prevent them from developing their basic nature. The modern world has found a label for this obstacle: they lack human rights. The latter means nothing but the availability of that living space which is "natural" for human beings because it leaves them with their original dignity. Therefore, normally the existence of

15. Similar to E. Jüngel, "Der Gott entsprechende Mensch. Bemerkungen zur Gott-ebenbildlichkeit des Menschen als Grundfigur theologischer Anthropologie," in *Entsprechungen: Gott — Wahrheit — Mensch,* BEvTH 88 (München, 1980), p. 300: Man's highest dignity is simply being here.

human rights should be assumed. We must not consider them as the payoff or premium for a worthy and disciplined lifestyle because they are the God-ordained framework in which a dignified life is possible. Thus, human rights are not to be granted, but kept.[16] No state has the right to abolish them. Thus, every citizen has the duty, if necessary, to fight for their restoration. Whenever human dignity is trampled on, first of all, the powerful in the country, but second, the whole society is responsible for this. Concern for human rights is, therefore, a political, public event that involves the general public.

In contrast, self-respect is not about individuals. Individuals fight with one another/among one another not for dignity but for self-respect. What lends a human being dignity, following the terminology used by Schiller, is gaining the victory in an ethical-spiritual endeavor not by defeating the "others" who are in competition with you but by defeating your own fleshly temptations in life. But we cannot see this as the root cause of man's dignity. We would use the term "self-respect" here and would also examine how Schiller's dignity and self-respect relate to the *doxa* of a human being elucidated in the Bible.

What can be defined as man's dignity *and* self-respect is expressed most clearly — even in philosophical terms — in the light of our relationship with God. Dignity *and* self-respect both signify an illumination, a glorification of our being which cannot be properly explained from an "immanental" perspective. War and honor, fatherland and honor, material status symbols and dignity, ethical asceticism and dignity — the list of aberrations, distortions, and self-delusions associated with *immanental* reasons for human dignity and self-respect is endless!

In conclusion, let us try to see dignity *and* self-respect in their proper context! We seek our *self-respect* in dealing with fellow creatures, but our focus on them does not signify an appreciation of their individual uniqueness as creations of God. Rather, it calculates the advantage for our own self-respect that we can gain from them. Thus, we do not appreciate others. But perhaps we will honor them "for tactical reasons," in the expectation that they will pay us back in kind. Uncertain of our own worth, we seek self-respect from one another and are at the same time incapable of

---

16. See G. Picht, "Der Staat und das Gewissen seiner Bürger," in *Hier und Jetzt II,* p. 204; see also Picht, "Zum geistesgeschichtlichen Hintergrund der Lehre von den Menschenrechten," p. 135.

affirming the other in his dignity as a creation of God. "How can you believe, when you receive glory *[doxa]* from one another, and you do not seek the glory that is from the one and only God" (John 5:44, NASB). How could it really be *glory* that is given to us when we "ascend" (elevate ourselves), seeking glory instead of descending?

Looking at the other in a wrongful and calculating manner leads to shame in this person, even if he is not responsible for the way he is seen. He experiences himself as being unappreciated and made into an object. Shame is man's ineffaceable recollection of his estrangement from the origin; it is grief for this estrangement and the powerless longing to return to unity with the origin.[17] To be ashamed is a very basic occurrence, which could not be said in the same way about the pangs of a bad conscience. When we are struck with pangs of conscience, the truth is not necessarily apparent. Often a bad conscience indicates that a person's self-respect or dignity has been impugned. But it is not always clear why this actually happened: often the actual facts are obscured. However, in his shame man does not escape the truth — he senses it. Unable to resist, he falls into God's hands, although he feels as if he ought to be able to hide from God. The coverings the ashamed person reaches for in his inability to flee are not without function and value. They are necessary to shield his eyes from God, and God uses them to reapproach the creature who had become separated from him and keep him safe above the abyss.

The most profound thing is the covering God gives himself — as if he, too, were ashamed by the human beings separated from him. I am talking about the incarnation of God. God at once reveals and hides himself in a human being.

God becomes man so that man does not think he has to become God. This is the *existential* purpose of the divine incarnation: to keep us in our humanity, even more to place us in the position of true, real humanity. The other aspect is also true: God became man so that we could become divine. This main idea in Irenaeus is not in conflict with what I said first.

---

17. D. Bonhoeffer, *Ethik* (München, [6]1963), p. 145; see also Bonhoeffer, *Schöpfung und Fall/Versuchung* (München, 1968), pp. 94ff., where man's conscience is peculiarly viewed as "shame before God in which at the same time our own wickedness is concealed" (p. 95). Bonhoeffer does not interpret conscience as the voice of God in the sinner, but as his resistance to this voice, which nevertheless as man's resistance points to the voice against man's knowledge and desire (p. 45). Quotation from English translation, *Creation and Fall/Temptation,* trans. John C. Fletcher (New York: Macmillan, 1959), p. 81.

For inhuman man elevates or humiliates himself into an inner void, but man in union with God discovers his destiny and truth as a creation of God. In this way God's incarnation signifies the highest possible recognition that can be given to us. Its goal is the glorification of what is human. It alone is the source of our splendor. The incarnation of God is the effective remedy for our lack of humanity, for our sin.

J. A Summary of the Propositions about Sin

Man

1. God created man in such a way that he called this living being by his name at the same time. God addresses human beings and encourages them in love to respond to him with their life.

1.1. Christians observe God's loving address most clearly in their fellow man Jesus of Nazareth — the Logos who took on human "flesh," who is called the Christ, the bearer of the good news of God for us (= gospel).

1.2. God does not deny human dignity to the sinner who fails to respond to him. He continues to *speak to* him in love.

1.2.1. But the danger exists that the sinner denies himself his human dignity, denies it to his fellow human beings or is denied it by other human beings.

1.2.2. Human beings accuse each other and also themselves of not having *earned* their life or their right to exist. Human beings live with the basic fear that they will not be allowed to continue living if they cannot prove to those around them by their deeds that they are worthy of living and entitled to exist.

1.2.2.1. In so doing, they overlook the fact that they all are entitled to exist and are given recognition because the Creator has given them life and significance.

1.2.3. Human beings rob their *fellow creatures* of dignity/self-respect by "enlisting" them in the process of self-justification. Human beings give up *their own* dignity/self-respect when they have incurred guilt and so ruined their chances for the future that they no longer see any possibilities for their life. (Conversely, they give up their own right to life when it seems as if only death can preserve their human dignity and self-respect.) Both of these things can be accompanied by deep *shame*.

1.3. Shame profoundly jeopardizes the human enterprise. Whoever is ashamed fears he will lose his humanity, his existence as a *human being*. This fear is a basic human emotion. At the same time it becomes apparent what man is actually meant to be when he is ashamed.

1.3.1. Whoever is ashamed misses — unconsciously — union with God. This is the source that lends his existence splendor and inner vitality.

1.3.1.1. God is working on human beings who are ashamed. Therefore, they are rightfully treated with a kind of awed respect.

1.3.1.2. If we follow our own experience, the opposite of shame is human *self-respect*. But on the basis of theological reflection, we can say with the same right: it is *faith*. In faith, too, it becomes apparent what man is actually meant to be. Faith is at the same time the power that keeps us living as *human beings*. It is not just something extra to "mere humanity."

1.3.1.3. Looking at anthropology as a whole, faith means the liberation of man from shame.

1.4. The believing individual also gives recognition to himself! But he considers himself worthy of living because God wanted him, not because he in any way earned the privilege of having his own existence.

1.4.1. Nevertheless, he will and may rejoice over successful accomplishments all the more because these are not necessary for him to prove that he has permission to live.

1.5. Man as a human being lives and dies by the prevailing judgments on his person.

1.5.1. In living as a believer, God's judgment of the person prevails.

1.5.2. Only the person who is certain of his own justification can give recognition to others in such a way that his opinion proves to be helpful to them in their life.

The Event of Sin

2. The core meaning of "to sin" is the inability to give recognition to anyone or anything. Sin is the inability to accept one's fellow creatures as they exist in themselves by virtue of their dignity as creations of God. The sinner is not even able to give recognition to himself in this way.

2.1. The sinner accepts others *only* as they fit into his own image. His image of reality is such that it is identical with his need to justify and assert himself.

2.1.1. The sinner sees only *himself* in all others as long as he tailors their appearance and existence to conform to what he wants to have from them: the justification of *his* person.

2.2. Sin is calculating. Sin often begins by bowing to others to make them well disposed to oneself. But it ends in exploitation and destruction.

2.2.1. Thus, the sinning individual miscalculates. At best, he gains short-term relief from his burdensome situation, but in the long term he definitely shoulders an even greater burden.

2.2.2. The sinner fails to recognize reality, and reality takes revenge for this.

2.3. Sin always and everywhere is structured in such a way that people misuse other creatures as a substitute for God.

2.3.1. These misused persons are supposed to play God for the sinner. Because this role is invariably too much for them to handle, in the end the sinner always fails to get what he desires, his actions are futile, and his being is empty.

2.3.2. As such, sin is that which is simply futile and in vain, that which never achieves its goal. Yet this does not at all mean that sin does not really destroy, does not really kill.

2.3.3. Sin is a misdirected hunger for God. It is precisely the sinner who *seeks* God. And the real God is closer to him than he, the sinner, thinks.

The Mystery of Sin

3. Only man can sin. But why does he sin?

3.1. Man sins because he lacks God — or seems to lack him.

3.1.1. Man is constantly *tempted* to ensure that God satisfies his hunger for justification by taking action on his own, that is, by exerting pressure on his fellow creatures because it seems so uncertain to him that God could satisfy his hunger. The fact that at first man is often successful when he takes this path explains his constant temptation to sin.

3.1.2. There is no one except God who can take responsibility for the fact that man is able to be tempted. But it *must* be assumed that God does, indeed, take responsibility for it. Following Jesus' advice, we ask God in the Lord's Prayer that he would not allow temptation to have a chance in our lives because our ability to be tempted was created by him and we can succumb to temptation. In plain English, this means: May he not lead us into sin.

3.2. Man does not fall into sin because he hates God or because he seeks his own freedom (to take action) and he, himself, wants to be like God. Rather, such hostility to God is always the consequence of sin that has already been committed.

3.2.1. Most likely it is *forgetfulness of God* (for reasons that are found in man or in God?) that first leads man into sin. Later sin always leads to more and more sins. We cannot say more than this. Man's entrance into sin remains God's secret whichever way you look at it.

The Meaning of Sin

4. If man is called a *sinner,* we rightfully believe that he is living contrary to the forces and laws that preserve and pass on life.

4.1. Sin brings about death and its tendency is anticreation. Sin does not take pleasure in being. Only superficially does it seem to be a zest for living.

4.1.1. The sinner leaves living nature's self-movement and self-organization; he moves against the stream and against the rest of creation's sense of direction (= not only a lack of instinct but of reason as well).

4.1.2. The sinner also leaves the realm of human laws and social orders, which are intended to compensate for the basic human conflict with nature (= a lack not only of reason but also of love).

4.2. There are two examples of how man goes his own way. Traditional theological terminology calls this dual phenomenon impulsive-addictive desire (concupiscence) and man's arrogance (hubris).

4.2.1. Concupiscence and hubris do not refer to any mental defeats or passions, and even less do they describe the moral vices of individuals; rather, they characterize man's universal situation.

4.2.1.1. For all living beings, man is the only nonintegrated creature who is still unsure of himself and still in need of his justification.

4.3. Man's certainty, justification, and integration enable him to live in loving harmony with his fellow creatures. These are specific meanings of the word *faith.*

4.3.1. Faith that is real is man's certainty, justification, and integration that are real.

4.3.2. The believing individual returns to fellowship with the Creator and comprehends love as the God-ordained purpose and direction of creation.

4.4. God saves creation and humanity from complete destruction even where faith does not exist, even where only sin exists. Sin does not completely achieve its goal.

4.4.1. Nevertheless, the sins of human beings as well as the evils still present in nature together cause serious and unjust suffering in many creatures.

4.4.2. On the one hand, humanity is inclined to sin and, on the other hand, inclined to believe. This is an indicator of creation's still unfinished and imperfect condition. (Unfinished does not mean bad. It is not a contradiction in terms that God wanted to have a world that was both good and unfinished. Likewise, those who describe a child or a symphony as unfinished do not mean that they are bad or deficient in any way.)

4.4.2.1. The creation is unfinished, however, in that it is not yet redeemed from its evils, but will be redeemed.

4.4.2.2. Given the continuing evils found in creation, humanity is dissatisfied that its perfection has not yet been achieved. Although God in principle shares this dissatisfaction, it also finds expression in man's sinning.

4.4.2.3. However, God does not agree with the sinner's "actions to improve life" if these actions do not spring from the joy man finds in life, but from hatred, envy, and disgust.

4.5. The possibility of faith granted to human beings is a concrete preview of the pending redemption of the world (it means that man can receive this redemption "proleptically").

4.5.1. As a sinner, man is the most harmful and most miserable of all creatures. As a believer, however, he is a revelation of creation in its perfected beauty, a preview of the glory of the redeemed world.

4.5.2. The history of humanity is the grammar of world evolution. The course of creation all the way up to redemption has found a language in humanity.

4.5.2.1. For this reason, human beings themselves are not the sole meaning and purpose of reality, either in sin or in faith; rather, they are always signs or letters in which God's action in and for the world is expressed.

4.5.2.2. The eschatological goals of creation are expressed in sin and in faith — both of these possibilities reserved for human beings. These goals can be seen both in what God has rejected and thus intends to eliminate from creation and what God has chosen and will raise up to be the sole reality in the redeemed creation.

4.5.3. As the bearer of God's eschatological grammar, not only humanity but each individual human soul is of ultimate, that is, eternally unchanging, value.

4.5.4. Even when man is sinning, he is participating in God's work of rejection, for God takes action to reject what is contrary to his will. Thus, man is a servant of the Creator, embodying his eternal will and capable of being redeemed. His soul, too, is of eternal value.

4.5.4.1. As God intended, the sinner reveals what is rejected by God and thus is no longer wanted by God in the perfection of the new creation. *In this way* what God wants and does not want regarding sin are *meaningfully* joined together.

God's Assistance for the Sinner

5. God knows the human beings created by him. In their struggle for dignity they *all* fall into sin, and he himself must assist them if they are to be kept from completely destroying themselves.

5.1. Even exceptionally gifted human beings in whom evil plays itself out are and remain human beings marred by sins and weaknesses. But they are "signs of God" among us. They are a door through which the lost splendor of creation returns.

5.2. The essence of the gospel of Jesus Christ is that God sees our sinning as a flaw for which he, the Creator himself, takes responsibility by sending a special gift of love to human beings — the incarnation of God!

SECTION VIII
THE MAIN ISSUES IN NEW TESTAMENT
HAMARTIOLOGY

A. Sin in Transition from the Old to the New Testament

Following the campaigns of Alexander the Great the age of Hellenism began for Palestine. At the same time this epoch was the age of *Judaism* between the Old and New Testaments. This Judaism shared in the widespread sense of anxiety in Hellenism, a foreboding feeling that disaster had come upon the world. The latest literary documents of the Old Testament — the book of Daniel, for example — make allowance for this hellenistic anxiety about the world with its apocalyptic visions. To be sure, this widespread feeling had developed organically out of Israel's history *as well*. Israel was increasingly rattled by theological questions that had remained open, such as the problem of Job. Israel expected sinners to suffer bad fortune but the pious to prosper, but in the case of Job this idea was clearly falsified.

In the period of Judaism between the two Testaments, Israel gained a (partially) deeper theological understanding of sin. The issue of how far the harmful effects of sinful deeds reach was more closely examined. On the one hand, the opinion that each person has to pay for his own sins gained currency. On the other hand, Israel saw sinful deeds from a different angle. They came to understand sinful deeds as a destructive impulse into the peaceful condition of the world and reflected on the conditions for an atonement that would heal this rupture.

The central idea was that sins could be "neutralized" if a righteous person sacrifices his own peaceful state and suffers vicariously. However, because it seemed to be evident that too few righteous persons could serve as substitutes in view of the many sins of human beings, they judged the present world pessimistically, doubting that it could continue to exist. For political reasons as well, Israel increasingly despaired and failed to hope that the promises of salvation given to the nation could be fulfilled through the continuous progress of history. The view that the present world order was intolerable and was an "old world" heading for destruction gained greater acceptance. All the people who thought in apocalyptic categories expected a qualitatively different, new world age that would soon break into history and in which suffering and tears would no longer exist.

In some cases such expectations had the effect of deepening their understanding of sin and evil, but there were also ideas circulating that revealed a growing superficiality in dealing with sin and in their understanding of sin. In view of the expected imminent end of the world, they began to calculate like businessmen whether there was a surplus of good over bad deeds. A kind of debit-and-credit mentality often marked their attitude to guilt and sin, to good and evil. At the same time sin and the righteousness of human beings were more intentionally subsumed under the priestly categories of "unclean and clean." Here, too, at least a tendency to externalize their understanding of sin could be detected. Just like that, "sinning" could now be understood as a process of violating the rules of ritual purification. It was obvious that this often resulted in attitudes that were wrong in both theological and human terms. Later Jesus expressly rebuked those who held such attitudes (for example, in the classic section of Mark 7:15ff.). What was already developing in Hellenistic Judaism found its clearest expression in parts of the New Testament. Whereas the Old Testament, especially in its older layers, tends to understand sins as specific, individual transgressions against God or against human beings, the New Testament frequently speaks of sin as a formative power that holds the whole world in thrall. The period between the Testaments had a heightened awareness of the corruption and lostness of the world, and this is in keeping with the New Testament's frequent practice of speaking of *ha hamartia* in a way that virtually personifies sin. For example, in the famous Pauline treatise on sin in Romans 7:15ff., we find not only statements about what *the* sinner does or does not do, but also statements about what *sin* does, what *sin* can do.

In addition, the New Testament (as well as the Old Testament) uses a number of simple, easily understandable words in common use internationally or religiously to describe the everyday event of sinning and incurring guilt. The Greek substantives used in the New Testament alone are a colorful mixture, which is probably also the case in most other languages and religions of the world. Besides the above-mentioned word *hamartia,* which is found most frequently and means that man misses his target like a poorly shot arrow or strays from his path, the New Testament also speaks of man's *adikia* (unrighteousness), *anomia* (lawlessness, asserting a selfish, human will against God's commandment), *hēttēma* (only found in Paul [Rom. 11:12 and 1 Cor. 6:7], meaning defeat, inferior works), *kakia* (malice, wickedness), *opheilēma* (for example, in the Lord's Prayer, Matt. 6:12: the guilt incurred in a creditor-debtor relationship), *parabasis* (the transgression of the law, *transgressio legis* — a term for sin used primarily by Paul), *parakoē* (disobedience), *paraptōma* (lapse offense — used more frequently in relationship to God than in relationship to human beings), *planē* (mistake, delusion of the heart), *ponēria, ponēros* (wickedness, meanness, dissoluteness, corruptness, every imaginable kind of evil), *porneia* (lewdness, also in terms of idolatry), and so on.

In spite of this abundance of terms comparable to what can be found in the Old Testament and in other religions, there is a conspicuous tendency to conflate the multitude of possible human sins and speak generally of *sin* (in the singular). This conflation not only has to do with the apocalyptic thought that emerged in the intertestamental period and even found its way into many New Testament writings. Rather, an even more significant cause is the pervasive *christological character* of the whole New Testament. Evil and sin was radically centered and condensed through the appearance of Jesus Christ. He often appears in the New Testament as the one in whom the humanity that is a part of the new, coming age is separated from the humanity that is a part of the old, perishing age. Jesus Christ *is* the decision because we must decide either to be with him when the new creation dawns or to remain behind in the world of corruption, in the world of evil.

Thus in the transition from the Old to the New Testament, the following change has taken place. The stand the individual takes on Jesus Christ reveals most precisely and most clearly what the word "sin" ultimately means and what evil ultimately means. "Sinning" now always means: rejecting Jesus Christ and the salvation that has arrived with him. *Sin* (in the singular) now appears as the basic attitude of hatred toward the light that came into the world with and in Jesus Christ. That is why it says in John 3:19, "This is the verdict: Light has come into the world, but men loved darkness instead of light because their deeds were evil."

Therefore through the mission of Jesus Christ, the theological understanding of sin was given a new form. In the New Testament, "sinning" was no longer understood only in the usual sense of violating one of Yahweh's commandments. Rather, at the same time "sinning" assumed the character of hostility toward the grace of God that appeared in Jesus Christ. "Sin" now took place in the form of a rejection of the gospel, a rejection of the mission and message of Jesus Christ. However, through this rejection, what the Old Testament prophets knew and said became clear once again — the idea that sin never simply represents the violation of a certain ethical commandment, but at its core is *unbelief.* Against the backdrop of this deepening understanding of sin that was made possible through Jesus Christ, Søren Kierkegaard could say: in the Christian understanding of sin, the equivalent of sin is not vice, the moral misdeed; rather, the equivalent of sin is unbelief!

I have already said that this development in the New Testament's understanding of sin did not signify a simple break with the Old Testament. On the contrary, it represents a focusing of the Old Testament tradition. The dominant aspect is its continuity with the Old Testament.

It seems to be a contradiction that the Old Testament sinner incurs guilt by violating an instruction of the Torah whereas the New Testament sinner becomes a sinner by unbelief, by rejecting the gospel of God in Jesus Christ. But in the final analysis, the Old Testament sinner as well always offended against the kindness and grace of God. He impaired the relationship of trust that Israel had with the God of covenant. By breaking the covenant law, he not simply violated a divine edict but offended against the kindness, love, and help of the God who had chosen Israel. On the other hand, our earlier observation that at its core sin is a violation of the first commandment is not invalidated by the New Testament approach that all sin is unbelief toward the gospel and a rejection of the grace of Christ. For this too means nothing but persisting in one's violation of the first commandment in spite of the kindness and nearness of God that appeared in Christ, making *such* recalcitrance superfluous and impossible. Faith in Jesus Christ should result in nothing but the reestablishment of the first commandment in the heart of sinners. This is why the Gospel of John is right in affirming what Christ said: "He who hates me hates my Father as well" (John 15:23) and "When he looks at me, he sees the one who sent me" (John 12:45).

B. The Relationship between Sin and Suffering (Sickness) in the New Testament

The New Testament continues to affirm an insight which gained acceptance in the later strata of the Old Testament. A sinner does not have to suffer in every case; his guilt is not simultaneously his burden in every case. Moreover, a righteous person does not have to be able to lead a life free of suffering, sickness, and disaster in every case. So this insight has become perfectly natural since then. Neither does sin make one sick in every case, nor does righteousness keep the righteous person healthy in body and spirit in every case.

That is why, in the New Testament, *the forgiveness of sins is not a priori identical with a recovery from physical or social ailments in every case!* But it aims at such a recovery — this must also be seen!

When a paralyzed man was let down through the open roof of a crowded house into the living quarters where Jesus was staying, everyone expected nothing less from Jesus than that he would heal this paralytic man, which the description in Mark 2 clearly shows. Because of this initial expectation (besides Jesus' tremendous claim to have authority), it was very surprising when Jesus first granted the paralyzed man forgiveness of sins. The man's physical infirmity was not healed *in this way* (Mark 2:1-12).

From this perspective the unity of sin and sickness, of freedom from sin and health assumed in several older sections of the Old Testament, is no longer in effect in the New Testament. There is also no indication that Jesus understood the paralytic's sickness as a consequence of this man's having committed especially serious sins.[18]

Yet it is the intention of this narrative to call our attention to the unity between *righteousness before God and health in a whole new way.* It expresses the truth that the mere physical restoration of a sick person does not yet mean that he has sufficiently recovered. The people who witnessed this scene were supposed to understand that, above all, the restoration of a human being to health requires the healing of his relationship with God. Only after that does Jesus perform the physical healing. It becomes apparent that the more serious infirmity, the more serious suffering, is the one that the people hardly ever really notice — their broken relationship to God.

In the New Testament Paul even talks about an ailment man is exposed to *because* he has come to faith and *because* his sins have been forgiven in Jesus Christ. For Paul continuing in the grace of Christ has nothing to do with a religious pharmacology that would prevent us from contracting any illness. On the contrary, Paul could put the goal of his faith in terms of wanting to "gain Christ" and "sharing in his sufferings" (Phil. 3:7, 10).

18. See John 9:1-3.

The righteous man must not only suffer much (Ps. 34:20), but he is *permitted to* suffer and is *able to* suffer.

Because the book of Job was added to the collection of Old Testament writings only at a late date, we find Job's complaint going in a quite different direction. He lamented the fact that he had to suffer, *although* he didn't do anything wrong. In the New Testament we find in Paul an Israelite who is convinced that he had become a righteous person by faith and therefore had to strive to become *conformed* to Jesus Christ in his sufferings, and even his death. From this point of view Paul is an anti-Job because he affirms that it is precisely God's friends who must suffer. His desire to lose even his salvation and be cursed if that could open the way to salvation for his people in Jesus Christ (Rom. 9:3) is typical.

Paul was not addicted to suffering. It is known that he resisted unfair treatment by the Roman authorities. For him, having to suffer was not an imperative in terms of the rule that can only be called nonsense: now that you have become a "committed Christian," you have to learn how to taste the bitter side of life. Rather, for Paul suffering is an indicative, that is, a fact of life for everyone who is grafted into the body of Christ. It is a part of reality for the life of the baptized. However, this does not mean that Christians must now become acquainted with the bitter side of life. On the contrary, it means that Christians experience the return of divine splendor ascending over the sorrowful fields of life because the members of the body of Jesus Christ are "always rejoicing," even in their sorrow (2 Cor. 6:10), if they are emulating Paul. Paul is both sorrowful and joyful because he belongs to both the old and the new age in his solidarity with Jesus Christ. To be sure, through his solidarity with Christ, Paul first sees the stark reality of the old age in all its unadorned sadness. Yet, he emphasizes that "our present sufferings are not worth comparing with the glory that will be revealed in us" (Rom. 8:18).

With this attitude Paul is still to a certain extent in continuity with the heritage of the Old Testament. For example, he interprets Jesus Christ in the light of the figure of the "suffering righteous one" who appears in Deutero-Isaiah (see Isa. 53:3f. and Phil. 2:7f.). Baptized Christians who have a share in Jesus Christ are incorporated into this "Suffering Servant of God" and thus are also given a share in his splendid glorification by God, which has already begun. All this signifies a lively forward movement in the Old Testament tradition.

C. Guilt and Forgiveness in the Fifth Petition of the Lord's Prayer

"Forgive us our debts as we forgive our debtors." In Luke *hamartia* stands for debt (Luke 11:4), a word that is often rendered by the English word "sin." Matthew 6:12 says: "Forgive us *ta opheilēmata*"! (God, forgive us the debts we have accumulated with you!) We continue by giving the gist of the next phrase: Do this, God, just as we are prepared to remit the debts our fellow debtors owe to us. Whoever interprets the fifth petition that Matthew passed on in this form should also cite its important parallel, the passage that is known as the parable of the unmerciful servant (Matt. 18:23-35).

A king remitted his servant the huge amount which the servant owed him but was not able to pay back. Unfortunately, then the servant did not treat a debtor under him in the same way. When we pray in the Lord's Prayer, "God, forgive our debts," we are asking our heavenly Father to remit the payment of our debt in the same way that servant asked his king to remit his debt. But at the same time we know that the fulfillment of our petition must imply our own willingness to forgive.

A parallel to this parable is found in the fifth petition of the Lord's Prayer. The first part of the sentence speaks of our relationship to God, the second of our relationship to our neighbor. The connection between our sin against God and the debt we owe to our neighbor is discussed here in a basic way. Of course, it is peculiar how little we who pray the Lord's Prayer are really used to considering the nature of the forgiveness we are asking for there. How many of those who pray the fifth petition have the feeling that the issue here is whether they can be released from their own debts, the debts they have incurred by sinning against *other people?* However, if we pay attention to the illustrative parable of the unmerciful servant, it becomes clear that in the Lord's Prayer we are asking only for the forgiveness of the debts we incurred by sinning against God.

In the fifth petition of the Lord's Prayer, it is not a matter of receiving strength to compensate for debts we have incurred in our relationship to our fellow man. For the fifth petition says: just as God as our creditor remits the debts we owe him, we should also remit the debts of our fellow man who is in our debt! The issue here is not that we must actively clear up our own debt owed to our fellow man. This practice played a large role in Pietism. Pietists believed it was necessary to clear up our own debt before we could receive forgiveness of sins from God. Rather, the issue here is whether we are willing to be reconciled at the point where *we ourselves have the right to sue for the recovery of debts owed to us by our fellow men!* The command that we, too, have to forgive those who are guilty of having sinned against us is placed alongside the divine forgiveness of our sin (against God) in the Lord's Prayer.

In the Christian realm, we often encounter this sweeping statement on the Old Testament: it is filled with vengeful thoughts, even with rejoicing at the fall and misfortune of their so-called enemies. Proudly and smugly, such Christian critics think they themselves no longer operate at this low cultural level. In pastoral conversations they confess that they are the kind of people who could never resent anyone for anything, especially not when they have empathized with the personality structure and the motives of others.

But is this understanding attitude really at a higher level culturally, even if such people are willing to forgive everything and are often more likely to accuse themselves? In fact, it holds a very serious problem that they have repressed. All people have every reason to treat many others who are guilty of having sinned against them with hatred or anger. But they cannot permit themselves these feelings. They are afraid that releasing these feelings would end in their personal destruction. Even if we can pray the Lord's Prayer "correctly" and do not twist its intention when we repeat it, the strength we ask for in this petition is (the first step) our ability to discern when others have diminished our happiness and wholeness. We should really *know* what it means to forgive our debtor!

If we inquire again about the unmerciful servant (the parable that illuminates the fifth petition of the Lord's Prayer), we find out that we are to forgive others what they can *never compensate us for!* We do not have to give the other a break because we are so good-natured; we do not have to spare him the cost of paying his debt even though he could very likely compensate us for it but doesn't want to because it is convenient not to do so and he feels a certain sense of shame. Rather, we are supposed to pardon the other for impairing our well-being and damaging our personhood. This damage affects our whole personality because it had its origin in the most profound depths of human twistedness. We should forgive our neighbor who incurred guilt by diminishing our own being. This happened when the other made an idol of us, even misused us as a substitute for God. The fifth petition of the Lord's Prayer comes from the recognition that human beings cause irreparable harm to each other and destroy each other not just sometimes, but daily and under the guise of moral normality or even goodness in this far-reaching way. Our whole life is interspersed with modified forms of idolatry. However, we can least of all compensate for what we did to those whom we have misused as substitutes for God. Every moral endeavor and every effort to compensate on our part are bound to fail.

It is difficult, extremely difficult, to forgive when human beings are confronted with the fact that they were actually abused in their childhood by their mother or father because their parents made an idol of them. The person abused as a child can forgive his parents for this only because the former child as well incurs guilt in a *similar* way, only because the former child as well would be lost if God would disassociate himself from him as a result of such guilt and would not "shine his light on the sinner's face" every morning anew as the "light from inexhaustible" (*Evangelical Hymnal*, no. 349).

The disastrous chain of idol making can really be broken only by God's forgiveness. It begins to work before we do anything. Peace can enter in where human life is infected by a vengefulness that destroys everything, often without this state of affairs being noticed even where it is completely repressed and produces its negative effects. The sufferings other people have inflicted on us can never be compensated for, yet even they can be transformed into productive new opportunities in our life when we understand suffering as sharing in the sufferings of Jesus Christ, who together with us is heading toward the splendor of the new creation.

D. Reflections on the Meaningfulness of Making a Distinction between Sin and Wrongdoing

In the previous section I primarily characterized our broken relationship to God as sin and broken interpersonal relationships as wrongdoing. But from the New Testament's point of view, this is not so compelling at all. In the New Testament a broader usage prevails and numerous concepts are used, one minute expressing our broken interpersonal relationships and the next minute our broken relationship to God, and then both in a single context.

Nevertheless, it is advisable in our present language situation within a secularized society to distinguish between sin and wrongdoing.[19] When we speak of sin, our broken relationship to God can be in view first. Yet Christians should not correct the language of fellow human beings using secular speech and use the word "sin" whenever they are used to speaking of wrongdoing. For then a further inquiry is very legitimate. By using exaggerated theological language to describe interpersonal wrongdoing, are you not putting other people under such pressure that it could produce neuroses? And conversely: Aren't you making it too easy on yourselves in dealing with your wrongdoing when you never understand interpersonal offenses as something that should be ironed out between the individuals concerned on their own if at all possible? Given the fact that such wrongdoing can be ironed out, don't you make it too easy for yourselves when you pray, "God forgive us?" *We should label others' violations that can be ironed out and modified by improved behavior not as sin but as wrongdoing.*[20]

In criminal law the concept of *expiation* has the meaning of atoning for wrongdoing by serving a sentence of equal weight. But this is a secularized misuse and misunderstanding of expiation. This concept has its place where compensatory works are no longer a possibility.[21] The concept should pale into insignificance and be removed from the penal code.

Sin is the kind of wrongdoing against our fellow men and fellow creatures and also against God that we can never make up for.[22] Sin can only be atoned for and forgiven, but can not be cleared up by compensatory works (it is understood that forgiveness does not leave out *possible* compensation as if forgiveness were an alternative to it instead of freeing people who offer it!). We can sin against human beings *as well*. But the removal of this offense, which is always at the same time an offense against God, presupposes *that first God himself comes out of his silence* (the silence that represents the appropriate outcome of human sin) and resumes his

---

19. See also N. Hartmann, *Ethik* ([¹1925]; Berlin, ³1949), pp. 23ff. and 817f.

20. But we should not overlook the fact that all wrongdoing also has an irreversible aspect to it.

21. W. Trillhaas, *Dogmatik* (Berlin/New York, ³1972), pp. 321f.

22. Trillhaas correctly says, "The fact that sin cannot be cancelled is a part of sin's essence. I can repair the damage and correct the mistake caused by sin, but I cannot correct the sin itself. Paul's phrase that the wages of sin is death points to the finality of sin" (Rom. 5:12-21; 6:23) (*Dogmatik*, p. 790).

relationship with us. And this forgiveness is to be distinguished clearly from a totally different question. How should we react when wrongdoing that calls for compensation is present? Taking people seriously as human beings means here not underestimating their strength and freedom to make amends or their insistence on providing compensation.

E. The Problem of the Sin against the Holy Spirit and Mortal Sins

Does the Holy Spirit work "irresistibly" in those who come to faith? Can anyone the Holy Spirit gets hold of resist God's call, can anyone evade God's entry into his or her own life? If the Holy Spirit would work "irresistibly" in this way, then no one could sin against the Holy Spirit. In the history of theology, the clarification of this issue has always been seen as especially difficult.[23]

The same thing is true of the following problems. How are we to evaluate a situation in which someone becomes a convert, a born-again Christian, a baptized believer with the assistance of the Holy Spirit, but later falls away from his Christianity and, sometime later, tries again to become a Christian? Especially during the time when Christians were persecuted in the early church, the question was asked, "Can a member who offered sacrifices to the emperor to escape martyrdom be readmitted into the church, into the eschatological people of God?" There are a few verses in the New Testament that venture to give a clear answer to this question.

Hebrews 6:4-6: "It is impossible for those who have once been enlightened, who have tasted the heavenly gift, who have shared in the Holy Spirit, who have tested the goodness of the word of God and the powers of the coming age, if they fall away, to be brought back to repentance. . . ."

Hebrews 10:26-29: "If we deliberately keep on sinning after we have received the knowledge of the truth, no sacrifice for sins is left, but only a fearful expectation of judgment and of raging fire that will consume the

---

23. J. Müller calls it the "touchstone for our views concerning the nature of evil." *Die christliche Lehre von der Sünde* (Bremen, [6]1889), 2:612; quotation from English translation, *The Christian Doctrine of Sin*, trans. William Urwick, 2 vols. (Edinburgh: T. & T. Clark, 1877), 2:418.

enemies of God. Anyone who rejected the law of Moses died without mercy on the testimony of two or three witnesses. How much more severely do you think a man deserves to be punished who has trampled the Son of God under foot, who has treated as an unholy thing the blood of the covenant that sanctified him, and who has insulted the spirit of grace?"

These verses from Hebrews say first: in the opinion of the author, it is possible in principle to fall out of the state of faith worked by the Holy Spirit and to return to the old being that is under the power of sin and death. In this view the Holy Spirit does not work irresistibly, at least not *in the sense* that he would force those whom he gets hold of to belong to him for the rest of their life. Moreover, the verses quoted from Hebrews show us that in the perception of its author, the Holy Spirit — he is *a fruit of the life and death of Christ* — represents the supreme and highest remedy that is given to us for our sins. If the Holy Spirit can accomplish nothing in the life of us sinners, then nothing can help us because his coming *is* the eschatological, the final advent of salvation. His coming *is* the new covenant of God. If a rupture occurs between us and the Holy Spirit, then there is nothing left that could heal this rupture. From these observations about Hebrews, we can now turn our attention to the verses in the New Testament Gospels that speak of a sin against the Holy Spirit. It is actually a matter of only a single statement which we find in Matthew 12:30-32, Mark 3:28f., and Luke 12:10. I quote first the perhaps more original Q form of the saying according to Matthew 12:30-32.

"He who is not with me is against me, and he who does not gather with me scatters. And so I tell you, every sin and blasphemy will be forgiven men, but the blasphemy against the Spirit will not be forgiven. *Anyone who speaks a word against the Son of Man will be forgiven, but anyone who speaks against the Holy Spirit will not be forgiven either in this age or in the age to come.*"

Jesus' dictum in Matthew — as in Mark — that blasphemy against the Holy Spirit is eternally unforgivable was placed in the framework of a *miracle story* by a secondary redactor:[24] after Jesus had driven out a demon, some tried to explain this act of healing in this way: He himself has an

---

24. H. Thyen, *Studien zur Sündenvergebung im Neuen Testament und seinen alttestamentlichen und jüdischen Voraussetzungen,* FRLANT 96 (Göttingen, 1970), asserts this on pp. 257f. (following R. Bultmann and F. Hahn).

unclean spirit, he is driving out the devil with Beelzebub. In Matthew 12:28 Jesus defends himself against this charge by correcting them: I am driving out the evil spirits by the Spirit of God, by the Holy Spirit, and, because I do this, the kingdom of God has now come upon you. According to Jesus, *the flight of the demons (the unclean spirits) is an indication that the Holy Spirit and the kingdom of God have arrived.*

Their suspicion that Jesus himself was possessed by a powerful unclean spirit and thus had the power to drive out demons prompted Jesus to make this sharp rejoinder — this is the redactor's intention. Let us keep in mind that Matthew 12:32, in exact correspondence with Luke 12:10, says: "Anyone who speaks a word against the Son of Man will be forgiven, but anyone who speaks against the Holy Spirit will not be forgiven,[25] either in this age or in the age to come." (Compare the parallel verse, Mark 3:28f., which leaves out the sin against the Son of Man: "I tell you the truth, all the sins and blasphemies of man will be forgiven them. But whoever blasphemes against the Holy Spirit will never be forgiven; he is guilty of an eternal sin.")

The Christian church for many centuries derived a remarkable idea from the version of Jesus' words found in Matthew that speak of the impossibility of forgiveness in this and the future age, an idea that is rather hard on Jesus' saying. Reinterpreting this statement, they taught *even in the hereafter, forgiveness of sin and even repentance is possible in itself,* and more precisely, forgiveness and repentance for *all* sins, *except* the sin against the Holy Spirit!

In the course of church history this peculiar understanding of the text was then combined with the verse from Hebrews 10 quoted above that speaks of the terrible expectation of God's judgment that will befall baptized Christians who have fallen away. It also speaks of the *raging* fire that will consume these poor people in the life to come. But, as early as the Middle Ages, this terrible picture was moderated again. The idea of *cleansing fire* took the place of *consuming* fire. However, this cleansing fire waits not only for those who have fallen away from the faith but also almost without exception for all those who have died.

Thus the church's doctrine of *purgatory* emerged through a complicated process. Today it is clear to all theologians working carefully with the texts that the exegetical foundation, that is, the New Testament basis, for this church doctrine is questionable.

---

25. See Thyen, pp. 257f. (following Tödt).

The dictum of 1 Corinthians 3:13-15 on the end-time judgment must also have played some role in the development of the church doctrine of purgatory: "His work will be shown for what it is. . . ." "It will be revealed with fire, and the fire will test the quality of each man's work. If what he has built survives, he will receive his reward. If it is burned up, he will suffer loss; he himself will be saved, but only as one escaping through the flames."

When Matthew's Gospel says that the sin against the Holy Spirit can be forgiven neither in this nor in the coming age, this should certainly not mean that all *other* sins could be forgiven, if not now, then at least after death in the world to come. For the future age, the *aiōn mellōn,* does not mean "life after death in the hereafter" at all. Rather, this coming age has already dawned with the coming of the Holy Spirit at Pentecost. In a certain sense it even dawned with Jesus' work on earth. Matthew 12:32 says, therefore (in terms of the objective situation that had been clearly discerned only from the perspective of Easter): Whoever sins against the Holy Spirit cannot be forgiven either in the old or in the new age, either in the old or in the new creation, either in this transitory world or in the kingdom of God *(basileia tou theou)* now dawning.

In the traditional Roman Catholic view the church not only has the authority to absolve the penitent from his sins in the context of the sacrament of confession and penance, but it also has the authority to remit punishments for purgatory in the hereafter (indulgence). *The assertion of an unforgivable sin against the Holy Spirit, however, does not play a role in the practice and in the teaching of the Roman Catholic Church.* Rather, the church considers itself qualified, in principle, to be able to forgive any sin that occurs among human beings.[26] Thus it is not the case that Roman Catholic dogmatics would draw a distinction, as many think, between "venal sins," on the one hand, that can be forgiven in the confessional, and unforgivable, very serious "mortal sins," on the other hand. Rather, the Catholic church debates in its textbooks whether one really needs to confess the "venal sins" at all (those sins that do not cause a distortion of the image of God in man or a distortion of his soul), or whether one has

---

26. See L. Ott, *Grundriß der katholischen Dogmatik* (Freiburg/Basel/Wien, [8]1970), p. 503: "The church's power to forgive sins extends to all sin without exception." Quotation from English translation, *Fundamentals of Catholic Dogma,* ed. in English by James Canon Bastible, trans. Patrick Lynch, 5th ed. (St. Louis: B. Herder, 1962), p. 422.

to claim the sacrament of penance for them at all because this sacrament is actually there for mortal sins and is intended to help believers move away from them — this is the prevailing doctrinal view.

Committing a mortal sin signifies the loss of grace and a distortion of the *imago Dei*. This is why such a sin can only be cured with a new gift of grace through the sacrament of penance. But in this way it *is* cured. Therefore, the theological concept of mortal sin does not mean a human offense whose tracks could never be covered up, or whose punishment has no end. *The concept of mortal sin simply has nothing to do with the idea of an unforgivable sin against the Holy Spirit.* It goes back to 1 John 5:16, where mortal sins are set apart from other sins that do not lead to death. Starting there, the church developed the doctrine of the seven mortal sins *(peccata mortalia* or *peccata capitalia).* These seven sins that can only be forgiven through the sacrament of penance are called by these names: (1) pride, (2) gluttony, (3) the pursuit of luxury or opulence, (4) greed, (5) (godless) sadness, (6) envy, and (7) anger. It is almost as if these mortal sins had to do with our *everyday sins.*

Luther and the Reformation rejected the distinction between mortal and venal sins. They taught that every sin is a mortal sin from which only God's grace in Jesus Christ can help extricate us. Unfortunately, a felt need to draw a distinction between minor sins and *one* very serious sin took root in later Protestantism, mainly in Pietism. For example, we find in the early Protestant orthodox Lutheran David Hollaz (1648-1713) the following statement: among born-again Christian believers, every sin is *venal,* as long as it occurs involuntarily and does not chase away the grace of the Holy Spirit indwelling born-again Christians, and does not extinguish faith. Rather in the same moment it is committed, pardon is there. However, it is terrible when someone knows God's commandment and saving will inside out yet nevertheless *intentionally* acts against this commandment and saving will after careful consideration. Hollaz feels that this is not only a sin that leads to death, but actually the sin against the Holy Spirit.[27] Thus, Hollaz has in mind a form of sin that weighs much heavier than the mortal sins of Roman Catholic dogmatics. It is a sin oscillating between "the most serious mortal sin" and the "sin against the Holy Spirit."

What makes it especially difficult to follow Hollaz in his theological

---

27. Hollaz, *Examen Theologicum Acroamaticum Universam Theologiam Thetico-Polemicam Complectens* (1707), pt. 2, cap. 4, pp. 542, 545, 556-650.

reflections is that he is working with the peculiar concept of a "willfully committed" sin. But what does it mean to commit a sin "willfully"? It is characteristic of the act of sinning that most of the time it occurs both willfully and unwillfully at the same time. Therefore I agree with Karl Barth when he says that distinctions between mortal and venal sins are to be theologically rejected. "The distinction between lethal and venial sins cannot be sustained. It is quite irrelevant." Indeed, "in the last resort it is to be rejected."[28]

Nevertheless, the nature of a possible sin against the Holy Spirit remains an open question when we take into consideration the modern surroundings of anthropological experience and the reality of today's church. This question cannot be seen as settled simply because we reject the distinction between mortal sins and venal sins. We now have to ask: What does it look like, what happens when a person blasphemes against the Holy Spirit? Is it tantamount to a person once converted to Jesus Christ leaving the path of faith in the course of his further biographical development? Is there only *one* conversion? Does the apostasy of those individuals who have already been born again represent something like an unpardonable, irreversible disaster? Or, for example, did Søren Kierkegaard's father commit the sin against the Holy Spirit by lamenting his miserable prospects for the future and cursing God when he was a ten-year-old shepherd boy standing on a boulder with his arms stretched out to heaven? Evidently, this event was associated with a horrible family depression, a despair embracing two generations and the feeling that the whole family must be wiped out by God as "an unsuccessful experiment." Kierkegaard's father clearly remembered it even as an eighty-two-year-old man.

It must be clearly emphasized *against* the above-mentioned assumptions that an anthropological verification of the offense called "the sin against the Holy Spirit" is not possible. I mean by this that this sin cannot be equated with certain forms of human despair, that is, depressions caused by religion and the concomitant feelings of being cursed. The enduring solid core of Jesus' warning about the sin against the Holy Spirit centers on the truth that God cannot be mocked (see Gal. 6:7: "Do not be

---

28. K. Barth, *Die Kirchliche Dogmatik*, 13 vols. (Zurich, 1932ff.), IV/2, p. 558, hereafter cited as *KD*; quotation from English translation, *Church Dogmatics*, vol. 4, *The Doctrine of Reconciliation*, pt. 2, ed. G. W. Bromiley and T. F. Torrance, trans. G. W. Bromiley (Edinburgh: T. & T. Clark, 1958), p. 493.

deceived: God cannot be mocked. A man reaps what he sows"). It is also a fact of pastoral care that Christians often sense when they have "grieved," "quenched," or "despised" the Holy Spirit (see Eph. 4:30), and that in their sadness about this they ardently wish they had not done this. However, the fact that man must bear the consequences of his deeds does not mean that God will never again treat a person kindly who has incurred guilt by sinning *against God.*

In the realm of Pietism the possibility that converted or born-again Christians can fall away from the faith is greatly feared. The horrible calamity that is described as the sin against the Holy Spirit in three Synoptic New Testament Gospels seems to lie in *this* possible outcome. In Pietism these verses in the Synoptic Gospels were frequently combined with the above-mentioned verses Hebrews 6:4-6 and Hebrews 10:26-29 to develop not a "doctrine of purgatory" but a doctrine of the eternal perdition and damnation that threatens converted Christians. But this exegetical combination must also be rejected for theological reasons. For example, it gives religious people a really bad conscience in an unchristian way and makes it worse for those who have a tendency to be depressed anyway. (This is also a dreadful medical situation because these people feel that their depression is a necessary consequence of religious failure. On the other hand, they never feel that their religious fear is a necessary consequence of their depression.)

It would be absurd to read out of the Synoptic statements about the sin against the Holy Spirit that a godless person can find justification by God and come to faith, experiencing God as undeserved favor "by grace alone"; yet a justified, "born-again" believer is eternally lost in the event that he rebels again against God. Moreover, it would be absurd to think a person could lose the Holy Spirit (and his gracious assistance) through his own guilty acts. This would assume that one could first *have* the Holy Spirit as a possession. In fact, this Spirit remains free and independent. He never becomes the personality of any spiritually gifted people whatsoever. Every baptized person is at the same time a person born again by God's Spirit; however, each person exists *simul iustus, simul peccator,* as a righteous person and a sinner at the same time. And his sins are not mostly just minor sins that he instantly regrets, that would no longer have a disruptive impact on his renewed relationship with God. In fact, they *all* disrupt this relationship.

The "spiritual health" of baptized and born-again Christians is, after all, not a "new being" that can be presented in anthropological terms, but a process of *becoming* healthy that is never finished in this life.[29] But, if this is the actual situation of born-again Christians, then they are hardly in danger of forfeiting once and for all a healthy *condition* they had already achieved and falling into a vacuum devoid of grace in which there would no longer be any more healing power. Furthermore, the opinion that there could be only *one* conversion in the life of an individual cannot be theologically substantiated.

A clear dividing line must also be drawn between the sin against the Holy Spirit mentioned by the New Testament Synoptics and mental problems, biographical conflicts, panic reactions, and diseases. It was Protestantism that *sinned* by often overloading such anthropological phenomena with the religious weight of an offense that has eternal consequences.

In the letter to the Hebrews the warning about the irrevocable loss of salvation and about the consuming fire of judgment served an important purpose. It deterred believers from avoiding martyrdom in the Roman Empire by falling away from Christianity. The end of the world and the return of Christ seemed to be imminent. The thrust of the argument went like this: How horrible it would be if a Christian would now turn down a salvation that was so near you could almost touch it!

In the Synoptic Gospels the warning about the sin against the Holy Spirit was intended to underline the decisive significance of Jesus' mission. They emphasized that the one who would like to wait for another savior will no longer find anyone else. According to the testimony of the verses I have mentioned, Jesus said (their authenticity does not need to be determined here): I do not want any fame for myself, but I call your attention to what is behind my mission — God's radical (eschatological) offer of salvation, which is now a matter of life or death. First and foremost, the unique significance of Jesus' mission in the history of salvation is underlined with these Synoptic references to the sin against the Holy Spirit. They are calling attention to the right path that leads to salvation; doubters are invited to go this way as well.

29. See Luther, WA, 7:337, lines 30-35.

SECTION IX
THE PROBLEM OF ORIGINAL SIN

A. Discussion of the Problem in the Twentieth Century

Original sin — I would like to speak of universal sin. It is the *peccatum* into which all human beings "fall." They fall by themselves. We fall by ourselves. No one can be the exception: the "essence" of the *peccatum commune* that represents our sinful nature underlying our individual sins has already been described:[30] We try to *ensure* by our "strategy of self-justification" that our own person is affirmed and recognized as good. We tyrannize our surroundings and put pressure on them to acclaim us. Whoever founders in the process rejects himself. In both cases, however, we imagine that we can be and, above all, have to be the principle of our own self — and this is freedom. The external mark of original sin is the absence of gratitude to God: the attitude that is mentioned in Romans 1:21. In ontological terms original sin is not a special, second sin alongside the sin we commit. Both are set apart only in intellectual terms. The former proves to be the root of the latter, or the bad omen set before every deed, even before otherwise good human deeds. Of course, the theological assertion of this universal human corruption at the root of his being has become a hotly contested issue in more recent times and is often denied. Its meaning is hard to understand, not least because many have become uncertain how this *peccatum commune* is related to the accumulated sins of the world or to the sinful surroundings of our society. We will see that these two aspects are not the same.[31] Could, then, these surroundings be properly understood as our universal human destiny from which only God's grace can extricate us? No. First of all, our own resistance is called for here — we argue this way and then are confused. . . .

Protestant and Roman Catholic theologies have frequently voiced reservations about the traditional doctrine of original sin. The most radical criticism came from the Catholic side. Yet, the discussion within the Roman church bore a different character than the Protestant discussion. The primary concern for Catholic theologians was to be rid of the pressure exerted by Rome and conservative systematic theologians to hold strictly

30. See p. 74.
31. See also pp. 229-232.

to a real *transmission* of sin from Adam and Eve, pressure that was felt beyond the middle of the twentieth century. In their view Adam and Eve were really to be seen as the two original human beings, as the actual *progenitors* of us all (the theory of so-called monogenism) in spite of the scientific teaching of evolution, a view that should be held in faith and in doctrine although a magisterial definition of the nature of original sin was never given. On the other hand, from the outset, the scientific teaching of evolution hardly presented any problem for European Protestant theologians in the twentieth century. (It would surely have been embraced by Schleiermacher if there had been a theory of evolution during his lifetime.)

For Protestants the heritage of the Reformation remained significant. In the case of Luther's teaching it amounted to a theological synopsis and an intertwining of original sin and sinful deeds. In contrast to the Reformation it has always been in keeping with Roman Catholic theology to distinguish clearly between original sin and sinful deeds. It has continuously taught that baptism cleanses the sinner from original sin (and, additionally, if they are present, of actual sins previously committed by the individual). A baptized Christian then faces only the problem of his *new* actual sins (especially what are known as mortal sins, which, however, can be forgiven with the help of the church's sacrament of penance), sins for which he is culpable, that is, which did not occur without the freedom of the will.

However, Luther taught a continuing influence of humanity's original sin beyond baptism in each individual sinful deed and impulse. Because of this continuing influence it is good for every Christian to "crawl back" into his baptism again and again.[32] Beyond the baptismal event Luther demonstrated the continuing effect of original sin in those dictates of the heart that amount to a rejection of God, an inability to love God or even follow the first commandment.[33] Luther wanted to stress that baptized Christians do not just have to struggle with sins committed against themselves and their surroundings, but that they are also always turning away from God while committing all these sins. In responding to Luther's

---

32. As Luther taught in many places, the essence of *repentance* seems to lie in nothing less than a *return to his baptism* that the Christian must make again and again. In this way Luther's theology of baptism brings out the aspect of man's active human response to God's grace.

33. See WA, 39I, pp. 84-86, especially p. 84, lines 22f. (eleventh thesis).

theology, this intention has often been misunderstood. It was thought that Luther's assertion of original sin's continuing influence beyond baptism signified that Luther categorized human nature as thoroughly corrupted by sin and thus found nothing good in human beings.

However, Protestant discussions of the problem of original sin in the twentieth century are largely free of this misunderstanding as far as Luther's theology is concerned. They additionally reveal their tendency to stick to Luther's close linkage of original sin to sinful deeds.[34] In no significant Protestant doctrinal study of the twentieth century was a desire ever expressed to do without a theology of original sin. But in all these presentations the theologians usually propose that the misunderstood words "original sin" should be replaced by another concept,[35] for example "Lebenssünde" (Karl Barth);[36] the universal, fateful aspect of alienation (Paul Tillich).[37]

Roman Catholics remember that they have always criticized the Protestant claim that a universal sinfulness outlasts even baptism. The memory of this criticism has flowed into many contemporary Roman Catholic discussions of original sin. Remembering this Counter Reformational position seems to have made it easier for many contemporary authors to criticize the dogma of original sin. In the period between 1960 and 1972 the Catholic theologian Julius Gross submitted a four-volume work on the history of the dogma of original sin. Volume 1 bears the title *A History of the Origins of the Dogma of Original Sin: From the Bible to Augustine* (Munich and Basel, 1960). Volumes 2-4, which have been published since 1963, give a "history of the development of the dogma of original sin." The final volume, published in 1972, encompasses the history of its development from the Reformation to the present. Gross prefaced this fourth volume with a sentence from Tübingen's Catholic Old Testament scholar Herbert Haag and took it as his motto: "Since the Western church has paid homage to a 1,500 year tradition led astray by Augustine, mo-

---

34. See A. Peters, "Die Sünde und die Sünden zwischen Glaube, Bekenntnis und Erfahrung," in F. Beisser and A. Peters, *Sünde und Sündenvergebung. Der Schlüssel zu Luthers Theologie* (Hannover, 1983), pp. 54f.

35. See G. Freund, *Sünde im Erbe. Erfahrungsinhalt und Sinn der Erbsündenlehre* (Stuttgart and others, 1979), pp. 47ff., 189-91.

36. *KD*, IV/1, pp. 11, 558 — Barth correctly considers the traditional Latin term for original sin, *peccatum originale,* to be incontestable.

37. Tillich, *Systematische Theologie* (Stuttgart, 1958), 2:46, also p. 65.

dernity is taking leave of 'original sin,' truly not too early — rather much too late."[38]

In the final section of the same fourth volume, Gross sums up: "Modern science has killed original sin. Since then Catholic theologians have been endeavoring at least to conserve its name. Recently they have been abandoning the name as well.

"Having outgrown the paralyzing belief that humans are entangled in the guilt and punishment of a sin committed in the dim and distant past, modern man resolutely prepares to struggle against evil in every form, convinced he is dependent on himself alone in this struggle."[39]

With a somewhat exaggerated emphasis Gross agrees with this whole development. He may be right when he says many today think that humanity is dependent on itself alone in the struggle against evil and that "no God" would help it in this struggle. But how does Gross back up his contention that the "modern man" who feels this way about God is now resolutely fighting against evil in every form? (If that were only so!) It is also not completely obvious whether Gross actually believes that in an earlier age people thought they were able to fight against inherited evil in the world only with the help of God when the dogma of original sin was still almost universally accepted. But now they take care of it all alone. If Gross should want to say this, he would do well to keep in mind that in church history original sin was never considered an evil that man had to fight with God's help or grace. Rather, since the time of Augustine, original sin was considered to be the disaster from which God *alone* could liberate us. This gracious liberation is received through the sacrament of baptism. It is *this* point which should be critically discussed today. Can such an understanding of the effect of baptism be maintained with biblical, theological warrant?[40]

Now we turn to another problem. We could ask if the arguments against the church's dogma of original sin drawn from recent findings in natural science are even worth reflecting on theologically or, instead, put us on the wrong track. The "scientifically" inspired evasive actions of theologians have often proven to be more of a tragedy than the traditional theological

38. Translated from U. Baumann, *Erbsünde? Ihr trad. Verständnis in der Krise heutiger Theologie,* ÖF, pt. 2, vol. 2 (Freiburg/Basel/Wien, 1970), p. 6, from Haag's accompanying letter.

39. Translated from J. Gross, *Geschichte des Erbsündendogmas. Ein Beitrag zur Geschichte des Problems vom Ursprung des Übels,* 4 vols. (München/Basel, 1960ff.), 4:352.

40. See Gross, pp. 306f.

doctrine of original sin itself. Time and again there has been a rash reaction to the latest scientific hypotheses on the origins of humanity. Since the end of the nineteenth century many theologians have attempted to take into account the foregone conclusion of science that modern humanity can be traced back to several different "first parents" and that the first human beings were primitive beings rather than superior beings capable of falling into sin. These new findings at least seemed to require a modification of the doctrine of original sin. However, today it must be noted that these new findings settle nothing for the theological problem of original sin.

Until recently certain Roman Catholic theologians took the opposite approach, trying to defend the dogma of original sin. This approach was equally problematic because they tried to prove and demand that everyone should be convinced of the historical existence of a single first human couple — Adam and Eve. Moreover, in this view, a Christian has to believe that sin came into the world through *this* first human couple and was then transmitted "from one generation to the next." Even philosophical and scientific efforts were made by Catholic theologians beyond the midpoint of the twentieth century to reject the hypothesis of scientific "polygenism" in a cogent form.

As early as at the First Vatican Council a group of theologians (whose main speaker was Franzelin) said that "polygenism" violates "both the dogma of original sin as well as that of the redemption of all men by the one Christ."[41] In the fifties Karl Rahner was tempted to come to the assistance of the encyclical *Humani Generis* presented by Pope Pius XII on August 12, 1950, and to test the sharpness of his thought by defending the theory of "monogenism" espoused in the pertinent section of the encyclical.[42] He believed that it was possible to provide "metaphysical" proof for this theory.[43] But in the sixties the whole theological climate in European Catholicism changed drastically.

41. See K. Rahner, "Theologisches zum Monogenismus," in *Schriften zur Theologie* (Einsiedeln/Zürich/Köln, 1954), 1:271, including n. 2; quotation from English translation, *Theological Investigations,* vol. 1: *God, Christ, Mary, and Grace,* trans. Cornelius Ernst (Baltimore: Helicon Press, 1961), p. 247, also pp. 247-48 n. 2.

42. H. Denzinger and A. Schönmetzer, *Enchiridion Symbolorum . . .* (Barcinone-Friburgi Briscoviae-Romae, [36]1976), p. 3897.

43. Rahner, 1:311ff. For Schoonenberg's critical response to Rahner, see his *Theologie der Sünde. Ein theologischer Versuch* (Einsiedeln/Zürich/Köln, 1966), pp. 225-30.

An example of this is P. Schoonenberg's *Theologie der Sünde* (Theology of sin) (imprimatur 1964). This monograph claimed to free original sin from biological misunderstandings. What was wrong about its traditional understanding was that the existence of a chain of guilt reaching back to Adam that had to be passed on from generation to generation was assumed to be true. The universal entanglement of humanity in original sin was explained biologically instead of historically or in relation to society. Schoonenberg attempted to understand original sin in a new way as a disaster that befell human beings by way of certain social and historical factors just as certain human phenomena which were considered to be biological transmission in an earlier time were declared anew in the twentieth century to be attributable to environmental factors. The individual commits (deeds of) sin in the context of a (sinful) "environment" in which what was earlier called "original sin" has its place (or what today should perhaps be called "the sin of the world").[44] This means we sin because of our being situated in a "sinful situation" that prevails throughout the world (the situation which has its source in sin and invites us to sin).[45]

In keeping with this view, Schoonenberg also tried to develop a more progressive understanding of grace. He criticized traditional Catholic theology for having often described the imparting of divine grace as the pouring out of a supernatural substance. Here, too, the significance of historical, social, and societal factors was neglected. But this teaching is correct in asserting that "there is no granting of God's grace in which the world and one's fellow man do not have a part."[46]

In particular Schoonenberg supported these theses with reasons that have a lot going for them. Yet on the whole his attempt to renew the doctrine of hamartiology is not unproblematic. The decisive question is whether the doctrine of original sin can be *put on the right theological track* by making a particular decision either for "biological transmission or social

44. Schoonenberg, *Theologie der Sünde,* pp. 115ff., 193ff., also p. 141; see also Schoonenberg, "Der Mensch in der Sünde, in *Mysterium Salutis. Grundriß heilsgeschichtlicher Dogmatik,* ed. J. Feiner and M. Löhrer (Einsiedeln/Zürich/Köln, 1967), 3:836ff., esp. p. 896.

45. Schoonenberg, *Theologie der Sünde,* pp. 121ff.; see Schoonenberg, "Der Mensch in der Sünde," in *Mysterium Salutis,* 2:894ff.

46. Schoonenberg, "Der Mensch in der Sünde," in *Mysterium Salutis,* 2:896; quotation from Piet Schoonenberg, *Man and Sin: A Theological View,* trans. Joseph Donceel (Notre Dame, Ind.: University of Notre Dame Press, 1965), p. 119.

environment," a truly vexing question. Since the main subject of original sin is a universal human transgression of man's proper relationship to God, the theory explaining it in terms of "society" is just as wrong as the theory explaining it in terms of "biology."[47]

In the sixties Herbert Haag wrote that the Priestly creation story in Genesis 1:1-2, 4a is limited to the statement *that* God created man. The biblical account basically leaves open the technical question about the "how" of humanity's creation. It also says nothing about whether human beings were beings of high intellect who were thus capable of falling into sin from the first moment of their creation. The biblical account speaks of the fact that God created *man* just as he created the trees or the animals. The gist of the account is the creation of the whole species of human beings: in view of humanity, Adam is *pars pro toto*. Thus Haag thought that his exegetical findings "are more likely to speak in favor of polygenism." The same conclusion also applies to the Jahwistic narrative of the fall in Genesis 3. It is a collective statement about an event that originally spoke of all human beings (and not merely of Adam and Eve misunderstood as two singular figures or as the two first human beings). Haag wanted to show that, for exegetical but also theological reasons, Bible scholars should move more along the lines of agreeing with natural science than along the lines of Vatican declarations on the issue of original sin.[48]

In the Dutch Catechism (imprimatur by Cardinal Alfrink, March 1, 1966), which has caused quite a stir in the German-speaking countries since 1968, the Dutch church made even more candid use of critical methods of Bible scholarship.[49]

In recent times it has been recognized that the biblical story of creation with its six days is a "wonderful stylistic invention."

47. Schoonenberg sees this difficulty himself, at least in part. He is careful to avoid trite alternatives and often prefers the form of a question to promote his reflections. He is cautiously thinking in terms of augmenting the classical view of the biological transmission of sin by considering the "sin of the world" through which every individual always finds himself in flawed moral orders (see "Der Mensch in der Sünde," in *Mysterium Salutis,* 2:931f.).

48. H. Haag, *Biblische Schöpfungslehre und kirchliche Erbsündenlehre* (The Bible's doctrine of creation and the church's doctrine of original sin), SBS 10 (Stuttgart, [¹1966] ⁴1968); see also the summary paper in Gross, 4:294f.

49. Gross 4:296: "The best Dutch theologians," such as E. Schillebeeckx, P. Schoonenberg, G. Mulders, A. Hulsbasch, and W. Bless, wrote this catechism.

It is a "poem" that must not be viewed as a "historical report."[50] A Catholic should know and acknowledge today that man is the result of evolution. "A species of animal, living in forests and plains, ascends the evolutionary ladder in a slow process of development that extends to . . . us. The life that flows through me comes from the animals." "We see the great spectacle better and better: the backbone that slowly straightens up, the skull that is filled with greater and greater intelligence, the animal that straightens up and becomes a human being." The Dutch Catechism explicitly states that as a Catholic, you no longer have to accept the idea that in the beginning there was once a paradisiacal state of intact nature and immortality.[51] For the modern Catholic it is no longer so important (as it seems to have been for our ancestors) to find an explanation in the first chapters of the Bible for how sin came into the world. Adam and Eve do not have to be used to explain the idea that in the distant past a serious mistake was once made that has been transmitted to the whole of later humanity. Today, it is probably enough to say that sin represents the "free expression of our own will."[52]

Under the guise of the most permissive renewal, the most daring challenge to dogma, the Dutch Catechism ultimately succeeded in speaking of sin in a very traditional (semi-)Pelagian way that has been allowed in Roman Catholicism for a long time. This is especially apparent in the answer that was given to the following question: Was it "necessary that sin came into the world"? "In reply we can only say that it must have happened with a certain measure of freedom — otherwise it would not be sin. And freedom signifies that it would have also been possible for man not to do it." (This is a clear decision regarding the figure of speech first used by Augustine: "posse non peccare — non posse non peccare.") In ambiguous language — now more understandable — the catechism

---

50. "The Proclamation of the Faith for Adults," Dutch Catechism, p. 58; see pp. 29ff. (on Genesis 2 and 3): "This incomparably excellent portion of Scripture will never be able to be replaced in its comprehensive portrayal of man before God. But it will probably have to be replaced as a description of the *beginning* of humanity" (translated from Dutch Catechism). What this text says about the "first sin" subsequent to the creation stories is likewise not to be seen as a historical recollection. It concerns us. Adam and Eve's sin happens "in us."

51. Translated from Dutch Catechism, pp. 13f., 303.

52. Translated from Dutch Catechism, p. 499.

adds: "But this does not mean that on the whole all sins could be avoided."[53] Still we give this Dutch attempt at restating the faith credit for consistently opening Catholicism to natural science and the historical criticism of the Bible. But although this attempt was long overdue, it is no longer enough to stop there in our modern age. For in this form it has not only continued questionable, old theological practices under the guise of progress, but it has also not even begun to make the necessary changes in the way it speaks of and defines original sin. This undoubtedly presents a series of problems that have not been sufficiently dealt with. What are the major irrefutable problems in connection with the dogma and with the idea of original sin as such? Criticism of the dogma of original sin has properly raised the question of its logical consistency again and again. It was said: if original sin is really a matter of a *sin* for which every human being incurs guilt, then it is out of the question that the guilt is an *inherited* shortcoming or fate because the individual could not be made responsible for an inherited fate.[54] Thus there seems to be a need to raise this critical objection to the concept of original sin: it is either the sin of every individual or it is inheritance, but not both together! The concept of original sin seems to be a wooden iron; it seems to contain a contradiction in terms.

But the problem under discussion here was not unknown to theologians of earlier times. Nevertheless, they always faced the compelling necessity of teaching a universal sin or original sin *(peccatum originale)* beginning at the root of humanity. How strongly they always felt compelled to teach original sin can be gauged by the fact that even the following problem did not keep the theologians from teaching it: To the present day it is disputed whether the Bible itself suggests a dogma of original sin. On the one hand, the opinion is held that there has been a dogma of original sin only since Augustine. Others believe that what Luther understood by original sin is already found in Paul in an objective sense. If this is true, then we must ask the further question whether such an understanding of original sin can also be verified in the Old Testament.

53. Translated from Dutch Catechism, p. 297.
54. See the critique of H. S. Reimarus (1694-1768) in his "Apologic oder Schutzschrift für vernünftigen Verehrer Gottes"; see also Freund's appreciation of Reimans's critique, pp. 13-32.

B. Biblical Aspects

Genesis 3 did not intend to establish a dogma of original sin! Although Israel knew that the whole nation could suffer from a common sin not only from time to time but that the sin of every individual compatriot *always* draws everyone else into the guilt, and although a single verse in the Old Testament — Psalm 51:5 (Surely I was sinful at birth, sinful from the time my mother conceived me) — even sounds like an early formulation of the classic church doctrine of original sin, nevertheless it has been proven that in its theological development, Israel more and more came to recognize that every individual is responsible for his own sin; no one has to atone for the sins of his fathers.

Ezekiel grappled with the fact that a number of Israelites still held the opinion that a son had to bear the misdeeds of his father. "The fathers have eaten bitter grapes, and the sons' teeth have become dull from them" (Ezek. 18:2). Ezekiel prohibited the use of this proverb in the name of God: "The son will not share the guilt of the father, nor will the father share the guilt of the son. The righteousness of the righteous man will be credited to him, and the wickedness of the wicked will be charged against him. But if a wicked man turns away from all the sins he has committed and keeps all my decrees and does what is just and right, he will surely live; he will not die" (Ezek. 18:20-21). To the Israelites living in Babylonian exile Ezekiel conveyed the message that they had the chance to begin again.

Without presenting all the additional Old Testament verses that could be considered for our problem, we can say in summary: in spite of historical developments and at least formally different views on guilt within the Old Testament itself, in the end the above-mentioned concern of Ezekiel expresses the sentiments of the whole Torah. But at the same time another statement about guilt also expresses the sentiments of the whole Old Testament: *all human beings do not respond to God's acts of kindness in an appropriate manner!* (Ps. 116:11f.: "And in my dismay I said, 'All men are liars.' How can I repay the LORD for all his goodness to me?") Human beings even respond to God's goodness with malice. To be sure, there may be much beautiful piety and many righteous human deeds in specific cases, but a great qualitative difference separates our righteousness from God's righteousness. This universal human predicament is not an original sin that is propagated from one generation to another. But it describes Israel's situation and the situation of all human beings in such a way that human beings generally could not live by what they have "deserved," but owe their life to "undeserved" divine goodness and forbearance.

From the perspective of the New Testament as well we can state that the "enlightened teaching" of Ezekiel as a whole is far more in keeping with it than the opposite teaching that the son of a sinful father is partly responsible for his father's sin. The son, too, must therefore bear the punishment for the sins of his father. (See John 9:1ff., where on the occasion of the healing of a man born blind, the question is raised whether the sins of the parents could have been the cause of his physical disability.) On the other hand, on the basis of the Christ event the New Testament speaks of sin in a form that is different from that of the Old Testament. As the firstborn of a new humanity, Christ is confronted with the perishing world which is understood as "sin" in its entirety. Even those believers grafted into the body of Christ still have a part in this all-embracing sinfulness of the perishing world. They still live in the "old aeon" as well. This is the decisive form in which universal human entanglement in "sin," the power of death, is found in the New Testament. Therefore, *Christian theology should interpret original sin more or less in this way: we should understand by it the condition of humanity not (yet) living in the light of Jesus Christ.*

It was always understood that the fifth chapter of Romans contains the main New Testament passage in terms of its relevance to the subject of original sin. In this passage Paul seems to be teaching the existence of a sin which has come upon all human beings since Adam in a kind of "biological chain reaction." But careful exegesis of this text can convincingly show that it is, in fact, not speaking of a biologically inherited disease going back to them.

Paul writes in Romans 5:12, sin (and death through sin) entered the world through *one* man — Adam. In this way death came to all men on the basis of the fact *(eph ho)* that all sinned (in the same way Adam sinned). Paul is pointing out here that all people fall into Adam's sin again and again. He is simply not interested in positing a sin that is biologically transmitted from generation to generation. He is more interested in asserting the much greater powerfulness of Christ's kingdom of grace compared to Adam's kingdom of sin. That is why we read in Romans 5:15, "For if the many died by the trespass of the one man, how much more did God's grace and the gift that came by the grace of the one man, Jesus Christ, overflow to the many!"

The teaching of "inherited" sin in the strictest sense of the word can also not be deduced from the New Testament.[55] But how valid are the reasons that led to the development of a doctrine of original sin in church history?

C. The History of the Doctrine of Original Sin

The New Testament and the apostolic fathers took it for granted that humanity was universally caught up in the power of sin, but they did not yet know and offer a specific doctrine of original sin. There has only been a *doctrine* of original sin since it became customary in church history to distinguish between two kinds of sin, the kind that we ourselves commit *(peccatum actuale)* and the kind into which we were born *(peccatum orig-inale)*. A theological need for the precise elaboration of this distinction arose with the gradual emergence of *infant baptism.* The fact that the forgiveness of sins is given through baptism was established without question by New Testament texts. The baptism of newborn children, however, confronted the church with the obvious question: What guilt did the infant bring upon himself, what sins of his can or must be forgiven?[56] In the sixth chapter of Romans, Paul had written about baptism. It results in the

---

55. We are most likely to do justice to the complicated New Testament textual findings and — changing — terminologies if we do not blur the distinction between a forgiveness of sins that individuals have *committed,* an act attributed to the earthly Jesus, and the deliverance from *sin* attributed to the exalted Jesus Christ. The former means that the New Testament would also like to speak of *sins* in continuity with the Hebrew Bible. Their forgiveness takes place on the level of an ethical command; forgive each other's sins. The latter — "the ransom" of all from the realm of sin by the death and resurrection of Jesus Christ — means that the New Testament, without canceling out the former meaning, would also like to speak of an eschatological event that affects the whole of humanity, representing a soteriological invasion of the realm in which sin/evil holds sway in the world. Only this latter meaning provides a theological bridge to speak of "original sin" from the vantage point of the New Testament. But it is questionable whether "original sin" is an appropriate designation for that sinister realm and that sinister power which the death and resurrection of Jesus Christ have invaded.

56. Seen historically, therefore, a path led from the *practice of baptism* to the theological doctrine of original sin. Reflecting on this in a systematic fashion, Schoonenberg neverthe-less puts it the exact opposite way: "The early church deduced the necessity of baptism from the calamity of original sin . . . thus in the process of developing tradition results often quickly become motives!" (translated from *Theologie der Sünde,* pp. 220f.). See sec. 7 n. 9.

sinful man being "buried," it is there to crucify "the old self" and to do away with the body of sin (Rom. 6:6). As far as human beings who have already reached maturity are concerned, this statement was felt to be clear and understandable. In the early church, many were anxious to postpone their baptism to the end of their life. Their intention in doing so was that they didn't want to saddle themselves with more new sins after baptism.

But when infant baptism became customary, it not only led to the question, From which sins must an infant be cleansed? but also to the problem that in spite of the cleansing, an ensuing sin-free life could not be expected. It had become unclear where the capacity to commit sinful deeds came from if the "old Adam" was drowned by baptism. The theological difficulties that had become so intense at this point led theologians to draw more precise theological distinctions between original sin and actual sins. In the following discussion I want to remind us of a historical situation that has long since been clarified and is well known.

Tertullian was a pioneer of the distinction that was drawn between *peccatum originale* and *peccatum actuale* and that was fully developed only by Augustine. At an early date he spoke of a *vitium originis* that is transmitted through infection from Adam to all his descendants. He also coined the image of the *tradux peccati* (the "tendrils of sin" that have kept growing from the time of Adam onward). His discussion of the *corruptio naturae,* the corruption of human nature, which was effected by the above-mentioned *vitium originis,* had especially grave consequences. Tertullian was not an advocate of infant baptism! But he paved the way for the later distinction between original sin and actual sins through his great interest in unmasking infant baptism as a meaningless custom. He asked: Why does one baptize infants? Is this not meaningless if these young human beings do not yet have any genuine, actual sins of their own? Why infant baptism if the newborn children are merely tainted with the *vitium originis* that cannot be attributed to any guilt on their part. Tertullian's doctrine of sin put all its emphasis on the *actual sins.* For Tertullian they were the essence of sin. Thus, according to Tertullian we should seek liberation from them through baptism.

About two hundred years after Tertullian the British monk Pelagius, a contemporary of Augustine, also basically believed that there were only "actual sins." Pelagius thought that everyone bears guilt for his own sins and that everyone has the freedom to avoid sinning. We should keep in mind what Pelagius and his followers were actually concerned about at that time because today more often than not the word "Pelagianism" is used incorrectly to describe a heresy. The Pelagians advocated the following three views:

1. Adam's sin did not come upon humanity in its subsequent history by transmission. If Adam's descendants sin, this happens more by copying the bad example of Adam and Eve. Our sinning thus occurs *imitatione, non propagatione!* (The Council of Trent in the sixteenth century commented that the reverse was true. Original sin is not propagated by imitation, but by natural procreation.)
2. The second characteristic view of Pelagius is that we must not regard either death or evil in the world as a punishment for our sins. Rather, death and evil are parts of the natural organization of the cosmos. They are effects of natural law.
3. The Pelagians did not, in principle, reject infant baptism. But they thought its purpose was not to cleanse a human being from his sin, but to graft him into the body of Christ, or incorporate him into the church. For the Pelagians this was the crucial aspect of each baptism.

Augustine laid the foundation for the development of the doctrine of original sin in the West by coming to grips with these Pelagian views on the one hand and with Manichaean views on the other hand. In doing so, Augustine had to surmount considerable obstacles that were also tied to a question that the natural science of that era answered in a controversial fashion. The question was: What exactly happens when a woman is fertilized by the male seed? Is a complete human being with body and soul generated by this act? Or is only a new human body generated while the soul is added later in special ways? If the latter is supposed to be correct, when and by whom is the soul added? And what does this lack of clarity about the origin of the soul mean for the problem of original sin? In the modern era, Augustine has often been called the one through whom the disparagement of sex entered the history of dogma. But for the most part modern critics forget to acknowledge that Augustine's attitude was formed against the backdrop of the debate about the origin of the soul. In those days it was inevitable that it would become a contentious issue. Augustine's doctrine of original sin becomes adequately clear only in the light of this historical debate.

One of the four theories about the origin of the soul considered in the age of Augustine was the doctrine of *the preexistence of the soul.* Those who advocated it believed that souls exist independent of the body. Souls exist from eternity *before* being connected to a human body. They have their own life close to God; they are free there and can even sin. Many advocates of the preexistence of the soul believed that when a soul enters a human body this is always the consequence of a fall of the soul prior to its bodily existence, and thus a punishment for moral transgressions before birth. The anthropology of the theologian Origen, for example, was in keeping with this view that had even been considered by Plato in an earlier time. But the Manichaeans as well believed in this theory on the origin of human souls.

Those who held to this theory had to come to the conclusion that a doctrine of original sin is totally meaningless. At any rate it seemed out of the question that evil reaches our descendants through the human progenitors Adam and Eve by way of heredity. According to the theory of the preexistence of the soul, evil has its origin in heavenly processes beyond time, in a fall of souls on the other side.

Following Augustine, the Christian church — for good reasons — rejected this whole set of ideas. Since then it has denied that a soul could lead its own life before birth and, in this context, even be guilty of moral transgressions.

A second theory on the origin of the soul discussed at that time was *emanation.* It states that human souls were created by an effluence from the substance of God. This is why they are the divine in man. For people who have a pantheistic experience of life, the acceptance of this idea of emanations is always obvious. Nevertheless, the early church also rejected this second theory. In doing so, it rejected — again for good reasons — an all too idealistic view of man as the sole divine, free being among all the creatures.

A third theory bears the label *generationism* or *traducianism.* The central idea here is that in human procreation body and soul are generated simultaneously; in other words, an ensouled body is generated. Those who hold this view do not believe, as would be the case within emanation, that souls are pieces of divine substance and as such enter a transitory earthly body. Rather, they are of the opinion that souls originate in the substance of the parents, just like the bodies of newly generated human beings. But this means that we would have to accept that human beings possess a "soul substance" that can be passed on. Just as modern science knows about genetic chains consisting of DNA, the two theories from that era, generationism and traducianism, imagined the existence of a chain through which the "soul substance" is transmitted. The designation for this chain was *tradux*. I have already mentioned this word introduced by Tertullian, which means "tendril." Generationism or traducianism teaches that in the act of procreation something of the "soul substance" of the parents is imparted to their descendants. The "soul substance" of our progenitors is also passed on and winds its way through all our descendants like a tendril in a vineyard. On the basis of this theory, a doctrine of original sin is, of course, very conceivable. If we have reason to assume that the "soul substance" of our progenitors was damaged by some occurrence, it follows with scientific necessity that this damage is also transmitted to our descendants. At that time this theory was bound to appear to be the scientifically most advanced in comparison to the first two.

In the early church, yet a fourth theory was discussed, to which its proponents later gave the name creationism. Those who believed in this theory were dissatisfied with the teaching of generationism or traducianism that parents are capable of passing on souls to their children in the biological event of procreation. The creationists believed this view would not do justice to the significance of the human soul. Therefore, they advocated the view that each individual soul is created directly by God from nothing and then added to, or poured into, the new life developing in the womb. In this view original sin could not be inherent in the soul or the spiritual nature of a newborn human being, but at most in his body. In this way the biological substance of the body and physical, sexual processes came to be marked by sin.

The theory of creationism has led to a discussion among its adherents about the question of the point in time when God gives the growing embryo a soul. Many set this point in time at a very early stage in its growth so that it moved close to the time of procreation; others put it at a much later time. Since the theory of creationism has been given a kind of privileged position in the dogmatics of the Roman Catholic Church, it even gained significance for the ethical discussion of the problem of abortion. Theoretically, an abortion would be ethically possible until the point in time when the soul is joined to the body by God. Or to put it a different way, only an embryo that has not yet been ensouled could be aborted if necessary.

In the early church Augustine vacillated between the third and the fourth theories on the origin of the soul. We can still agree that he was right not to endorse the theory of the preexistence of the soul or the theory of emanation. He was right to separate himself from the Manichaeans on the one hand and the idealists and pantheists on the other hand in his basic interpretation of anthropology. He supported the view on the origin of the soul that made the most sense from a scientific point of view in his time. His vacillation between creationism on the one hand and the theory of generationism or traducianism on the other hand argues in favor of his caution. Of course, in doing so, he accepted a scientific, anthropological foundation that made a doctrine of original sin a virtual necessity. Subsequent church history emphasized the doctrine of original sin to varying degrees depending on whether one was more inclined to accept creationism or traducianism (generationism). The pure creationists classified the corruption of original sin in the end as a less fateful occurrence or phenomenon than the real supporters of the third theory because the creationists believed that at least an uncorrupted core, the soul, enters all human beings. But for the firm supporters of generationism or traducianism man is corrupted by original sin even in the depths of his soul. It is clear that a theologian such as Luther believed more in this last-mentioned theory, while the Council of Trent could best tie its interests in the field of theological anthropology to the fourth theory, creationism.

On the question of original sin Augustine reached the following conclusions: At first it was possible for Adam to avoid sinning in paradise. However, after the fall occurred, it was no longer possible for Adam and all his descendants to stop sinning. *Post lapsum Adae* — and this is said directly in opposition to Pelagius — there is no longer a *posse non peccare*. *Post lapsum Adae* there is no longer any ability not to sin. Now each person *must* bring forth actual sins. The loss of *iustitia originalis* is what has been transmitted to us from our fallen ancestor Adam. All of Adam's descendants inevitably fall into disobedience to God as well as into a sinful attitude of pride or arrogance by having lost this original position of righteousness. They are joined by a fourth sinful characteristic, "evil lust and desire" *(concupiscentia)*. In recent times scholars have been right to stress that Augustine did not just mean sexual lust when he used the term *concupiscentia,* but men's evil desires in a comprehensive sense. However, to Augustine sexual lust was at least in the foreground of the discussion when he spoke of *concupiscentia*. He was convinced that sexual desire pulls man into sin with exceptional force. Man becomes weak and almost loses his free will — this is an example of sin occurring with exceptional intensity.

Augustine's propositions served as a foundation for all subsequent Western conceptions of Christian hamartiology. The marks of his historical influence on the doctrine of sin can be found in the second article of the Augsburg Confession of 1530. On the subject of original sin, it teaches: "After Adam's fall, all men begotten after the common course of nature are born with sin; that is, without the fear of God, without trust in him, and with fleshly appetite; and this disease, or original fault, is truly sin, condemning and bringing eternal death now also upon all that are not born again by baptism and the Holy Spirit." The Pelagians are rejected, and so are all who deny that the original fault is a real sin.

However, the *church in the East* followed a different path. The doctrine of sin does not have the significance for them that it has in Western theology. To be sure, from the beginning the East also spoke of the fate of death coming upon human beings through Adam and weakening our moral strength. However, in Eastern Christianity they did not understand this weakening as a fundamental *non posse non peccare*. Consequently, until the present day the Orthodox doctrine of grace has not concentrated as strongly as the Western doctrine on the question of forgiveness of sins. In the East, this was and is more important: *the idea of grace as a force that rescues us from the transitoriness, the futility of earthly existence and from bondage to death.*

A suggestion of the divergent doctrinal development in the West and in the East that lay ahead can already be seen in Augustine. Augustine defended himself against the charge brought against him by the "Greeks" that he introduced a dogmatic innovation with his doctrine of original sin. In his writing "Contra Julianum," Augustine explained that the absence of a doctrine of original sin in several of the significant Greek fathers merely stemmed from the fact that they were in the midst of a combative situation in which such a doctrine would have been unfavorable or misunderstood. When these fathers, similar to many Pelagians, portrayed sin only as the reprehensible, personal guilt of an individual Christian, this has to do with the fact that they constantly had to resist an understanding of man (with his soul ostensibly imprisoned in the dungeon of his body) shaped by dualistic Manichaeanism. This is the sole reason they did not speak of original sin. Augustine believed this does not alter the fact that proper Christian teaching must reject Manichaeanism and still speak of man's original sin in a way that is based on Scripture.

In the course of the Middle Ages Western theologians learned how to express themselves even more precisely on the difficult question of the *specific meaning* of original sin — in contradistinction to actual sins. They noticed that in any case arrogance or concupiscence must not be described as the meaning of original sin. Although they were certain that baptism wipes out original sin, it obviously does not have the effect of definitely ruling out arrogance and sinful desire in the baptized person. But in what guilt or false way of living can original sin be found, since it should be distinguished from actual sins? The following answer was generally received: The meaning of original sin is found in the absence of the original grace of creation which makes man pleasing and holy before God. This is why medieval theology said Adam and Eve fell from their original position of grace by committing their sin together and thus lost their original position of righteousness that had made them holy. Therefore, original sin was defined as a flaw, a *carentia,* regarding the *iustitia originalis* or supernatural grace, which amounts to the same thing. And, in keeping with this idea, baptism was understood as a sacramental event through which supernatural grace was again infused in those who were baptized.

In the Middle Ages theologians also set out to answer the practical question: What will become of children who had to die unbaptized? What fate will they suffer in the other world in view of the fact that sanctifying, supernatural grace could not be infused in them? This was a question that unsettled medieval people. And they were instructed by their dogmaticians that there was no possibility that their unbaptized children could enter heaven. But in the afterlife such children were also not doomed to languish in hell. This would be inappropriate for those who had not yet committed a single actual sin. Thus they taught that children who passed away early with their unpaid-for original sin had to endure a punishment *(poena),* but a very mild one: *mitissima omnicum poenarum poena,* which Augustine laid down in these terms. The vision of God would be withheld from these children, but they could possibly even be happy in the next world. They all came to a special place *in front of* hell, "the limbo of children," the *limbus infantium.*

Manifesting such clear features of an unwholesome dogmatism that takes logical consistency to the extreme, this doctrine is an indication of how the West has gotten stuck in a problematic rut with its distinction between original sins and actual sins. Defining two kinds of sin, which Luther later tried to reverse, was a mistake from the beginning. The fact that the doctrine of original sin received such an exceedingly bad press in the modern era is not simply to be interpreted as a lack of theological understanding or as a philosophical repudiation of Christianity. Even if the reasons why the doctrine of original sin was rejected were often questionable, modernity quite rightly perceived an inner problem with this dogma that had already arisen in the early church. This problem surfaced in conjunction with early theological reflections on the character of infant baptism as a sacrament that effects the forgiveness of sins.

The fact that the traditional Western doctrine of original sin speaks of a universal entanglement of humanity in sin was and is not wrong. Nor is the fact that it states that sinning continues from generation to generation. Rather, the dogmatic technique of subdividing sin into two and even several different kinds of sin and, wherever possible, assigning each kind of sin its own sacrament that blots out sin was and is wrong. What was wrong about this is that the church understood itself as a kind of therapy center, as an indispensable, salvific institution where the deadly poison of sin can be treated with the proper antidotes.

The profound problems associated with this self-understanding of the church were an essential contributing factor to the Reformation in the sixteenth century. Unfortunately, the Reformers were not able to complete a *common* new version of the doctrine of original sin. To be sure, all of the Reformers knew that the church's understanding of sin and grace was due for a theological renewal. In addition, they were all unified in emphasizing that man received salvation by grace alone. But each Reformer went his own way in renewing the doctrine of original sin and actual sins.

The Zurich Reformer Huldrych Zwingli wanted to untie the knot in such a way that he considerably diminished the significance of original sin. He thought original sin must be judged to be a handicap, but at the same time he did not see it as an individual's guilt. It is a weakness, a shortcoming.

On the other hand, Luther's student Matthias Flacius (1520-1575) clearly overestimated the theological weight of original sin which Zwingli seemed to have underestimated. He taught that original sin is the substance of human nature making all people so incapable of doing good that man is like a wooden block or a stone *(truncus aut lapis)*. But his theological opponent, Melanchthon's student Victorin Strigel, asserted against Flacius that every individual has the freedom to act and thus can decide to do good or to do evil. Strigel taught along these "semi-Pelagian" lines, which in our context is also predominant in the Catholic history of dogma.

The inner imbalance in the Reformers' teachings on sin is again reflected in the widely accepted doctrinal formulation of the second article in the Augsburg Confession. Here, statements on original sin were placed alongside one another although they are not on the same level, but are linked together in a very illogical and unclear fashion.[57] We are clearly on the level of theological speech or the level of doctrine when the fact that man no longer fears God is cited as the meaning of original sin. But, in one leaping bound, the Augsburg Confession, Article 2, shifts from this theological level to a philosophical, ontological level by further saying that the descendants of Adam live with a profound corruption of their nature. This corruption is portrayed as a biological defect resulting in human missteps. From this speech level the *Confessio Augustana* then jumps into an ethical context by saying that human beings do not keep God's commandments on account of original sin. From the ethical level the descriptions eventually border on psychology when it talks about evil lust and the evil inclination of human beings. The fact that in Article 2 of the Augsburg Confession such highly diverse speech levels have been pulled together in such an unclear way indicates that the new dogmatic formulation of the doctrine of sin had not yet advanced far enough. It is obvious that such a situation had to result in doctrinal formulations at the Council of Trent that rejected "the" Reformational understanding of sin. But the Roman Catholic objections at this council also contained a problem in a formal sense. It wrongly assumed a unified Reformational teaching on original sin and thus objected to a dogmatic construct that could not be adequately verified either by Luther's texts or by Calvin's texts. Through this development in the sixteenth century the overall situation in the field of hamartiology became more complicated.

The following small parable attempts to express what can now be said — against this historical backdrop — regarding original sin (and our liberation from it), and how this should be said theologically. Six theses follow the parable.

57. The following observations on the Augsburg Confession are found in Freund, pp. 48f., in more detail.

D. A Parable

A child has run away from his father's house. Now we know this story . . . the child wants to discover the world on his own and make use of its beautiful things. He ends up in a great forest and gets lost. Now the story becomes more and more familiar . . . the initial pride of the child who had taken a trip into freedom turned into consternation, fear, and regret.

A while later he comes across an older brother. This brother is walking through the forest with confident steps. The child is especially happy to be able to join him, because he was already afraid he would never be able to find his way out of the strange, dark forest. "Where are we here?" the child asks. "On our father's property," the brother answers. "But didn't I run away from our property?" "No, you were always wandering around inside the property. It is much larger than you thought."

After this brief exchange the same corner of the forest that had seemed so strange and dark to the child just a short time ago immediately grows more familiar. A friendly light penetrates the leaves. *Still walking through the forest, the child's experience* is becoming antiquated. He no longer thinks the forest is the far country. Although the child is still in the place where he was on account of having run away, he is no longer in the place he thought he was until then. The future which he thought was walled in is once again open to him. The child is redeemed.

Dogmatics should interpret "the grace of the forgiveness of sins" just as this parable does! By God's grace we are indeed in a different place at the same place. In our mind the system of coordinates we have superimposed on things changes so that the far country becomes our home and the splendor of the home sky and light returns to the gloomy place.

Our inadequate interpretations of what happens when our sins are forgiven often result in a misunderstanding of the sacraments as a spiritual purgative or laxative. Instead, the parable says: The forgiveness of sins is not an event of cleansing, but the return of an awareness of God in my person and the return of splendor in my world. It is grace by which I perceive myself to be in a different, an incomparably better place. But *original sin* qualifies every individual sin as darkness. Its outcome is a wrong way of seeing reality as well as the damage resulting from this misperception.

When we sin, it is not just our awareness of God that is not right. Rather, it always leads to a misinterpretation of earthly things and misguided behavior because we are wrong about God and his realm of power.

E. Six Theses concerning Original Sin

1. Original sin is that flaw which explains humanity's universal need for redemption and defines that need. But our interest in a doctrine of original sin should not be focused on demonstrating human shortcomings that exist everywhere but on pointing out the universal divine will to bring redemption demonstrated in historical deeds (and especially in the new covenant in Jesus Christ)!

2. What the meaning of the sin called "original sin" is should be stated from the vantage point of *Christology:* When we imagine all of mankind without Jesus Christ, without his Spirit, without the things he lived for on earth, also without the opportunity for us to recognize ourselves in him and him in us, then we get the exact meaning of what the word "original sin" means, then we see exactly what is left. For then human beings would only be the brothers and sisters of Adam and Eve and not at the same time those who belong to Christ as brothers and sisters. What a gloomy situation that would be!

3. Thus it follows for our *understanding* of original sin: original sin is that darkness hanging over humanity which is most adequately observed when the radiant light shining on humanity from Christ is noticed and recognized. It is the shade we see most clearly in the light of Jesus Christ. It is the "absence of God," the missing nearness of God Jesus Christ's mission is intended to overcome.

4. The concept of original sin refers to what is sinful about all sin, what is repeated in every new sinful action. Therefore, the discussion of original sin means that all sinning is only a variation of *one* basic sin. This is why original sin and actual sins should not be separated, but at best only differentiated. They form an indissoluble unity. We must talk about original sin in such a way that we infer the individual is not responsible for his guilty offenses. We must talk about individual actual sins in such a way that their origin in a universal, human blindness to God or distance from God is not ignored or overlooked.

5. Original sin is that maelstrom creating the need in all human beings to perform the act of justifying creatures, an act that is solely God's prerogative. Therefore, original sin basically takes place as a declaration of justification (with its negative consequences) — or as the withdrawal of justification! — not only in our own human strength but in our limited human dimensions. (In relation to original sin the New Testament gospel

is the message God gives me again as the subject of my justification. At the same time he exposes self-justification as the cause of ruined relationships. The force that is sufficient to counter original sin in the individual is not, therefore, the church's administration of baptism, but faith. But original sin itself is ultimately unbelief.)

6. We must rethink the significance of the sacraments regarding the problem of original sin. The church's awareness of the power of the sacraments to forgive sin is in a crisis. This is not surprising if we look back at its long history in which sacraments were misunderstood as a pharmacological remedy for sin (or its consequences). But sacraments such as baptism and the Lord's Supper do not simply wash away sins. Rather, they reveal God's nearness, they reconnect us with God. At the same time they overturn situations that have become socially destructive. They redefine our existing relationships to the world around us.

SECTION X
IS THERE COLLECTIVE GUILT
AND COLLECTIVE FORGIVENESS?

A. The Problem of the Nation's Guilt

We know from church history before the twentieth century that Christian confessions of sin were usually the confessions of *individuals*. Corporate confessions of sin and the acceptance of collective guilt were rare exceptions. But don't we encounter both kinds in the Old Testament? Time after time Israel knew about the whole nation's guilt. To be sure, these incidents took place under unique conditions. It is hard to make a distinction between the nation-state and the religious community in ancient Israel. But in looking at Christian people we must ask whether in certain situations membership in the *church* does not at least require and make possible a common confession of sin. Or must we go even further and, should the occasion arise, speak to *nations* about collective guilt (and also about forgiveness)? Since they understand themselves as sharing a common national identity, we will examine this first by looking at a section of the Old Testament from Lamentations (5:1ff.).

> Remember, O LORD, what has happened to us; look and see our disgrace. Our inheritance has been turned over to aliens, our homes to foreigners. We have become orphans and fatherless, our mothers like widows. . . . We submitted to Egypt and Assyria to get enough bread. Our fathers sinned and are no more, and we bear their punishment. Slaves rule over us. . . . Women have been ravished in Zion. . . . Princes have been hung up by their hands. . . . Woe to us, for we have sinned! . . . Restore us to yourself, O LORD, that we may return; renew our days as of old!

Hardly any other Old Testament text was felt to be such a direct parallel to the situation of the Germans after the end of World War II. On October 18 and 19, 1945, the Evangelical Church formulated its well-known Stuttgart Declaration of Guilt, in which prominent church leaders who knew they were not only in a "community of suffering" but also in a "solidarity of guilt" with all Germans confessed as representatives for all Germans: "Unending suffering has been brought upon many peoples and countries by us." On August 8, 1947, the "Darmstadt Word" of the Brethren Council of the Evangelical Church in Germany commented on "the political path of our nation. We must allow ourselves to be absolved of our total guilt, the guilt of our fathers as well as our own"; we must allow ourselves to be called home "by Jesus Christ, the Good Shepherd and from all the false and evil paths on which we Germans have gone astray in our political intentions and actions."

These declarations were gratefully received by part of the population but were at once vehemently contested by another part. Not only the subject matter of the declaration was contentious, how in particular the guilt of the Germans and especially of Evangelical Church members had been seen and portrayed, but also the collective form in which all were included in the confession of guilt. From the grass roots the desire was often expressed that the guilt of the victorious powers against Germans should also be mentioned.

Did the above-mentioned church declarations really want to ascertain a collective guilt of the Germans?

The problem of guilt weighing down the whole German nation was understandably an important subject in many German worship services in the summer of 1945. In the context of a sermon delivered in a local church, the Lutheran Hans Asmussen, a leader who served the Confessing Church well, stated: "The German citizen . . . , who for the sake of his peace sacrificed justice, is guilty." "The sword and this dire situation did not come over us without reason. The German subject must declare himself guilty."[58]

The event of such isolated penitential sermons in Germany was already well known to an international delegation of ecumenical church representatives who had come to Stuttgart in October 1945 to reestablish contacts with Protestant Christians and probe the possibility of providing material assistance. Within the delegation there was the opinion that an official confession of sin on the part of German church leaders would facilitate the reestablishment of relations and relief funds from overseas.

On the other hand, they recognized that such a confession of guilt among partners that were not equally free had its difficulties. (A bishop in England expressed his opinion shortly after the Stuttgart Declaration had been issued. He said that now that the Germans had confessed their guilt, a similar confession should be issued in Allied circles. This statement cost the Anglican bishop dearly in his own country.)

---

58. Asmussen quote translated from G. Besier and G. Sauter, *Wie Christen ihre Schuld bekennen. Die Stuttgarter Erklärung, 1945* (Göttingen, 1985), p. 17.

A further difficulty with the Stuttgart and the Darmstadt Declarations was that their sentences partially took the form of a *personal confession,* which was bound to lead to this critical inquiry: Should a personal confession take place so publicly, should a confession of guilt before God take place so spectacularly and include all fellow Christians, indeed, all fellow citizens? Should such a confession of one's own guilt not be left to *every individual?* Could the personal confession of German church representatives not be misunderstood and politically misused by foreign leaders who neither understood nor respected the total context of the Stuttgart Declaration? Hans Asmussen had such fears when he read the Stuttgart Declaration in front of the ecumenical delegation on October 19, 1945. That is why he explained after reading the text: "Only because the German churchmen had already confessed before God the sin mentioned in the declaration were they now able to repeat what they had said before God in front of the foreign visitors." He added: "Do your part to make sure that this declaration is not misused politically, but serves the purpose we want to achieve together."[59]

Finally, the Stuttgart Declaration had to contend with a third difficulty. Its authors happened to speak for all Protestants and certainly spoke without authorization for the German people, which was understandable considering the limited opportunities for travel and the structural reorganization of the Evangelical Church that had not yet been completed. Asmussen believed he could say to his brothers from the ecumenical movement: "I have sinned against you as a member of my people" because he — Asmussen — had to exercise the priestly office in Stuttgart as a member of the body of Christ. Asmussen felt that he was a *mediator* called by his own conscience and by his ordination. On the other hand, he believed he could and should secure exoneration and pardon for those guilty Germans who were not able at that moment to declare their own guilt. Thus, only the *priestly character* of his confession of sin made it possible for Asmussen to take responsibility for the whole nation.

Many questions remain unanswered. Did Asmussen adequately assess the form and content of what objectively happened in Stuttgart? Furthermore, did he adequately assess the form and content of the Darmstadt Word formulated in advance by Hans Iwand (and rejected by Asmussen himself)? Yet our remarks on the background events of 1945 show that

---

59. Quote translated from Besier and Sauter, p. 32.

leading German church personalities did not claim for themselves the right to establish a collective guilt of all Germans in agreement with a sweeping foreign condemnation of the German nation. And this is a good thing because the assertion of a collective guilt is always questionable. This concept must be avoided.[60]

"There is no such thing as the guilt or innocence of a whole nation. Guilt, like innocence, is not collective, but personal. Sometimes the guilt of human beings is disclosed and sometimes it remains hidden. There is guilt that human beings have confessed or denied. Let everyone who experienced the era (of the so-called Third Reich) fully aware quietly ask himself about his involvement."[61]

The general guilt of a nation cannot be articulated politically or legally but, at best, in the language of faith within the church, and in such a way that church members who face the public with a clean record *voluntarily* place themselves under the indictment and penalty for the sin committed by the people for the benefit of their seriously incriminated fellow citizens. Such "solidarity of guilt" may be called a priestly service or be given a different name. At any rate, it possesses a liberating power; it really helps to erase guilt. It helps human relationships to blossom once again, facilitating the return of splendor. This solidarity alone entitles us to speak theologically not only of individual, personal guilt but of guilt that has *become* collective — through voluntary intercession. Voluntary intercession as a priestly service is a noble opportunity (not at all tied to ordination) for members of a Christian church to profess their faith and practice solidarity. Such an occurrence not only means following Christ in costly discipleship but is profoundly in keeping with the piety of Old Testament Israel, as the most familiar verse, Isaiah 53:4, testifies.

On the other hand, the Old Testament does not know the idea of a

60. See the explanations of P. Tillich, *Systematische Theologie* (Stuttgart, 1958), 2:67f., which I affirm.

61. The address of Federal President R. von Weizsäcker at the ceremony of the Bundestag and Bundesrat commemorating the fortieth anniversary of the end of World War II on May 8, 1985, documented in, and translated from, *Jk* 5 (1985): 275 (274-79). Likewise Jaspers explained with great authority in 1946: "There is necessarily such a thing as collective guilt in terms of the political liability of the state's citizens, but not in the same sense as moral and metaphysical guilt, nor as criminal guilt. Assuming political liability is surely hard in its terrible consequences, even for each individual . . . but this liability as such does not affect the soul" (translated from K. Jaspers, *Die Schuldfrage* [Heidelberg, 1946], p. 56); see also his discussion on pp. 50-72.

possible "collective guilt" of Israel. At first glance an Old Testament passage such as Lamentations 5, quoted at the outset, seems to point in the direction of establishing a collective guilt. But a really careful exegesis is essential here. We must consider the fact that the Old Testament is more or less familiar with the repercussions of guilt that impact the whole nation, but not with a collective accusation of guilt that would include innocent people in the charge. Strictly speaking, the text quoted from Lamentations 5 does not even take the form of a confession of guilt, but of a *lament*. The misery the people have to suffer on account of their fathers' guilt is brought before God. This thought is being expressed: "God, you are having us bear the consequences of earlier sins! How much longer?" The person praying and asking this question articulates the hope that God will allow the situation to become as good as it once was.

The vital, present-day need for a whole nation to undergo an internal and external change is not in view in this passage from the Old Testament Lamentations. They pin their hopes more on a change in God. Could he now let the punishment the whole nation endured be sufficient payment for their fathers' sin? Even the statement of Lamentations 5:16, "Woe to us, for we have sinned!" is neither a confession nor a profession, but a lament that the repercussions of the sins committed in the nation and God's punishments are so severe and prolonged.

Dietrich Bonhoeffer, in his dissertation *The Communion of Saints: A Dogmatic Inquiry into the Sociology of the Church* (1930), written *before* the so-called Third Reich, gave his own more objective opinion about the issue of possible collective guilt than we have to. At that time he drew a somewhat too sweeping, dogmatic picture of the Old Testament nation of Israel and its prophets. Again and again the prophets demanded: "The nation should repent as the people of God. It is not individuals who have sinned, but the nation. Thus, the nation must also be comforted" (Isa. 40:1). By developing the sociological theory that there is a "greater personality" of whole peoples and institutions, the so-called collective persons besides human individuals, Bonhoeffer can advance this thesis: "It is not only individual Germans and individual Christians who are guilty; Germany and the church are guilty too. Here the contrition and justification of individuals is of no avail; Germany and the church themselves must repent and be justified." This is an analogy to the situation in Old Testament Israel because, then as now, not just the individual but also the nation (the community as a whole) is God's partner and stands in the presence of God, "in God's sight." The community is willed and created by God and therefore, Bonhoeffer believes, must also seek repentance. He is arguing here from the vantage point of divinely given orders of creation, or orders of community, being able to use this unbroken approach more readily than we can today. In this context Bonhoeffer approaches the idea of a *vicarious priesthood* by expressing the following idea: "It is clear" that repentance/change must be made, specifically by *individual* human beings, and "yet it is not the individuals, but the collective person *(Gesamtheit)* who, in the individuals, hears, repents and believes. The centre of action lies in the collective person. Thus the collective guilt of a community is something else than guilt as a social phenomenon in the community. The 'people' is to repent, but it is not a question of the number who repent, and in practice it will never be the whole people, the whole church, but God can regard it 'as if' the whole people has repented."[62]

With the image of the collective person which he applied to every people, every nation, Bonhoeffer blurred the distinction between Israel and other nations. The fact that he also relates the justification of the sinner to the collective person is likewise problematic. But we understand Bonhoeffer properly if we assume that it is not right to detach such theological teaching on the guilt of a whole nation from the context of its spiritual rationale. Thus it cannot be used to vindicate collective national guilt under international law. Moreover, Christian communities/congregations/churches should know that they vicariously shoulder the burden of the whole nation's guilt or the guilt of all nations. This theological truth is the proper focus of Bonhoeffer's work.

In fact, "We have sinned" is construed corporately in Old Testament Israel in such a way that either the sins of their ancestors and their own similar sins merge together; or in such a way that an oppressive significance is attributed to the transgressions of the fathers, and the descendants have to bear this heavy burden for a while longer. But only for a while! *This certainty of faith is the actual background of the lamentation quoted earlier.* Israel believed and knew: God punishes the children for the sin of the fathers to the third and fourth generation. But this limit is set. Moreover,

---

62. D. Bonhoeffer, *Sanctorum Communio. Eine dogmatische Untersuchung zur Soziologie der Kirche* (1930), in *DBW*, ed. J. v. Soosten, vol. 1 (München, 1986), pp. 74f.; quotations from English translation, *The Communion of Saints: A Dogmatic Inquiry into the Sociology of the Church*, trans. R. Gregor Smith (New York: Harper and Row, 1963), pp. 83-84.

it is a certainty for this Old Testament Israel that God's gracious action quantitatively far outweighs his punitive action. As a reward for devout good living God grants his blessing that will have an impact for a thousand generations (see Exod. 20:5; 34:7; Num. 14:18; Deut. 5:9). Israel *lives,* Israel draws its hope for the future from this great excess of divine mercy over God's wrath.

Jewish people involuntarily experienced a quite different kind of corporate or collective liability in the Diaspora. For example, in Berlin, the "protection money" that had to be paid by the Jewish community was drastically raised in 1786 under the reign of the enlightened Frederick the Great. It was tied to the stipulation that the Jewish community also had to assume liability for all of its members' offenses "irregardless of whether it is a matter of theft or a bankruptcy caused through no fault of their own." It was made clear to the Jewish community that they were under threat in their entirety on account of one "unrighteous" person in their midst.[63]

It is not unintelligible that many Germans found it difficult and impermissible after 1945 to be treated on the basis of this legal "model." But it is also not unintelligible that a way of thinking fell back on us that did not even first arise in fascist ideology, but came out of *our own traditions,* reaching much further back into our history. Of course, this way of thinking does not possess any biblical dignity whatsoever — on the contrary!

As I have said, there is no Old Testament idea of the occasional existence of collective guilt in which all fellow Israelites would be made equally responsible for past injustice. Of course, the sin committed by a few or many individual compatriots affects all; thus the whole nation suffers the consequences of God's punishment. But if it can somehow be overlooked, a few or several or all individuals excluded are from this ruin. In Genesis 18:16ff. God not only patiently bore or heard with joy Abraham's intercession for Sodom, "Will you sweep away the righteous with the wicked?" but expressed his willingness to spare the whole city even if only a fraction of the inhabitants were found to be righteous. Even in situations where the Bible speaks of the *burden* of guilt spreading to the sons from the fathers (the sons having to bear the consequences), Israel's theological interest is focused on *limiting* and *ending* this situation. The relatives and

---

63. Translated from B. Harenberg, ed., *Die Chronik Berlins* (Dortmund, 1986), p. 135.

descendants of guilty persons who have to bear what comes upon them act the same way. They do not let this situation become an occasion for self-accusation, but for lamenting their plight before God. Their understandable and legitimate desire in so doing is to see the community return to an experience of God's blessing as soon as possible and as individuals to get away from the burden that comes from the guilt of strangers or their own guilt as soon as possible.

When the Hebrew speaks of *'awon* that must be borne, then we sometimes have to translate *'awon* with "sin," sometimes with "punishment." Frequently this idea is found in the Old Testament: Whoever commits an *'awon,* his own *'awon* affects him too. His sin is simultaneously his punishment (compare Wis. Sol. 11:16: "Everyone is plagued by the sin they commit"). In Genesis 4:13 Cain says after God cursed him and allowed him to flee, becoming restless and unsettled: My *'awon* is greater than I can bear.

The *'awon* is, therefore, a *transgression with an oppressive weight.* In Israel the impression was not dominant that moral reproach is brought upon the one who sins from the outside; rather, he is under great strain from the weight of his own deed. In comparison with today's sensibilities, guilt was seen much less as a moral category. Rather, it seemed to interfere with God's world order, almost automatically provoking his angry and "wrathful reaction," a highly unwise action in light of the knowledge of Torah.

In spite of our considerable historical distance from this Old Testament pattern of thought, such language about sin gained a large measure of new attractiveness after 1945. This language seems to be clearer and ethically more comprehensible than Christian discussions shaped by the long and complicated processes of doctrinal development.

And yet the widespread modern assumption that Old Testament forms of recognizing and dealing with guilt have gained a new relevance also poses the danger of self-deception to which many theologians today actually succumb. This is the difference: the "nations coming from Christianity" do not have a form of existence in which the religious cultic community and the political community are *one* as they were in the ancient nation of Israel which was chosen by God. In addition, the nations coming from the rationality and morality of the modern Enlightenment and secularization do not live with an awareness of being committed to God through the Torah. Modern secular-political interpretations of guilt and forgiveness and their interrelationships start with completely different presuppositions than those that were prevalent in the Old Testament. Thus, it is more likely that any "structural parallels" only seem to be related and, in observing them, the significance of the Enlightenment and secularization was overlooked.

Moreover, in our present situation, the task that faces a Christian theology called upon to develop an improved, renewed understanding of sin is *not* to attempt a return to Old Testament hamartiology! The task for which there is no alternative must rather be the complicated inheritance of Christian history (which has always included the Old Testament inheritance anyway), must always be entered on anew — and, looking into the future, must continue to be developed by constantly reexamining its christological formulation and by including modern anthropological changes and contemporary historical-political questions. Here it must be expressly stated that it will prove to be wrong, even impossible, to return to a time prior to the Western developments of a highly individualistic, highly subjective, and highly personal approach to sin and guilt, to return to more archaic, collective, perhaps even "national" forms. Here, too, a promising path to follow would probably be the further development in which the inwardness and subjectivity achieved until now is carefully preserved. Such continued development could lie in renewing structures of intrachurch socialization.

B. Systematic Issues in a Political Interpretation of Guilt

Today's conditions as well as numerous attempts by the church to deal with sin in a timely fashion seem to contradict what I have just delineated. In recent years, for example, individual confession has become a rarity in the Catholic church; most of the time a common confession of sin and common absolution are "occasionally" desired in a worship service of the congregation. In the past several decades theological pleas for a de-individualization in our understanding of sin and forgiveness have increased, countering the Western practice of relating sin and forgiveness to individuals only. *Political theologians agreed in their demand to sweep away the illusion of theology and the church that all change and improvement on a small scale, as well as in the larger political context, can only begin in the hearts of individuals who must be converted.* Since the individual (indeed!) is often the victim of "unconverted anonymous structures," the collective and political aspect of our involvement in sin and our coming to terms with sin should occupy the attention of theologians more than it has up to now, and the individual aspect should receive less attention.

In fact, modern theology faces the task of charting the right course between giving appropriate consideration to sources of corruption undermining the structures of society and giving appropriate consideration to what must be said about the individual's sinful heart as in the past. In doing so, it must note that sin does indeed always undermine and destroy networks of social relationships, but that the opposite is not automatically true: When networks of social relationships are destroyed, they produce sins in the individual or rather a distorted humanity in the individual sphere. *Of course, most of the models of political theology draw precisely this opposite conclusion: they regard the disrupted social conditions as the actual cause of individual human transgression and individual misfortune.* Therefore, concerning sin and guilt they consider it an urgent task of the churches to do their best to help heal shattered social and political structures.

But opinions are divided on this: Is not the main task of the church in any case Christian proclamation with its goal of offering individual, personal words of encouragement and comfort as it proclaims the gospel of grace and forgiveness and describes the new opportunities for abundant living that come from God? And is not Kierkegaard right in his thesis that sin or guilt has been increasing quantitatively in the course of human history but, nevertheless, each individual falls into sin on his own in terms of a qualitative leap? If Kierkegaard were not right at this point, then it would only be logical for the churches to dissolve themselves, merge with political parties advocating justice, and abandon their entire theological religious background, for whatever goes beyond an appeal for justice would be ballast. *However, if we agree with Kierkegaard, then it must be conceded that even successful political and moral endeavors to change unjust, sick social structures — which should by all means take place — nevertheless do not prevent the emergence of sin in all members of society.* It is hard to make this understandable because criminality, for example, can indeed decrease when social conditions improve (whereas edifying sermons in the worship service hardly change anything when it comes to criminality outside the four walls of the church). Strictly speaking, it is important to give efforts for social improvement every possible chance to succeed, on the part of the church as well, but to evaluate them objectively. Throughout the history of humanity they have been at best relative improvements, quantitative progress toward better conditions, but never a defeat of the forces urging us to commit sin in the human heart, never a defeat that begins at the root of the problem.

Therefore, the churches are not doing everything that should be done about sin and guilt by struggling against "structural sins," against "evil that has become objectified in society." Of course, the *one thing* that should certainly be expected in this regard is the solidarity of Christian churches with the oppressed. But the *other thing* that should certainly be expected from Christian churches is that they view and address *all* people, even the oppressed, as subjects and perpetrators of their sins (and not merely as the objects and victims of others' sins). If they abandon the latter task they have ceased being Christian churches. The church and theology should notice collective immorality and socially determined alienation, but this should not make them forget that sin and guilt remain categorically tied to our *personal life,* to our own human conduct and the responsibility we assume for our own life. Nor should they forget that *all* who are given recognition as *human beings* must *also* be seen as independent subjects of sin and guilt.

It cannot be denied that when many Christian theologies apportion blame to the individual, it carries the negative connotation of a clerical "father confessor mentality" because, in fact, social constraints (or the social changes not yet sufficiently registered by the church) are the real issue. Nevertheless, when the church and theology begin to see sin and forgiveness in this situation primarily or even exclusively as "collective events," they ended in a dead end. For what happens then?

At first, it only looks as if this course were a rather complicated but tempting, dangerous tightrope walk. We immediately see that an avalanche of stones could slide down to our left and to our right. In other words, we can see: on the one hand, a collective understanding of guilt can exonerate the individual. It tells him: Your personal sufferings and social injustices in general are not the kind of things that could be done away with or influenced by your private awareness of sin or by your private, religious relationship to God. You don't need to take personal responsibility for all this. These evils are all determined by a false consciousness that encompasses the entire society or by collective immorality (or at least by the immorality of the powerful). On the other hand, the individual is put under a considerably greater strain by collective interpretations of guilt than by the individual, personal interpretations. The individual is also told:

even if you have not had a direct role in causing the social injustices that have put great pressure on public life, you are partly to blame for them as a member of this society, *you are partly responsible for all of them.* You cannot exclude yourself from partial liability by making private excuses.

Thus, two exactly opposite effects are the possible outcome of collective interpretations of guilt and forgiveness. Actually, one or the other can be appropriate in individual cases — also from a theological viewpoint. Many a scrupulous Christian who accuses himself can experience help when he learns to discern for which unjust situations he has to assume responsibility and for which unjust situations he does not have to, and should not have to, assume responsibility. Many an unscrupulous Christian who is, in fact, only easing his own conscience can experience help when his partial liability even for evil that takes place far from him is elucidated for him. The only question is, will Christians really recall the effect of the collective interpretations of guilt and forgiveness meant for *them?* Will not the scrupulous one put additional pressure on himself on the basis of such interpretations, and will not the self-satisfied one not make life even easier for himself? The *inability* of liberation theologians to rule this out is the dilemma of their political theology, which is fixated on this new way of discussing sin, guilt, and forgiveness.

Political, secular hamartiologies of the modern era have made it their number one priority to stigmatize the individual for his partial responsibility in perpetrating public injustices and abuses and then to refuse him the desired absolution. Dorothee Sölle, for example, understands those of us who are members of the rich industrial nations as "sinners." She believes that we are all de facto "collaborators" with powerful, anonymous systems of oppression. She even interprets *peccatum radicale,* that is, original sin, politically.[64] She sees our public involvement in sin within the context of an exploitative society in which *every* member must shoulder his share of the entire guilt of this society, even if he is only a consuming member of society and has not become active as a political offender or a public figure who helps to create public policy.[65] In spite of its moral evidence this kind

---

64. This seems theologically wrongheaded to me because real original sin reaches the individual and his sinful deed not from the unjust structures, but on the contrary reaches the general public from the individual. Original sin is not that which *precedes* the actual sin of a human being, but it is the sin active in the wrongful deed.

65. D. Sölle, "Sünde — zur politischen Interpretation eines theologischen Begriffs," *ThPr* 6 (1971): 249f.

of hamartiology is surely untenable both from a theological and Christian perspective. This teaching understands sin exclusively in terms of the love or solidarity that is denied to our fellow human beings, but not at the same time in terms of the trust in God we failed to give him. She indicts the unloving, egotistical, isolated rich man who is unhappy in his prosperity. But how will she motivate him to love more? By making threats? Or by appealing to him to lead a more fulfilling life? How does the vital Christian perception of sin as *unbelief* occur in this model? What right does she have to say that God can *only* be offended in our exploited and humiliated *fellow man* when she speaks of sin judged to be an insult to God? Is not *God* also in this fellow man (apart from the fact that we also sin in our dealings with nonhuman creatures)? This is not an issue of nuances, but of the place and function of belief and unbelief as it relates to sin.

If we follow Sölle's model, we must *also* allow faith to be absorbed into *mutual human cooperation* marked by idealistic, trusting relationships, and develop the thesis that we can believe in God only by living and working together in such harmony. Thus faith is redefined as human solidarity that has not failed and not collapsed. But this thesis was full of unsolvable puzzles. When and whom must I *first* trust? First God, then human beings? Or are both intertwined? *But where does our help come from? How can that which is destroyed between human beings or is in bad shape become whole again?* I would not know what else Christian theology could teach except that God himself must first provide what he lacks in our life and this is something that he wants to do. Who else could do it?

Whoever is concerned to see more love and more dignified, meaningful living conditions among us human beings must pray that *God* is manifested in his divine love and power, in his holy splendor in the midst of our activities. Love does not increase among us by itself or by social-ethical admonitions, as urgent as they may be. More love among human beings — and who wouldn't want this? — requires that in the midst of our general activities there are points of entry where God's nearness and powerful holiness are experienced. But these points of entry are found where individuals come to *faith,* that is, where they find the One who can provide what they lack in life *in the midst of the evils of this world.* This may well be only a few people. But a single saint (who always has a community of faith as well) counts a lot as a point of entry for divine nearness and divine splendor.

CHAPTER 4

The Forgiveness of Sins —
A Renewed Church and
the Renewal of the World

SECTION XI
THE CONCEPT OF THE FORGIVENESS OF SINS
ON THE BASIS OF THE NEW TESTAMENT

As a formal description, the forgiveness of sins means:

1. *Deliverance from death and reintegration of those living separated from God — an event bringing wholeness and safety, but also freedom, peace, and future, and in particular —*

1.1. An event that *seeks* sinners, *pursues* them. To be sure, in the New Testament not a few needy persons went to Jesus on their own to find help. Yet with regard to sin, this statement is true: Not the one separated from the "fellowship of salvation" seeks his Savior; rather, the Savior seeks him. It is not the sinner who finds his Redeemer, but the Redeemer who finds him.

1.2. God and man bearing other people's trespasses in terms of a debt that can no longer be paid off. It enables and obligates the discharged debtor to forgive others who can no longer pay off their debts to him in the same way.

1.3. An event that overcomes resistance, that brings home the poor, the sick, and those "excluded" for other reasons and restores them, an event that takes place against the resistance of the righteous and healthy.

At the same time the self-satisfaction and self-definition of the righteous and healthy are interpreted in more detail. On the surface their life looks respectable. But it is racked with hypocrisy and an attempt to justify themselves. A lack of love and godlessness are found behind their facade.

1.4. An event the healthy and righteous need although they do not need a doctor according to Mark 2:17. The fact that they have no future is hidden from them and can only be overcome when they find their way back to the fellowship of sinners and tax collectors who had previously lived in separation from them.

2. *An event linking us with God/Jesus Christ, more precisely:*

2.1. An event that brings God himself close to man, who has become a slave to his idols and thus, in fact, exists godlessly. Through this event man learns to set God apart from the world and to love God — which is in keeping with Israel's faith.

2.2. An anticipation of the Last Judgment, already offering the believer living now peace with God and a reason for hope beyond death.

2.3. The incorporation of those "who believe and are baptized" (Mark 16:16) into the risen body of God's Son and, thus, the event that creates the church.

2.4. The creation of the pure and holy "new man" (see Eph. 2:15) in whom Christ "dwells." But this new man is never found in the singular. He is never only the individual whose sins were washed away as a "private person." For the cleansing event making the "new man" includes the event in which barriers that had separated human beings from one another with insurmountable force until now are torn down. Those who have come together in this way are "new men" engaged in mutual cooperation.

3. *An event moving forward the eschatological renewal of the world, more precisely:*

3.1. A reevaluation of familiar values initiating the future world with seeds and signs of hope, the kingdom of God in the midst of this present world that is passing away.

3.2. An event separating light and darkness in human life, an event by which evil is clearly defined and seen for what it is.

3.3. The historical appearance of greater glory than was ever there before.

3.4. The beginning of reconciliation not only between one human being and another but also between human beings and nature.

SECTION XII
THE DISAPPOINTMENT OF TODAY'S CHRISTIANS
OVER THEIR EXPERIENCES WITH
THE FORGIVENESS OF SIN

A. The *Proprium Christianum:* Grace

The purpose of all religions is to lift human beings out of their "deficits" and place them on the path that leads to redemption. But the conditions attached to this path to salvation are diverse. In one instance, sacrifices must be offered or propitiatory payments must reach the deity. In another instance human beings must radically change their lives and keep drastic, far-reaching laws. In still another instance they are to cleanse themselves by means of certain rites or procedures conducted by priests. The penalties that are used to threaten the offenders are also diverse. The ranks of those who even enter the army of the redeemed in a religion vary in size.

There is no question and no doubt that of all the redemptive religions (the phrase contains a tautology!), Christianity has reached a zenith in terms of easing the burden of human beings, who do not have to perform works to be free from their sin and guilt and in terms of proclaiming a universal, divine, saving will meant for the whole of humanity — indeed, for the whole world (see 1 Tim. 2:4; Rom. 11:32). God himself could not bear more of the burden for the redemption of the world, and more grace could not be showered on humanity than is the case in the Christian faith. Here God himself provides men with the atonement. And that is why it is correct to say that the whole of Christianity comes down to God granting the forgiveness of sins. In this regard Christianity does not recognize a type of forgiveness, atonement, or cleansing that is tied to specific human works or the mediating services of priests. The "saving act" has taken place once and for all in Jesus Christ for the sake of the whole world (Rom. 6:10; Heb. 9:26). Everyone who believes this is already pure and is already saved by allowing what God has objectively "done" for him and all people long ago to be true for himself.

In Christianity redemption as grace is logically thought out. Christianity can never be surpassed in this by any other religion. Its gospel is the message of divine forgiveness without conditions. The unconditional nature of the gospel comes from the belief that God himself has fully produced the results required for our *restitutio in integrum*.

The *church* can have no other purpose than spreading this faith among us and making this gospel known. The church exists to enable human beings to share in the forgiveness of sins understood in this way — or there is no church at all; then it exists nominally at best.

The New Testament is full of traditional concepts of atonement, cleansing, and forgiveness whose meaning has been stretched to describe radical grace. Christ is the *sacrifice* for our sins — there will never again be such a sacrifice after this one. At the same time he is the *high priest* who performs this final sacrificial act in Hebrews. However, those who apply this act to themselves and consequently assume that no longer will anything at all ever be able to make them impure are called Christians. Christians are those who recognize that they have been *sanctified* in this sacrifice of Christ.

A beautiful, rather old book (H. Windisch, *Baptism and Sin in Earliest Christianity up to Origen,* 1908)[1] correctly demonstrates that it was a fundamental conviction of the early Christians that the baptized had nothing more to do with sin; they were radically converted to God and entered into life.

(Given the occurrence of sin even among Christians that could not be overlooked), the early church reluctantly felt compelled to consider the problem of sin theologically *subsequent* to the fundamental act of repentance and cleansing which the transition to Christianity (baptism) signified. To be able to do this, the early church adopted from Judaism certain distinctions between serious, mild, inadvertent, and willful sins, etc.[2] Only mild and inadvertent sins committed by Christians were taken into consideration. For this rule was still valid: true Christians are sinless people in their essential nature. Yet this now became "an ideal with compromises."[3] Windisch believes that the Lutheran *simul iustus et peccator* deviates from Paul's doctrine of justification insofar as he would not yet have allowed the Christian a permanent "life of sin."[4]

This opinion of Windisch could be examined on the basis of Romans 7:15f.: the old interpretative problem of whether the "wretched man" described here who does not do the good he desires to do should stand

---

1. H. Windisch, *Taufe und Sünde im ältesten Christentum bis auf Origenes. Ein Beitrag zur altchristlichen Dogmengeschichte* (Tübingen, 1908).
2. See Windisch, p. 33.
3. Windisch, p. 507.
4. Windisch, p. 527.

for the apostle Paul himself, or his situation in life *before* his encounter with Christ (the prebelieving state). Bultmann decided that he is obviously talking here not about the daily experiences of the apostle, but of the conflict in his life before his decision of faith, and in such a way that in retrospect being human is revealed to be contradictory from the perspective of faith.[5] In so doing, Bultmann properly moved away from the debate about whether Paul was speaking of the "unconverted" or the "converted" Christian. We must also follow Bultmann in not interpreting the conflict described by Paul as a conflict between desire and performance, but more fundamentally as the existence of "prebelieving" man.[6] And yet Bultmann does not seem to have adequately considered the problem of the "prebelieving" condition that remains a problem for the believer. Besides, in his interpretation, the scope of Romans 7:15ff. does not really become clear. This might be found in Paul's intention to point out that the problem of sin could not be solved by man's own efforts.[7] On a positive note, Paul wanted to emphasize simultaneously the complete and sole "sufficiency" of Jesus Christ to solve the problem that is not solvable for us.

Was Windisch's thesis supported by this? Was he correct in observing a theological chasm between Luther and Paul with regard to the problem of *simul iustus et peccator.* Probably not. There is no reason to attribute an "undialectical" understanding of faith to Paul that would have overlooked the Christian's lifelong need of redemption or the continuation of his "prebelieving" state even in situations where God has given faith. However, Windisch's main observation remains historically accurate that early Christianity knew it was separated from the "old" world of sin that is passing away as if by an incision (baptism!).

In view of their liberation from all sins by the merit of Jesus Christ on the cross, a certain "mood" prevails in the New Testament that can no longer be easily comprehended by us today. A love for God never known before flows through the one whose sins are *completely* forgiven, who consequently has become a *new man* (see Eph. 2:15). The first command-

---

5. R. Bultmann, "Römer 7 und die Anthropologie des Paulus," in *Exegetica,* selected, introduced, and edited by E. Dinkler (Tübingen, 1967), p. 198.

6. See Bultmann, "Römer 7 und die Anthropologie des Paulus," p. 209.

7. E. Fuchs, *Gesammelte Aufsätze I: Zum hermeneutischen Problem in der Theologie* (Tübingen, 1959), pp. 284f.; Paul's line of argument in Romans 7:14ff. has as its goal a demonstration of "how futile life is without faith"; see E. Käsemann, *An die Römer,* HNT 8a (Tübingen [¹1973], ²1974), p. 190.

ment is reestablished in his heart. He no longer has to misuse his fellow creatures as substitutes for God: he is *reconciled* to God himself. Thus in the New Testament this statement applies to all human beings who have become Christians: They have crossed over from the sphere of falsehood into the sphere of truth, from the sphere of darkness into the sphere of light. They are the ones who had been lost, "alone, separated from God and without joy," but have now been found again. They are the ones who had previously existed in sickness and alienation but who have now been healed. They are the ones who had previously been slaves (of sin) but have now been released into freedom. They are born again from the dead — a profession that mainly characterizes Christian baptism. The *new creation* (2 Cor. 5:17) has already dawned in *faith,* which always signifies a "dwelling" of Christ in the believer and of the believer in Christ from the New Testament's post-Easter perspective.

The superabundant *doxa* (glory) which is found in the grace of God (thought out in the Christian kerygma) was originally intended to be the message that would fill the whole world with great joy (see Luke 2). Yet in the meantime it is no longer certain whether this kerygma still brings joy even to the members of the churches. Indeed, it is no longer even certain whether Christians themselves still understand this proclamation and whether it is even clear to them that the whole of Christianity comes down to the forgiveness of sins understood in the above-mentioned fashion.

I believe I am not mistaken in observing that even among the members of the contemporary church shaped by Western culture, there is a considerable aversion to both the theological axiom of the radical sinfulness of man (see Rom. 7:15ff.) and to the traditional forms in which the forgiveness of sin or grace is applied in the church.

The fact that Christians in general are still happy today and that God allows them to "make a fresh start again and again" through their faith can surely be recognized. Nevertheless, the central significance of the forgiveness of sins in Christianity and the church is often misunderstood or rejected. Already in Immanuel Kant it was a set phrase that "hopefully" Christian grace would not deliver us from our own moral efforts (at self-improvement) as well. And in the age after Kant the fact that the gospel of Jesus Christ has the power to save sinners (1 Tim. 1:15) is no longer what modern man actually expects from Christianity and is looking for in the church. Unfortunately, this is no longer always what we actually find when we live in our congregations today. In addition, a considerable difference has emerged between the dogmatic, traditional claim that the power of the forgiveness of sins can renew our whole existence and our *experiences* with the church's way of imparting grace or forgiveness. We often get the impression that the words expressed in church are inadequate because they seem to be higher and more glorious than what actually goes into our life. Generally speaking, what are known as the sacraments are frequently offered and recommended as sources of the forgiveness of sins (and, therefore, to use Luther's phrase, of "life and salvation"),[8] but in a way that is not at all identical with the realities of the church and the personal experiences of the "recipients of the sacraments." The "intended content" and the "actual content" diverge.[9]

It was never easy for the Christian church as a whole to live up to its calling to proclaim its own message of the radical grace of God. For example, the Reformation had to expend a lot of effort to uncover it again and extricate it from the legalisms ("Pelagianism," "semi-Pelagianism") that had taken hold in the church. Yet, even the churches of the Reformation were not equal to the task of proclaiming the gospel they had uncovered as history progressed. They, too, began to oscillate between a new legalism and much too cheap proclamation of God's radical grace. The problems I have suggested here are the actual, the true reason for every church's constant need for reformation. A need for the Reformational renewal of the church always exists, especially when we look at how the contemporary church deals with grace and its respective understanding of sin.

8. "Where there is forgiveness of sins, there is also life and salvation" (translated from Luther's Small Catechism, BSLK 1967, p. 520).

9. See C. J. Jung, *Erinnerungen, Träume, Gedanken,* recorded and edited by A. Jaffé, special edition (Olten/Freiburg i. Br., 1984), pp. 58-61: After Jung had been confirmed by his father in 1890, an event that was extremely boring for the boy, he pinned his "last hopes" on Communion. He hoped to experience the essential aspect of Christian faith in Communion, upon which his father "seemed to place so high a value." But he experienced a stiff ceremony that "tasted flat," a pitiful commemoration in which literally "nothing at all happened." A religious union with Christ did not take place for Jung, and neither did the great deliverance from sin. "Slowly I came to understand," he remembered in old age, "that this communion had been a fatal experience for me. It had proved hollow; more than that, it had proved to be a total loss. I knew that I would never again be able to participate in this ceremony. 'Why, that is not religion at all,' I thought. 'It is an absence of God; the church is a place I should not go to. It is not life which is there, but death.' I was seized with the most vehement pity for my father. . . ." Quotations from English translation, *Memories, Dreams, Reflections,* recorded and edited by Aniela Jaffé, trans. Richard and Clara Winston, rev. ed. (New York: Pantheon Books, 1973), pp. 52-55.

B. The Sacraments and the Forgiveness of Sins Today

When baptism is desired today, this presumably happens — as far as the motives of the people in the so-called state churches are concerned — least of all because of their prospects for "receiving" the forgiveness of all sins (which was still crucial for early Christianity!). Anyway, the word "reception" (it seems hard to dispense with this term in the language of theology) tastes like a decaying mushroom. Even in the Lord's Supper, the forgiveness of sins is probably no longer of immediate importance in terms of the recipient's expectations — especially since its "reception" in the liturgical order of the worship service often seems to be classified more as a kind of "technical requirement" that enables one to participate "easily" in the celebration of the Lord's Supper a short time later. Today it is theologically disputed whether the Lord's Supper even has to form a "marriage" with confession and with repentance and absolution. Whoever rejects this will cite arguments for it that are based on recent findings in the exegetical study of the New Testament. The only problem is that in claiming these findings, an important "theological implication" is sometimes ignored. This fact is overlooked: Whoever considers *the strengthening of the Christian community* as the main purpose of the Lord's Supper in appealing to recent exegetical findings should again focus on the issue — which does not always happen any longer — of what disrupts fellowship among human beings. Then from the angle of the "fellowship issue," we would once again encounter the core problem of healing for our sins, as "undesirable" as this may be!

At this point we must not overlook the fact that the *sacrament* of *penance,* which aims at confession and absolution (which became *rudimentary* in the Lutheran churches and mainly followed the Lord's Supper in its regressive form), is today exposed to a process of fading away that encompasses all denominations. Many theologians are now trying to break out of the front of those who lament this process. The hypothesis that the forgiveness of sins is not at all as centrally anchored in the New Testament's understanding of "salvation" as has been assumed in the history of church dogma is found among the arguments they use to make this point. But this hypothesis is untenable. It makes the solution to the problem much too simple for itself because it fails to explore the historical causes for why the sacrament of penance and our "awareness of sin" have faded. But we cannot save ourselves the work of coming to terms with these causes by "resorting to exegesis."

Certainly, when an open confession of sin immediately precedes Protestant celebrations of the Lord's Supper (in which we speak the words of confession "from our heart," stating that "I regret my sins and am sorry for them"), and when the pastor as "the ordained servant" "grants" absolution and thus puts us in a position to partake of the Lord's Supper, then this rite, even if its vocabulary is modernized, is not in any case equivalent to Jesus' dealings with the tax collectors and sinners before he had table fellowship with them. But it must be asked if our Lord's Supper must correspond to these fellowship meals at all. Indeed, it is even disputed by scholars whether the historical Jesus "granted" any people the forgiveness of their sins.[10] For only in the profession of the post-Easter community of faith did the crucified and risen *Kyrios,* Jesus Christ (who has become for us wisdom from God — that is, our righteousness, holiness, and redemption, 1 Cor. 1:30), become the personified forgiveness of sins, so to speak.

Now at least there does not have to be any dispute by the exegetes about the fact that the historical Jesus sought the lost sheep of the house of Israel. He pursued those who had ended up among the separated members of the house of Israel because of some difficult situation or personal guilt. His table fellowship thus served to restore the unity of God's chosen people. As such it certainly had something to do with "the forgiveness of sins." Therefore, those who want to align the church's practice of Communion today more closely with the behavior of the historical Jesus are not at all justified in detaching the forgiveness of sins from the celebration of the Lord's Supper. How are we able to understand the table fellowship of Jesus in any other way than this: Jesus made himself the one who shared in the destitution and guilt of those he endeavored to bring back into the community of the whole nation of Israel. "The only way their guilt is taken away is by Jesus living in close companionship with them."[11]

On the other hand, the post-Easter significance of the forgiveness of sins is not fundamentally different. Only the universal aspect was added. All of humanity is now potentially its "recipient." Christian theology can

---

10. P. Fiedler, *Jesus und die Sünder,* Contributions to Biblical Exegesis and Theology, vol. 3 (Bern/FFM, 1976), pp. 271ff., objected to the view that the historical Jesus forgave sins and conferred on his disciples the authority to do this.

11. Translated from P. von der Osten-Sacken, *Grundzüge einer Theologie im christlich-jüdischen Gespräch,* Abh. z. christ.-Jüd. Dialog, no. 12 (München, 1982), p. 80.

learn from the historical Jesus' get-togethers with the tax collectors and sinners that the church must beware of a one-sided understanding of repentance that sees remorse, confession, the desire to change, and, in the end, the absolution of the sinner as *preconditions* for admission to Christ's table. For in fact it is always the Lord *(Kyrios)* who must first come to the door and to the table of the one who is not worthy (see Matt. 8:8; Luke 7:6) so that his burden is relieved and he is given the desire to change. A theology that is able to make adequate distinctions when it teaches about repentance must see that repentance represents a complex divine-human event and that on the human side alone, various acts are part of this event which occurs partly *before* and partly *after* our awareness and experience of being accepted by God's grace. Thus the claim that the proper order is "first repentance, then grace" is just as wrong as the opposite claim that "repentance always comes only after the reception of grace." That is why the liturgical "location" of the sacrament of penance (or its historical remnants) immediately *before* Communion is in fact at least not clear and also not compelling. It would be advisable today to develop a common theological framework for understanding the power of forgiveness granted both the historical Jesus and the post-Easter Christ, thus enabling us not only to make careful distinctions about repentance but also to speak clearly about it. The "releasing" of both the forgiveness of sin and thus of repentance interprets each other.

Bonhoeffer's Finkenwald experiments, which were concerned about regaining *individual confession* in the Protestant church,[12] were probably not very promising for the future. Bonhoeffer believed it was essential to overcome one's own arrogance and pride on a regular basis and to ask any available fellow Christians (not a friend whom one trusts and with whom one is joined together in mutual support) to hear one's confession and grant absolution. But the central idea of individual confession suffers not only from the difficulty of putting it into practice and not only from the existence of diverse sources of opposition that saw the danger of a Christian elite being formed. The institution of confession as such has entered a crisis in our time, and this factor carries more weight. However, this is not only caused by its frequently mentioned competition with psychotherapy. It probably seems almost ridiculous to many Christians today to see

12. See D. Bonhoeffer, *Gemeinsames Leben. Das Gebetbuch der Bibel*, ed. G. L. Müller and A. Schönherr, in *DBW* (München, 1987), 5:93-102.

salvation expressed in such egotistical and individualistic terms. In the traditional sacrament of penance they are supposed to try to save their own soul by expressing sorrow, confessing their sins, being willing to offer satisfaction and change their ways, and finally by receiving absolution while at the same time the entire human society seems to be drifting toward the brink of disaster. It is well known that most Christians who are still interested in being absolved from sin now prefer common confession, which is made possible in various forms in the services of worship. The gathered congregation says *pars pro toto,* "We have all sinned." The rest of humanity would have to confess more or less the same. Of course, the opportunity for a *new beginning* promised by the pastor (if he does not merely quote "a word of grace" from the Bible that is in keeping with the church year and is kept remarkably "more modest" than an explicit absolution) refers once again only to the group of members in attendance. What is the situation for all the others? May and can they make a new beginning? Do we "at least" have to hear personally the words of absolution in the service of worship? This much seems to be clear: Even common confession and absolution in the worship service can hardly be considered a successful way out of today's difficulties with individual confession and with the traditional sacrament of penance in general.

The flaw is not that common or open confession unites whole groups of people and their offenses into a single category almost without distinction. Rather, a shadow is cast on it because it, too, does not solve the problems associated with individual confession. Today we simply do not come very close to getting at the heart of what destroys people's hopes and understandably fuels their fears with confession and absolution in its present form. The fact that this ecclesiastical form of "dealing with guilt" still even exists in the highly developed countries most likely has to do with their unconscious search for an authority where guilt is still called guilt and evil is not played down or excused. This severity is sought after — the opposite of *tout comprendre et tout pardonner.* Of course, if this assumption is correct, it is even more questionable if the present way the church deals with sin, confession, and absolution does justice to the task it faces.

Fortunately, the church's sacrament of penance is not the only gate through which God's grace can stream into the world. Fortunately, the church's "office of the keys" (that is, its mission to bind and loose) is also not exclusively tied to the church's sacrament of penance, which most

Protestant churches are not familiar with anyway. But where are we more likely to break through to God's renewing action than by staying with the possibilities of the institutional church? We should openly ask this question because it is already being dealt with on a broad front, at least in a "latent" sense. And for a long time now it has not always found a satisfactory solution. Thus, we must beware of the opinion that we actually need only to pull man's *"repentance"* or *"conversion"* out of the "ruins" of the traditional church sacrament, and then we would *have* the place where God wants to intervene in our world to renew it. It will not work this way. For repentance and conversion run the danger of being misunderstood legalistically if they are detached from the gift of divine grace that is a part of the traditional sacrament. It could then easily come to the point when even this theologically unacceptable advice is given: You had better not rely so much on the forgiveness of sins that can "be had so easily" and can "be done so easily"; *instead,* try hard to change — as if one could be had without the other.

It must be assumed that the forgiveness of sins, rightly understood and rightly practiced, will *always* be the nerve center of church life, of a living church. However, in the course of history, the forgiveness of sins was made relevant in different forms and at different places time and again. This means that it can also happen today outside of the confessional and even outside of the church building. But it is certainly also made relevant today far from strident moral demands for change which come along without religion and without grace and lack the splendor of divine compassion. If we are concerned about the forgiveness of sins and the return of splendor in our world, then for the time being the call for an urgent *conversion* of Christianity (the church, humanity in its entirety) that is so widely accepted and considered "thoroughly Christian" must no longer be trusted so easily.

C. The Widespread Aversion to the (Wrongly Proclaimed?) Gracious Message of the Forgiveness of Sins

Let us now enter a difficult terrain guided by the key issue — what *inhibits* the acceptance of the Christian proclamation of grace? Where does the aversion to grace come from? There would seem to be several reasons: partly "deep-seated" reasons touching the spiritual roots of Christianity, partly more "superficial" reasons that could perhaps be positively influenced by more decent theological work and more conscientious church leadership.

As far as the "deep-seated" aversion is concerned: It is identical with a fact accurately recognized by all perspicacious theologians of church history, yet seldom adequately understood by the "foot soldiers" of the church. We all look as if we were happy to hear "your sins are taken away from you; you will not die, but live." However, in fact, we don't desire *any* divine grace, indeed, do not have such a hostile attitude toward any other reality of this life than the grace of God that has been lavished on us![13] The gracious God is natural man's greatest enemy. And that faith in God which alone enables us to cease being "natural men" and enemies of God is the greatest of all miracles because man desires to be gracious to himself, desires to save himself and does not at all want to give up the support of his physical and mental life that he has constructed for himself. This is why the gracious God gets in his way at the place where he has put down deepest roots of his life. Following Kierkegaard, we would have to be very poor sinners, despairing about ourselves, in order to exist in a way that is open to God's grace. Nevertheless, making us into such very poor sinners, even though this is precisely what we do not want, is the greatest accomplishment and the actual work of the Holy Spirit in the history of the church.

The work of the Holy Spirit must also remain *his!* Good theology fulfills its task at this point by allowing just this insight to prevail and by strictly renouncing all efforts to help this work achieve better success by instituting new programs of theological education or church reform.

But the situation looks different, quite different, when it comes to modern man's aversion to the central Christian message of the forgiveness of sins which is fueled by experiences Dietrich Bonhoeffer called "cheap grace" in his book *The Cost of Discipleship* (1937):

"Cheap grace is the deadly enemy of our Church. We are fighting to-day for costly grace.

"Cheap grace means grace sold on the market like cheapjacks' wares. The sacraments, the forgiveness of sin, and the consolations of religion

---

13. See *Luthers Werke,* Weimarer Ausgabe, 18:633, line 5 (hereafter cited as WA); also K. Barth, *Die Kirchliche Dogmatik,* 13 vols. (Zurich, 1932ff.), II/1, pp. 148, 151, 154 (hereafter cited as *KD*).

are thrown away at cut prices. Grace is represented as the Church's inexhaustible treasury. . . .

"Cheap grace means grace as a doctrine, a principle, a system. It means forgiveness of sins proclaimed as a general truth, the love of God taught as the Christian 'conception' of God. . . .

"Cheap grace means the justification of sin without the justification of the sinner. Grace alone does everything, they say, and so everything can remain as it was before. . . .

"Cheap grace is the preaching of forgiveness without requiring repentance, baptism without church discipline, Communion without confession, absolution without personal confession. Cheap grace is grace without discipleship, grace without the cross, grace without Jesus Christ, living and incarnate. . . ."

The people in our geographical location "became Christian and Lutheran, but at the cost of true discipleship. The price it was called upon to pay was all too cheap. Cheap grace had won the day.

"But do we also realize that this cheap grace has turned back upon us like a boomerang? The price we are having to pay to-day in the shape of the collapse of the organized Church is only the inevitable consequence of our policy of making grace available to all at too low a cost."[14]

This aversion to the church's message of grace is the obvious result of Christian seriousness and being deeply moved by the true message of grace that Christianity proclaims. It is aimed at cheap grace which is eagerly consumed by many but then proves to be useless, even harmful. Bonhoeffer's aversion comes from inside the church. It comes from his pain at seeing the most sacred treasure being sold off dirt cheap, orchestrated by an opportunistic church organization that was ultimately cutting its own flesh in the process. And this process continues to the present day.

Bonhoeffer's rightfully famous text also alludes to problems associated with modern secularization: The Christianized European world that partially went through the Reformation in which grace became an imminent part of everyday life has to lament the following lapses in the church. "[The church] baptized, confirmed, and absolved a whole nation unasked and without condition. Our humanitarian sentiment made us give that

---

14. D. Bonhoeffer, *Nachfolge* (1937) (München, [10]1971), pp. 13f.; quotations from English translation, *The Cost of Discipleship*, trans. R. H. Fuller, with some revision by Irmgard Booth, rev. ed. (New York: Macmillan, 1949), pp. 45-47, 58.

which was holy to the scournful and unbelieving. We poured forth unending streams of grace. But the call to follow Jesus in the narrow way was hardly ever heard."[15] Bonhoeffer's subject here is despicable European "churchianity" and Christianity that provoked the mockery of Voltaire and other Enlightenment philosophers. They had all come into conflict with the church's doctrine of grace to an extremely high degree. At the same time they tried hard to introduce more morality in the European political community. It is obvious that Bonhoeffer tries to show that their criticism was legitimate and yet at the same time takes the wind out of their sails by pointing out the way Christianity should be, the way of strictly following Christ. His theology is moving here on two tracks. First (in conjunction with criticism intended for the church itself), it is opening up to that "secularized" modern European that can only think and feel "worldly" after all that the history of Christianity has produced. Second (with the goal of renewing or restoring Christianity and the church), it puts a stop to the useless and undignified selling off of the sacred to the "world." It appeals to the church to rediscover the *arcanum* and, above all, to preserve it.

"Costly grace is the sanctuary of God; it has to be protected from the world, and not thrown to the dogs. It is therefore the living . . . Word of God, which he speaks as it pleases him. Costly grace confronts us as a gracious call to follow Jesus. . . ."[16]

Opening to the world *and* simultaneously narrowing the door to the church — this is the particular tension that characterized Bonhoeffer's theology during the final part of his life. The modern (atheistic) critique of religion, the focus on this earthly life and the secularization of life, is largely accepted. But at the same time he speaks of church discipline. Moreover, a "christological concentration" uniquely shaped by Bonhoeffer's own theology is attempted: concentration on grace which is found, as he says, by strictly following Jesus Christ.[17] In an extremely bold

---

15. Bonhoeffer, *Nachfolge,* p. 25; quotation from ET, p. 58.

16. Bonhoeffer, *Nachfolge,* p. 15; quotation from ET, p. 48.

17. Here Bonhoeffer's theology connects with Karl Barth's breakthroughs in the modern era. They consist primarily of a theological reappraisal of human achievement and human self-realization through moral action. Moreover, Barth's teaching, in spite of definitely following the tradition of the Reformation, does not show any reluctance to see divine law *as gospel,* similar to liberal theology; and it shows no fear of a basically positive assessment of the need to do "good works as a sign that divine grace is active in the believer in spite

intensification of the doctrine of grace Bonhoeffer attempts to interpret discipleship as *grace,* the kind of radical change (expressly including ethical improvement) that takes the cross of self-denial upon itself. In this context Bonhoeffer espouses the view that medieval spiritual life in the monasteries, with its development of strict forms of Christian life together and with its attempt to follow the special "evangelical counsels" of Jesus' preaching, could still be extremely relevant to the modern era. To be sure, Bonhoeffer could not approve of a special spiritual estate elevated above the general population with a set of instructions for living a strictly regulated monastic life, something the Reformers also taught. But life based on the "evangelical counsels" would have to become the lifestyle of *all* Christians, of the entire "worldly" laity — together with its Magna Charta, the Sermon on the Mount!

This was Bonhoeffer's attempt to find his way back to costly grace. It can remain left open as to how one should judge the issue of how close this experiment comes to new legalistic priorities in the church which are supposed to be given legitimacy by Bonhoeffer's theological inheritance. We must now discuss an additional, third source of contemporary resistance to the "Christian message of grace," now that we have heard this important voice of protest against the way the church currently handles its responsibility of granting the forgiveness of sins.

This third source is the fact that *the world has changed* since the introduction of nuclear weapons, or, better, since humanity has been given the possibility of destroying itself. As this historical development was occurring, Christianity appears to have failed historically. It was put in the dock and was accused of having driven humanity and the earth into a dead end. Regardless of how legitimate this accusation against Christianity is, its "promises" are no longer enticing for many people, at least in the form in which they are usually "proclaimed." Its "means of grace" are often considered to be useless. "No God will help us to preserve this earth. Disappointment about the fruitlessness of Christian ethics or about the problematic ethical fruit of Christian faith is prevalent on a large scale.

---

of the possibility of works-righteousness and self-justification." I have attempted to interpret all this not as a break with Luther's theology nor as the continuing unbroken influence of Calvinism, but as a legitimate continuation of Reformational theology by Barth in different historical situations in Gestrich, "Die hermeneutische Differenz zwischen Barth und Luther angesichts der neuzeitlichen Situation," *ZThK. B.* 6 (1986): 136-57.

Meanwhile, many pastors have gained the impression that the gospel proclaimed by them is simply no longer getting at the root causes of the evils that have taken their toll on us today and that have led us to feel anxiety about the future. This has made many of them tired."[18] Seen from a sociological vantage point, Christian faith seems to appear for the most past as a private attitude virtually without ethical and political significance. Seen from a psychological vantage point, Christian faith hardly saves us from using one of the psychological therapies from the toolbox of today's human sciences. We all still need the latter even if we "go to church." And then *they* often uncover the "true roots" of the trouble whereas the church's proclamation no longer seems to succeed in doing this.

Thus many people in our civilization are tired of hearing the church's "message of grace" about a "reconciled world," given the extremely unreconciled overall situation in the world. What we hear, then, is useless and obscures the facts. At best the teachings of *Judaism* which were previously so often judged to be "religiously antiquated" or "blind" by representatives of Christianity are still finding some "acceptance" (in the churches sometimes great acceptance). Its ostensibly greater realism anchored in the history of salvation does not call unreconciled reality "reconciled" and evaluates *merciless* historical outcomes as a clear absence of grace. This realism is being eagerly embraced.[19]

All this may be a caricature of what should "actually" be proclaimed in the church. But the idea that something is being "proclaimed" to the people from the churches has become strange and is not covered by reality! The church's preaching is in a crisis today that, seen as a whole, can neither be denied nor solely attributed to the people's different way of life and different leisure time habits, to prosperity and the competition of the mass media. Its diminished response comes *from within*. Thousands of theolo-

---

18. See my essay "Sündenvergebung als Problem und als Wirklichkeit der Kirche," *ZThK* 80 (1983): 325.

19. This problem became very clear in the dialogue between P. Lapide and W. Pannenberg, *Judentum und Christentum; Einheit und Unterschied: ein Gespräch,* Kaiser-Traktate 60 (München, 1981), p. 40. The latter put it this way: "The uniqueness of Christianity is its belief in the reconciliation of the world in Jesus Christ and in the presence of his Spirit, a world that is otherwise still unreconciled." Lapide remarked on this statement: "My simple Jewish mind no longer comprehends this: either the reconciliation is here or I cannot in any way accept a reconciliation that is not perceptible for me as a real reconciliation" (both quotations translated from the German).

gians and pastors have run out of things to say. They are taken aback by the historical situation in which they "have nothing to say" or "do not know how to say anything." In short, it has become very difficult for the churches to spread their own unique message among the people — the announcement of God's enabling nearness as a comfort for all who lack God or no longer expect anything from God given their objective situation (perhaps also given the system of religion prevalent today). Today's sermons that don't know what to say are those that say all kinds of things, but no longer know how to bind and loose.

Three important causes of modern man's aversion to the gracious message of the forgiveness of sins have been described: First, the hostility to grace which *is always* present in man because he wants to be his own god; second, the traditional spreading of "cheap grace" by the churches; finally, modern man's disappointment with the fruitlessness of the "spiritual enterprise," given the situation in the world today. These three totally different causes work together. They force us to ask the question: How should a Christian church that wants to stick to its own cause or find its way back to it react to this rejection syndrome?

D. The Church's Crucial Need to Correct Itself

The church's poor performance today in granting the forgiveness of sins is not just one of many imperfections inherent in the church; rather, it really jeopardizes the church. It reaches so deeply that even superbly devised "church growth programs" can not get at the root of the problem.

A theological mistake of many "church growth programs" is that they pursue "church renewal" as its own subject and goal — aside from the fact that there is often a real danger of going beyond the existing church to a theoretical church. When all is said and done, it is the people who are missing in this approach. For a new and, above all, better church will come into being only when a better understanding of a central issue of faith is achieved; more precisely, when a heresy is defeated that has gained a foothold in the churches. Real growth only happens in this way. Today a beginning must be made by focusing on the issue of the forgiveness of sins and scrutinizing church theories and practical traditions that have taken a beating. Without theological renewal at this point, strategies for church growth cannot become "important" in any case.

Modern theology inquires too little about the specific conditions for the forgiveness of sins. I do not mean "preconditions," but the place and the circumstances in human life in which the forgiveness of sins should play its role. *One* important place is, without a doubt, the church service, because Christians in worship are often open to the "encouraging word" that sins are forgiven. They hear in the worship service that *God* no longer regards them as sinners (and that they should, therefore, no longer see themselves in this way). What now? "I've heard it, so now I'm going home." (Perhaps a pastor brought the encouraging words of a worship service directly into my living room — via television.) Whatever the case may be, in hearing those "words of encouragement," it remains to be seen what my relationship to the church (the congregation) will be in the usual practice of today's church. I have received absolution without the question of this relationship having been broached. Should not the "heretical point" I just inquired about be located *here?* In fact, a better understanding of faith *at this point* ought to become the gateway to a renewed understanding of sin and grace!

The church is — objectively — always in a dual relationship to sin. Here is what I mean: the church not only has to speak "loosing words" into the "world"; that is, it is not merely a dispenser or mediator of the divine forgiveness of sins. Rather, it is itself the first recipient of forgiveness. The church itself comes into being, grows, and prospers through the gospel's power of forgiveness. For the one whose sins are forgiven by God is (re)grafted into the body of Jesus Christ as a member who had been lost but is now found (this is expressed in the event of baptism, for example).

Compare Ephesians 2:14ff. to this: In this text, the event by which the church comes into being is described as one in which human beings who have been separated by an insurmountable chasm find their way back together again. "Jews" and "Gentiles" — the most well-known example — who could not eat at one table find their way to each other. The *faith* that Jesus' death has been rightfully interpreted and proclaimed as a peacemaking sacrifice of reconciliation caused this miracle, Ephesians says. "A new man" was created out of those who had been so deeply separated before, and the idea of *one* new man could be emphasized. They became members together in *one* body of Jesus Christ. Probably inspired by Paul, the letter to the Ephesians established a paradigm for the forgiveness of sin. For he reminds us that something disruptive, something hostile and divisive was "dismantled" in the person of Jews and Gentiles through faith in Jesus Christ. Jews are proud of not having to be Gentiles. Those classified as "Gentiles" (always by Judaism first of all!) react to this with hostility and injured pride. The irreconcilable relationship between them is especially tangible in their mutual polarization. But such mutual polarization and exclusivism is ultimately the result of living in the mode of *self-justification*. Ephesians reminds us that only the word of Christ's atoning death accepted in faith could silence this self-justification. In this way, Jews and Gentiles found their way to one table. And the permanent lesson from this is clear: The word that is able to break such self-justification *establishes* the *church* — then and now.[20]

This aspect of the forgiveness of sins that creates the church has been largely ignored in the church's contemporary theory and practice. Thus, the way in which such granting of forgiveness became the current practice can only be called heretical — the issue of *the commitment of the members of Christ's body to a shared life* does not play a role at all. Consequently, the mistake is found in the fact that the "encouraging word of forgiveness" is allowed to be one thing, the issue of participating in the life of the church another; the latter is seen as separable or detached from the former.

The actual handicap of the present-day forgiveness of sins is not the diminishing intensity and willingness of man to confess his sins, not the increasing preference for confession in unison, not the lesser knowledge of our own sins in comparison to earlier times (and the less intensely felt remorse, if we disregard our guilty feelings for a moment). The widespread failure to produce genuine fruits of repentance and good deeds that flow from conversion is also not the actual cause of the degeneration of the forgiveness of sins. It is not behavior on the "receiving side" that creates the actual problem, but on the "giving side," on the side offering itself in

---

20. That is why the Confessing Church, for example, can really not acquit itself of great failures during the so-called German church struggle between 1933 and 1945. As long as it did not declare its allegiance to Christian-Jewish community or do its own calling to enter the fellowship of "Jews and Gentiles" and make it the first priority of its confession of faith in this historical situation, it contributed next to nothing to saving the church! It was also not "given" the opportunity to uphold fundamental truths of the faith-Christology, the justification of the sinner — at some other point. For if these truths had been in full force in the Confessing Church, it could not have lost a single Jewish Christian. This verdict is not meaningful as a moral-theological censure of the Confessing Church by the younger generation; rather, it gains power and becomes helpful when it is made by those who had a part in shaping the life of the Confessing Church at that time.

service. For the root of the damage is that the person who — supposedly — received the forgiveness of his sins *remains private,* and this is accepted by the church.[21] If it were to recognize that the forgiveness of sins signifies eo ipso an actual coming to life (again) of a Christian among his fellow Christians, it would not discuss absolution in isolation from the interaction of church members. Rather, it would theologically reappropriate forgiveness and even grace in such a way that they are not discussed as something that is secondary and different compared to the social and service dimension of faith. This is exactly what Bonhoeffer also wanted.

It is not enough to *imagine* theologically that a person who believes the church's message "your sins are forgiven" subsequently comes to life again in his family or among his colleagues, thus enabling his relationship to his social environment to be renewed. Such an assumption would really only be a "theological idea" anyway — with an uncertain grounding in reality. But this is one of the mistakes of modern theology — it is not and does not want to be particular about telling the difference between those friends and acquaintances of a church member who are part of the church and those who are not. Many people in our social environment are not Christians; they do not belong to the church. We must ask this question: "Does this make any difference?" Focusing on the event of the forgiveness of sins, however, we must not forget the — unrecognized — point that a renewal of life together or new opportunities to work together with other members of the body of Christ *must not be missing* from this event.[22] If this is

21. It is often claimed that we can no longer understand sin in private terms, but only in social, political terms, and that is why the granting of forgiveness is no longer valid. But the opposite is the case. Forgiveness becomes difficult not because we no longer understand "sin" in private terms, but precisely because we do this!

22. This raises the question of the extent of the body of Christ. Is the church/community of faith to be understood exclusively as this body whose head is Jesus Christ (Eph. 1:22; Col. 1:18)? Or is Jesus Christ the head of the whole world? This problem, discussed by Barth in *KD*, IV/3.2, pp. 863ff., has become pressing especially in Europe through the emergence of the "post-Christian situation." The solution to this problem must surely not be sought in the direction of blurring the boundary line between the church and what is not the church, and relativizing its importance. Yet this boundary line must surely not be equated with the boundaries of existing church organizations. This theological statement does not detract from the dignity and necessity of existing churches at all. The church organization alone does not make the body of Christ; rather, the body of Christ makes the church organization. That is why the membership of individuals in the church is decided by Jesus Christ's relationship to them and their relationship to him — independent of legally framed memberships! Seen in this light, the relationship between human beings

missing, nothing else will be renewed or made possible. Everything has remained and will remain the same in our hearts, in the church, in the world. Again and again the church has misunderstood the theological truth that the "recipient" of every single forgiveness of sins is never only the individual, but always only he *and* his "community of faith," he *and* the church.

---

who are members of the body of Christ is something special, something different from their human relationship to non-Christians: Christians are called to work together in a unique way that is totally irreplaceable — starting with their common praise to God. The purpose and necessity of this special interaction are often misunderstood by today's Christians, or no longer understood. This is why they strangely do not mourn the loss as many baptized human beings are presently leaving the churches. These people are now missed where members either did not or were not supposed to work together. The damage has started to spread throughout the large churches and can only be healed by a clear and radical change in our understanding of baptism and baptismal piety.

SECTION XIII
THE REALIZATION OF RENEWAL

A. Atonement

The diverse options the Bible offers to express the divine *event of grace* come from the rich history of Israel's religion. Among the predominant terms we find the word "atonement." All human beings are considered as being dependent on the expiation of their sin.[23] In the Bible the word "atonement" *(expiatio, hilasmos)* frequently intersects with the word "reconciliation" *(reconciliatio, katallagē)*. The death of Christ on the cross is considered the "all-sufficient," once-and-for-all sacrifice of atonement (see Rom. 6:10; Heb. 9:26-28) that reconciles humanity with God. In this sacrifice of atonement Christ is the "substitute" of us all.

"God was reconciling the world to himself in Christ, not counting men's sins against them. And he has committed to us the message of reconciliation." God made him who had no sin to be sin for us, so that in him we might become the righteousness of God (2 Cor. 5:19, 21). "Since we have now been justified by his blood, how much more shall we be saved from God's wrath through him. For if, when we were God's enemies, we were reconciled to him through the death of his Son, how much more, having been reconciled, shall we be saved through his life!" (Rom. 5:9-10).

Harking back to archaic insights ("blood"), the Bible's discussion of atonement does not fuel the suspicion that God's gracious action is a pardon that can be had at a "cheap" price. What must be expiated with blood is not only a most serious violation of the world order established by God and of the confidence and blessing we had previously received, but also — and first of all — a violation of God. The healing is costly. The death of the ungrateful violator and offender is the only "solution" — unless an atonement of *equal weight* becomes possible. The archaic origin of "the idea of atonement" does not argue as such against the idea

---

23. Israel has been familiar with an actual *sacrifice* of atonement only since the Babylonian exile. In Israel's priestly theology it is the focal point of the cult (H. Gese, "Die Sühne," in *Zur biblischen Theologie. Alttestamentliche Vorträge,* BEvTh 78 [München, 1977], pp. 90f.). See also O. Hofius, "Sühne und Versöhnung. Zum paulinischen Verständnis des Kreuzestodes Jesu," in *Versuche, das Leiden und Sterben Jesu zu verstehen,* ed. W. Maas (München/Zürich, 1983), pp. 33, 43.

that "atonement" should play a good, supportive role in the faith and life of modern men. Its historical roots reaching back to time immemorial, its extensive dissemination in the history of religion and the eminent malleability of its subject matter, speak in favor of this idea! It was shortsighted of liberal theology in the nineteenth century to reject the entire field of language and symbolism associated with "atonement" in the Bible as "no longer relevant for our age." (For the most part they did not take offense at the religiously reduced, civil application of the "idea of atonement" in criminal law!) Even today many Christians have considerable reservations about theological formulations of grace in Christ that use propitiatory concepts. The parts of the New Testament that speak in such terms are still often left out. The idea of a Father God who sacrifices his Son or allows him to be sacrificed so that he can get along better with the rest of humanity (and it with him) seems to be "subethical," even a downright anti-Christian religious delusion. This "sacrifice" also seems to have accomplished nothing: human beings continue to sin.

A more careful exegetical study of the propitiatory statements in Scripture probably does not play a role in such a principled rejection of the propitiatory understanding of grace. It is more likely that such people are referring back to ideas like the ones S. Freud presented in *Totem and Taboo* — ideas about a primeval event in which the father's wrath is vented on sons who desired women shielded by a taboo. The father then kills the offending son. The son's death gives him "satisfaction." But the killing of the father by the rest of the sons, the "brothers," creates "incessant guilty feelings."

Imagine how many speculations are possible! However, the New Testament tells about a historically verifiable human sacrifice that really "happened" under Pontius Pilate. In trying to find the correct interpretation, we must remember that the New Testament texts continue Israel's traditions of sacrifice and atonement, which in turn all experience a new interpretation in the New Testament. They are seen as *pointing to Jesus Christ.* Many verses interpret the sacrifice of his life not as providing *God* satisfaction for a loss suffered on the part of humanity, but as God giving sinful *humanity* "enough" to cover their sin and guilt, to heal the rifts human beings brought or bring into their life, and to fill the emptiness in their souls. This is also largely in keeping with the Old Testament's theologies of sacrifice: God is not the recipient, but the subject, the giver of atonement.[24]

---

24. All these theologians agree: Gese, Hofius, Janowski, and even Koch.

"Neither in Paul . . . nor . . . in any other writing of the New Testament can theories be found of a 'God demanding a bloody sacrifice of atonement.' The teaching of a *satisfactory* and *propitiatory* sacrifice of atonement Jesus offered before God and for God is a completely . . . unbiblical teaching." Paul did not assume a mutually "hostile relationship" between God and man that would have to be reconciled, but *man's* hostility against God. Thus, the atoning death of Christ does not effect a satisfaction of God's wrath. In Paul the "expression *orgē theou* (God's wrath) does not mean an emotion of God but an objective state of affairs: the coming eschatological judgment of wrath that must bring the sinner who has forfeited his life as an enemy of God the final sentence of death." "The reconciliation granted by God in the event of the cross *results* in those reconciled being rescued from the coming wrath," or, in Paul's words, "not being damned in the final judgement."[25]

However, critics have often found fault with this view. Above all, they believe it is ethically incomprehensible, even offensive, that God would allow an innocent person to suffer vicariously and atone for human beings who had incurred personal guilt. This fateful "idea of the scapegoat" incredibly spares the actual guilty party his deserved punishment, and consequently remorse and repentance as well. In their view we must protect the death of Jesus Christ from such interpretations[26] — even if there is a hint of this interpretation in the New Testament itself.

Today's scholarly Bible exegesis makes this argument against such views. Both in the Old and New Testaments the recipient of the propitiatory action is included in the sufferings of the innocent substitutionary victim of the sacrifice. He does not get off "free." With H. Gese we could characterize the idea found in this theology of atonement as the teaching of an *inclusive substitution*.[27] Sinful man is part of the atoning event because sin does not just weigh on man externally like a detachable piece of luggage or dirt on the skin that can be washed off. The sinning person cannot distance himself from his sin. We are sinners at the core of our personhood. This is why the wiping out of sin actually means taking away, killing the person! Only through his own death is the *homo peccator* free of his sin. This is still the case when a substitutionary victim exists. Only when the

25. Translated from Hofius, pp. 27-30.
26. See Gese, p. 85.
27. Gese, p. 97.

sinner could go through his own death *without* finally dying would there be hope for him.[28]

The postexilic parts of the Old Testament actually grant such hope! God himself gave Israel "means," laying the foundations for such hope. When the human being who incurred guilt, or his representative, the priest, lays his hands on a sacrificial animal, then what is actually impossible begins to be possible. Of course, this gesture does not signify any dumping of one's own sins on the animals, but in this process the one offering the sacrifice personally *identifies* with the animal sentenced to death. Thus, it has to do with a rite of identification. This rite guarantees that an "exclusive substitution" does not take place; "instead, in cultic atonement the sacrifice of the victim's life is a substitution that includes the one bringing the sacrifice."[29]

The fact that such an event — also providing the structure for a change in the "story" — still possesses outstanding significance is probably too little recognized in most Christian churches today.

1. The Necessity of the New Testament's Sacraments in a Theology of Atonement

In the New Testament the identification of the sinner with the victim of the sacrifice (and the reverse, the identification of the substitutionary victim with the sinner) which is at the center of atonement mainly takes place in the *mystery of baptism* and the *mystery of the Lord's Supper*. Baptism drives the baptized individual into death together with Christ (Rom. 6:3f.). In the Lord's Supper the communicants gain a share in Christ's mortal wound, in his shed blood[30] *(koinonia tou haimatos)* and in his broken body *(koinonia tou somatos)*. Luther translated: in "fellowship" of the blood/body (1 Cor. 10:6; see Phil. 3:10).

28. See Hofius, p. 35.

29. Gese, p. 97; quotation from English translation, *Essays on Biblical Theology,* trans. Keith Crim (Minneapolis: Augsburg, 1981), p. 106; B. Janowski, *Sühne als Heilsgeschehen. Studien zur Sühnetheologie der Priesterschrift und zur Wurzel KPR im alten Orient und im Alten Testament,* WMANT 55 (Neukirchen/Vluyn, 1982), p. 359.

30. This blood does not simply point to suffering and death because for Israel, "in a cultic sense, blood is the life substance that has been set free" (Gese, p. 98; quotation from ET, p. 107). Thus, the "fellowship of Christ's blood" means the transmission of *vitality* to the sinner doomed to die. At this point the event of the cross is already associated theologically with the "resurrection from the dead." See Gese, p. 106: "To speak of atonement means death and resurrection together" (quotation from ET, p. 116).

Without a doubt what are known as the sacraments have their deepest theological significance and necessity in "carrying out" the inevitable death sentence on the sinner (the recipient of the sacrament!). But they do this in a way that grants the sinner life after death. In baptism and Communion we die with Christ. It has to do with the rites of identification given to the church which personally unite Christians with their sacrificial victim: They "share" their guilt with him, he "shares" his righteousness with them. It is not as if Christ were "sacrificed" again, given over to death for us again when the sacrament is administered. Rather, the meaning is that now *we*, too, are taken into his death. If the New Testament could totally dispense with an explication of the salvation event in terms of a theology of atonement, then it — and we today — could also totally dispense with baptism and the Lord's Supper and be satisfied with the "encouraging words of salvation" contained in the sermon. The issue of whether baptism and the Lord's Supper are necessary thus depends on the issue of whether atonement is necessary. It would be an error to emphasize the indispensability of these so-called sacraments in one form and interpretation or another but to reject the idea of atonement or to reject the necessity of atonement and the interpretation of Christ's death *as an atonement.*

The crucial aspect of baptism is not the incorporation of the baptized individual into the "body of Christ," into the community of faith, into the church. The crucial aspect of the Lord's Supper is not the testimony that the "members" belong together, with Christ as the reigning head of the church. Rather, the crucial aspect of the sacraments is that they make possible for us the *death* that is our due on account of our sin. *This* should be made possible for us for the sake of our life, for the sake of receiving new life from God. This is exactly what baptism and Communion accomplish! Everything else about the so-called sacraments, especially the above-mentioned gifts and effects, are ultimately only consequences and concomitants of the basic sacramental event I just mentioned: the event of identification described in the theology of atonement. Moreover, baptism and the Lord's Supper have a basic theological message that is in full agreement. When it comes to this key aspect of the sacraments, they intend and say the same thing. Yet if we want to discern a difference and a sequence, a "sequential relationship" between them, we can only point out that the symbolic content of baptism (drowning, cleansing, etc.) speaks more the language of a uniquely preparatory, an initiatory event, whereas the Lord's Supper speaks the language of togetherness among intimate friends, those who have belonged together for a long time and meet at table regularly.

2. The Central Christian Category of Substitutionary Action

Since we must not release the so-called sacraments, baptism and the Lord's Supper, from their original shared identity with the biblical theology of atonement, if we do not want to let them degenerate into arbitrary "church events" that we can interpret any way we like, we must ask this fundamental question: Do we still need this archaic theology of atonement? Is it indispensable for Christian faith? Does a Christian need both main sacraments? Are not interpretations of Christ's death sufficient which avoid the idea of atonement? Is the substitutionary suffering and death of Christ without any discussion really the root from which everything *must* grow if it helps to bear the name "Christian"?

Such questions are obvious today because in any case Christian discipleship, the ethics of Jesus, the loving behavior of Jesus and his proclamation of love, and, finally, the prophetic Jesus who threatens the rich and unrighteous with judgment are all basic components of what we rightly call "Christianity." Besides, there are numerous misunderstandings centered around the concept of atonement (the bloody payment of satisfaction) — and this is mainly because of the application of an undoubtedly unchristian "principle of atonement" that has been used in church history. These facts carry such great weight that they do not allow us to reemphasize immediately the atoning death of Christ as the *centrum Christianum* with great fanfare — after a certain correction of our theological course.

However, it is essential that the church — in a generally recognizable way — declares its faith *anew* in the atonement rightly understood and *comes to terms with* mistakes that were made in the history of Christianity over this issue. An understanding of the atonement that points the way ahead must disclose the significance of *substitution* in Christianity with theological precision.

We must begin with the following exegetical fact: When the Bible speaks of substitution in conjunction with the atonement, this does *not* mean that in place of the sacrifice that is due and the suffering of the actually guilty party another must be killed to whom perhaps a lesser value is ascribed. Especially the Old Testament animal sacrifices that were used to atone for sin do not take place on condition that God would (or should) also be satisfied with *cheaper substitutes.* Substitution in the Bible never means "cheap substitute"![31] On the contrary, it means the enabling of the one who is actually stricken.[32] The actually guilty person is also enabled to atone in his own person and in this way regain his status as a child of God. First of all, the substitutionary victim offered up — it may be a rather weak, poor being — is supposed to make possible a breakthrough to the realization of one's own guilt and then remorse, repentance, etc. The guilty person sees himself in the substitutionary victim; he sees his own poverty and weakness. It thus leads the actually guilty person exactly to the "places" he must occupy with his person (even if he strives to evade this in his sin): on the one hand, to the place of the person rejected by God and before God; on the other hand, to the place of a child living near and with God. Above all, the latter is the place in which the *homo peccator* did not want to be up to that point. This is why he fell into sin and brought about evil. Nevertheless, we will now live in this place according to God's will. God achieves this by leading the *homo peccator* to identify with the sacrificial victim. God provides him with the opportunity for atonement. In this way God makes sure that the guilty person — even he — actually occupies the place provided for him in the *familia Dei,* in the house of God.[33]

N. Hoffmann, in his studies on the biblical understanding of the atonement and substitution, has especially developed the *trinitarian* anchoring of substitution. As a human being, Jesus Christ himself, the Logos, assumes the position in the divine being that God granted to man. God in his triune being adds humanity to himself in the person of his Son. However, human beings resist this. They do not want to fill their position in the being of God.[34]

Sin "in its actual, revelational sense" is "the deed of a 'son' as such, the resistance of this son to his sonship." It does not just end up hurting the

31. On the necessary distinction between "substitution" and "replacement," see mainly D. Sölle, *Stellvertretung. Ein Kapitel Theologie nach dem "Tode Gottes"* (1965), Um ein Nachwort erweitert Neuauflage (Stuttgart, 1982), pp. 17, 60 and passim. Gese points out the difference between our legal concept of atonement and the biblical concept, "Die Sühne," p. 87; see also Janowski, pp. 3ff.

32. See N. Hoffmann, *Sühne. Zur Theologie der Stellvertretung,* Sammlung Horizonte N.F. 20 (Einsiedeln, 1981), p. 69.

33. See Hoffmann, pp. 54f.

34. Hoffmann, p. 52.

Son, but also wounds the Father — sin thus reaches into the divine Trinity.[35] "Basically the sinner negates the Trinity." The Son "drifts away" from the Father. "Sin is the plunge toward the *nihilum trinitatis*." The word "hell" signifies precisely this nothingness![36]

The biblical secret of substitution must, therefore, be unfolded in Christian theology from the perspective of the substitutionary event in the triune God himself; that is, from the perspective of the loving existence of the Father for the Son, the Son for the Father, the Spirit for the Son and the Father, etc. N. Hoffmann wants to see the Trinity virtually as the "original matrix of every substitutionary act."[37]

When Jesus was crucified on Golgotha, the continually occurring inner-trinitarian act of substitution prevailed "*ad extra* over its negation by sin."[38] Properly understood, this cross is not an event "between Jesus and sinful humanity in which human beings cast their misdeeds on him or he — as the 'Lamb' — convicts them of their . . . wickedness." Rather, Jesus' "bearing of the world's sins" is, so says Hoffmann, with H. U. Balthasar, "an event between him and God the *Father*."[39]

"Christ, in so far as he is the great one who atones for our sins, makes it possible for us sinners to atone and, thus, to be sons of God. He not only marks the 'place' in which *man* finds his Christian identity. He is even more the 'place' in which *God* himself proves his identity."[40]

Is Christianity at its core the religion totally focused on substitutionary action? Must we expect every proper Christian anthropology and ethics to understand man as a being dependent on substitutionary action?[41]

35. Translated from Hoffmann, p. 53.
36. Translated from Hoffmann, p. 54.
37. Translated from Hoffmann, p. 49 n. 136.
38. Translated from Hoffmann, p. 57.
39. Translated from Hoffmann, p. 60.
40. Translated from Hoffmann, p. 95. I concur with Hoffmann's reflections (in the preceding five paragraphs). But I question Hoffmann's description of the event of atonement made elsewhere as a *transformation* of sin (see p. 65). Christ imparts to us the strength "to turn sin into the suffering of the Son" (because of the Father's love that we do not reciprocate!) and thus to carry and destroy sin (p. 89). On the cross of Jesus sin was transubstantiated into "the Son's suffering love." In this way it became an atonement (p. 59). Hoffmann is not only seeking to link it to the Roman Catholic mass, but to lay a better theological foundation for a "heart of Jesus" — piety marked by the idea that the church itself can "transubstantiate," "destroy" guilt — must we not stay with the encouraging word that it is *God* who forgives sin?
41. See the corresponding thesis by Sölle, *Stellvertretung*, p. 49.

When it understands itself correctly, does Christian faith see in substitutionary action the basic law of the new creation? Therefore, should the Christian church intervene in world history as an "event of substitutionary action"? Every question I just asked seems to fit exactly with D. Bonhoeffer's view. According to him Christianity and vicarious action not only belong closely together; rather, it must be said: Christianity *is* vicarious action.[42]

Bonhoeffer distinguishes between *ethical* and *personal* substitutionary action. Ethical vicarious action (its greatest case is described in Schiller's "Bürgschaft") takes place where a person voluntarily sacrifices anything he owns, even his own life, for another. Thus, the substitute sacrifices the things another should have come up with. Yet the substitute cannot really take the place of the other person. He can, for example, bear the consequences of another's evil deed, but these consequences do not become the punishment for *him,* the substitute. For the substitute did not personally commit this deed. All ethical substitution encountered among human beings ceases where the sphere of the individual is violated.[43]

Bonhoeffer concludes from this that every attempt to build community "on the foundation of Adam's humanity is illusory." "Everyone remains alone as a person." The love and the vicarious action of the other end in the prepersonal realm. They do not reach the other person. But this ability to reach the person of the brother/sister is found in the vicarious death of Jesus Christ. "*The substitutionary act of Christ* is more than ethical. This act is not only about a sacrifice of possessions, but a substitutionary sacrifice of the person."[44] This is why Luther was right to emphasize that Jesus Christ not only bore the *consequences* of our sins but also the *punishment* for them, because he was enabled and called to be a personal substitute.[45]

---

42. See E. Jüngel, "Das Geheimnis der Stellvertretung. Ein dogmatisches Gespräch mit Heinrich Vogel," *BThZ* 1 (1984): 68ff., for a critique of Bonhoeffer's concept of vicarious action that he not only frames in christological terms, but also gives an ecclesiological and anthropological cast from the vantage point of the idea of the church as "the body of Christ." See also K. Koch, "Sühne und Sündenvergebung um die Wende von der exil. zur nachexilischen Zeit," *EvTh* 26 (1966): 223.

43. D. Bonhoeffer, "Das Wesen der Kirche" (The essence of the church), in *GS* (München, 1972), 5:243.

44. Translated from Bonhoeffer, "Das Wesen der Kirche," p. 243.

45. D. Bonhoeffer, *Sanctorum Communio. Eine dogmatische Untersuchung zur Soziologie der Kirche,* in *DBW,* ed. J. v. Soosten (München, 1986), 1:99.

However, because the Christian christological concept of personal substitutionary action contains "deep problems of social philosophy," we could have great ethical reservations about it. For the ethical person obviously wants to answer for his own good and evil deeds before God. How can he put his sin and guilt on another person and get off scot-free himself? Bonhoeffer answers this question he himself had asked: It is *God's will* that we should have the burden of our sins taken from us because we are not able to carry them ourselves. At this point "man ought to abandon his standpoint of moral self-responsibility," because this "counts for nothing in God's sight." At this point man should accept Christ's *personal substitutionary act.* The latter is a special "offer from God." It is "in force only in Christ and his church. It is not *a moral possibility."*[46]

Bonhoeffer shares the opinion he already had found in Augustine that the forgiveness of sins — and this is the outcome or product of personal substitutionary action — is found *only* in the church, the community of the saints.[47] From the vantage point of this social concept, Bonhoeffer says the church represents a *community,* not a society, association, or crowd. For each "member" is a permanent lifelong part of the church. Every member is fully supported by it; every member is committed to the same tradition. The church, Bonhoeffer likes to say, "the community of faith," is even a "community of persons," thus, a fellowship in the original sense.[48] It is also possible for the members of the church to take personal substitutionary action on behalf of one another! It occurs because of the universal priesthood of all believers. In the community of faith every person needs the other as a priest. In Bonhoeffer's view, this is the meaning of the language about the universal priesthood (mostly misunderstood in individualistic terms). "The brother who is in the community of Christ vicariously becomes Christ for me." In Harnack and Troeltsch, but even in Barth, the knowledge of God and the *individual* Christian's relationship to God come first, the relationship of Christian members of the church to each other is regarded as something that has been or must be deduced from this.[49] But in Bonhoeffer the first level of Christian life is the community of faith/the fellowship. *It* is the

---

46. Bonhoeffer, *Sanctorum Communio,* p. 99; quotations from English translation, *The Communion of Saints: A Dogmatic Inquiry into the Sociology of the Church,* trans. R. Gregor Smith (New York: Harper and Row, 1963), p. 114.

47. Bonhoeffer, *Sanctorum Communio,* p. 126.

48. See Bonhoeffer, *Sanctorum Communio,* p. 177.

49. Bonhoeffer, "Das Wesen der Kirche," p. 261; see p. 238.

subject of the knowledge of God and of being a Christian even before that which the individual Christian recognizes and does. In the community of faith/the fellowship it dawns on the members what God is all about when one snatches another away from hell in his priestly service — and all along it is *God* who does this.[50]

But what church is Bonhoeffer talking about? About the one that exists? Or is he talking about a theoretical church? Bonhoeffer wants us to understand that he is talking about the empirical church that is actually present among us, provided that we grasp its being and its significance *in faith.* "Christ existing as community. This can not be seen, but only believed."[51] Christ faces us as a brother. "He vicariously stands where my brother should stand for me. My physical brother can not be a brother by himself, because he can not penetrate my personal sphere." "The category of thou is closed to him. Christ is our brother. But for that reason our brother can now become Christ for us."[52] The church members' mutual care and concern take place in a threefold structure of substitutionary action: as "a sacrifice for the neighbor," willing to risk everything, then in "intercessory prayer," finally in the "forgiveness of sins."[53] The latter is an exclusive "present" and "right" that Jesus Christ gave to the church.[54] "In the Old Testament, it was still impossible" for one to grant forgiveness of sins to another.[55] Whoever forgives the other's sins takes his sin "upon himself, because he knows that Christ bears his sin. Therefore, he can take the sin of the other."[56]

"Through the Christian principle of vicarious action the new mankind is brought and held together. In it the material particularity of the basic Christian relationships consists."[57] A Christian is dependent on the community of faith. "Each man sustains the other in active love, intercession and forgiveness of sins through complete vicarious action, which is possible only in the church of Christ, resting as it does in its entirety upon the principle of vicarious action, that is, upon the love of God. But all are

50. Bonhoeffer, "Das Wesen der Kirche," p. 262.
51. Translated from Bonhoeffer, "Das Wesen der Kirche," p. 248; see also p. 255.
52. Translated from Bonhoeffer, "Das Wesen der Kirche," p. 248.
53. Bonhoeffer, "Das Wesen der Kirche," p. 265.
54. Bonhoeffer, "Das Wesen der Kirche," p. 267.
55. Bonhoeffer, "Das Wesen der Kirche," p. 216.
56. Translated from Bonhoeffer, "Das Wesen der Kirche," p. 269.
57. Bonhoeffer, *Sanctorum Communio,* pp. 99f.; quotation from ET, p. 114.

sustained by the church, which consists in this action for one another of its members."[58]

The basic idea of Bonhoeffer's whole theology might be that God calls us in Christ to be *priests* for one another. In calling all baptized believers to be priests, God is calling forth the "new humanity," the community of substitutes. The authority for church members to be personal substitutes for one another comes from the atoning death of Christ. Standing in the tradition of Judaism, the goal of Christianity is to enhance the quality of human life which occurs when it is structured by mutual care and concern.

3. Predestination and Substitutionary Action

The category of substitutionary action the young Bonhoeffer boldly called "the Christian principle" not only forms the horizon of the biblical theology of atonement, but also the core of the church's teaching on predestination.[59] With Karl Barth this can be developed from the perspective of faith in Jesus Christ, who is elected and rejected in our place. Jesus Christ takes our place[60] so that we are enabled to take our place with God (to be God's children). As human beings affected by God's election, we do not lose our human independence and all human freedom; on the contrary, we gain both first and foremost by being elected. The sinner who becomes personally "identical" with the elected and rejected servant of God from Nazareth is lifted out of his shame and enveloped by the divine *kabod,* God's glory.[61] The life of election is a bright, shining life.[62] If existence

58. Bonhoeffer, *Sanctorum Communio,* p. 128; quotation from ET, p. 136.

59. Being elected by God means being appointed by God to be a substitute.

60. Barth, *KD,* II/2, pp. 132f. Cullmann illuminated "election" and "substitutionary action" as the two pillars in the New Testament's line of thought on salvation (*Christus und die Zeit* [1946], pp. 100-102). "The principle of God's gracious action is "the election of a minority to redeem the entire human race, or put in different terms, it is the principle of substitutionary action."

61. In the priestly theology of Scripture, the place in which God's glory "settles" is at the same time the place in which atonement can be found: (Hebrew) *kapporet*/(Greek) *hilastērion* = the lid of the ark of the covenant in the tabernacle, or, later, the Most Holy Place in the temple. According to Romans 3:25f. — the key verse of Paul's atonement theology — the crucified Jesus is this *hilastērion.* He is now the place in which God is present, "in which the transcendent God is near in his glory *(kabod)* . . ." (translated from Janowski, p. 353).

62. See Barth, *KD,* IV 13.1, pp. 89ff.; see also C. Gestrich, *Neuzeitliches Denken und die Spaltung der dialektischen Theologie. Zur Frage der natürlichen Theologie,* BHTh 51 (Tübingen, 1977), pp. 211ff.

under sin is characterized by a lack of splendor, a lack of speech, and a lack of communication (no word that points the way ahead is available), in the life of election the night that banishes our existence into darkness disappears: The new day dawns, the splendor and the word return.

A Christian dogmatics can assume many tasks. But if it does not forcefully develop the inner connection between atonement, predestination, and substitutionary action, and if it makes no attempt to consider issues of ontology, anthropology, and cosmology *from this position,* issues of general concern to all theologians, then it is not assuming its responsibilities at all! Then it will suffer from an irrelevance it has caused itself.

B. The Unfinished Task of Fleshing Out the Relationship between the Forgiveness of Sins and Substitutionary Action

1. An Attempt to Define More Precisely the Institution of Substitutionary Action

We do not know enough about substitutionary action. Therefore, what follows can only be an attempt in need of improvement and refinement by others. It is true that the christological and trinitarian and, to a lesser extent, the ethical significance of substitutionary action has long since been analyzed by not a few very capable theologians, among whom Anselm of Canterbury still deserves a place of honor. However, the ontological significance of substitutionary action has always been too little developed. We should first notice (and neither Bonhoeffer nor Sölle has done this) substitutionary action that is also encountered in nature and in all non-human creatures. It takes place there not voluntarily but "programmatically." Occasionally certain beings or organs in nature assume the functions or tasks of others, who "do something else" during this time. I am speaking of an ontological quality inherent in substitutionary action as defined by this universal institution of nature.

In a special way substitutionary action is related to the phenomenon of time. The main example is surely the behavior of many male and female creatures toward their newborn offspring. During the initial period "parents" still assume responsibility for getting food and providing security to the point of giving up their lives while fighting for them. In this sense they are acting as substitutes for their young. Meanwhile the offspring can grow stronger and be preserved from premature extinction in many ways. In this connection the emotional development of the human child in which the self can develop plays a large role. A human child neglected or abandoned too early can hardly develop a healthy self-image. He is impeded on his way to becoming his own "person"!

Substitutionary action in nature is a precondition for more complex structures of life being able to develop. Because other beings and organs are active in a way that is also useful for third parties, for a while all are able to dispense with certain tasks required for self-preservation. In diverse ways others are working for all so that the burden of all is eased somewhere, and in this respect they do not have to provide for their own life. For the first time this phenomenon in nature makes possible the emergence of "special capabilities" and "more complex structures of life." Through their further development, the "more advanced" creatures gain usefulness for the others. (What the old, naturalist theologians so much admired while looking at nature is this meaningful teamwork of the creatures that complements, supports, and moves each other forward.)

We must distinguish between the phenomenon of existence in *time* to which all created things, all that exists, are *subject,* and the phenomenon that a creature can *have time.* Plants and animals exist in time or in a temporal way. They are subject to time. But they do not have any time. Never. The fact that a temporal being can have time (among all creatures only man has time — a distinctive feature that is worthy of note!) is tantamount to a present of additional time. We are (largely) free to use this time as we want.

The fact that human beings "have time" again and again is possible only because of a *special kind of substitutionary action.* It will later be characterized as "ethical substitutionary action" — without this being identical to what Bonhoeffer also called by this term. People who "lack time" lack this special kind of vicarious action. On the surface it sometimes seems as if we had worked hard to achieve our own leisure time: for example, by quickly finishing tasks or by consciously dragging them out. But on closer examination this does not yet explain how we really have time. During these free blocks of time the continuity of that basic social commitment or mutuality which all other creatures must always have as long as they are here must be largely broken off or interrupted — by others! We must be released from this commitment and given time — for ourselves! Thus, even more substitutionary action must be taken for us than is usual in nature. Only then do we have "free" time. Only then do we have time which we can use as we see fit, if we want, even for social tasks.

Man is the living being who is temporarily given time by his own kind and released from the basic social commitments of the living beings who all often need and support one another in the context of nature. Man could not develop as man without such a temporary release, which is in addition to the substitutionary action already "programmed" into nature. He needs this free time. This is why he also needs this special substitutionary action. He needs members of the same species who treat him so kindly that they temporarily free him from his basic social commitments. Both the universal-natural and the exclusively humane, ethical substitutionary action I just presented are prevalent among human beings. Both are needed. The person who lets man have time for his specifically human needs is the one who takes ethical substitutionary action. Without these needs being met man could not live humanely, with human dignity (and precisely for that reason he could not act "ethically" himself!). The ethical substitutionary action so prevalent among human beings is the root both of our freedom and of our having time, which is actually a gain of additional time. And in a certain sense we can seriously say that man has also emerged from free time or leisure time, and he emerges from it again and again. He is at any rate the creature who is in special need of the "Sabbath" and its interruption of many work commitments.

From what has been discussed up to now we may infer for *ethics* that the basic principle "each according to his performance" is foolish. Even the offer of society to grant everyone material recognition and support "according to his capabilities," kindly added onto this principle in Marxist ethics, remains insufficient. The principle of a humane society (from which, of course, all presently existing societies still keep their distance) must be: "To each according to his needs!" The longer-term interest and well-being of all can only be accepted and the beneficial institution of substitutionary action be utilized in this direction. However, ethics should make itself useful by working through the difficult question of how the particular needs of the people can be adequately ascertained without giving out petty grades.

In evolution human beings have come onto the scene in connection with a natural ability to increase their substitutionary actions. Human beings are the ones who use the institution of substitutionary action existing in nature for their own benefit. We *must* assume this because without the working of such "increased substitutionary action" the human enterprise will always and everywhere immediately collapse. It is also true that human beings do *not* always grant each other the vicarious action they require. We are very familiar with the breakdowns in human society by this. And we know that man is not at all the epitome of a "free" soul in comparison with animals. (Because of a lack of ethical substitutionary action) he is often even decidedly "unfree," a slave, whereas animals are neither one nor the other. Human beings actually destroy each other, including that "core" of their being that makes man into a human being. Such events that also definitely affect nonhuman nature have been called "sin" in this book.

2. Sin and Substitutionary Action

We can now see how sin actually repeals man. It works against the reality of human life. Under its influence the release that would give us time for ourselves is not granted. On the contrary, sin impedes this release. It takes it back, makes it ineffective. The "good word" from which humane living is fashioned is not only opposed, but also made inaudible. Our ears become deaf to it.

Under the influence of sin man is actually free in only *one* sense. He is free to refuse biological-natural substitutionary action besides the ethical. For example, he can neglect his parental duties, which an animal is simply not free to do. (Presumably we are theologically justified in speaking of man's freedom to sin only in this sense. Sin frees the individual to dispense with all the substitutionary duties "programmed" into all natural beings if he feels so inclined.) Thus the universal, natural system of substitutionary action can be attacked and partially suspended by human beings. Thus humanity poses a far-reaching danger to the world. It reaches as far as man's "perverted freedom" under sin reaches. From this viewpoint it becomes obvious that the sins we traditionally call "actual sins" — for example, stealing, lying, committing adultery, murder — are the actualization of this specifically human freedom to abolish the mutuality, that is, the mutual care and concern creatures have for one another that has been programmed into the natural order.

It is part of the distinct nature and reality of the sin event that more complex living structures are again reduced to simpler and most simple forms. Moreover, it is part of the distinct nature and reality of sin to work against the institution of substitutionary action that is producing the higher forms in evolution. Here we can give a kind of definition to sin that makes it possible for us to speak of sin in and with the nature sciences as well. Moreover, this goes to show that the inner trend of evolution toward more and more spirit, love, etc., that some claim to see is questionable because humanity, which should actually be the "spearhead of evolution," becomes a retarding factor in evolution and even exerts a counterforce on it.

Sin is so threatening to us and the whole word that we human beings generally try to resist and escape its destructive force through *ethics*. But all the various systems of ethics are ultimately the attempt to strengthen or reactivate the institution of substitutionary action that is threatened by sin. (What matters is not necessarily the concept of vicarious action, but when the ethicist is not even properly aware of the full magnitude of the institution as such, which is often the case, this is a limitation, indeed, a shortcoming of his model.) It cannot be disputed that every system of ethics would like to ensure that community services essential for a decent life are provided for as many creatures as possible. Ethical behavior in the church's situation urges us to give one another what we should hand over to one another and forgive the debts we owe to one another for the sake of the common good. It showers praise on substitutionary behavior that preserves, regains, or even enlarges our room for personal growth. Of course, when all is said and done it is questionable whether ethical behavior can be a successful instrument in view of this objective. The old theological reservations about an ethical optimism which fails to recognize the power of sin are well known. However, they are not of interest at this point. For the basic ethical question is at least not objectionable. "How do we save the institution of vicarious action?" This question is encouraged time and again because it is *amazing* that in spite of evil "there is something at all — and not nothing instead." Human beings recognize there must evidently be counterforces that oppose the destruction that human beings constantly and vehemently perpetrate. The powers that resist the destruction could even be the stronger forces; and perhaps we can somehow ally ourselves with them.

Theology calls such forces *grace*. In addition, it teaches that these forces ally themselves *with us*. However, theology should show where and how such things occur ontologically, how the effects of sin are curbed or even neutralized, and that in spite of evil love and spirit are "making headway" (and together with them all that is good, true, and beautiful). Theology should also show that individuals are "making headway" and the leveling forces are being restrained; it should show where and how it is occurring. This, too, must and will happen wherever the substitutionary action essential for human affairs exists. Christian theology obviously attributes the possibility of this happening to grace. (Grace is focused on safeguarding the individual's existence — on the other hand, sin "works" on its dissolution; grace is focused on freedom; on the other hand, sin destroys it.)

3. The Way in Which Substitutionary Action Eases Burdens and Heals

The principle by which the institution of substitutionary action becomes ontologically effective is the rule that those who are better able to carry the burden *now* temporarily shoulder it. Substitutionary action always and everywhere means that others or another temporarily assumes certain tasks which "this person here" should actually assume. This is a more or less far-reaching action; for example, substitutionary action can free "this person here" from the responsibility of personally taking care of certain tasks at a certain time and at a certain place. Meanwhile "this person here" can personally do other things somewhere else. Others or another is making things easier for him. Now he is not being asked to assume more responsibility than he can handle. This will do him good and in the longer term also enhance his "social skills" and his usefulness for the general public.

Substitutionary action allows more time to those who need more time. Without this additional time they would spend their time in less constructive ways and their life would have a more negative impact on themselves and on others. Sometimes they might live in a way that would have a devastating effect on others. The intervention of a substitute gives them an extension. Later they can also do justice to the demands they would not be able to meet now in a constructive way.

Substitutionary action is a recognizably "intelligent" institution of nature. It utilizes excess power by directing it to places where for the moment shortcomings still exist. Substitutionary action is the ontological substitute on which loving, mutual care and concern — love — could occur in the course of evolution. If we like the word "secret," we will imagine that the "secret" of substitutionary action is found in this truth: A life structured by mutual care and concern always achieves more than when the individual creatures care exclusively for themselves. The institution of vicarious action works by utilizing temporal differences — just as a public utility does when it takes electricity from the net during the night in order to pump the water that had flowed down into the reservoir up the mountain again in this period of low demand.

Finally, it can be said of the natural institution of substitutionary action that healing power radiates from it as well. The heavy strain put on certain creatures is cut short because they are given a substitute. This is nothing short of a soothing of their emotions, enabling sick, damaged creatures who have overdone it to recover again. In nature such a cessation of the strenuous activity for a limited time is often enough to heal damaged lives again. Even in human medicine one of the greatest opportunities for healing a doctor can use is simply breaking the vicious cycle in which patients get caught. Two examples:

I. A heavy strain has been placed on nature — water, earth, and air. To be sure, it is part of their normal functioning to "digest" the garbage and waste left behind by living creatures. However, modern man asks too much of nature at this point. The result is that water, earth, and air appear to be "poisoned" and in fact do not function as they should; they have gotten off track. Now we must raise the question whether those who have placed excessive demands on nature until now are bringing relief to it. Do they have sufficient resources to meet this challenge? Until now something else has been happening. Man has been sidestepping the responsibility that has come to rest on his shoulders. For example, the toxic waste of influential, prosperous nations is being shipped from them to the other side of the globe. It is being dumped for low fees in industrially less developed, poor countries that are biologically still rather healthy. This reprehensible behavior, taking some of the strain off their own environment and in return using up new land (a classic paradigm of sin!), has not created any *substitutionary solution,* but in fact only a *makeshift solution* that only appears to be a way out in the short term. The dilemma has been postponed. However, in contrast to the makeshift solution, substitutionary action would mean that the waste disposed in highly industrialized societies is taken over by partners who are able to handle it in terms of their capacities. The action of these partners who are willing to be substitutes would mean a real solution to the problem. But this much is clear: Nature in Africa or in yet more distant parts of the earth cannot be the substitute for Europe's nature. Moreover, the governments in those regions are not the kind of partners who could handle Europe's ecological problems by acting as substitutes for them.

Only one solution can be considered. It is *the citizens of the highly industrialized countries themselves* who should ease the burden they have placed on their hard-pressed environment/nature by drastically reducing the quantity and the chemical-biological danger of their toxic waste, by completely easing up on endangered regions for a rather long period of time and by making sacrifices for this. The Europeans must take on the job they still expect nature to handle today as its "usual function." If this would really happen, much would improve. In time we would get a more intact, safer environment in Europe. Besides "helping out" an overburdened nature, it would do our own lifestyle a lot of good. We would become more healthy ourselves.

This example can teach us two lessons at once: first, human beings can also become substitutes for nonhuman creatures, and, second, substitutes must often come from the circle of those who until now have put too heavy a burden on partners who are in need of a substitute and who have refused to act as substitutes. But in what way has their burden been eased before that would give them the capacity to behave in a totally different way?

II. A Roman Catholic priest rescues a Jewish family from being taken away to Auschwitz. He passes himself off as this Jew. He later dies in the camp. But that Jewish family can be saved. Almost fifty years later it already has descendants numbering more than fifty persons.

The priest took this substitutionary action on his own initiative. He orchestrated it without having been sent by anyone. No one could ask him to do what he did. Those who were in need of his substitution in this situation could at best wish that the priest would act this way. Their cry for help in their hour of need was sufficient justification for the act of substitution. For them this happy turn of events came to pass because another recognized on his own who had suddenly become his neighbor in this situation. Or to put it a different way: The priest recognized that he had become the neighbor of this man here and now.

In the case of this priest we now speak of a sacrifice. This is not without good reason. But we should make careful distinctions when we handle this word "sacrifice." The priest did not make a sacrifice like that of the crucified Christ. No one could ever repeat this sacrifice. And above all no one has to do this. However, the priest had many different motives for his act of substitution. We cannot understand them all. But it is of no significance at all whether they were all or mostly of an altruistic nature. It must be assumed that he mainly drew strength from the life and faith of his church. From this point of view he was certainly lonely in Auschwitz, but in a religious sense he was not alone.

His former sufferings still create blessing. They benefited and still benefit the entire relationship between the church and Judaism. We can probably say they have brought a new spirit to this relationship and in any case have helped to ensure that a new, future Auschwitz is no longer thinkable. The impact of this one individual's substitutionary action shows in exemplary fashion how one shining deed can generate the power to head off disaster in the long term and spread its blessings to wide areas of life. Here we can begin to comprehend that good has a chance in the world even if it apparently happens much more rarely than evil.

4. The Consequences of Understanding the Forgiveness of Sins

A breaking of the vicious cycle brought about by substitutionary action must occur whenever that which is called the forgiveness of sins in Christianity really takes place. An inner calm and a gain in time must become real in connection with this. The forgiveness of sins brings peace of mind and allows us to gain additional time. It counteracts overexertion and relieves the stress of wrong priorities. Christian "conversion" — for many this is a clearer designation for the thing intended than the words "forgiveness of sins" — is actually a *remission* in the medical sense of the word — a return of health brought about by God's healing assistance, a turning back onto the road of health. Understood in these terms, repentance/conversion is neither a precondition for the forgiveness of sins nor its consequence, but the event of the forgiveness of sins itself.

But *where* does this happen in real life? When confronted with this question theologians in this situation are quick to speak of Jesus Christ as the "actual place" of all healing, beneficial substitutionary action. But this has become a formula accompanied by too little understanding. Surely it is not wrong to interpret Jesus' life and death as an event of substitutionary action through which the "nature" of all substitutionary action could become clear to us. Only then the many substitutionary events in the world would also have to come into focus so that we could observe them. But modern theology has largely failed to observe such substitutionary action today. Too little consideration is given to the idea that Jesus Christ is not in *himself alone* the epitome of healing, beneficial substitutionary action. He is also not the only place of such action. He is rather a door to the substitutionary events in real life that would perhaps not even be observed without him and would perhaps not even be made use of. The least that everyone can observe in him is the possibility *and* reality of healing, beneficial substitutionary action. The laws of nature, the order of being — they are at least not opposed to such substitutionary action (and the enhancement of life that occurs as a result of it).

We may speak of the possibility *and* reality both of natural and ethical (specifically human) substitutionary action. This means that the institution of vicarious action exists and is also used by everyone, at least unconsciously and in certain areas of life. But it could be used even more extensively — and, then, consciously. There are more possibilities in it than we utilize. Here there is a difficulty. It is not only essential that we recognize the existence of this institution and understand the way it works. The point is that we have the desire to use it and actually do use it. The masterful, diabolic skill with which sin spins everyone into its net is also evident in the fact that human beings certainly recognize the reality of substitutionary action and can even understand and affirm it as a beneficial reality — and yet are in the habit of not using this opportunity, but even stabbing it in the back. In this way sin proves itself to be a highly intelligent "institution." It can always obscure its own ability to bring its own influence to bear effectively because we can even "intellectually" affirm what we then deny and combat with our actual behavior. The "ancient foe" is winning — and on his part he needs the ability to outwit us. But we are not able to outwit him. What can we do now?[63]

---

63. This question corresponds to the complaint of E. Lévinas that reality ("existence as we experience it as human beings") "is actually 'the evil.' But existence is evil not because it is finite, but because it is without boundaries." We are directly exposed to this unbounded existence *when we suffer,* and there is no evading it and no place to go for refuge. Because existence is without boundaries, we are "driven into a corner" when we suffer. Lévinas expresses what is as long as there is not sufficient, unforced human substitutionary action. But such human action is actually not possible if there is no divine grace. Translated from *Die Zeit und der Andere* (Hamburg, 1984), pp. 24, 42, the German edition of *Le temps et l'autre* (1948), pp. 29, 55.

People who are always blocking substitutionary action require extraordinary assistance to know how to use the healing, beneficial institution of substitutionary action that is so effective against sin. Two things would have to be achieved (and for the time being it is an open question whether they can really be achieved): the fear that *excessive ethical demands will be placed on us* by a life in the mode of substitutionary action must be taken away from us; secondly, we would have to be spared the "intense experience" of consistently practicing human substitutionary action: the experience of absolute loneliness and Godforsakenness that Jesus had to endure on the cross. This experience would be *an excessive spiritual demand* for us.[64] In what follows I will attempt to show that we human beings actually enjoy such extraordinary divine assistance that sin can be broken and a life of substitutionary action becomes humanly possible — without being driven into an ethical or spiritual situation that demands too much of us.

The task before me now of demonstrating this is difficult because "sinning" usually appears less demanding in comparison to fulfilling the "law of Christ," "carry each other's burdens" (Gal. 6:2). The "yoke" of following Jesus — in spite of Matthew 11:30 — does not appear to be "easy"; instead, we deem it incompatible with the actual conditions of our existence. The unending debate about the practicality of the Sermon on the Mount is the striking example. We sin so that we do not have to overdo it. But at this moment we are blind to the fact that right now we (and others) are overdoing it and putting a great a strain on ourselves — whereas the "life of substitutionary action" would not only have avoided this, but would even have healed the consequences of such overexertion.

Of course, *forgiveness* not only extricates the sinner from his sin, it also heals the consequences of his sin! Let us remember that the word "sin" signifies the destructive human tendency to put too great a strain on creatures for the purpose of "justifying ourselves" or getting for ourselves what only God could give. At the same time sin is our attempt to gain the enhanced quality life that results from living in the mode of substitutionary action *without* intervening on behalf of the other *by forcing others to support our own person (leading in the end to a diminishment of life, to a*

---

64. These explanations parallel — in part — the forceful statements that are central to the thought of E. Lévinas, *Die Spur des Anderen. Untersuchungen zur Phänomenologie und Sozial-philosophie,* translated, edited, and introduced by N. Krewani (Freiburg/München, 1983), pp. 320-21.

decline in the quality of life and wasted opportunities). Such an occurrence is at the same time our human attempt to push God the Creator out of his creation.[65]

It is not God who needs human help; rather, it is we who need his help. This has not changed *post Christum natum;* also not in the twentieth century! At this point, we must follow the theology not of Sölle and certain Barock mystics, but, for example, Karl Barth — and Paul too. Giving up this truth would mean the end of all theology, even of feminist theology (and at the same time the abandonment of Christianity and its Jewish, Old Testament roots). Besides, when we speak of the distress, sufferings, and pain of God caused by human sin — which is undoubtedly permissible — we should not abandon the foundations of a theology that pays careful attention to God's divinity (not masculinity!).

However, the human creature who has become *poor* by committing sin that has diminished his life or by replacing God is able to "find" God, who desires to "fill" *this need.* God wants to be called on and found *in our distress and guilt. On his own* initiative he reveals and proves himself to the "poor in spirit, to those who have lived deficient lives, who have 'gone into debt.'" He "chooses" such people and restores them to a life of

---

65. Through Bonhoeffer's *Letters and Papers from Prison* (the letters of July 16 and July 18, 1944, as well as the poem "Christians and Pagans"), talk of *God's powerlessness* and of God allowing himself to be pushed out of the world by the *homo peccator* became theologically popular. This talk has obviously been misunderstood. God has not "become" powerless in the sense that he has been increasingly weakened and replaced in our modern age by human beings who have become more and more autonomous (and thus has increasingly come to need *human* substitutionary action and help). For example, D. Sölle in her book *Stellvertretung* (English translation, *Christ the Representative*) seems to feel this way. And she appeals to Bonhoeffer (pp. 168ff.), with whom she thinks she agrees. But — and this is Bonhoeffer's opinion — we should under all circumstances believe and teach that God is never powerless or weak. He is always strong; only not necessarily strong as defined by what we call "masculine strength," or as of late, "feminine strength" as well. *Both* anthropomorphic ways of understanding strength fail in relation to the doctrine of God. God's power is of a special nature. His power is made perfect in weakness (see 2 Cor. 13:9). This is also something quite different from the strength of "female" devotion, "earthiness," or a forceful, dynamic social nature marked by interdependence. God's kind of power works by means of human powers we do not consider powerful, but *ineffective* and insignificant. With them, he kills, heals, lifts up, and creates — as nothing else can kill, heal, lift up, and create. Of course, *we* comment on this with talk of "divine weakness" — but this has nothing at all to do with the modern Enlightenment. Paul used this term, too, but he said, "The weakness of God is stronger than man's strength" (1 Cor. 1:25). This is the key point.

splendor, making *more* out of them than they "originally" would have been, that is, without the effects of sin.

Of course, he elects the weak and the despised "to nullify the things that are, so that no one may boast before him" (1 Cor. 1:28f.). Whomever God chooses in this way is — in a broad, biblical consensus — also immediately elevated to the status of *substitutionary existence,* thus used by God as a tool of healing and of the return of splendor in the world (or as instruments to carry out his mission and build his "kingdom"). Those elected by God in their poverty of spirit henceforth work *in covenant* with God. *However, substitutionary action is the entrance gate of God, of love, of the return of splendor in a reality distorted and diminished by sin.* From this vantage point we can keep these provisional results in mind: by sinning we always strive to protect ourselves from the excessive "demands of God" or seek to make life easier for ourselves, yet in fact by sinning we always saddle ourselves with more than we can cope with. Nevertheless, this whole complex development is annulled by the electing God. From this perspective it is God who "ultimately" takes care of these "excessive" demands. However, even the elect sin, and — logically — this is why it looks as if the process of canceling out sin must start all over again.

Now it is a peculiarity of sin that it not only appears here or there as "a diminishment of life," but links together the individual "holes" in reality like a net. This means that if I am dealing with the burden of sin here or there, I am dealing with *all* sin.[66] As we will see, this is why the query of the person who had been asked by Jesus in the New Testament to love his neighbor (who is my neighbor? Luke 10:29) is very understandable. If I have to deal with the burden of my neighbor, then a lot more is riding on this than first meets the eye: the deficits are ultimately interlinked — and every act of love and compassion is always only a small beginning. So who wants to intervene on behalf of his neighbor?

From this vantage point the central message of the New Testament is clear — on the cross Jesus had to carry the *entire* burden of sin — the burden of the "whole world." The burden of all fell on him because he was able to intervene on behalf of his actual, individual neighbor and his "deficits." And in this situation the "struggle" of this unique "substitute" culminated in the experience of Godforsakenness. In this experience God seemed to stand on

---

66. Impressively formulated as an *experience* by F. M. Dostoyevski, *The Brothers Karamazov,* p. 431; see the quotation of Kuschel, p. 178 (page numbers from German edition).

the side of all the others and not on the side of Jesus, who instead hung there himself as the one completely abandoned by God as *the epitome of sin;* for he hung there alone and as an isolated individual. *None of us can be expected to endure the loneliness of this experience, nor is it even possible.*[67] If substitutionary action would require *this* at all times and places, it could not become our concern. If following Jesus would have to be a "discipleship of the cross" in this sense, then its yoke would in fact not be "easy," but unbearable for us. Then we would also have abolished the distinction between Jesus Christ and Christians (or the church) in an inadmissible way. This then is our second provisional result — no Christian must or can become Christ for the other in terms of taking upon himself those moments of Godforsakenness on Golgotha for his neighbor. (In addition, when someone does not want to become a victim but seeks to avoid it as much as possible, it must not be held against him. This is all right because the assumption that a human being wants to become a victim represents a human problem. The idea of a human being becoming a victim *should* have come to an end with Jesus' death on the cross.)[68]

Because "the whole misery of humanity" is *not* laid on us, the argument that it is of no use to help our so-called neighbor proves in the end to be a lazy excuse! The commission Christ gave us to forgive, to act as substitutes and work for healing, is limited by the measure of what is humanly possible.[69] This should be clear for the members of the church. In the church our mission of proclaiming God's grace as *unlimited* forgiveness must be strictly set apart from our own limited, ethical mission as members of the church.[70]

67. H. Gollwitzer emphasizes this in *Von der Stellvertretung Gottes. Christlicher Glaube in der Erfahrung der Verborgenheit Gottes. Zum Gespräch mit D. Sölle* (München, 1967), p. 43.

68. G. Bader, "Jesu Tod als Opfer," *ZThK* 80 (1983): 431, 420-21 n. 28.

69. Christ's word in Matthew 18:22 that his disciples should forgive "not seven times but seventy times seven" is not opposed to this. This word does not impose on the disciples an unlimited bearing of the whole world's sin, but it forbids them from calculating an unreasonable limit on their own duty to forgive that is not proportional to the forgiveness they received from God. The above-mentioned sentence objects to the thesis of D. Sölle, *Stellvertretung,* p. 142, that is right in principle: "The person who represents someone, and so makes himself dependent, must be prepared for the worst" (quotation from English translation, *Christ the Representative: An Essay in Theology after the "Death of God,"* trans. David Lewis [London: SCM Press, 1967], p. 124). Substitutionary actions as a Christian attitude and as a possibility for the church must not mean this!

70. See below, pp. 331-337.

C. Binding and Loosing

The "authority of the keys" delegated to the disciples or apostles in the New Testament (the authority to bind and loose) comes across to modern Christianity as a big question mark. What has become of it in our churches?

". . . you are Peter, and on this rock I will build my church, and the gates of Hades will not overcome it. I will give you the keys of the Kingdom of heaven; whatever you bind on earth will be bound in heaven, and whatever you loose on earth will be loosed in heaven" (Matt. 16:18f.).

Jesus said to the disciples, "I tell you the truth, whatever you bind on earth will be bound in heaven, and whatever you loose on earth will be loosed in heaven" (Matt. 18:18).

The risen Jesus steps into the midst of the disciples on the evening of Easter Sunday. . . . "As the Father has sent me, I am sending you" (John 20:21). And with that he breathed on them and said, "Receive the Holy Spirit. If you forgive anyone his sins, they are forgiven, if you do not forgive them, they are not forgiven" (20:22-23).

Never in the later history of the church was this delegation of authority classified as an unimportant matter. In the doctrinal tradition of Protestantism the "authority of the keys" is one of the few basic marks of the church. It is one of the *notae ecclesiae*. Wherever such a basic mark is missing, the church is nonexistent. Because this is so, the fact that the churches of the modern era are hardly noticeable as places of the binding and loosing word should actually alarm us. Even theologians can no longer clearly envision what the "authority of the keys" consists of or how it is properly exercised. Does binding mean not forgiving someone, with the result that it stays that way forever? Or does it mean exercising "church discipline," thus acting to educate church members with the goal that the loosing word could still be imparted later? Does it mean ensuring that grace does not become cheap grace, something that is taken for granted? Or does binding mean determining the scope and content of Christian dogma, which then becomes binding on believers? In other words, is its teaching authority meant? Then "binding" would mean to "declare something binding." And "loosing" would mean to "declare something nonbinding." Another question would be to clarify *who* should do whatever might be meant by binding and loosing. Every pastor, every church member, the congregation as a whole, the church leadership, a synod, the council of the whole church, the bishop, or ultimately only the pope as the "successor" of Peter? And finally: What means are available to the church to exercise the office of the keys?

The New Testament's talk of binding and loosing goes back to Jewish-Rabbinic terminology. The highest religious figures in Judaism are an authority which in certain cases can release a Jew in advance from his duty to fulfill the law or to pay for an offense that has already been committed. They can do this with binding authority. Of course, this does not mean they have any general authority to forgive sins.[71] But in the New Testament, binding and loosing mean either not releasing human beings from *all* their sins (= binding) or completely releasing these human beings from their sins (= loosing). The translation "declare binding"/"declare nonbinding" is, nevertheless, not exactly wrong.[72] On closer examination it is compatible with the above-mentioned meaning of binding and loosing.[73] Whenever representatives of the church say in binding terms what is true and what is not true, they are not making statements about factual issues as defined by natural science; rather, they are interpreting the gospel and applying its contents ad hominem. *Expressing in binding terms what is true in the church must always mean a message about salvation — in contrast to disaster or ruin in time and eternity.*

Therefore, binding language from the realm of the church *always* refers

---

71. J. Jeremias: "In the Rabbinical literature 'binding' and 'loosing' is almost exclusively applied to the teaching decisions of the Halakah: the teacher of the law binds (declares something to be forbidden) and looses (declares something to be permitted)" (translated from Jeremias, Art. A, "Die verschiedenen Wendungen des Schlüsselbildes im NT," Art. B, "Die Schlüsselgewalt," in *ThWNT*, III, p. 751).

72. But Jeremias is correct when he writes, "Limiting Matt. 11:19 to teaching authority hardly captures the meaning of this verse" (translated from p. 751).

73. Many commentaries on the Gospel of Matthew correctly see the purpose of this statement as affirming an authority which extends both to the forgiveness of sins and to teaching authority *(potestas docendi in ecclesia)*. This is also Luther's view (see E. Mühlhaupt, ed., *Martin Luthers Evangelien-Auslegung*, 2 pts. [Göttingen, ³1960], pp. 522-63). Luther stresses that the authority of the keys aims at the forgiveness of sins. It must never be exercised like a worldly ruler — unlike the way the pope exercises this *potestas* (p. 533). But the keys *also* mean "authority to teach" (and this means especially "preaching"), "not just the authority to absolve" (p. 542). The pastor exercises this office on behalf of the congregation (p. 542; Luther does not deny that the pastor is commissioned by Christians; rather, the pastoral ministry is identified as a ministry that belongs to every church member — and has only been delegated to the pastor by the congregation for practical reasons; see p. 550). Luther sees in Matthew 16:19 above all an affirmation of the necessity that man is *granted* the divine forgiveness *from the outside*.

to the question of how human beings addressed by the church stand before God. But then all binding language in the church involves precisely the question of our redemption from sin and the terror of death.[74] The church's binding language can never happen by producing unchanging dogmatic formulas that ignore the *present situation in which the proclamation occurs*. Rather, the church's binding language must always at the same time do justice to Christ, the present situation, and the pastoral care of human beings. Then it has binding and loosing power.

There is no serious theological reason for opposing the idea that Christ's mission of binding and loosing can be properly and authoritatively fulfilled by issuing church memoranda, pronouncements, etc.

Now I will examine more closely the event of binding and loosing.

In the New Testament *loosing* means even now releasing a human being from this passing age, removing him from the world of sin and death, thus removing him from his own guilt and guaranteeing to him that in this way he will be saved from condemnation at the Final Judgment. Jesus Christ gave his own disciples authority *(exousia)* to make decisions about human beings that would be met with approval in heaven and anticipate the outcome of the Final Judgment. The person loosed by such an apostolic exercise of the "office of the keys" knows too that he now belongs to the community of the "redeemed." He sees in himself an individual who has been personally touched by God's gracious election. To be sure, at the end of the world even more members of the kingdom of God will come to light than the church has even had in terms of baptized members and

---

74. This binding language of the church is the actual object of *dogma* or *dogmatics* as the science "of decisive belief" and of the "assertive speech event" in the church (G. Ebeling, *Theologie und Verkündigung. Ein Gespräch mit R. Bultmann,* HUTh 1 [Tübingen, 1961], pp. 106ff.). Of course it also has to do with preaching and professing the faith. The above-mentioned statement that the binding language of the church always concerns or should concern redemption provides the most important basis for ecumenical conversations about preaching an understanding on the *church's teaching office.* Above all the Catholic side can say: Every Catholic dogma wants to and has to be measured by whether it relates to the truth of Christ that is essential for salvation and exclusively serves *this truth.* This is the only way it can counter the Protestant distrust of the Roman Catholic teaching office which in their view always defines new truths of the faith on their own authority and formulates additional dogmas that lead us away from what is essential for salvation. No other kind of church dogma would be admissible. Regarding the question of who *holds* the "teaching authority," it could be kept in mind that hierarchical officeholders do not decide on dogmas alone in any Catholic church without faith in the parishes playing the greatest role.

members certain of their "acceptance." But whoever has been loosed by an authorized representative of the church is a coheir of the kingdom of God who even now knows about this status of his.[75] Whoever has been loosed in this way is necessarily also a "member" of Christ and the church. Therefore, he becomes aware that he no longer belongs to this world.

Loosing understood in New Testament terms does not mean absolution from individual sins in a certain period of his life. Rather, it signifies man's comprehensive transition into an indestructible life that is seen as being irreversible. Every baptism was originally understood as such a loosing.

But what does *binding* mean? The disciples/apostles definitely did not think they were free to judge which person they did not want to loose but wanted to keep bound to his sins and to the old world that is passing away. They did *not* have instructions and authority to perform the opposite of loosing in specific cases, excluding specific individuals from salvation for all eternity. Their mission and their authority was to *open* the kingdom of heaven.

It is easy to realize the historical and objective correctness of this thesis when we are oriented to the original New Testament situation of the term "binding and loosing." Its origin lies in the early post-Easter era. It was mainly Bultmann who emphasized this, with good reason.[76] The returning Lord was expected. It was essential to win as many as possible in the time still remaining! Of course, this initial situation in which the term was defined must be kept separate from the development of the church's understanding of the office from the third century on, which disproportionately shaped its later understanding of the office of the keys. Its understanding of the church office was given a legal cast from the third century onward, which can be

75. Protestant Christians, insofar as they know why they are Protestant, consider the Roman Catholic teaching on the necessity of believers' ultimate uncertainty about their final state of redemption and acceptance to be unacceptable. This question about the certainty of salvation was the *pivotal theological issue* of the Reformation, although it has been noticed much too little. This controversy is of much greater theological significance than the issue of recognizing the pope's "Petrine ministry" in the church.

76. R. Bultmann, "Die Frage nach der Echtheit von Mt 16,17–19," in *Exegetica. Aufsätze zur Erforschung des Neuen Testaments,* ed. E. Dinkler (Tübingen, 1967), p. 277, assumes that belief in Jesus' resurrection first established the *ekklēsia* of Christ. He thinks it is conspicuous that the word *ekklēsia* is found in Matthew exclusively in 16:18 and 18:17 in words attributed to the earthly Jesus. This fully convinces Bultmann that these verses are a post-Easter interpretation.

verified mainly in the church order of Hippolytus of Rome. The charisma of the officeholders became the legal right of the officeholders. This authoritative dictum first appears in the West, that is, in Rome and Africa, and later in the East as well: The bishop alone has the right to administer the Eucharist; he alone can delegate this right to whomever he pleases. At about the same time "a special official dignity" is bestowed on the bishop with this legal meaning; significantly he also receives "the authority to grant forgiveness, the right to actually readmit mortal sinners into the fellowship of the church." At this early date the church is already dealing with the issue of *r*eadmitting individuals into the church when mortal sins are present (for example, when Christians offered sacrifices to the emperor in times of persecution). Calixtus I of Rome submits this authority to forgive to the approval of the bishop, which was only granted to the martyrs until then. Previously the martyrs could readmit mortal sinners into the church without any official approval. Now, the bishop decides: All forgiveness of mortal sins by martyrs must be confirmed by the bishop.[77] Exercising church discipline, the bishop can now "retain" the sin of an apostate, thus refusing him readmission and absolution.

At least since the Reformation this has been recognized as a problematic development in the office of the keys. By then this office was used as a punishment or a means to exert pressure by not admitting Christians to the sacrament. It was not at all used as it was intended to be, *sine vi sed verbo.* But even in the Reformation the dubious aspects of this general understanding of the keys were not entirely cleared up or overcome. Article 28 of the Augsburg Confession deals with the *potestas ecclesiastica* under the heading "On the Authority of Bishops." Following John 20:21f., it says that the bishop's "authority of the keys" to forgive or retain sins is properly exercised only with the teaching and preaching of God's Word and with the administration of the sacraments. But these are sources of *eternal goods,* thus not of goods that have something to do with power in this world. Here its teaching on the office of the keys becomes an apology for the doctrine of the two kingdoms! It says the church's authority of the keys does not at all "hinder" the police and the whole "secular government." However, at the same time the office of bishop should never be a secular office either. In Luther's Small Catechism, the question, "What is

77. The historical overview "on the development of the pastoral office" given in W. Bernet, *Weltliche Seelsorge — Elemente einer Theorie des Einzelnen* (Zürich, 1988), pp. 29ff., was quoted, translated from the German. The quotes are found on pp. 30-32.

the office of the keys?" was added on later. The answer, "It is a special authority Christ has given to his church on earth to forgive the sins of penitent sinners, but to retain the sins of the unrepentant, as long as they do not repent." This one-sided emphasis on church discipline with regard to the office of the keys was an educational tool used to produce a repentant attitude in believers by exerting gentle pressure. It is likewise a questionable development of the pertinent New Testament statements.

We will take our bearings from the original situation and say: Binding occurs not when the disciples/apostles/servants of God's Word refuse to "open the door," but when an individual closes his mind to the kerygma of Christ, to the opening of eschatological salvation that has now taken place. Moreover, no present-day pastor, no present-day Christian should ever "bind" a human being in any situation. How would he ever come to take such action which is confirmed in heaven and will never be revised? No, the church that is not mentally disturbed does not perform the act of binding. It only performs the act of loosing. This is not irresponsible, frivolous speech which no longer wants to know anything about church discipline and the law of God.

Church discipline is a completely different matter.[78] It does not signify

---

78. Today we seem to be further from a proper understanding of church discipline than before — it has always been a problem! Today it can no longer be said that the larger churches are even struggling to gain an appreciation for church discipline!

Various writings in the New Testament show a familiarity with congregations that observe a boundary between behavior that is acceptable in the church and behavior that is no longer acceptable. They are also familiar with congregations being encouraged to conform their behavior to what was desired in the church. A variety of steps are mentioned by which a wayward member is to be won back. When those who refuse to listen to reason are excluded from the community of salvation (excommunication), this step seems to be the *ultima ratio* (1 Cor. 5:1-6). Of course, the desire that his spirit (might be) saved on the day of the Lord underlies this disciplinary action. For Bonhoeffer, who frequently quoted this Pauline text in the context of his discussions on church discipline, the pastoral, restorative character of *all* church discipline was, of course, essential. Naturally he understood church discipline as an exercise of the New Testament commission to bind and loose. "Church discipline is the necessary visible consequence of properly exercising the office of the keys within the congregation" (translated from "The Authority of the Keys and Church Discipline . . ." [in German], p. 374). But the word "consequence" should be underlined here because it at least makes a distinction between the office of the keys and church discipline.

This distinction must be maintained — perhaps, even *against* Bonhoeffer's detailed suggestions on "remitting sin" (absolution) and "retaining sin" (retention) *within* the

the eschatological binding of which the New Testament speaks. Likewise the preaching of the law is a completely different matter. It, too, does not signify eschatological binding, but is actually done for the sake of the "loosing" gospel.

It has been said that a person can reject the good word of God, the gospel he has heard, and in so doing bind himself. The preachers of the gospel bind him by their proclamation, although they intend the opposite. The gospel (and not the law, as many have thought) can also have a binding (that is, hardening) effect. However, God himself ultimately stands behind this regrettable hardening of the hearts of certain individuals. The mystery of his intention that takes effect here cannot be solved in a historical time frame. However, we can surmise from the context of Israel's hardening discussed by Paul in Romans 9–11 that even this hardening serves to augment the rule of God and in the end flows into it.

To summarize: The sentence "whatever you bind on earth will be bound in heaven" means: If some people cannot be won by *your* apostolic preaching of the gospel, but remain bound, then this is meant to be God's will; this is in keeping with an eternal divine decision.[79] The subject of binding and loosing leads us to ask "ultimate questions," especially questions about double predestination. Many Christians down through

---

church. These suggestions are described in detail in the book *The Cost of Discipleship,* on which we will not elaborate here.

What is called "binding" *in the Gospels* is absolutely not identical with holding back or refusing absolution for reasons of discipline within the church!

Ebeling as well (*Kirchenzucht* [Church discipline] [Stuttgart, 1957], p. 54) writes cautiously that church discipline *rests* on the New Testament's establishment of the office of the keys. Therefore, it is *not* identical with holding this office. Ebeling (p. 55) correctly points out that we must not only relate binding (and also loosing) to church discipline, but the latter actually refers to the "problem of the church's boundaries." However, Ebeling says that the church's boundaries "bear witness to themselves" whenever the proclamation of the church is *rejected* (p. 30).

Today more than ever it must be kept in mind that church discipline cannot be an independent theological subject, but always represents the natural flip side of each congregation's understanding of God. Moreover, the educational form and practice of church discipline appropriate for today could not be a copy of New Testament considerations on discipline since both the situation of the church and education methods have changed.

79. That is why it is not correct to understand "binding" formally as the authority to state and speak in *binding* fashion what is Christianly true and valid in God's eyes. For this could signify *loosing* of all things!

the centuries of church history have believed that the unpenitent and those who are among the "weeds" were predestined for hell even before the beginning of creation. They are excluded forever. But this opinion defies the entire logic of Christology, which says: God "wants all men to be saved and to come to a knowledge of the truth" (1 Tim. 2:4). It is also not biblically necessary.

This much is clear. The disciples/apostles/preachers of the church did not and do not first have to bind those whom *God* had *already* predestined "negatively." Certainly (in terms of what I said above), the apostolic preaching of the gospel could have the effect that those rejected from all eternity harden their hearts. Only, it is not compelling to think that the hardening of their hearts and their divine nonelection apparently fixed from the very beginning would necessarily have to mean their *eternal* lack of opportunity and a divine decree of suffering and hell. The impenitence and reprobation decreed by God for certain human beings *can* signify as a nonelection decided even before the beginning of creation that their separation from God will not last an eternity and will not result in (meaningless!) punishment, but can be restricted to a role God always intended them to play when "the old world" is abolished and the form of this world passes away. Then they will have fulfilled the purpose that was determined for them in advance, which has been revealed as a special kind of divine service. Therefore the reprobation can possibly be limited to the time "of this time and space world." This is why double predestination confronts us with a mystery — because we know *nothing* here. Therefore we can also not rule out that "can." The gravity of the gospel that is after all the key to eternal life is not underscored by adding on homiletical threats in any form that announce the "weeping and gnashing of teeth" to people who harden their hearts. Moreover, such threats and announcements do not mean "binding." It is merely pseudopastoral care. The gravity of the gospel cannot be articulated in this way. Instead it will become clear only when the proclaimer is able to announce accurately the essence of the gospel and thus find a "loosing" language. The greatness and beauty of what can be said by Protestants will also determine the gravity of the gospel.

D. The Sermon[80]

A crisis of relevance in preaching is a given whenever preachers no longer understand their job of *loosing* and when as a result no one knows any longer what it means to be bound.[81] Never in the history of the church have there been so many textbooks on preaching in print as today. By this measure it should now be a pleasure to preach and listen to preaching. But it is more likely that the glut of literature has to do with the seeming impossibility and difficulty of solving the problem.

Preaching that takes "loosing" seriously should also be able to achieve its goal in the modern era. But preaching which does not get serious at all or only seems to get serious will not be happy at any point. But what does "serious" mean here? It means that the effective verdict on our life is disclosed to us now, the verdict God stands by in time and eternity. It means that God declares the sinner "righteous." Preaching should pass on this verdict in an appropriate way, which at any rate must not be delivered in the style of "I think so" and "if you can personally accept it this way." As people felt without hesitation in the New Testament, it is a mind-boggling responsibility to be given the authority to preach this way; yet it is not strange. No one has to take responsibility for the verdict of justification pronounced on the sinner. This becomes and is solely possible *insofar as God on his initiative replaces what the sinner takes away from God's creation.* This is the foundation of all forgiveness of sins.

In this exact sense bad is replacing what has been destroyed by the sinner and his sin. An *eschatological new creation* is now continually taking place on God's initiative. This also means *kainē ktisis* (the new creation has a very close connection with the forgiveness of sins and the justification of the sinner because forgiveness draws God into our life and into this world and in so doing completely *renews* life and the world). The solution that emerges for the world in this way is not a cheap divine "overlooking" of our sins, not a stereotyped and weak divine general pardon for our aberrations and evil deeds that reach down to horrible depths. Rather, it is the greatest and most holy event ever to occur on the earth. The Creator comes to his creation. God comes to sinful man and associates with him.

---

80. This section is dedicated to my colleague in Berlin, Wolf Krötke.

81. See Luther: "Ligare et solvere prorsus aliud nihil est quam Evangelium praedicare et applicare" (WA, 12:184, lines 32f.).

He looks into everything we have achieved and forfeited down to the smallest detail. "No one and nothing is forgotten." The flaws and imperfections we inflict on existence become splendorous "scenes" of creation renewal — as soon as God himself "enters" them. The most incredible thing proves to be true: sinner, sin, and God belong together! This is so because God comes to the world precisely by way of man's sin, making his own choice and decision. (Which is, therefore, not a category of human moral failure, but of divine self-determination.)

In view of what I have just elaborated on in our present historical situation, we will seldom have to face the objection — which is not well founded anyway — that such an approach negates human freedom and responsibility for sin and "frivolously" burdens God with this responsibility. But we do have *one* problem with what has just been said, a problem that must not be hidden, especially in connection with preaching: all of what has been said occurs — so it was said "revealingly" enough — *as soon as* and *if* God arrives on the scene of our human circumstances. But why does he not always do this? Why does he very often at least take his time? Why does he leave out so many opportunities — until in our impression it is too late for God's coming?

Handling these questions is part of every sermon preparation. It is the most decisive aspect of sermon preparation. If these questions are avoided when the sermon is being prepared, questions that by their very nature are not impossible but theologically and existentially difficult to address, the finished sermon is rubbish. For every sermon has only one purpose — *making people certain of the outcome* of things in spite of all their understandable and legitimate doubts about God's coming to the world and his overcoming of all the imperfections in the history of humankind. Preaching should free us from the fear that a quite different outcome of things is coming. It should illuminate real life in the world as the place where God is paving the way for this outcome. The church exists only where such a speech event is possible. The real church stands and falls with the occurrence of such speech.

At the same time what is known as the dogmatic content of Christianity is found in this kind of language even though it is not easy to achieve. Thus it is wise to spend time studying the dogmas of the Christian faith that have been established in centuries of exegesis. Such study is generally part of sermon preparation. Surely many a "preacher" is afraid of this reflection because he suspects that the dogmas represent an additional obstacle to speaking and transferring Christian truth to the modern congregation. Instead, he would have every reason to hold the Christian dogmas to their task of emphasizing *what* in all the world argues in favor of *man,* who is after all such an immense source of corruption in every single case. Correctly understood, the "dogmatic" aspect of every good sermon is that it emphasizes what argues in favor of man in a way that is homiletically and pastorally appropriate. Whoever preaches in the Protestant tradition defends man. Although so many facts are arrayed against his vision, the preacher speaks out against the obvious assumption that we are moving into a future that is futile or that in time will do away with ourselves morally and physically.

The talk of working through the dogmatic truth of Christianity is actually the basis of our preaching skills. A minister would be very mistaken if he thought the sermon in the worship service would only become exciting and appealing if he brought in facts and stories from modern history. No, the sermon becomes appealing, relevant, and of current interest — all this together — when the quality of its dogmatic content is undiminished. The sermon stands or falls on the question whether it participates in the dogmatic truth of Christianity and expresses this truth in its message. The sermon is the real test case for dogmatics. But dogmatics is also the real test case for preaching. (Does a work of speech deserve the label of "sermon" if it nowhere forges ahead to predestination and evil?)

An encouraging sermon (even the most serious sermon should be encouraging!) speaks about the truth that in an unexpected way much more argues in favor of us than against us — without failing to recognize or ignore our miseries. The actual test for the Protestant sermon is whether it could be called edifying in terms of its form, content, and impact. This test shows whether it was able to give back to its listeners their joy in being human and whether the listeners literally experienced their dignity during the sermon.

Of course, Protestant preaching cannot draw its content or, better, its dogmatic substance exclusively from books and also not exclusively from the church's faith tradition. If the listeners (and why not the readers as well?) are to gain certainty about what has been communicated to them and thus be *edified,* they must experience *more* than only a reminder, for example, of Paul's line of reasoning that no one can get anywhere against the person for whom God himself is interceding in Jesus Christ (see Rom. 8:31ff.). An appeal to authoritative words is not enough here. A sermon (for that matter dogmatics as well) needs "spirit," and the subject for that is the individual author. "Spirit" means here the capacity to bring out the dogmatic truth with reasons that are easy to understand. We need to say in our preaching or dogmatics: "Contrary to all that seems to indicate our base nature, there are many good things we can say about us; indeed, our prospects for the future are bright because we have been 'rescued.'" *Yet whoever preaches this way must be able to show in real life itself what actually supports this verdict.* If it is to be persuasive and bring joy, better reasons must be advanced than those that argue against us. And these reasons must prove their worth much better in real life. We must not take what argues against us from real-life experiences but then on the other side draw the gospel and dogmatic truth only from books. This would not only be a bad homiletic practice, but also a bad dogmatic mistake. Not just the sermon looks at real life; dogmatic theology must do it too. (And "homiletics" is anything but the task of mediating between dogmatic theology or a "desired dogmatic content" and real life. There would be nothing to mediate if there were no other way dogmatic theology could find its reasons, if it were to seek reasons by skirting real life. It is not without good reason that dogmatic theology must be "written" again and again.)

A common task of dogmatic theology and preaching is their search for a language which does not yet exist. It is incumbent on them both to *discover* reasons for hope. Motivated above all by the New Testament, they are searching in the midst of our reality for a *promising reality* that is not infected by the germ of diminished life, that is, of sin. They are to discover *God at work* renewing and rescuing his creation.

Friedrich Nietzsche looked for what was strong and healthy in history. Correctly understood, his longing is not surprising for Christianity. Christian faith as well hopes to strike gold by looking in this direction (even if it does not think it is successful when it discovers the "will to power"). Nietzsche was right in pointing out to the church of his time that its dogmatic language was distancing itself from real life.

A teacher of homiletics has reason to point out the good example of most philosophers, who take a persistently *questioning attitude* toward life. In the theology of the twentieth century this attitude was sometimes judged to be an expression of philosophy's limitations compared to those of theology. Moreover, they believed that theology has answers. But they were mistaken about "having" answers. Today it is essential for theology really to *practice* solidarity with those who seek.

This must be said in such a pointed fashion because preaching is important. It is not a form of instruction about the past. It *remains* the central way the church expresses itself. It is the church's opportunity to offer its "loosing" word. In saying this we must stress this fact: Not just the religious address in the worship service should be designated by the word "sermon." It is advisable to define "sermon" in much broader terms. It ultimately means that the church is looking for and finding a contemporary language for God's work. And here too we must stress: Only the seeking church is a finding church.

God desires to be sought. It seems to me that a key deficit in modern sermons is our much too limited amount of patience and strength in seeking God. It is true that preachers are trying hard to deal with this or that particular problem in our life — but are they seeking God? Are they seeking the only One whose nonappearance must cause a *sermon* trouble? In our present situation it is hard to guard against the impression that authors — and not rarely atheistic authors from societies in which the voice of the churches is sounding only a muffled tone — are often doing much more patient and sensitive work in seeking answers to the question of God. Furthermore, it is hard to admit that Protestant preaching could achieve *its* purpose with a knowledge of reality and a language ability that is inferior to good novels. Certainly it is not a matter of allowing only theologians with poetic talent to get into the pulpit. Rather, my crucial point is that the sermon should be able to stand up to reality and remain in a questioning mode long enough. There is no dogmatic bank account from which the preaching Christian can effortlessly withdraw his messages. And why should people show an interest in sermons whose declarations do not bear the character of *precious words* that have been acquired through hard work?

But *where* are we to look? In two areas. First, wherever sin is committed and, second, wherever substitutionary action takes place.

The first point: Sin is God's "special place" in reality. Although he "is" *there,* it is very difficult for us to discover him there. He is found *there* by us only in connection with our efforts *to come to terms with our past.* The task of preaching is to counteract the way we repress guilt and to offer an interpretation of the past (that expands and surpasses the knowledge of self and history that had previously existed). This interpretation cannot be had easily. It cannot be simply extracted from any textbook of systematic theology. Yet it belongs in the center of every Protestant sermon. The traditional, *unique* potential of the sermon to liberate human beings so that they can come to terms with what they have repressed reminds us modern men and women of psychoanalysis; yet this potential must not be underestimated. What, then, is its effect? The listeners (or readers) previously thought it was *inevitable* that they would get caught up in sin and guilt. But the sermon traced back this entanglement in sin to the point where things could still be influenced. While not in any way fostering the suspicion that the theological doctrine of sin explains away human freedom, it attempted to get back to the point where freedom to make a better decision was still an option, thus avoiding guilt. The sermon did not do this to shame listeners but to lead them into the realm of freedom. Looking back and discovering the point at which things went bad has a liberating affect. Exposing and naming this point take away the fear that the same failure will be repeated at the next opportunity. It just goes to show that it is possible to get to the bottom of the unplumbed depths of the human soul and demythologize imaginary human demons. The sermon has proven to be a factor in genuinely enlightening its listeners. It has single-mindedly pursued the question of *truth* against all kinds of resistance for the benefit of man. And the truth has exposed sin's banality and lack of mystery! It goes to show that it is certainly useful when preachers also possess something of the virtues and capabilities of *good historians.* We can recognize them by their ability to find a clarifying word in the struggle for the correct interpretation of the past. (A psychoanalytic therapist does *not* seek or speak this clarifying word at the climax of his treatment, but the sermon should forge ahead to it!) Its precise role is enabling man to assume responsibility for his real past by tracing back the confusing threads of guilt to the point where he could still have had the upper hand over this matter. He faces up to his sin! Now he knows about real guilt. (Does this happen in psychoanalysis?) And this rehabilitates him morally. Every sermon that has reached its goal at this point is a true source of encouragement and delight to its listeners. It has helped its listeners to replace previous delusions with self-recognition and a new feeling of being equipped to "make better decisions." Looking at this part of its job we can say: this special word event, the "sermon," is not there to instruct people about this or that; rather, its purpose is to do away with existing delusions.

Second, in quest of the word to be preached we should *discover* where substitutionary action occurs in our real life — and where it should still occur. I demonstrated this point earlier. Through the institution of sub-stitutionary action, the sick circumstances surrounding our life can regain their health. A human existence that had become "impoverished" by sin can be restored to its original fullness because divine grace uses this institution as a gateway. If I have just spoken of preaching in the interest of coming to terms with the past, I am also concerned about shaping the future. And both aspects of the sermon are actually one. If the crucial question had just been, "What is — in retrospect — the truth?" the aspect of the preaching task I will now discuss focuses on how to love today. And here it is important to realize that the truth about the past and love in the present are only two sides of the same thing. Moreover, it almost goes without saying that man can hardly provide better for the future than by loving today. The sermon should first find out where substitutionary action is taking place among us. Therefore it will point out encouraging events, even if it were only a matter of isolated signs. The question we must seek to answer could be put in these terms: Where can we find today what can be seen as promising for the future, how can we identify today what will put things right tomorrow? If the sermon yields positive results in the framework of these questions, it will be able to go a step further and point out additional promising ways that are needed to lead man out of a meaningless existence and extricate his life from the precarious situation of having hardened his heart. But is not the "salvation" of which the sermon should speak to be found in Jesus Christ? Well, the formulaic mention of this creedal phrase does not yet disclose this "salvation." It must be disclosed in our real life — this is what preaching means — because salvation in Christ only comes into proper focus as an opening to life. Of course, it surpasses the ability of any individual theologian to be familiar with all the areas of real life that must be considered and properly incorporate them into the sermon. If the preacher draws his knowledge of reality only from his own life, then his "guidance" becomes too subjective and narrow (legalistic) or too vague and general (non-specific). Both are the result of inadequate knowledge of reality. Therefore, the life experiences and the professional knowledge of his contemporaries, perhaps of his ancestors as well and especially of his church members, must play their part in the sermon. Thus, the sermon should have coauthors and, in a certain sense, be presented as an open-ended manuscript. The sermon may also borrow from others. Its originality and freshness is another story. We must ask: What is called for in this sermon about God and the subject at hand? Is it being said at the right time to the right people? And what is "called for" consists of command (what is demanded) and offer (what is offered and passed on to us). The sermon is encouraging and brings us joy when it discloses and introduces attractive ways of better sharing life together that have yet to be discovered. The sermon achieves its goal when it not only tells us that we should take one path or another that we have already known for a long time, but when it opens up new paths for us as a genuine "speech event."

The sermon belongs in the *worship service,* insofar as its "message" regularly awakens the congregation's need to praise and thank God. Not intercession, but praise and adoration are the most obvious response of a congregation to sermons that belong in the worship service, that is, the response to which the "Amen" is spoken with grateful, heartfelt approval. Other sermons, which by their very nature *cannot* succeed in joining this "Amen," are not necessarily connected to the worship service. In isolated cases, it would also be advisable to check to see whether these speech products are really sermons with the two essential features I just mentioned (coming to terms with the past and opening up to the future). From the perspective of the preachers and perhaps also of the situation, it is not always possible for the "sermon that belongs in the worship service" to succeed, that is, the sermon that offers "the loosing word" in which Jesus Christ, as it were, becomes our "contemporary." The service itself is not invalidated when this "loosing word" *cannot* be spoken for whatever reason. *There does not have to be preaching in every worship service.* Pastors should be put in a position of enjoying an inner freedom that gives them permission time and again not to preach in the worship services they conduct. Less would often be more. With its rich liturgical possibilities the worship service is also able to lend expression to that adoration of God which always both edifies the worshipers and elevates them to a position of dignity. It cannot be stressed enough that the sermon is essentially *not* a "fixture of the worship service" but the breath of the whole church by which it lives and acts even when there is no preaching at the moment.

Finally, we must discuss an issue on which Karl Barth raised our theological consciousness: Is the sermon, so to speak, a holy event, is it in fact the crucial sacrament by which God himself speaks to us most clearly? Taking all pertinent information into account, I intend to answer as Barth would. The preached word, just defined as a "loosing" word, is not God's own Word. It remains a human word. And it is not the devout hearing of the preached word that "brings about" the "salvation of the soul" or "the forgiveness of sins" or "the believer's incorporation into the new being," as current phrases put it. The "word" of the sermon is not this coming of God, but it *testifies to it.* It does not *bring* redemption, but it *testifies to it.* "Testify" is the proper term. It combines the human activity of "pointing to God's redemption," "standing up for God," and "being deeply moved by what God has done." It guarantees the serious nature of preaching mentioned at the outset without "sacramentalizing" it.

Whoever preaches testifies that he knows that he himself is addressed by God. He testifies that he believes in divine *deliverance* from death (to be clearly distinguished from the ardent desire of many to be "kept from dying!"), and therefore that he himself believes *in* the forgiveness of sins as it is defined in the third article of the Apostles' Creed. As in the case of the historical Jesus, the faith of the preacher is combined with *parables* of what is believed as soon as the preacher expresses himself. True preaching cannot exist without new parables continually being told. And nothing but this truth is expressed in them: The preacher refers to his own experiences of how Christ has stripped death and sin of its power. Preaching lives by the certainty that its authors have discovered such things in real life, experiences that are powerful and redemptive. It does not compete with Christology in terms of a "natural theology"; rather, it means Christology in the form of preaching. As soon as preaching begins to make discoveries like this, it also "flows." (Homiletics should pay close attention to the question of what actually constitutes this "flowing of a sermon." It often takes a long time before "it flows." And that is the way it should be. But for the one who wants to preach, the onset of this "flowing" is probably a sign that he is now ready to preach.)

In conclusion this point must be stressed. The fact God is and can be our deliverer from death and sin does not at all depend on whether there is preaching, or "preaching that is done properly." God *is* this Deliverer. Fine preaching discloses this good news by continually making new attempts — with good reason! It can achieve a worthy goal when it succeeds. More and more human beings will recognize God and then no longer have to understand reality as a blind mixture of good and evil. Life becomes an opportunity for them to live meaningfully and to link up with realities that will never lose their validity and their value. This is what we can live *and* die with. Disclosing this is the sole purpose of the sermon.

E. Divine and Human Forgiveness:
Prospects for the Future of Ecclesiology

The event of forgiveness must now be portrayed *concretissime.* As we said in the previous section, preaching points to God's forgiveness. But at the same time its aim is to bring about human forgiveness.

We are once again working on the assumption that the sinful misuse of our fellow creatures as substitutes for God and salvation always means at that same time that we go into our Creator's debt and into his creatures' debt (including the sinner's own person!). The theft of opportunities for living and the destruction of creation by sinners create factual results that can no longer be reversed, or at least not without God's help. The ugliness and dullness of the fragments left behind by the sinner must be compared to seeing objects in a garbage dump. The objects that have arrived there cannot be restored. In the best-case scenario grass will grow over them in time. Yet the aftermath of these "bequests" left by sinners even resembles toxic waste, which contaminates future generations as well.

Forgiveness is the — only — possibility of preventing the consequences of sin from "eating away" at us. Forgiveness interrupts the process (advance) of sin. It also rescues and restores what can still be rescued. An endless chain of evil can be broken by a single act of forgiveness. When a fellow human being forgives me, canceling my debt to him that I could not repay — what happens to me then? What happens to him? The relief and liberation I feel are combined with an inner revival of moral integrity which is mainly necessary to restore my self-esteem. This integrity brings splendor and joy back into my life. Moreover, gratitude in all directions is not difficult now.

On the other hand, *forgiving* seems difficult. What happens in the one who forgives? He has to wrestle with — understandable — feelings of hatred and the need for revenge. Aggression against the debtor fills him. He wants as much atonement as possible — even if it will never be enough. What could dissuade him from embarking on this course of action? What could give him the insight that he, too, is a sinner and that others likewise have endless claims against him? What could trigger a change in him that allows him to see that revenge makes the current of evil rise instead of containing it, and that we all need forgiveness? He has to be filled with something that is greater than revenge and hatred. We do not have to speak now of "God" or of "love," but at least of an awakening to a view of reality that quickly sees how things can turn out all right. It is not commendable personal generosity that makes forgiveness possible (generosity would only be a weakness here), but grace that comes over the one who has been wronged, persuading him to become an instrument of reconciliation and renewal.

A special relationship is built between the person wronged and the person whom he forgave. It is not as if the one who was forgiven now had to bear the burden of feeling obligated to be "eternally grateful." Especially not that! The forgiver was and is not a benefactor in the usual sense of the word. He was motivated to forgive by a value system or authority he himself felt was higher. The spirit of this value system or authority is now passed on to the person who was forgiven. We can say that the forgiver has won over a human being. A special bond, a committed relationship, was forged between the two persons. But this relationship is not marked by psychological dependency, but by that higher authority which made this relationship possible. A closer examination of this special relationship brings to light that the forgiver has become a substitute in two respects. First, he "remitted" the other's debt (in New Testament Greek: *aphienai*), which the "debtor" could not have repaid. The forgiver assumes the loss caused by the "debtor." He bears the consequences of the act for which the other person should have assumed responsibility because the other person cannot assume this responsibility. Second, the forgiver is a substitute of that higher authority which prompted him to forgive. He has become its representative.

At this point we must speak once again about the church. One would think that the church would be the driving force behind the *pro-cessus* of forgiveness in the world. But whenever the church deals with the forgiveness of sins, it is in immense danger. The church, of all institutions, could become the greatest barrier to the real occurrence of forgiveness. It prevents forgiveness when it gives people the questionable opportunity to "settle" their debts with God in such a way that they already feel liberated and all right without forgiving others and, above all, without having received forgiveness from others. Such a misguided attitude is reinforced when the church portrays *the priest* as the representative of that "higher authority" from which the grace of forgiveness issues forth, instead of the person who is wounded by sin and yet who forgives his "debtor." So they go to the priest as the mediator and representative of God and find "the forgiveness of sins" in him and through him. But there is no encounter between those who incurred guilt and those who were wounded. At best they will meet in court. And it is possible that they will cope with their mental anguish through their own direct relationship to God or through the mediation of the church's priest if he is willing to be a party to that. Certainly there is a better, more acceptable understanding of the priesthood. But no one can deny the danger that churches, irrespective of the denomination, can foster a fatal competition between divine and human forgiveness in which the divine forgiveness wins in a dubious way and in a dubious linkage with a dubious priesthood and sacramentalism.

The sermon and the sacrament have suffered a modern loss of relevance, and this is connected with the widespread impression that here a liberation from sin and guilt is being "granted" to me or us without the substitutionary bearing of wrong that must take place at some point in the process. The practice of granting absolution from sin in which God/Christ alone are supposed to be the ones who bear the wrong without human beings or creatures being given a similar significance in bearing wrong is heretical. Of course, the practice of granting absolution from sin in which only a fellow creature bears the wrong in our place or in which only a sinner offers "satisfaction," but in which God/Christ are not in the picture in any way as sin-bearers, and as the reason for the forgiveness of sins, is also heretical. The former heresy overlooks the fact that it is hard to imagine human society without human sacrifices and substitutionary actions if it is not to become completely inhuman and perish. The latter heresy overlooks the fact that forgiveness without the intervention of God/Christ would become too demanding and legalistic. Without God coming to our help, there would be no forgiveness. Rather, the earth would be ruined by man (yet in fact the opposite thesis is true: Because there is forgiveness and we can count on God, it is *impossible* for the earth to be ruined by man).

The church believes that Jesus Christ has made a powerful beginning by winning our forgiveness. By personally breaking through sin and by releasing and liberating human beings from the bondage of sin, he has created a community of faith — the church. It was formed by people who accepted *one another* as brothers and sisters, having been "attracted" by him, having personally experienced relief from the burden of sin and thus having gained new motivation. The sin that weighs so heavily on human beings lost its destructive capacity among them. The church cannot only call to mind this original situation in its celebrations, but it can and should always return to it. It is useful for the church to be thrown back to its beginnings. Here it encounters its source of power, its "sacred ground," which it must not demystify by seeking to explain it. The ordained "of-ficeholders" of the church should keep its origin pure and use the language that is an integral part of it with utmost care — at the right time and at the right place. They should do this in such a way that human beings become capable *of drawing themselves from the original source of the church and following their own calling to take substitutionary action.* Where the ordained ministry of the church is understood in these terms, there is no need to reflect on the "church come of age." Then the truly promising basis for a common, ecumenical understanding of "ministry" is already achieved. It is an honor for the pastor to pave the way for as many members of the body of Christ as possible to become substitutes by whom God's gracious action gains ground at the place of sin. (The Christian's calling to take substitutionary action is not an imperative, but an *indicative.*) But the ordained minister is completely misunderstood if he is seen as a "dispenser of grace" who could "procure" what "wipes out" sin among human beings because of special ceremonial rites he can perform. If the critics of sacramentalism want to attack this image of the priest, every Christian denomination must emphatically agree with it for theological reasons.

The church has a mission in world history. It is to make possible human substitutionary action in such a way that it is no longer too much for us to handle and no longer makes substitutes forsaken victims. It is to make substitutionary action humanly possible. Or to put it another way: As God's instrument it is to ensure that human beings do not refuse to accept healing, beneficial substitutionary action by making sinful excuses and that it takes place on a larger scale to meet the need. We have seen above that substitutionary action which releases the brother/sister from his/her obligation and grants him/her time for his/her own life quickly reaches the limits of what is humanly possible. It is always true that the individual does not have sufficient time and strength for the other. But in the church the burdens that must be carried here can be carried together. We must also read the church's idiomatic expression "among brothers and sisters" in this way. They are close enough to one another that they do not have to allow individual fellow Christians to be saddled with the whole burden of human substitutionary action. They do not only have to share material possessions, as is so often demanded; above all, they can share the burdens and the strain with one another!

It is precisely in the church that human beings should make sacrifices. But no one should become a victim. The best of all *imperatives* — and this is its mission in world history — should be broadcast from the Christian church: No human being, no one should any longer have to become a victim! It should no longer be necessary to purchase social harmony with the "inevitability" of a shockingly large number of people who fall victim to the disastrous consequences of technological change — all the way from the world economic system to automobile traffic. Where society cannot (yet) do it "differently," the church must not resign itself to a system that creates more and more new victims. On the contrary, *its* place in history is here: It must take the side of the victims and work for change so that the sacrificial victims are devictimized and the sources that create victims are cut off. The church can (could!) easily endure the conflicts with the authorities that can be expected to emerge from this situation because no individual Christian is the creator of conflict or the one affected by conflict (who would therefore have to become the victim himself sooner or later); rather, once again it is the community of church members. If they were in reality far from willing to endure such conflict and instead were inclined to tear the church apart by splitting into political factions of the left and the right, they must in the end be prepared not only to tolerate the church's involvement with the victims but to help support it. The action of a church that does not have its eye on the approval of this or that political authority, but in a theologically clear and emphatic way leads the battle against those who create victims and fights for the victims, cannot be contested by anyone who wants to be part of the church himself. This course of action must be supported by all Christians!

In keeping with its mission, the church seeks to save human *psychai*, that is, souls *and* lives. Worship and preaching both serve this purpose. This purpose is also served by proper church instruction in which from an early age the *formation of conscience* must not be neglected. Its goal is to enhance the capability of human beings to build relationships and develop their perceptive faculties and be set free from a life that is curved in on itself. Its goal is also to enable human beings to break away from antiquated methods that are no longer in keeping with the times. Evil is also a particularism in a temporal sense. We split off the present time we cherish from modern developments and cling to what is outmoded. Of course, what would be desirable in this situation cannot be achieved by issuing moral appeals. A movement toward such goals presupposes *formative events* in which man is deeply affected by a vision of the whole encompassing God, the world, and man. Such events must be in keeping with the forgiveness of sins, which is itself nothing other than this vision of the whole.

If we ask what the "Christian" element of Christians' ethical involvement in society actually is, we must look for this in the following direction: The involvement is "Christian" when it takes place as a natural response to instructions given by Jesus Christ about forgiveness and substitutionary action. It is not action that takes place under pressure. It hardly understands itself as "commitment," but is action that has begun effortlessly. It is accompanied by a joyful awareness that in this wicked world a counterforce to sin has in fact become possible and that humanity has not proven to be a creation destined to despair but one that is actually pushing toward great beauty. Moreover, Christian life, surrounded and enveloped by personal faith and by brothers and sisters who care, gives birth to and fosters what is called *culture* by no longer having to "mimic strength," but by discovering human strength in what is thought to be weak. The church has an inner inclination to foster culture, that is, a truly humane civilization.

When Christians *pool* the resources that are at their disposal to intervene on behalf of the victims, neither a tendency to "fall down" observed by Nietzsche nor a preference for "what is weak" will appear in this action, but rather the best opportunity to realize true humanity will emerge. It is not even possible for Christian faith to be found in one place but the human spirit in another.

I am of the opinion that it is no longer acceptable for the church to be so undemanding of its members that they are *not* expected to make themselves available on a regular basis, to "help out" together with several other church members, at least *in one place* acting as a substitute and bringing relief to human beings/creatures who become victims or are in danger of becoming victims. The church would be more attractive and more credible if such substitutionary action was expected of its members. Indeed, only in this way *is* it the church. Only in this way does its willingness to forgive sins become credible. Only in this way is the forgiveness of sins fully able to unfold its healing, beneficial effect. Only in this way is the church built up.[82]

Christians must know that they exist in the church under privileged conditions. What the church is able to bear can often not be handled today under different conditions. This is why the church must beware of using its authority as a custodian of morality too forcefully. The church should more often become active itself on the front lines where victims are struggling instead of issuing moral appeals to many or all leading political institutions.

The church likes to call itself the "new people of God." Christendom in its entirety is also called the "people of God." But this "holy nation" is nothing to write home about. How much better could the church accept

82. It is a matter of actualizing what Luther called the *blessed exchange*. This exchange takes place in the church not just between Christ and the individual believer (Christ transfers his righteousness to the believer and in exchange assumes his sin), but — as a result — among the members of the body of Christ. In his sermon of July 30, 1522, Luther said (WA, 10 III, p. 220, lines 32-34): A virgin must put her wreath on a prostitute; a devout woman must put her veil on an adulteress. As a lofty goal Luther mentions a situation in which a Christian even gives up his own righteousness and lets it serve his neighbor's sin (WA, 10 IV, p. 217, lines 11f.). In short, the guilt and shortcomings of the other should and can be carried by Christians.

But we must ask: How far does this task go? Does it really go as far as giving up one's own salvation for the other (as P. Althaus, *Die Theologie Martin Luthers* [Gütersloh (1961), ²1963], p. 268, interprets Luther's idea of the great exchange)? Would such an active abandonment of one's own salvation even be a possibility, a choice? And we must ask another question: Does this task of making the exchange and acting as a substitute apply only to brothers and sisters who belong to the church (the one who stands ouside the realm of shame vicariously assumes and carries the other's shame)? What about this "blessed exchange" taking place, for example, between a baptized member and an unbaptized, "post-Christian" freethinker? The question seems to answer itself. Of course Christians should simply direct the strength of their sheltered life to those who need it — without examining their faith in advance. Yet it is not just a question of material assistance for the socially needy — and nothing else. The "exchange" that Luther has in mind aims at assuming the burden of strangers' sin. The Christian who bears the burden of strangers does not merely become a benefactor, but an instrument of *justificatio impii*. This is a spiritual event. When an *impius* is deeply effected by it, it is always equivalent to being a part of the church of Jesus Christ. The church of Jesus Christ is simply broader than church organizations are, and a Christian's mission to be ready to "make the exchange" is much more far-reaching than a charitable activity that bypasses the soul of another. The aim of this mission is to see human beings break away from the power and agony of evil and to see the "return of splendor in the world." (What happens in the churches under the name of *diaconal service* should obviously be conceived and practiced in terms of this faith.)

responsibility for its mission if Christians were not *more* assimilated by their national (mostly pagan or secularized) customs and traditions than by the international fellowship of their fellow believers! *Christendom still awaits the day when it will become one people.* In *this* respect the ecumenical vision has a clear and necessary goal.

In the preceding discussion I demonstrated how important it is for the "world" that the Christian church facilitates substitutionary action by limiting its scope. This limitation also signifies a depersonalization of substitutionary action. It must no longer be that mentally and physically exhausting process in which two partners "personally" and "completely" surrender themselves to each other in any form. Certainly Christian substitutionary action must not be lacking what it really means to intervene on behalf of another person. But the opportunity for this intervention never impacts the Christian as an individual, but always as a member of his church. As a member who uses his spiritual gift, he should work together with the other members and their spiritual gifts. His substitutionary action is thus always a matter of concern for other Christians as well. Perhaps he is now irreplaceable as an individual in a particular role. He should not think that others would take care of what has to be done if he does not do it now. But when he does it himself, he is neither alone nor autonomous, that is, he wants to have the advice and support of his fellow Christians as much as possible.

Surely nothing of the interpersonal character of forgiveness should be taken away from it. But we must also not overlook how many people and other creatures are sinned against without the guilty parties ever physically facing the wronged person who would perhaps forgive them under certain conditions. Perhaps he has died, been killed, or destroyed and thus can no longer "face" the guilty party in any way. We are confronted then only with the "resulting victims" of the sin that was committed and with a web of damage. The guilty parties can establish no personal relationship to the subsequent victims of their sin, and, therefore, they can no longer win any forgiveness. (It is possible that the wronged persons are the only ones still living and their "debtors" are dead.) Now it would be disastrous and totally wrong from a theological perspective to divide the *forgiveness of sins* for the reasons just mentioned into a group where "only God" can still forgive (because the injured party has died) and into a group where the human beings involved should try to achieve forgiveness among themselves (because the direct partners are still living). Who, then, would not want to wait, postponing the problem of dealing with guilt until the injured party is no longer within reach? Of course, in reality the death of the person injured by the sins of a fellow human being does not "simplify" the problem of forgiveness, of bearing or coming to terms with guilt at all. It is also not true that the guilty party could "only go to God" now — and thus would no longer have any obligations. It is correct to say that the person first injured by the sin can no longer forgive him. But he must still come to terms with the snowballing aftereffects of the wrongdoing he set in motion when he committed his sin. This far surpasses anything individuals could deal with on their own. Now it is the job of the community to join the effort and help make the partial amends that are still possible. The church should be urgently expected to offer the assistance and the incentive that enables him to meet his moral obligation realistically.

The church must *distinguish* between the issues of guilt and forgiveness that must be clarified in a human being's personal relationship with God and those aspects of his sin and guilt that need to be dealt with objectively in the context of the interrelationships between large groups of people that transcend the individual. For example, an alcoholic needs both pastoral care (an issue of the sin and guilt that cannot be denied in spite of his addictive disease), but at the same time objective help regarding those aspects of his life that show him to be the victim of others' sins. Bearing the sins bunched together in this one case means not only helping the alcoholic to win the personal forgiveness that will make life easier for him, but also *helping* him and working for actual improvements in deep-rooted, social pathologies in the arena of politics and the church's charitable ministries. This charitable work (needing a "team" and making its influence felt beyond the individual) is part of the process the church is rightly involved in when it acts to extend forgiveness and vicariously bears the burden and guilt of others. This, too, is meant by the keyword "depersonalization."

When Christianity made it possible for substitutionary action to place *limited demands* on the individual, making it appear "easy," it introduced a new phenomenon into world history. But what really makes this limitation of substitutionary action possible! After all, there really is an extreme need for it, and its demands are also placed on every individual human being in an extreme fashion. The power Christianity calls *grace* is the reason why "adequate" substitutionary action that does not at the same time make excessive demands can become a real possibility. It sets the limit beyond which substitutionary action would become a curse. However, on this side of the limit it can occur joyfully. God bears whatever lies beyond this limit.

If this is the content and the message of grace, it should never be said that God puts us to shame by such undeserved favor. After a long history of language abuse the term "grace" must also be stripped of its moralizing connotations. It is not a shameful pardon and not a substitute for human good works; rather, it makes good works possible. If theology knew this again with certainty, its conversation with philosophy would be made much easier.

In view of the working of grace[83] that sustains us in our limitations and *in our life as a whole,* Christians can also echo this sentiment of the philosophical idealists: God will supply whatever goes beyond our strength.[84] He has already supplied it. Of course, not "there," but "here."

83. Not "gratia non tollit naturam, sed perficit" is meant, but "natura non tollit seipsam, quia sustinetur gratia."

84. An allusion to the poem "Lifelines" (To Zimmer), which was one of the last poems written by F. Hölderlin. It ends with the words: "What we lack here, God will supply there / with harmonies and eternal reward and peace" (translated from the German).

Index of Names

Index of Scripture References

OLD TESTAMENT

APOCRYPHA

Wisdom of Solomon

NEW TESTAMENT